HEARTS
AND
MINDS

BOOKS BY HARRY S. ASHMORE

An Epitaph for Dixie
The Negro and the Schools
The Other Side of Jordan
*Mission to Hanoi: A Chronicle of Double Dealing
in High Places* (with William C. Baggs)
The Man in the Middle
Fear in the Air
Arkansas: A History
*The William O. Douglas Inquiry Into
the State of Individual Freedom* (editor)

HEARTS
AND
MINDS

The Anatomy of Racism
from Roosevelt to Reagan

HARRY S. ASHMORE

MC GRAW-HILL BOOK COMPANY

*New York   St. Louis   San Francisco
Toronto   Mexico*

1 2 3 4 5 6 7 8 9 D O D O 8 7 6 5 4 3 2

ISBN 0-07-02456-1

LIBRARY OF CONGRESS CATALOGING IN PUBLICATION DATA

Ashmore, Harry S.
Hearts and minds.
1. Afro-Americans—Civil rights. 2. Afro-Americans—Civil rights—Southern States. 3. Afro-Americans—Social conditions. 4. Afro-Americans—Southern States—Social conditions. 5. United States—Race relations. 6. Ashmore, Harry S.
I. Title.
E185.615.A83   305.8'96073   81–20734
ISBN 0-07-002456-1   AACR2

Book design by Roberta Rezk.

For Nathaniel,
and all others similarly situated

Contents

We come then to the question presented: Does segregation of children in public schools solely on the basis of race, even though the physical facilities and other "tangible" factors may be equal, deprive the children of equal educational opportunities? We believe that it does. . . . To separate them from others of similar age and qualifications solely because of their race generates a feeling of inferiority as to their status in the community that may affect their hearts and minds in a way unlikely ever to be undone.

Earl Warren, Chief Justice,
for the Supreme Court of the United States,
Brown v. Board of Education of Topeka,
May 17, 1954

1

The Old Folks at Home

*I*n 1931, when I was in my second year of high
school, the eminent scholar and critic, Lewis Mumford, wrote of me and my kind: "The Southerners themselves
are exactly like the Old Regime in Russia as portrayed by
Tolstoy and Chekhov: lazy, slow-moving, torpid, imperturba-
ble, snobbish, interbred, tolerant of dirt, incapable of making
effective plans of organization." I came across this characterization almost half a century after Professor Mumford set it down
in the course of a visit to the University of Virginia, and by that
time I was well aware that the most exalted American intellectuals had long held a similar view. Ralph Waldo Emerson found
the Southerner "ignorant as a bear, as irascible and nettled as
any porcupine, as polite as a troubador . . ." Henry Adams
held that "strictly, the Southerner had no mind; he had
temperament."

Reflecting on those who surrounded me during my teen-
age years in Greenville, South Carolina, I find that the Mum-
fordian catalogue could hardly be said to apply as a whole to
any one of them. They were undoubtedly interbred. But those
who were snobbish were usually intolerant of dirt, imperturba-
bility did not necessarily equate with laziness, and the passage
of the years has demonstrated that a fair number were capable
of sound planning and effective organization. After having
spent the latter third of my life among non-Southerners, my
guess is that the incidence and distribution of these qualities
among my classmates would not have differed significantly
from that to be found in a public high school in any city of
comparable size in which the older American stock remained
dominant.

This is not to argue that we were not, in important

respects, outside the American norm. We were different; even as teen-agers we knew it, and some of us had begun to polish up the hallmarks of our Southern identity, while others, looking to distant, greener pastures, had begun to slough them off. There was, most conspicuously, the matter of accent. The speech patterns of up-country South Carolina had little in common with the soft, slurred drawl commonly called "Southern." Indeed, a ranking linguist who specializes in American idioms, Raven McDavid of the University of Chicago, concluded that the discourse of educated upcountry Carolinians provided the best example of proper spoken English to be found anywhere in the land. Since Professor McDavid grew up two blocks from me I am naturally partial to his view that the nation would be well served if the speech patterns of our old neighborhood were accepted as the American standard. Still, perhaps for that reason, our accent was distinctive enough to attract attention when we traveled abroad—even the two hundred miles to the Carolina lowcountry, where speech was marked by broad *a*'s and liquid *u*'s and often lapsed into the cadence of the tobacco auctioneer.

The obverse of Professor Mumford's ascription was the characterization of the Southern accent and the manner it denotes as charming, at least when it is associated with a blue-eyed belle or a handsome gallant. Southerners were pleased to accept this aspect of the stereotype; if they recognized it as patronizing it still served to temper the latent hostility it often cloaked. But to acknowledge, and even exploit, what is seen as eccentricity by the larger national community was also to accept the brand of parochialism. The consciousness that this was our lot was firmly fixed by the time my classmates and I got to Greenville High. As we grew older and began to sharpen this perception through personal experience with outlanders it would seem to pose a choice between pride and shame, and most chose pride.

I don't know exactly when I first became aware of the special identity the past had imposed upon me. I suspect the revelation came early. Arnold J. Toynbee recalled that in his boyhood he accepted Britain's Diamond Jubilee as proof that the Empire was on top of the world and would stay there forever; the future historian was aware that there was a thing called history but he thought of it as something unpleasant that happened to other people, and he was sure that he would have felt the same had he been a native of New York. "Of course," he added, "if I had been a small boy in 1897 in the Southern part of the United States I should not have felt the same; I should have known from my parents that history had happened to my people in my part of the world."

It was not that those around me were, as Southerners are often pictured, obsessed with the past to the point of ancestor worship. I do not recall any mourning for the Lost Cause, and the old men who bore scars from the late unpleasantness seemed no more disposed to relive their youth than were the veterans of later wars. My grandmothers took pride in their late husbands' records on the battlefield but seemed to have no enduring regret that their valor and sacrifice had been rewarded by defeat. The consensus was that it was probably for the best that the union had not been sundered, and this had what amounted to an official imprimatur. The standard history used in the grade schools of South Carolina was a revision of an 1840 work by the state's most distinguished literary figure, William Gilmore Simms. In bringing the text up to date his granddaughter, Mary C. Simms Oliphant, wrote:

South Carolinians were wholly mistaken in two of their most cherished beliefs: First, they felt that slave labor was necessary to the South because farming was the chief interest of this section; second, South Carolinians honestly believed that there were so many slaves that their freedom would mean that the South would belong to the black race . . .

Time has proven how mistaken they were. We know now that we can farm successfully without slave labor, and that the freeing of the slaves has not Africanized the South. The pity is that South Carolinians had not taken the lead themselves in freeing the slaves and thus saving the country from a brothers' war. Instead . . . South Carolina led the Southern states out of the union.

So we came to understand that what made Southerners different, and accounted for our tragic past and present condition, was the presence among us of the descendants of those black slaves who had populated the lower seaboard colonies along with the early settlers. In 1931 the great majority of these were still in the Confederate and border states, and most were still working the land as their ancestors had been brought from Africa to do. No longer slaves, they were not yet citizens. And, as depression accentuated the South's endemic poverty, they were at the nadir of their fortunes.

I CANNOT claim that Greenville typified the South, which is far more various than those who fashioned its stereotypes have ever recognized. The first settlements spread from the ports along the estuaries, where there was rich, flat land suited to the plantation economy created by European colonial powers as they hopscotched across the Caribbean; the initial centers were Tidewater Virginia, Charleston, and Savannah on the Atlantic seaboard, Mobile and New Orleans on the Gulf. Their plantation-based culture, with its aristocratic forms and pretensions, survived more or less intact as it was transplanted to the rich river valleys of the interior. But it suffered drastic alteration as Southern settlers pushed on to the Mississippi and beyond, and began to populate upland areas that required different patterns of agriculture. It was here in the towns and cities of the upcountry that what came to be called a "New South" emerged with the advent of a truncated version of the industrial revolution that had already transformed the states to the north.

Greenville passed through all the stages except the very earliest. When it was still the wilderness domain of the Cherokee there were Englishmen of yeoman stock in the piedmont country that lies across the apex of the South Carolina triangle. By 1700, traders were crossing the mountains to bring back furs from as far away as the French territory in the lower Mississippi valley, and the export of peltry had become the most thriving business developed at Charles Town under the Lords Proprietor. There was still Indian fighting to be done when a trading post was established by Capt. Richard Pearis at a crossing on the Reedy River; the village that grew up there was first called Pleasantburg in recognition of a salubrious climate that attracted summer refugees from the malaria-ridden coastal communities; by 1931 its rechristened descendant was surrounded by satellite cotton mill villages that made Greenville County the most populous in the state.

At least it can be said of the place of my growing up that it was not atypical of the South. It did not, it is true, maintain the aristocratic conventions of the lowcountry, but then it never had. The growing city had not yet severed its ties to the agrarian past; the doomed effort to raise cotton on the exhausted red soil of the foothills went on as before, and there were black sharecroppers whose situation had not been changed significantly by emancipation. The cotton mills had provided a refuge for many of the poor whites, but not all, and one-horse farmers still tried to eke out subsistence on the few leached acres that represented the family inheritance from six generations of hard labor. In the western quarter of the county, where blue mountains rise steep and tall, hillbillies cherished their isolation and maintained the primitive life-style their progeny implanted in remote coves of the Smokies and Ozarks.

None of my family's amateur genealogists ever determined exactly when the Ashmores arrived in the upcountry. Presumably the first to set foot on American soil was William, a member of the crew of the *Dove*, who sailed from Cowes in November 1633, with Lord Baltimore's expedition to Maryland. But he probably was not the founder of the line, since a William Ashmore is listed as the only casualty suffered by the Marylanders in a 1634 territorial dispute with Virginia. In any case, the name was common in the Greenville District before the Revolution, and by my own time Ashmores were numerous enough to constitute a force in local politics. My father's first cousin, John, who occupied the county supervisor's office most of his adult life and passed it on to his son, held a politician's pragmatic view of the family connection. "The way I look at it," he said, "we're kin to everybody in this county, white or black, one way or another."

On my mother's side the roots were more readily traced. She was a pure product of the Protestant Scotch-Irish, who began a great migration from the North of Ireland in 1717. By the time of the Revolution more than a quarter of a million had arrived, most through the port of Philadelphia, and their settlements had spread from Pennsylvania through the uplands of Virginia and the Carolinas. This was the transplanted lowland Scottish stock that came to dominate the South Carolina upcountry; by 1790 the immigrants from Ulster constituted a majority of the 115,534 whites who shared the territory above the fall line with 29,679 slaves—a racial proportion that already had put them at odds with the 28,644 whites in the low-country, whose plantation economy was sustained by 79,216 blacks.

My maternal grandfather, Archie Scott, did not arrive until the great migration had about run its course; he was born in County Antrim and was three years old in 1847 when his father, John, decided to join the relatives who had established farms in the area centered by the Lickville Presbyterian Church, sixteen miles down the Augusta Road from Greenville. "I am well satisfied with the place and the country," John Scott wrote back to his wife in Kilrea, instructing her to pack up the children and join him. "In a word, it is a land of freedom and plenty."

"The search for aristocrats among the early Scotch-Irish will prove futile," James G. Leyburn wrote in *The Scotch-Irish: A Social History*. "These people were doubly a 'decapitated society,' for they had migrated twice. The move from Scotland to Ireland had been made by the optimistic poor; the move to America once more left behind most of those who had risen to prominence." Although their Calvinist heritage inspired them to plant Presbyterian churches and accompanying schools wherever they went, and some of the elders delighted in arguing the fine points of predestination and infant baptism, they had no difficulty in accommodating to the Protestant sects of the nonconformist English, Germans, and Swiss who shared their upland domain. The tombstone of John Scott's wife, Sarah McCullough, in the Lickville churchyard notes that she "was a consistent member of the Methodist Church at Bethesda and lived a Christian life . . . and died in a full faith of a blessed redeemer." My mother never entirely overcame her Presbyterian bent, but she followed the practice of the day and joined my father's Baptist congregation.

From the beginning, Leyburn notes, these Ulstermen seemed to waive their ethnic and cultural identity; when, as so many did, they pressed on to the west and were asked who they were they invariably replied, "A Carolinian," and let it go at that. Indeed, it is Leyburn's thesis that they were natural-born exemplars of the rising American middle-class:

Their optimistic self-reliance, with a conviction that God helps those who help themselves, was to become the congenial American folk philosophy of the next century, not far removed from materialism and a faith in progress . . . Holding the attitude they did, and being present in such large numbers throughout most of the United States, they afforded the middle ground that became typical of the American as he was to become. The Scotch-Irish element could be the common denominator into which Americanism might be resolved.

ARCHIE SCOTT married Jane Terry, who bore him ten children, and when Jane passed on he wed her maiden sister, Elizabeth, who finished the job of raising them. My paternal grandfather, William Ashmore, married Sylvia Anne Greene, and sired eleven children. In time, Grandfather Scott turned over the farm to his eldest son and brought the younger members of the brood to Greenville, where they settled in a tall old house near the center of town. The pattern was similar for the Ashmores; when the children were grown, or near to it, my widowed grandmother sold the home place, and only her son Van and daughter Alice remained behind on the land. This sizable company of aunts and uncles, plus the mates they took and the cousins they produced, filled my childish consciousness with regular visitations and occasional great family gatherings. It was, I suppose, what is now called an "extended family." The aged and homeless were passed around among the young marrieds, country cousins came to live with us so they could attend the city schools, and in return my brother and I were shipped off to enjoy pastoral summer pleasures on the plantation whose proprietor had married one of my maternal aunts.

In all this there was a minimum of that treacly quality called "togetherness"; the elders treated the children with a sort of detached affection, assuming that we properly belonged at one remove from the adult world. The front they presented to us was that they displayed to casual acquaintances, a polite facade of Victorian convention that avoided unpleasantness at the expense of candor. But a child's ear could pick up a hint of the broad, earthy strain that ran through their private conversation and provoked their frequent laughter. And a child's eye could detect the marked differences in temperament among these men and women who were so similar in manner. Looking back, it seems to me that those who were blood kin were likely to differ as much, one from the other, as they did from the relatives they acquired by marriage.

As I grew older and began to circulate beyond the inner circle of kinfolk, I found that these farm-bred newcomers could not be distinguished from those who had long lived in town. One Ashmore uncle became a Baptist minister, and a Scott was chief of the fire department, but most went into business, usually on their own. And in the boom years of the First World War all prospered, at least to the point of maintaining the minimum trappings of the middle class. If none became wealthy enough to be reckoned a real power in community affairs, they were on easy, first-name terms with those who did; in what was now their home town there was no public place, and no private parlor, where they would feel alien.

In their manner, and in their ambitions, they were, I suspect, not significantly different from their counterparts in, say, Cedar Rapids, or any other small American city just getting its growth with an influx from the countryside. Of course, a novelist who probed beneath the surface would have found human comedy and Gothic tragedy, as Thomas Wolfe did when he set out to fashion a chronicle of the Gant family of Asheville, sixty miles up the Buncombe Road.

When I grew old enough to share in their gossip, and that of their contemporaries, I found that most of my uncles had private lives at variance with their public mien; if this was also true of the aunts, convention prevented discussion of any failings beyond those that identified a few as shrews. A fondness for the bottle was a family trait; at least two uncles lapsed into alcoholism and one borderline case replied to the suggestion that his consumption was getting out of hand, "I always know when I've had enough to drink—I'm asleep." One fancied cockfighting, and, it was widely believed, could also be found in the hidden places where dogs were pitted; another was a womanizer of awesome reputation; the purported business reverses of several were believed to have resulted from gambling losses. They were, as I suppose their Cedar Rapids contemporaries were, torn between the conformist demands of middle-class respectability, and the powerful individualism of their nonconformist heritage.

Cousin Sue Scott, a maiden schoolteacher, compiled a record of the six brothers who came from Antrim, and noted that in all their long lives at least two never were known to agree on a public matter. When the bottle was broken out, she wrote, "peace and harmony did not always reign supreme—especially on political issues." Yet, the remarkable fact was that these volatile men and women, subordinating their own differences and joining with their traditional antagonists in the low-country, formed a solid front in national politics and held to it for a hundred years. Their fealty to the Democratic Party yielded only to the superior military force that ended their effort at secession and supported what amounted to a Republican occupation in the years following the Civil War, and to the opportunity to get rid of the interlopers through the "Bargain of 1877." They scuttled their party's presidential candidate, Samuel J. Tilden, in a deal that settled the contested election and ended Reconstruction in South Carolina and Louisiana. C. Vann Woodward, the historian of Jim Crow, wrote: "In effect, the Southerners were abandoning the cause of Tilden in exchange for control of two states, and the Republicans were abandoning the cause of the Negro in exchange for the peaceful possession of the Presidency."

It was, then, the race issue that created and maintained the monolithic Solid South, and gave it disproportionate power in national affairs. Legal segregation, as had the predecessor slavery, remained a peculiar Southern institution, and their identification with it denied Southern Democrats national office; but, as they had demonstrated in the case of Al Smith in 1928, no Northern Democrat could be elected if the party leaders overrode the Southerners' veto on the nomination. Yet, in the face of this controlling political reality, the Southern leaders insisted that there was, in fact, no race issue—that the region, in the spirit of noblesse oblige, had repaired the havoc wrought by the misguided social experimentation of its conquerors, creating in place of slavery a separate-but-equal accommodation necessary to protect disadvantaged blacks against naturally superior and sometimes predatory whites.

In retrospect, it seems incredible that sensible and often sensitive men and women could have taken this proposition seriously, but I am sure my relatives did. And if their political antagonists in the North did not believe it, they still accepted it—at least to the point that there was no effective pressure for an end to legal segregation, nor any effort to restore within the system the civil rights denied the black minority. For forty years after the United States Supreme Court gave constitutional sanction to the separate-but-equal doctrine in *Plessy v. Ferguson*, the South enjoyed the only relatively quiet time the region had ever known. There were no racial agitators abroad in the land, certainly none who had any direct influence among the isolated Southern blacks. The brief resurgence of the Ku Klux Klan in the twenties was an irrelevant caricature, never supported, and soon deflated by the Southern leadership. By 1931 the deepening depression had begun to demonstrate that the quiet of this pause in the historic progression had been that of stagnation, but initially the economic decline only served to increase competition for scarce dollars and reduce even further the minimal priority given to racial matters.

The segregated society had produced, and continued to require, a sustaining mythology. My relatives considered white supremacy a fact of life, as indeed it was if measured by the material condition of the two races. Although I do not recall the matter ever being discussed—and that, in itself, is a fact of some significance—I am sure most would have conceded that there were blacks who were their equals in morality, intelligence, and energy: Booker T. Washington, say, or that fellow Carver, the peanut man. But this was an abstract consideration; the blacks they knew were semiliterate at best, and so far as they could see showed no disposition to infringe upon the exclusive social domain of the whites. They could sustain that view because the urban white middle class, which now dominated the affairs of the South despite occasional political skirmishing with agrarian populists, had effectively isolated itself from the mass of blacks. The only personal contact was with household servants or those employed in menial jobs in the business community. These they treated with what they believed to be a beneficent paternalism.

Although there were certainly mean-spirited men and women who deliberately exploited the helplessness of the blacks with whom they dealt, those who openly flaunted the accepted norm did so at the price of forfeited respectability. I recall the discomfiture of the more proper of my relatives when they were reminded that one of their own enjoyed a handsome return from his investment in black housing; a slumlord, in their view, was not much better than the proprietor of a brothel.

Good manners on both sides marked the relationship between blacks and whites, and this at least reflected a genuine concern for the dignity of those in the inferior position. I was accorded one of my mother's rare whippings when she overheard me using the proscribed "nigger" in the presence of a house servant. If the pay was low and the hours long for these cooks and nurses and maids and yardmen, I doubt that their treatment was any harsher than that suffered by domestic servants anywhere. And certainly the professed bonds of mutual affection were something more than convenient fictions to improve the lot of the black and ease the conscience of the white. Old Uncle Ben, a former slave of my Uncle Walter Griffin's family, was kept on some kind of retainer long after he had passed beyond any productive work around the house and yard. When he died we were dressed in our Sunday best and taken to the Afro-Methodist Episcopal Church for the funeral, and I cannot doubt that the tears that flowed down white cheeks were evidence of genuine, shared grief.

White Southerners had come to accept segregation as ordained, subject only to the most gradual change. They believed, with deep conviction, that only they, whose long experience with blacks was unique among Americans, understood the problems inherent in race relations. The excesses of Reconstruction, still green in the folk memory, demonstrated to their satisfaction that only havoc could result if zealous outsiders were permitted to tamper with the existing social order. These were the articles of their faith and, unlike their slave-owning forebears, they no longer had occasion to test them against the reality that afflicted the mass of blacks.

WHEN we were still in grade school my brother, Cousin Walter Griffin, Jr., and I were regularly put aboard the Piedmont and Northern interurban train and dispatched to Belton in the lower part of the county, where we would be met by Uncle Hayne Lewis, Aunt Tee (for Tecora), and our cousins, Clarence and Archie, and driven to the plantation where, in collaboration with some twenty black families, the Lewises farmed twelve hundred acres. Looking back, I can see that this operation was an anachronism. The rolling land, never well suited for row crops, was rapidly shedding its topsoil and erosion was cutting gullys deep into the red earth. Cotton prices had begun the downward slide that would soon go past the break-even point, and out there in the far reaches of the section called "Possum Kingdom" you could hear the work song's mournful refrain,

> Ten cent cotton and forty cent meat,
> How in hell can a poor man eat.

But in the long days of those summer visits, the old place seemed idyllic to a city boy. We were each assigned a black of similar age, and this constant companion, wise in country ways, would serve as guide and protector as we roamed the fields and explored the streams that laced the wooded hollows. Mine was Nathaniel, and he remains vivid in my memory although we were lost to each other more than half a century ago. He was waiting each morning when we came out after breakfast, and at noon he shared the meal Aunt Tee handed out to us on the back porch, where we sat on the floor among the sleeping beagles, bare feet dangling over the edge of the weathered boards. There was a rough equality in this relationship. When we raced for some common objective or wrestled on a grassy slope, he was not expected to give quarter and usually won. In all aspects of woodcraft, and in knowledge of the sexual and other intriguing habits of the animal population, he was clearly my superior, but I, in my turn, could tell him of things he had never seen and could hardly imagine. On my side the consciousness of racial difference vanished under this intimacy, but I doubt that it ever did on his, for he could not forget that when dark came on and we headed home he would pass on to one of the shacks across the road as I turned into the big house to wash up and join those who were his masters.

Yet, at all levels the black and white worlds overlapped. The plantation had come down from the past typical of the upcountry pattern, comparable only in function to the great estates maintained by lowcountry grandees. The two-story big house was plain and square, with long porches front and back; it was served by a well, a privy, and a springhouse for cooling milk and butter, lit by kerosene lamps, and heated by fireplaces and the great wood range in the kitchen. There were sheltering mulberry trees, and grass and flowering shrubs in the front yard, but the grounds to the rear were mostly bare dirt where chickens, geese, turkeys, ducks, and guinea hens left deposits to be scraped off bare feet. Beyond were the smokehouse, barns, stables, pigpens, corn cribs, a shop that housed a blacksmith and a carpenter, and a commissary where the sharecroppers drew their rations. All these, like the tenant houses, were innocent of paint and had long ago weathered to a soft silver gray. These were the accouterments of a self-sufficient community, and it was the only home many of the blacks had ever known.

The sharecropping system had emerged in the straitened aftermath of the Civil War. Over most of the region cotton was the only cash crop, and its cultivation required substantial acreage suitable for gang labor. Whites still owned most of the productive land, but their capital investment in slaves had been wiped out and with it their credit; the freedmen in effect provided them labor on loan, receiving in return subsistance and a share of the profit when the crop was sold. The system has been duly condemned as a form of serfdom which effectively bound blacks to the land and left them subject to exploitation by unscrupulous planters. But, as I saw it in operation in that time when it was already entering its terminal phase, sharecropping was producing little material benefit on the white side of the equation.

Uncle Hayne owned a Model-T Ford, but this was the only piece of modern machinery on the place, and it was useful only for necessary trips to Belton. The roads over which he made his dawn-to-dusk tours to oversee the work in the fields were so bad he traveled by buggy. Mules drew the plows, and the planting, chopping, and picking was done by men, women, and children, so that about half the total cultivated acreage had to be kept in subsistence crops to feed the animals and the hands. One ate well in the big house, where there were bountiful supplies of home-cured meat, poultry, game, garden produce, fruits, and berries, but that was about all that could be said for the master's life-style. I doubt that any comparable investment of capital, energy, and constant worry would have produced so miserable a return in terms of cash or comfort.

In a sense, everyone involved was trapped. There was no way to make the operation more efficient without destroying its basic character—and this, of course, is what did happen when tractors, increasingly sophisticated farm implements, pesticides, and weed-killing chemicals began to transform all of American agriculture. This was a process that would benefit the surviving few by dispensing with the services of the many— those surplus whites and blacks whose roots were generations deep in the land. Before the wave of the mechanized future reached Possum Kingdom, Uncle Hayne and Aunt Tee had given up, and the old planter spent his last days vegetating on the front porch of a little house on the edge of Greenville. I can only assume that Nathaniel and the other blacks of my generation were caught up in the great diaspora that in our lifetime has denuded the Southern countryside of people and repopulated the slums of major American cities.

SOME migration had been spurred by the dislocations of World War I, and through the twenties there was a steady trickle from the countryside to the Southern towns and cities. In 1931 more than a quarter of Greenville's residents were black. No more than half of these were domestic servants, or found steady employment in the menial occupations where the lily-white hiring practices of the cotton mills and mercantile establishments did not apply. Most lived a hand-to-mouth existence, huddled in the dilapidated, overcrowded housing available in the several "niggertowns" scattered among the white residential neighborhoods. I was afforded a close-up look at these blacks as the depression worsened their condition, and my own.

My father was an early victim of the general economic collapse; bankrupt and in declining health, he lost his mercantile business and was forced to sell off the property he had accumulated, and my mother, in the resolute fashion of her kind, took over and rented a big house two doors from the one where Archie Scott had reared his brood. By taking in boarders she managed to keep us afloat, and I helped out by taking a paper route. The morning *News*, where I began my career in journalism on the delivery end, called its carriers "little merchants," selling us papers at wholesale and leaving it up to us to collect enough weekly subscriptions to pay the bill and net a profit. The routes were usually laid out so that each had enough well-paying white customers to keep the carrier solvent, but also extended into a black neighborhood, where sales were easy and could be counted in total paid circulation, but collection was well-nigh impossible. In this fashion I inadvertently subsidized my access to the bleak underside of the community most whites never saw.

My exposure came in the worst of the black neighborhoods, an enclave of jerry-built shacks that had sprung up on the edge of the city to accommodate recent arrivals who could not find a place in the more stable communities where domestic servants lived close to their employers. Some years later, with the benefit of broader perspective, I attempted to describe the scene as it was imprinted on my consciousness in those high school years:

One boundary of my daily round was the embankment of the Southern Railway tracks, where the Crescent Limited thundered by in remote grandeur and the long freights crawled past with a burden of the dispossessed covering the cars like roosting birds. The other was a festering creek that in occasional flood carried away that considerable portion of sewage the primitive outdoor plumbing could not, or did not, accommodate. There was no pavement here, and in truth no streets; the stilt-legged shotgun houses were set along muddy tracks that began, curved and ended without perceptible pattern.

My youth, and the satchel of papers that slapped my thigh in the early mornings, or the route list in my hand on collection days, gave me innocent passage. I came to be accepted as part of the natural order, and the pulsing life went on around me without the sudden dead pause that usually greeted the appearance of a pale face . . .

The sights, the sounds, and the smells were certainly different from anything I had known in the prim neighborhoods across the tracks. There was music in the soft voices and the liquid laughter, and a kind of subdued anguish in the song that was sounding always somewhere. The cutting edge of poverty had left visible marks: the swollen bellies of rickety children, the scabs of pellagra, the hollow cheeks of the tubercular. Yet there was an astonishing vitality, too, in the broad-shouldered bucks swinging off in the dawn to their muscle-straining jobs, and in the heavy-lidded, earthy women who marked their passage with white-toothed approval. It showed even in the very old, the gnarled uncles and grannies who poked at the black iron washpots and tended the swarming children through the long days when the able-bodied were at work, or looking for it. Moving their tilted split-bottom chairs with the sun, sitting loose as they said, they simply refused to die.

The community was close-knit, despite its obvious impermanence; and the spirit, of necessity, was communal. Only in extremes of weather were the openings of the close-set shacks closed; normally one saw through from front door to back, and the hum of conversation carried without interruption from window to window and from porch to sagging porch. No man owned the land he lived on, and the coming and going of persons of all ages kept the population in constant flux. With rare exceptions family relationships were casual. The usual conventions were relaxed; bastardy carried no permanent stigma, nor venereal disease, nor a prison record. Yet there was a code here, too. Everyone knew privation, but no one starved; the fatback and greens were a shared necessity and the Saturday night bottle was in the public domain. Sudden flares of violence, the flashing of bright blades and the stain of red blood against dark skin, were acceptable, but cruelty was not; transgressors guilty of sheer meanness were promptly cast out.

I can't claim that these sights and sounds suffused me with moral indignation. I had been conditioned to accept inequality as the natural order, and I did not then equate it with injustice. I could see that these blacks were materially deprived, certainly, but even an adolescent may have entertained doubt that such life-affirming people were any worse off spiritually than his own kind, who were suffering severe trauma as the depression undermined the verities and spread despair through the middle class. Of one thing I am certain: I did not see these blacks, or those I had known on the plantation, as exotic. They were my people—not in any proprietary sense left over from slavery, not in obeisance to some romantic notion of noblesse oblige, not in subliminal acknowledgment that our bloodlines may very well have been mingled, but in recognition of the inescapable entanglement of shared history and common experience. I still cannot imagine the South that gave me my identity without that pervasive black presence. When the continuing dispersal to the great cities of the North and West reached flood tide in the 1950s I wrote a book from which the preceding passages are quoted, and called it *An Epitaph for Dixie.*

2

The Uses of Rhetoric

*I*n a remarkably prescient passage in her history text, Mary C. Simms Oliphant closed a section titled "The Greatest Problem" with a warning: ". . . to this day South Carolina has a white man's government. The welfare of two races living in one small state is a problem you will have to face when you become citizens." I can recall no indication that this injunction left any impression on the incipient citizens who made up the depression-shrunk freshman class at Clemson College when I arrived there in 1933.

Blacks were virtually invisible on our isolated foothill campus, where the student sons of financially strapped white families were available to perform the most menial chores. In our bull sessions we argued the merits of the early New Deal reforms, pro and con, but the matter of race was not on our agenda. Neither was it on that of the keepers of the state's political verities, the old Bourbons, who had been left in disarray by the impact of the general economic collapse; most had rallied to the standard of Franklin Delano Roosevelt and only a few had begun to suspect that his wife, Eleanor, might turn out to be a latter-day abolitionist.

In my first year out of college, when I was still finding my way around the city-side beats as a reporter for the afternoon *Greenville Piedmont*, President Roosevelt made the famous speech in which he identified the South as the nation's number one economic problem, repeating for emphasis, "the nation's problem, not just the South's." No one in Greenville had any reason to question the diagnosis; the state's farmers were bankrupt for all practical purposes, and the cotton mills were often reduced to two- and three-day shifts when they were open at all. The textile unions were embarked upon their long

series of futile organizing efforts, and there was some unrest among the poor whites in the countryside. But for the
most part the classes, never precisely demarcated among
the intricately interrelated whites, were united by shared
privation.

I observed all this in the bottom-up perspective afforded
one who spent the days and a good portion of the nights
around the police station, the courts, and the city and county
offices where human misery showed up in bold relief. The
rescue operations of the New Deal were under way and blacks
were included on the periphery, sharing in the benefits trickling down from the effort to shore up the collapsed farm
economy and relieve the suffering of the urban poor. But, as
Mrs. Oliphant reminded, it was a white man's government, and
the disfranchised blacks were without leverage to insure fair
treatment by those who dispensed the federal largesse, or to
protect themselves against the brutality of those who thought it
prudent to keep the niggers in their place.

In due course I was transferred to the morning *News* and
assigned to cover the legislative sessions in Columbia and the
statewide election campaigns. Here I first came to appreciate
Malcolm Muggeridge's dictum that newspapering is the ideal
profession for those who find power fascinating and its exercise
abhorrent. "The only fun of journalism," he wrote, "is that it
puts you in contact with the eminent without being under the
necessity to admire them or take them seriously." In my
formative view, politics appeared as a sporting contest with
high entertainment value, as I conceded when I wrote in
retrospect of that early experience:

The guns of World War II were already sounding in Europe, but only
the echoes of battles long since fought could be heard there in the old
Statehouse, where General Wade Hampton stands guard on his
rearing bronze charger and the damage inflicted by Sherman's
cannon is left conspicuously unrepaired. And yet, even in the light of
hindsight, I recall the South Carolina General Assembly as a great
human comedy, identical in antic spirit with the legislatures I would
later frequent in North Carolina, Georgia and Arkansas. In all the
years I did journalistic battle with them, I never lost a genuine
fondness for the assorted jackleg lawyers, farmers, undertakers,
hardware merchants and the like who stream in from the hills and

plains to serve their interests while transacting the people's business. The proportion of mountebanks and scoundrels runs fairly high, but few are mean. I cannot plead them innocent of the consequences of their action—and lack of it—when the racial crisis finally broke upon them, but I am sure that few were touched by black hatred. For most, the emotional range never rose above a sort of foot-stamping petulance, aroused because the demand for Negro rights would not, as they had promised the voters, simply go away.

In the late thirties there was as yet no indigenous agitation by blacks, and in South Carolina very little on their behalf, and I doubt that a single member of the legislature gave serious thought to the possibility that something should, and could, be done to improve the plight of the minority race. Elected officials had long ago insulated themselves against such considerations by establishing the Democratic Party as a private club entitled to set its own qualifications for membership, the requirements being a white skin and willingness to support the party's nominees against all comers. The effect was to confine the election process to the restricted Democratic primaries, rendering meaningless the general election presumably conducted under the provisions of the United States Constitution and its civil rights amendments; blacks who could clear the hurdle of the poll tax could vote, but there was no substantive opposition ticket to vote for after the Republican Party virtually disappeared with the end of Reconstruction.

One result of the one-party system was to insure long tenure for politicians who combined personal charm with high oratorical skills. Those so endowed were perfectly suited to carry out the real objective of the controlling Bourbons, which was not to promote governmental action, but to minimize it. The folk memory of the political activism that produced secession and its aftermath gave laissez-faire a powerful attraction, and it was this, as much as simple racism, that kept unfurled the banner of white supremacy. Having proved its efficacy in the rout of the carpetbag Republicans, the race issue still served to rally, and divert, the poor whites, as the prototype Southern demagogue, "Pitchfork Ben" Tillman, had demonstrated with his bastardized populism at the end of the last century. Tillman's political heir, Coleman Livingston Blease, added the textile workers to the coalition of the disadvantaged and established a durable voting base that made him a perennial candidate. "The common whites clung to Cole Blease, indeed," W. J. Cash observed in *The Mind of the South*, "but they kept him in the United States Senate, where his single service to them was to keep before the startled gaze of the nation the vision of their eternal assault upon the black man."

The same verdict could be rendered on the career of Ellison Durant Smith, who established a course record for longevity in the United States Senate, serving six consecutive terms and yielding his seat only to a summons from his maker. "Cotton Ed" Smith was a lowcountry planter and never allowed anyone to forget it; his normal garb in the summer campaign season was a white linen suit, a string tie, and a broad-brimmed panama hat; from first to last he stood four-square on the three-plank platform of the antebellum slavocracy: states' rights, tariff for revenue only, and white supremacy. "If it was good enough for John C. Calhoun," he proclaimed, "it is good enough for me."

In 1938, following him in the course of the marathon joint primary campaign in which all candidates for statewide office appeared together in every county, I saw Cotton Ed swallowed up in admiring clusters of redneck farmers and lintheads from the cotton mill villages—this despite the fact that he had consistently opposed the New Deal measures that earned Franklin Roosevelt the devotion of these same voters. I once asked him how he would describe the campaign technique that made it possible for him to rise above, or sink below, the so-called belly issues of voter self-interest. "I get out there and mingle," he said. "I'll shake hands and break bread with any sonofabitch who's qualified to vote, but when he shakes my hand he knows he's shaking hands with *some*body." W. J. Cash put it more elegantly: "The hand on the shoulder of the commoner, the inquiry after the health of Cousin Elvira and the last baby, the jests, the rallying, the stories, and, of course, the confiding reminders of the proto-Dorian bond of white men . . ."

Person-to-person campaigning, however, could go only so far. This was the summer when President Roosevelt concluded that the nation's number one economic problem couldn't be solved unless the Southern obstructionists in the Congress were purged in the Democratic primaries. Cotton Ed was at the top of the list, and, en route to Warm Springs, FDR stopped his train at Greenville to instruct the faithful that they could best serve their own interests by keeping their senior senator at home.

Cotton Ed's counterattack was what came to be known as "the Philadelphia Story." This oratorical marvel was the senator's version of how, and why, he had walked out of the Democratic National Convention two years before. First, he said, he thought he had gotten into the wrong hall and fallen among Republicans when he found the convention floor sprinkled with black delegates. Then, sitting in the blessed lily-white sanctuary that was the South Carolina delegation, he had received the ultimate shock when a black preacher—in Cotton Ed's lexicon a "slew-footed, blue-gummed, kinky-headed Senegambian"—walked out on the platform to deliver the invocation. "And he started praying and I started walking," went the peroration. "And as I pushed through those great doors, and walked across that vast rotunda, it seemed to me old John Calhoun leaned down from his mansion in the sky and whispered in my ear, 'You did right, Ed. . . .'"

This was live theater. Television was not yet born and radio rarely reached out to the hustings, where someone in the crowd was bound to interrupt Cotton Ed's high-level overture with a cry of, "Oh hell, Ed, tell us about Philadelphy!" So far as I know the speech was never recorded, but Turner Catledge, who came down from Washington to cover the campaign for the *New York Times*, and I later reconstructed it from memory. Catledge considered it a gem of demagoguery never surpassed even in his native Mississippi, and was frequently called upon to render his version at private gatherings of the nation's political elders. In *An Epitaph for Dixie* I cited it as a remembrance of things past:

The Philadelphia Story had all the basic ingredients, and it carried the senator along to a victory climaxed by a stirring scene on election night when, with honest tears coursing into his grizzled moustache, he posed for photographers on the statehouse grounds wearing the red shirt of Reconstruction and clutching the rear leg of Wade Hampton's bronze charger. I suppose The Story shocked many of the outlanders who heard it, or read about it; and certainly the success of the run was a grievous disappointment to President Roosevelt. Yet to the initiated, to the orator and the audience, there was a sort of innocence about it. The white men who gathered under the chinaberry trees to whoop and holler as Ed built his climaxes didn't really object to being prayed over by a Senegambian, and didn't believe Ed did either. And, most remarkable of all, nobody enjoyed the performance more than the Negroes who stood, white teeth gleaming in the dark, at the rear of the crowd. "Hot damn," they would chortle, "Old Ed's pourin' it on tonight."

The style of this theater of the absurd was unique to the South, but its basic elements can be found wherever the process that sustains popular government is allowed to degenerate into particularized single-issue politics. In this case, all other considerations were dissipated by the racist appeal of white supremacy floating out of the past on a cloud of inherited fears and misconceptions. It was an emotional protest vote that allowed Cotton Ed to overcome denunciation by the most popular president in modern times while turning back two formidable opponents, the populist governor, Olin Johnson, and Edgar Brown, the wily boss of the state senate. Brown provided a postmortem: "Either Olin or I could have handled Ed on the race issue, but we were both licked the day Roosevelt came out against him. The most powerful force you can turn loose in a political campaign is the voter's feeling that some outsider is trying to tell him what to do." The anti–New Deal incumbents survived in every one of the Southern states where the presidential purge was attempted.

THE FACTOR of race has always made it difficult to apply the usual political labels in the South. Gunnar Myrdal found the region "the only place in the world where one can get a reputation for being a liberal simply by urging obedience to the law." South Carolinians had used "radical" to identify the black Republicans and carpetbaggers of Reconstruction, and the etymology was somewhat skewed when, as they usually did, proper citizens employed the term to indicate personal distaste for Ed Smith, Cole Blease, and their cohorts. It was not only that they considered the overt display of racism unseemly, they viewed it as unnecessary since it was employed to arouse poor whites against a threat of potential black domination that clearly did not exist.

Well-placed whites in the cities and towns, where most such were now situated, did not see more equitable treatment for the minority race as posing any conceivable threat to their interests. And some of the more thoughtful, accepting the New South doctrine of the Atlanta editor, Henry Grady, had begun to recognize that the urban middle class would benefit economically from the increase in purchasing power that would come with improvement in the condition of the mass of blacks. This, at least by contrast, was the liberal view on race, and it was held almost exclusively by men and women who in most other respects would be considered conservative. There was no tenable political position to their left; those who believed in their hearts there should be no social distinction between the races kept their heresy to themselves, or voiced it outside the region.

The moderates who held or sought elective office never met the race-baiters head on. Their tactic was to treat white supremacy as so firmly entrenched as to be politically irrelevant, and they simply ignored the dark fancies peddled by the demagogues. Their supporters would accept as disassociation, if not condemnation, their silence in the face of such outrages as Cole Blease's endorsement of lynch law: "Whenever the Constitution comes between me and the virtue of the white women of the South, I say to hell with the Constitution!" The conservative politicians would leave it to their allies among the newspaper editors and clergymen to condemn Blease for such a reckless invitation to mass murder and hope that this would prevent any more hapless blacks from winding up at the end of a rope. When a mob actually was in the streets, they usually could be counted on to take a stand in the name of law and order.

In the South, as everywhere in the nation, men of property ultimately dominated the political process: planters, industrialists, bankers, utility magnates, merchants, landlords, and the professional men who looked after their interests. They might lose an occasional skirmish to reformers who sought to increase their taxes or impose legal limits on their operations, but never a major battle. If some of these were disgusted with the way Cotton Ed hollered "nigger," most were simply amused, and could afford to be since they knew the senator would do them no harm. And they were always able to keep some men in office who shared their basic pragmatism and could be counted on to counterbalance the "radicals" when their own fortunes might be improved by government action. Thus, in the years when Cotton Ed was inveighing against the New Deal, the other South Carolina senator, James Francis Byrnes, was serving as Franklin Roosevelt's legislative leader, employing his high political skills to shepherd the administration's key measures through Congress and, incidentally, guarantee that South Carolina got her full share of federal bounty—and possibly a little more.

Born poor in Charleston, Jimmy Byrnes early in life moved to the upcountry to establish what soon became an unassailable political base. From 1911 to 1925 he served in the lower house of Congress, returning to Washington as senator in 1931. His faithful service to the Roosevelt administration was rewarded by appointment to the United States Supreme Court in 1941, but in 1942 he left the bench to join FDR in the White House as director of mobilization, the most powerful domestic post in the wartime government. In 1944, had he been able to clear his nomination with the labor leader, Sidney Hillman, he probably would have become Roosevelt's fourth-term vice-president and successor. As it was, he served the man who got Hillman's nod, Harry S Truman, as secretary of state.

These were milestones in the career of a national politician of the first rank, and the contrast between this sophisticated political operator and the Claghorn caricature presented to the world by his colleague, Ed Smith, was absolute. Similar disparities could be seen in the congressional delegation of any Southern state. There were always posturing showmen in Washington to play the role of the firebrand Dixiecrat, but the distinguished, able, usually conservative Southerners who dominated the key committees of both houses avoided racial matters as best they could, and when they couldn't treated them with all the restraint they thought their constituents would tolerate. If this seemed to indicate endemic schizophrenia among electors who simultaneously supported the likes of Ed Smith and Jimmy Byrnes, it could be attributed to the paralyzing effect of the emotionally charged issue of race upon rational political alignment.

ONE trying to interpret the political process in South Carolina found himself necessarily looking to the past. The standard political oratory was a burlesque of the state's history, and the political system itself was an anachronism. Moreover, the usual equation of economic and political power didn't seem to provide a wholly satisfactory explanation for the phenomena I was observing. It was true enough that the view of South Carolinians at the top of the economic scale usually prevailed in all matters of public policy, and by this test they might be identified as a ruling class. But preservation of the status quo seemed to depend more on inertia than upon the conscious manipulation of a self-perpetuating oligarchy. At the operating level, in fact, there was considerable factional infighting and the power balance within the Democratic monolith, where the counters were political patronage and influence, was likely to shift perceptibly from election to election.

Not even the most talented demagogue was able to convert his personal following into a durable political machine; his power did not extend effectively beyond the office he held, and any effort to exploit his popularity on behalf of other candidates was likely to be counterproductive—or, as in the case of Huey Long, fatal. In South Carolina, the closest thing to an ongoing political organization was the courthouse ring, which in most counties included a leader of long standing, and an inner circle reputed to be able to deliver the local vote. A county boss might or might not hold office, but in either case he was known as the man to see when someone needed something from government. Like their big-time counterparts in Tammany Hall, they traded constituent services for votes, and at election time some were known to sweeten the memory of past favors with a little cash and a drop of whiskey.

Within this loose coalition there were power brokers who plied their trade at the state level. In my day, Edgar Brown was far and away the most successful of these. A lawyer who shared his dominance of lowcountry Barnwell County with another ornament of the bar, Sol Blatt, Edgar was for many years the leader of the State senate, paired off with Sol as Speaker of the House. As a neophyte legislative correspondent I relied upon Edgar for instruction in the inner workings of the system, and, while there were limits to his candor in regard to his own operations, his sardonic humor made him an entertaining tutor.

The first requirement for a political operator was to

maintain flexibility, and Edgar illustrated the point with an anecdote I have since heard in various adaptations in political back rooms from coast to coast. In Edgar's version a county boss had seen his candidate for governor eliminated in the first primary, and had called in his local leaders to instruct them to switch their followers to Cole Blease in the run-off. "But Mr. Tom," one protested, "just last week you said Cole Blease was the worst sonofabitch in South Carolina." Mr. Tom replied, "I said it, and he is, but he's *our* sonofabitch now!"

As a matter of course Edgar referred to most of his colleagues as sonsofbitches, prefacing the title with approving, disapproving, or sometimes simply descriptive adjectives. Sitting alongside the gentleman from Barnwell on one of the black leather sofas at the rear of the old senate chamber I would be treated to a catalogue of vice and virtue as his fellow solons took the floor. One would be identified as a decent sonofabitch, another as a pusillanimous sonofabitch. Some required explanatory asides: a revolving sonofabitch was a sonofabitch no matter how you looked at him, while a lying sonofabitch was one who would tell a lie when the truth would do just as well. When I told him a pompous preacher-member had bitterly objected to being labeled a sanctimonious sonofabitch, he said, "All I know is, the last time I went out to his house his mother ran out from under the porch and bit me on the ankle."

If there was a difference in style, I doubt that there was any real difference in form or effect from the usual organization of the political system in non-Southern states. With the benefit of hindsight and broader experience, I would estimate the extent of actual corruption as somewhat below the national norm. The often perverse individualism of the voters provided a fairly effective brake on excessive peculation. Edgar Brown estimated that in any statewide election about one-third of the votes could be bought, one-third could be arranged—that is, delivered by the county bosses—but that the rest had to be persuaded. Persuasion of this critical third meant overcoming a deeply ingrained suspicion of all politicians. In Brown's case this proved to be the ultimate bar to his ambition to go on to the United States Senate; his very success as the preeminent insider at the state capital made him vulnerable to Cotton Ed's custom of referring to him on the stump as "Satchel Edgar."

The political process was essentially negative. It did not in itself provide a means by which the rich could exploit the poor, but neither did it provide any protection against such exploitation, which, in fact, was almost an act of nature in the face of an increasing surplus of labor fed by the decline in opportunities for gainful employment on the land. While they might be higher in the pecking order, those who presumably belonged to the ruling class had no immunity to exploitation; by national standards, there were very few wealthy men in South Carolina, and almost none who was not beholden to outside interests.

In the only manufacturing industry of consequence most of the early cotton mills had passed to foreign corporate ownership, and those that came later were transplants from New England. The landed gentry were still politically potent, but I doubt that there was then a planter in the state who could have liquidated his agricultural holdings for as much as a million dollars. The nation's number one economic problem bore the hallmarks of an economic province, and the sense that this was so produced a broad populist strain in the electorate that prompted the demagogues to inveigh against Wall Street and the trusts even as they waved the banner of white supremacy. If the issue was exploitation, the real targets were foreign, not domestic.

The effects of the lost war and Reconstruction were bound to be exaggerated in the folk memory of a community where the elders had, as children, actually experienced the impact of military occupation, but there was a harsh reality beneath the romantic embroidery. In 1938 Jonathan Daniels concluded *A Southerner Discovers the South* by attributing the region's pervasive poverty to "the imperial advantages which New England took as its loot after the Civil War."

Cato the Elder was no more implacable than the Brahmans of Boston who came after the Abolitionists with considerably cooler heads. The South was not plowed up and planted with salt as Carthage was. If no more generous, Bostonians (citizens of a region and attitude and not a town) were less wasteful. They recognized that the South kept in its place (a place in the nation similar to that of the Negro in the South) might be useful and profitable. It was.

With the black portion of the proletariat sealed off as an impotent caste, and the white portion convinced that it was not a separate class but an integral part of a cohesive white society, there was no prospect of revolution from below; if fundamental change was to come from above, the impetus would have to be initiated from outside the region.

Under the circumstances it was understandable that many voters approached electoral politics as a kind of summertime diversion, and that the more intelligent practitioners usually discussed their own roles with broad irony. The process was essentially irrational, almost wholly divorced from the reality under which the electorate actually labored. The gallows humor was a measure of the more discerning politicians' frustration over the limits on freedom of action imposed by their state's tragic past. The principal continuing element of that tragedy, of course, was the presence of a mass of unassimilated blacks, and this was particularly galling to those who were largely free of the more corrosive forms of racial prejudice—and many were, since a successful career in politics requires a tolerant and accommodating nature. They found themselves maintaining a status quo they recognized as bearing little relationship to the myth that sustained it, or to the needs of the citizens who suffered under it.

As MY perspective broadened I began to recognize that the anachronistic quality of South Carolina politics involved more than the standard practice of blaming all the state's ills on the Yankees and the frequent, usually fanciful, allusions to the past that colored campaign oratory. When I turned to history to try to improve my understanding of contemporary political reality I found that the shaping events long predated the firing on Fort Sumter. The aristocratic ideal that still informed politics in the South went back to the beginning of the Republic, when it was shared by all the founders.

This is not to say that aristocrats controlled the political process or, indeed, that those who exercised real power in the state were necessarily or even usually descendants of the original Bourbons. But the belief was still widespread that governance should be entrusted to men in position to take an elevated, disinterested approach to public affairs. The voters knew, of course, that it usually wasn't, but they thought it ought to be. To the extent there could be said to be a coherent prevailing political philosophy, it was libertarian as opposed to egalitarian. And the presence of a near majority of blacks imposed the same basic concept on the populists, who in South Carolina never made any attempt to form the kind of biracial coalitions that existed briefly in Georgia and North Carolina.

Equality and liberty were considered twin ideals in the body of Western political thought upon which the founders drew, and Thomas Jefferson managed to include both in the Declaration of Independence. However, in the intellectual circles of London, which set the style for leading American colonists, Samuel Johnson aroused little support when he condemned slavery as a violation of his Tory version of natural law. His biographer, James Boswell, dismissed this as an eccentricity inspired by "zeal without knowledge." His own judgment reflected the prevailing view of the dominant Whig politicians: "To abolish a *status*, which in all ages God has sanctioned, and man has continued, would not only be *robbery* to an innumerable class of our fellow subjects, but it would be an extreme cruelty to the African savage, a portion of whom it saves from massacre, or intolerable bondage, in their own country, and introduces into a much happier state of life."

The men charged with the practical matter of chartering the new American Republic found liberty and equality incompatible. The word *equality* did not appear in the Constitution until it was amended in the wake of the Civil War. A primary reason was that the concentration of slaves in the lower seaboard states was a compelling fact of life when the founders gathered at Philadelphia. But the word *slavery* also was unmentioned in the Constitution except for three brief references, one of which provided that a black man should be counted as three-fifths of a white. The fractional count was for the purpose of determining representation in the new central government: without some acceptable means of balancing this source of power there could be no United States of America.

The Federalist exegesis of the Constitution's philosophical underpinning also swept slavery under the rug. There was, in fact, no real ideological division among most of the founders. Those who owned slaves said they wished they didn't and agreed that the new nation would have been better off had not Britain—as they complained in the Declaration of

Independence—rejected the pleas of the colonies, Southern as well as Northern, for an end to the trade in human chattel. The consensus was that it was now too late to abolish a system upon which half the new states had become dependent; the best that could be done was to limit the growth of the peculiar institution. To that end they included a provision prohibiting the importation of slaves after 1808.

The extraordinary company of men of affairs who established the new government rejected inherited rank along with the rule of the British monarchy, but they were aristocrats nevertheless—"natural" rather than born, as Thomas Jefferson would have it, but still a self-conscious cut above the norm in property, and, by that token, social standing. When their authority began to decline with their advancing years and the advent of partisan politics more attuned to the felt needs of common men, they still served as idealized role models.

The early Southern leaders exhibited fealty to the concept of disinterest by joining with their Northern counterparts in an effort to find a way to eliminate, or at least minimize, the moral blight of slavery. In the early part of the nineteenth century abolitionist sentiment was as widespread in the South as in the North, with leading men voicing the view that human bondage was an abomination in the sight of God and man—"blackest of all blots, and foulest of all deformities," Charles Fenton Mercer of Virginia called it.

But Southerners alone would have to deal with the practical consequences of summarily eliminating a system that was seen not only as a source of labor but as a means of maintaining a social order based on the assumption—generally shared by all whites of that era—that blacks came of inferior racial stock. Upon emancipation the few slaves in the North would disappear into the small, segregated minority of black freedmen. In the South, where the proportion of whites and blacks was more nearly equal, emancipation could gain popular support only if accompanied by an effort to remove, or greatly diminish, the black presence. In the course of the 1820 crisis over the Missouri Compromise the sainted Jefferson wrote:

There is not a man on earth who would sacrifice more than I would to relieve us from this heavy reproach in any practical way. The cession of that kind of property, for so it is mis-named, is a bagatelle which would not cost me a second thought, if in that way a general emancipation and *expatriation* could be effected . . . But, as it is, we have the wolf by the ears, and we can neither hold him, nor safely let him go. Justice is on one scale, and self-preservation on the other.

The American Colonization Society, which included among its supporters such diverse luminaries as Daniel Webster, Henry Clay, and John C. Calhoun, managed to return enough slaves to Africa to found the Republic of Liberia, which named its capital after the Virginian, James Monroe. But the movement faded after 1830 as the plantation system spread beyond the Appalachians. The burgeoning Cotton Kingdom produced a new, expansion-minded landed gentry largely devoid of the qualms that beset the seaboard aristocrats. The importation of slaves did end in 1808 as scheduled, but by 1860 reproduction had increased the four hundred thousand blacks then on hand to four million, providing black majorities in South Carolina and the Gulf Plains states. For the generation that came to maturity in the second quarter of the nineteenth century the consuming issue would be containing the spread of slavery in an expansionist era. This accentuated the sectional division until it came to dominate national politics, and the pressures it generated ended any possibility that the peculiar institution might be voluntarily dismantled.

SOUTH CAROLINA was a logical place to look for the roots of sectional cleavage. The founder of my college, Thomas Green Clemson, the son-in-law of John C. Calhoun, bequeathed the family estate as a campus. My dormitory room overlooked Fort Hill, the handsome plantation house where the frustrated Scotch-Irishman, finding himself on the wrong side of the central moral issue of his age, employed his philosophical genius in an effort to convert slavery from an unfortunate necessity to a positive good. Calhoun's doctrine doomed the loose coalition of high-minded Northern and Southern patricians who had sought to reduce, and ultimately eliminate, the slave system. Those who accepted Calhoun's philosophy rejected any such necessity, and this in turn convinced the more passionate Yankee abolitionists that such gradualist schemes as African repatriation were a subversive means of disarming the righteous. In 1831 William Lloyd Garrison launched his fire-breathing

Liberator with a demand for immediate, unconditional abolition. The thunder out of Boston, as Garrison no doubt intended, was interpreted in the South as a declaration of holy war.

From the outset the moral issue was entangled with economic interests, and these were not limited to the planters' capital investment in their labor force, which often exceeded the value of their land. The first great confrontation came on the federal tariff, which produced a division between the protectionist North and the free-trading South. Calhoun, who had begun his career as an outspoken nationalist, reversed himself to argue that the central government was created by a compact among sovereign states, each of which retained the right to nullify within its borders any federal order it considered inimical. This was the states' rights theory ultimately elaborated in support of secession.

In the Senate Robert Y. Hayne of South Carolina, as surrogate for Calhoun, who was confined to the presiding officer's chair as Andrew Jackson's vice-president, argued the case for nullification, facing Daniel Webster of New Hampshire. Webster did not mention the peculiar institution in his cool lawyer's brief, but, in reference to the sectional conflict in the new states beyond the Appalachians, he cited the calm, orderly settlement of Ohio by New Englanders in contrast to the speculation and disorder across the river in Kentucky. Hayne construed this as an attack upon the Southern way of life, and cast Webster in the role of Yankee invader who would pierce the Southern heartland with his pernicious doctrines. But he was in fact replying in kind to William Lloyd Garrison when he cried:

He has crossed the border, he has invaded the state of South Carolina, is making war upon her citizens, and endeavoring to overthrow her principles and institutions. Sir, when the gentleman provokes me to such a conflict, I meet him at the threshold—I will struggle while I have life, for our altars and our firesides; and, if God gives me strength, I will drive back the invader discomfited. Nor shall I stop there. If the gentleman provokes the war he shall have war. . . .

In this forensic skirmish Webster was clearly the victor. "On this occasion the divisive idea of a united South had been routed," William R. Taylor wrote in *Cavalier and Yankee*. James

Madison, congratulating Webster, said of the debate, "It crushes nullification and must hasten the abandonment of secession." The former president, unhappily, turned out to be a poor prophet. The oratorical war had not ended, but was only beginning. In 1833 Garrison summoned his growing company of militant followers to Philadelphia to launch the American Anti-Slavery Society. There he proclaimed a nullification doctrine of his own, declaring that all laws admitting the right of slavery are "before God utterly null and void, being an audacious usurpation of the Divine prerogative; a daring infringement upon the law of nature; a base overthrow of the very foundation of the social compact; a complete extinction of all the relations, endearments and obligations of mankind; and a presumptuous transgression of all the holy commandments." Within five years the Anti-Slavery Society had 1,305 local chapters, with a membership pledged

to secure to the colored population of the United States all the rights and privileges which belong to them as men and as Americans—come what may to our persons, our interests, or our reputations, whether we live to witness the triumph of LIBERTY, JUSTICE, and HUMANITY, or to perish ultimately as martyrs in this great, benevolent and holy cause.

A phalanx of Southerners, equally willing to welcome martyrdom, arose to reply in kind. The exchange of oratorical shot and shell would continue with mounting intensity until it was replaced by the real thing.

Here it seemed to me, was the beginning of the gap between rhetoric and reality that still characterized the issue of race when I first began to think seriously about it a century later. In the abstract, the Garrisonians obviously had the best of the moral argument—but the abolitionist prescription was clearly unworkable. Calhoun's attempt to meet it by imbuing slavery with civic virtue was not only morally offensive but precluded any attempt to find a rational solution through gradual means that might have been acceptable to the majority of Southerners, who owned few if any slaves. Neither Hayne's bombast nor Calhoun's cool exposition proved persuasive to the state's political leadership, and unionist sentiment prevailed when nullification was first put to the test. As late as 1858, when

Congressman William Porcher Miles asserted that all Southerners were either absolute unionists or secessionists, Sen. James Hammond denied that such polarization existed. Mile's formula, he wrote, ignored "999 in every 1,000 of the voters and 49 in 50 of the substantial and influential men of the South."

Those who pitched the national debate over slavery on a moral plane were, for the most part, positioned outside the immediate political arena. The abolitionists and their Southern antagonists were an elite remnant of the old seaboard stock and, South as well as North, they scorned the compromising officeholders who were trying to hold the union together. Most of the practicing politicians of that day, like their successors a hundred years later, tried to avoid the issue as best they could, and minimize it when they couldn't. This only served to inflame the true believers on both sides.

"I do not wish to think or speak, or write with moderation," Garrison proclaimed. "No! No! . . . I will not equivocate —I will not excuse—I will not retreat a single inch—*and I will be heard!*" And heard he was, particularly by his Southern counterparts, who used his fulminations for their own ends. They found themselves in full agreement, if for opposite reasons, when Garrison borrowed from the prophet Isaiah to pronounce the Constitution "a convenant with death and an agreement with hell," publicly burning the hallowed document, and advocating that the North secede from the South. If the Garrisonians and the Southern Ultras alarmed and alienated the mass of voters, the epithets they hurled at each other, and at the pragmatists who tried to stand between them, steadily sharpened the two edges of the issue that would sever the union.

I would hear echoes of that confrontation throughout my career on the periphery of politics. I did not leave the moral issue behind when I departed from the South and began to deal with race relations as a national phenomenon; it reappeared in full fervor as a principal factor in the rising of the New Left in the 1960s.

3

⚜️

The Uses of Mythology

My first protracted exposure to the great world
beyond the Mason-Dixon line came as a result of
my first, and last, effort to exploit the ingrained defensiveness
of my fellow Southerners. In 1938, as I began to emerge from
cub reporter status on the *Piedmont*, my city editor, George
Chaplin, suggested the possibility of an expenses-paid vacation
which would also provide him with copy defending the honor
of our hometown. Greenville, which billed itself as the "textile
center of the South," had become a prime target for Northern
journalists bent on exposing the low-wage, stretch-out practices
that prevailed among the militantly antiunion Southern cotton
mills. These forays increased markedly after President Roosevelt designated the South the nation's number one economic
problem. Some were the product of honest journalistic enterprise; some were designed to produce pro-union propaganda
to bolster the faltering efforts of the Textile Workers Organizing Committee; and not a few were intended as counterblows
against the Southern promotional campaign to "bring the
cotton mills to the cotton fields," which had succeeded well
enough to leave behind a substantial residue of structural
unemployment in the older industrial cities.

Whatever the motive, the often sensational charges of
exploitation and degradation rankled the ordained protectors
of the South's good name. The proprietors of my newspaper
were in that number, and I found immediate sympathy for a
proposal that I cast back the stone by undertaking a foray of my
own into the Northern industrial slums. A mail canvass brought
in acceptances of the proposed series from twenty-two major
Southern newspapers ranging across the region from the
Atlanta Constitution to the *Dallas News*. On the basis of this

response, I persuaded a solvent uncle to co-sign a bank note to underwrite my expenses and headed north for what once had been—and so far as most of my incipient readers were concerned, still was—enemy territory.

I had no difficulty in finding ample evidence to sustain my prefabricated conclusions. The smart-alec quality of the enterprise attracted the attention of *Time* magazine, and produced this summary in its "Press" section:

A patriotic and industrious son of the South is 22-year-old Harry S. Ashmore, reporter for the Greenville (S.C.) *Piedmont*. Irked by the heart-rending accounts of the South's shortcomings by itinerant northern journalists, Reporter Ashmore decided to spend his two-week vacation in the "deep North to see how they managed to cast the first stone." New York City, the indignant reporter found, was "the sweatshop capital of America," its slums squalid and crime-breeding. New England's textile cities seemed to him "not far from being industrial ghost cities." In Philadelphia he found more slums and "the universal fear" that industry would move away. In the shadow of Bethlehem's steel mills he saw "filth and depravity" and the same methods that Southern manufacturers use to resist unionization. In Washington he found statistics to show that "low wages, long hours and primitive working conditions can be found anywhere."

In six snappy articles, the purposeful vacationist concluded that the North was as bad as the South.

By the time the articles reached print any indignation I may have felt was beginning to give way to contrition. As the predictably favorable reaction began to pour in, I recognized that this kind of tit-for-tat journalism only served to provide an excuse for exploitation of Southern workers—and was, indeed, a continuation in its own way of the anti-Yankee countermoralizing I had begun to see as a diversion which prevented Southerners from facing up to their own problems in their own terms.

Yet my experience in poking around the back streets of the great cities left me with no doubt that the Northern view of the South was, when not actively hostile, badly skewed. It was my first sustained experience of being treated as a stereotype; my accent and looks were enough to identify me as alien in those working-class neighborhoods, and when I managed to open up a conversation it often led to a remarkable outburst of unabashed racism—this despite the fact that there usually was no visible black presence to account for it.

Most of the workers I interviewed were those who would be identified in today's shorthand as ethnics, typically the children of European immigrants. Once they identified me as a Southerner they hastened to assure me that they shared my presumed racial prejudice. Insofar as they had had any personal experience with blacks it had usually been as competitors for scarce jobs, and in those days they kept their neighborhoods, and their unions, lily-white by whatever means came to hand. It was, in fact, in the presumably left-wing union strongholds that antiblack feeling was most outspoken—understandably, since blacks had often been used as strikebreakers in the early years of the century.

When I talked with Yankees of more elevated status, usually politicians, bureaucrats, and fellow journalists, race rarely entered the conversation unless I introduced it. Those of liberal bent saw the effects of prejudice as a problem, but an abstract one to which they did not assign high priority. Proudly cosmopolitan New York was in most respects more thoroughly segregated than any Southern city; with the exception of a small coterie of intellectuals, musicians, and entertainers there was little traffic between the white world and the black enclave in upper Manhattan called Harlem.

Later I would come to know Northern whites who had, and sometimes acted upon, a genuine concern with race relations. Some were political radicals, treating racial discrimination as an extreme outcropping of a class system under which the rich exploited the poor. Others were liberal heirs of the abolitionist tradition, who lent their support to such reformist interracial organizations as the Urban League and the National Association for the Advancement of Colored People. But most simply felt a vague compassion for blacks, expressed in a conviction that something ought to be done to redress the obvious injustices of legal and de facto segregation—although they usually didn't know exactly what. Almost without exception their goodwill was matched by their total lack of exposure to the realities of black existence, North or South.

It was their very sympathy that imposed upon the black leaders of the pre–World War II era the "double-consciousness" W.E.B. Du Bois described in *Souls of Black Folk*: "this sense of always looking at oneself through the eyes of others, of measuring one's soul by the tape of a world that looks on in amused contempt and pity." Of the well-wishers in the genteel circles into which he, as a Harvard alumnus, found his way, he wrote:

They approach me in a half-hesitant sort of way, eye me curiously or compassionately, and then, instead of saying directly, How does it feel to be a problem? they say, I know an excellent colored man in my town; or, I fought at Mechanicsville; or, Do not those Southern outrages make your blood boil? At these I smile, or am interested, or reduce the boiling to a simmer, as the occasion may require. To the real question, How does it feel to be a problem? I seldom answer a word.

When I was exposed to these circles I found that a Southern white usually encountered something of the same tentative approach. In 1941 I was appointed a Nieman Fellow at Harvard, a dispensation that included admission to such sanctums as the Faculty Club. In Cambridge I discovered that possession of two Confederate grandfathers not only aroused curiosity, but, to my embarrassment, often also invoked a measure of the compassion Du Bois cited—this based on the assumption that my appointment to faculty status certified an enlightened view on race, and that this must make me a pariah, if not a martyr, in my home environs. The conviction that one could not be pro-Negro without being anti-South was as firmly held among neo-abolitionists as it was among Daughters of the Confederacy.

In the Cambridge community of that day, with its token handful of blacks and Southern whites, there still flourished the enduring myth that Southerners and Northerners were, and always had been, divided not merely by geography and diverse economic development, but by historically differentiated cultures and even bloodlines. In *Cavalier and Yankee* the social historian, William R. Taylor, described this legendary past, which had, as he noted, produced a fictional sociology:

. . . the North had been settled by one party to the English Civil War, the Roundheads, and the South by the other, the royal party of the Cavaliers. The Yankee was a direct descendant of the Puritan Roundhead and the Southern gentleman of the English Cavalier, and the difference between the two was at least partly a matter of blood . . . Under the stimulus of this divided heritage the North had developed a leveling, go-getting utilitarian society and the South had developed a society based on the values of the English country gentry. It was commonly felt, furthermore, that these two ways of life had been steadily diverging since colonial times, and there were many after 1861 who believed that these characteristic differences between North and South brought on the Civil War.

This reordering of history had advantages on both sides for those who manned the rhetorical ramparts during the great debates that raged through the 1840s and 1850s. It was easier for the Yankee abolitionists to find a substantial portion of their fellow citizens guilty of perpetrating unmitigated evil if they did not have to treat the malefactors as kinfolk. In accepting the myth of Cavalier ancestry the Southerners divorced themselves from the crass commercialism of the North and elevated slavery to an act of noblesse oblige primarily intended to bring the blessings of Christian civilization to benighted blacks. A hundred years later, these fantasies still colored the rhetoric of those who sought to exploit sectional political and economic differences, North or South.

ENSLAVEMENT of members of a different race or tribe was a universal practice when it was instituted in the North American colonies, and had been throughout recorded history. The movement to ban the outright ownership of one man by another that began to spread across the civilized world in the eighteenth century did not go beyond that minimal recognition of the sanctity of human nature. Serfs bound to the land, peasants consigned to an inferior class, craftsmen locked into their trade, societies rigidly demarcated by caste—all these practices continued and left the great majority of the earth's inhabitants less than free. Viewing its residue at first hand, it occurred to me that the form of chattel slavery that continued in the South after it was abandoned throughout the Western world could be understood, and properly judged, only in the context of its own time and place.

So at Harvard I spent most of my time with the historians. The one who seemed to me to most successfully avoid the ideological imprint left upon American history by the moral issue of slavery and its aftermath was Frederick Merk, who inherited the mantle of the great historian of the American frontier, Frederick Jackson Turner. Professor Merk believed American history could best be understood by tracing step by step the course the pioneers followed in pushing back the frontier, and figuring out why they and their successors settled where they did. He tended to take ethno-cultural considerations for granted; when the westward movement across the Atlantic began to accelerate in the seventeenth century it naturally followed the latitudes, depositing those from northern Europe in the temperate zones of North America, consigning the Latin peoples to the subtropics and the continent still further south. The fact that most northern Europeans were Protestants and most Latins Catholics would have cultural and political consequences in the New World, as it did in the Old. But it was Merk's thesis that the great determinants of initial settlement, and of much that would follow, were the varied combinations of climate, soil, vegetation, topography, and mineral resources as they occurred in a vast land whose aboriginal occupants had not advanced beyond the Stone Age.

The first frontier examined in Merk's *History of the Westward Movement* was the Atlantic Coast. Among the English pioneers who landed there could be found the classic figure of the refugee from royal tyranny and religious persecution. But men of this kind, and the adventurous spirits motivated by an urge to explore the unknown, were a small minority; most came out of extreme economic necessity, and functioned within the framework of what was essentially a commercial operation. Responsibility for opening up the new domain beyond the sea was delegated by the English monarchs to development companies which expected return on their capital. The investors provided transportation and the initial costs of maintenance; in return they required the colonials to produce commodities suitable for export. This meant goods convertible to cash on the London market—initially furs and nonperishable agricultural products that could stand the long sea voyage.

Tobacco was the first cash crop in the first of the American colonies. In 1613 John Rolfe brought in a strain from the West Indies suitable to the taste of Londoners, and within a dozen years its production in tidewater Virginia and Maryland dominated the market. The experience was a harbinger for the South. The lucrative return from "sotweed" created a one-crop economy in the James Valley so extensive the planters were soon forced to import food for the gang labor such mass production required.

The first plantation laborers were white, reduced to temporary serfdom by the Virginia Company, which recruited poor English men and women who wanted to improve their lot but did not command the means to do so. "The answer to the problem was offered to the commercially minded," Merk wrote. "Every man or woman had assets—a body, two good arms, and freedom to sell these for a brief span of years." These indentured servants contracted to provide from four to seven years of uncompensated labor, the term depending upon skill and age. The seafaring men who served as agents in these transactions considered them natural to their calling; they purchased and delivered a cargo of laborers and brought back a cargo of tobacco. "The idea accorded well with the law of supply and demand—oversupply in England, undersupply in America," Merk noted.

From two-thirds to three-fourths of the colonists who arrived before the Revolution were indentured. A minority came from western Europe as "redemptioners" who sold ancestral lands and paid part of their passage in order to reduce their terms of bondage. At the other end of the scale some fifty thousand convicted felons were given reprieves from English prisons in return for seven-year indentures. A sampling of the migrants was provided by the official records maintained at Bristol from 1654 through 1686, in which 36 percent identified themselves as farmers or husbandmen, 22 percent as artisans, 10 percent as unskilled, 1 percent as gentlemen, and 25 percent as women.

Cavaliers of noble lineage certainly were involved with the Virginia Company, and a few actually came to settle in the James River country. This was also true in South Carolina, where the initial settlement was charged by Charles II to a group called the Lords Proprietor. But these were investors, not immigrants. The first settlers at Charles Town came not from the great houses of England but from the Caribbean island of Barbados, where the plantation system was already firmly emplaced. There were few noble genes in the pool that determined the character of those who made up the founding population.

The initial objectives sought in the settlement of Massachusetts had a touch of idealism—"the winning of freedom of worship and the building of a community of the godly." However, the colony established at Plymouth Rock by those Merk identified as "religious leftists" did not thrive and numbered only seven thousand in 1671 when it was taken over by the Massachusetts Bay Company. This enterprise, based at Boston, was firmly in the charge of "Puritans bent on establishing communities of their own faith in the New World," who were, as Merk noted, also "moved by a desire to acquire free land in the wilderness."

The climate, soil, and topography of New England, wholly unsuited to a plantation economy, led to the creation of villages with central lands held in common while individual parcels suitable for family farming were granted to settlers. The time soon came when the older villages ran out of land, and as new settlements were made the original proprietors were granted proportionate shares as absentee landlords. "The proprietors, when they voted not to add to their numbers, became a privileged landholding group," Merk wrote. In some of the towns proprietors were forbidden to sell their land rights to foreigners, a definition that included even non-Puritan English. The insular, homogeneous character of these New England settlements lasted a long time, but it could not hold as those who had become landed aristocrats turned their talents to the creation of a mercantile society that would make Boston a national center of commerce and finance.

FROM the standpoint of those engaged in it, no major amendment of the marketplace rationalization that justified the trade in indentured servants was required to ease the conscience of ship captains who began to substitute cargoes of blacks destined for the plantations of the South. But for those brought involuntarily from Africa, and bound for a permanent rather than a temporary period of service, the difference was profound, and it would prove fateful not only for the slaves but for the society into which they were forcibly introduced. There were blacks among the earliest settlers in Virginia and Carolina; most were slaves but many were given a form of indenture that permitted them to become freedmen. It was not until the early years of the eighteenth century that slave labor became a vital part of the Southern economy.

In 1698 the British crown ended its monopoly on the trade, opening the traffic to enterprising shippers from all the civilized countries of Europe, and from Puritan New England. Blacks, particularly those already conditioned by service in the Indies, were welcomed by planters discomfited by the impermanence of a work force of indentured white laborers, many of whom ran away and disappeared into such frontier areas as North Carolina where land could be had virtually for the taking.

If the record of the original North-South division in American politics has been obscured by mythic embroidery, no impartial record of the slaves, whose presence caused it, ever existed at all. Virtually all sources are secondary; the nearly universal illiteracy imposed upon the black immigrants meant that only a few obviously exceptional freedmen left written records of their own experience. Contemporary oral accounts of slavery by those who endured it were relayed by whites, most of whom were conditioned by their predisposition for or against the institution. Even in the case of the valuable oral history compiled in the 1930s from WPA workers' interviews with surviving ex-slaves there is the difficulty of memory blurred by age, and the inhibition imposed by the fact that most of the interviewers were white.

The first thoroughgoing scholarly examination of slavery was undertaken by Ulrich Bonnell Phillips, a Georgian who gave a strong economic cast to the works he began publishing in 1918. Phillips established the generally accepted standard of twenty or more slaves to qualify a farming operation as a plantation, and concentrated his attention on the fifty percent of blacks who provided the gang labor required for the great cash crops of cotton, rice, and sugar. He has been accused of thus giving a class bias to his work, neglecting the other half of the black population dispersed among the small farms and towns of the antebellum South.

Phillips' work is now regarded as tainted by racism, as it inescapably was in the light of the prevailing scholarly precepts of his day. The assumption that blacks were genetically inferior to whites was virtually universal in the academic community prior to World War I. No savant anywhere in the western world arose to challenge the conclusion of the famous 1910 edition of *Encyclopaedia Britannica*, assembled under the supervision of the faculties of Oxford and Cambridge: ". . . the negro would appear to stand on a lower evolutionary plane than the white man, and to be more closely related to the highest anthropoids." And Phillips insured the special ire of a new wave of leftist revisionists when he wrote of himself in the introduction to *American Negro Slavery*: "For him . . . who has known the considerate and cordial, courteous and charming men and women, white and black, which that picturesque life in its best phases produced, it is impossible to agree that its basis and its operations were wholly evil, the law and the prophets to the contrary notwithstanding."

But Phillips was no mere apologist. He did manage to see past the ubiquitous stereotypes that in the decades before and after the Civil War portrayed either a faithful black Sambo, happy with the lot Old Massa prescribed for him, or a brutalized black victim of the white man's whip, bloodhounds, and lynching rope. In the course of the renewed interest in the slave period set off by the civil rights movement of the 1950s, Phillips became an indispensable source for many historians who disagreed with his conclusions. He was staunchly defended by the socialist, Eugene D. Genovese:

The harsh truth is that racists like Phillips, until recently, have taught us much more about the South, and the Southern black man, too, than their Northern liberal detractors have ever been able to do. I am sorry about that. It is terribly annoying. But there is not much to be done about it. In my opinion liberal assimilationist historians would have long ago ruined us, had it not been for the opposition of Southerners, white and black, racist and anti-racist, who could not stomach the ideological cant we have been served up as "scientific" history.

Genovese, applying Marxian analysis, saw antebellum Southern society not as an aberration of the American capitalist norm, which he disapproved in any case, but as the reflection of a significantly different class structure. "The slaveholders," he wrote in *In Red and Black*, "presented the only politically powerful challenge to liberal capitalism to emanate from within the United States. It was they . . . who questioned the assumptions of liberal society, denounced the hypocrisy and barbarism of the marketplace, and advanced a vision of an organic society and a collective community."

IN the course of my explorations with the Harvard historians I was impressed by the fact that most scholarly critics of slavery had subordinated, or perhaps simply rejected out of moral outrage, the central point stressed by Genovese—that the plantation was, for better or worse, a genuine community. There were certainly harsh masters and cruel overseers, and in some respects the system had an inherently brutalizing effect upon all those involved in it, owners as well as slaves. But there were inherent limits on physical abuse and material neglect; you could not run a plantation with hands who were unfit or unwilling to work; the whip could, and did, serve as an instrument to maintain discipline, but any sensible planter severely limited its use, if for no other reason than to protect an investment that ran as high as fifteen hundred dollars for a prime field hand. The operating principle for a successful plantation was paternalism, and if this served to stamp an enduring brand of inferiority on the slave, it usually provided a safeguard against deliberate cruelty or inhumane neglect.

The external evidence bears out Genovese's finding that on the average the slaves were better off in terms of housing, diet, health care, and working conditions than were contemporary farm laborers anywhere in the world; their vitality is attested to by the fact that they constituted the only slave population that continued to increase—tenfold in fifty years—without further importation of Africans or the wholesale miscegenation that was common in the Latin countries. Genovese's Marxist bias led him to observe: "Were anyone perverse enough to bother, he might find that the living conditions of a large minority or even a majority of the world's population during the twentieth century might not compare in comfort with those of the slaves in Mississippi a century earlier."

Cotton was ideally suited to the South's climate and soil,

and to the use of slave labor. After the cotton gin and power-driven machines for spinning and weaving opened an expanding world market, the spread of the plantation economy was inexorable. There has been, however, a running argument as to whether cotton planting was profitable in the long haul. Phillips thought not, contending that the capital investment in labor, plus the inefficiency engendered by the lack of a profit motive for the slaves, had doomed the system. Others, analyzing the books of plantations in the newer sections, found an annual return of as much as 35 percent on the investment, considerably better than could have been had from a comparable operation using free labor. But plantations enjoyed such prosperity only when land was first brought into cultivation, so that the boom on the Gulf Plains was accompanied by bankruptcy and decay on the Atlantic seaboard, where cotton and tobacco cultivation had depleted the soil.

For many of the seaboard aristocrats the plantation system continued as a way of life after it had become a losing commercial proposition. This was the case with James Chesnut, United States senator from South Carolina, one of the drafters of the Confederate constitution, and a colonel on the staff of Jefferson Davis. A graduate of Princeton, as his father had been before him, Chesnut lived on one of the family plantations that embraced five square miles near Camden. Among his blessings was a remarkable wife, Mary Boykin Chesnut, daughter of another leading South Carolina family, whose highly literate *Diary from Dixie*, first published posthumously in 1904, provides an extraordinarily candid and perceptive picture of Southern high society.

Life at that level tended to block out the horrors sometimes visited upon slaves who lived in less fortunate circumstances. In Mrs. Chesnut's time her long-settled in-laws had never bought or sold a black, although the hundreds they had acquired by inheritance and propagation provided far more hands than the plantations required. She had spent much of her girlhood at boarding school in "innocent, slumbrous old Charleston, where like other inhabitants, I saw no wrong, and am sure that I would never have questioned any existing institutions to my dying day." But in her teens her father established a plantation on the raw frontier of the Cotton Kingdom in Mississippi. "I received there," Mary Chesnut wrote, "my first ideas that negroes were not a divine institution for our benefit—or we for theirs." She was in Washington in the years when the abolitionists held forth in Congress; her husband resigned his Senate seat in protest against the accession of Abraham Lincoln, but she confided to her diary: "Sumner said not one word of this hated institution that is not true . . . God forgive us, ours is a *monstrous* system."

Like other Southerners of similar view, Mrs. Chesnut did not extend her moral condemnation of the institution to those who now went to war to defend it. She never compromised her loyalty to her husband, or to the Confederate cause. She deplored slavery not so much for the degradation it imposed upon blacks as for the burdens it imposed upon their masters. In her diary the frequent references to Harriet Beecher Stowe were tinged with envy. The author of *Uncle Tom's Cabin* could live in a nice clean, sweet-smelling home, shut away in her library, exercising a literary talent the well-read Mary Chesnut no doubt felt was inferior to her own. "Now consider what I have seen of my mother's life, my grandmother's, my mother-in-law's," she wrote. "These people were educated in Northern schools, they read the same books as their Northern contemporaries, the same daily papers, the same Bible. They have the same ideas of right and wrong." But now they were fated to live in what amounted to Negro villages, whose inhabitants "walk through their houses whenever they see fit. . . ."

These women I love have less chance to live their own lives in peace than if they were African missionaries. They have a swarm of blacks about them like children under their care, not as Mrs. Stowe's fancy painted them, and they hate slavery worse than Mrs. Stowe does . . . My husband supported his plantation by his law practice. Now it is running him in debt. Our people have never earned their own bread. Take this estate, [her father-in-law's] what does it do, actually? It all goes back in some shape to what are called slaves here, called operatives or tenants or peasantry elsewhere. I doubt if ten thousand in money ever comes to this old gentleman's hands. When Mrs. Chesnut married South, her husband was as wealthy as her brothers-in-law. How is it now? Their money has accumulated for their children. This old man's goes to support a horde of idle, dirty Africans, while he is abused as a cruel slave-owner.

The plantation system conferred few, if any, benefits on the large numerical majority of small farmers who could never be classified as truly prosperous, and none at all on the marginal population of poor whites. The scholars are now virtually unanimous in the verdict that for the South as a whole slavery was economically disadvantageous. The system tied up capital in labor in a fashion that denied the region the means to develop the infrastructure it needed to gain and maintain the independence its leaders ultimately sought.

IN his thoroughgoing examination of every aspect of slave life Genovese took the measure of the stereotypes that still survive from the assault on the institution by Yankee abolitionists, and its uncritical defense by their Southern counterparts. These usually result from the effort to portray the worst of the abuses, or the best of the treatment, as typical, if not universal. Miscegenation, for example, was inevitable among people living in such close proximity, and the practice, cloaked in the most blatant forms of racist hypocrisy, not only degraded helpless black women but outraged their white mistresses. Writing of a neighboring planter whose light-skinned offspring were readily identifiable in the slave quarters, the redoubtable Mrs. Chesnut found that "his wife and daughters, in their purity and innocence, are supposed never to dream of what is plain before their eyes as the sunlight," noting in reference to the villainous libertine in *Uncle Tom's Cabin,* "You see, Mrs. Stowe did not hit the sorest spot. She makes Legree a bachelor."

The external evidence indicates that miscegenation was the exception rather than the rule; the census of 1860 showed only 13 percent of blacks with white ancestry, and the incidence was highest in the border states and lowest, from 5 to 9 percent, in the states with the greatest concentration of slave population: South Carolina, Georgia, Alabama, and Mississippi. "The plantations hardly emerge from the statistics looking like the harems of Abolitionist fancy," Genovese wrote.

Another of the durable horror stories, the supposed maintenance of slave-breeding operations on the worn-out plantations of the seaboard to supply hands for the new lands opening in the West, has little substance, although it is true that slaves were sometimes "sold down the river" in a fashion that callously divided husbands and wives, parents and children. But here again, the prevailing practice was to encourage stable family life in the quarters, whether out of a sense of Christian obligation or out of recognition that it improved the performance of the work force.

Although the only means of protest available to them were passive, the slaves could and did impose limiting conditions on their servitude, with the result that the planters were providing them with a steadily rising standard of living right up to 1860. It was because they did have something to lose beside their chains that slave revolts were relatively few and historically insignificant, except for the effect they had in feeding the fears of those who believed the abolitionists were sending down agents to foment a general insurrection. This has continued to be a source of frustration for those who have attempted to superimpose a revolutionary tradition upon the heritage of modern-day blacks. The Marxist interpreters, Genovese wrote, only "drew attention away from the slaves' deeper cultural and social resistance and from the organic relationships inherent in the slaveholders' hegemony."

Some, including W.E.B. Du Bois, have argued that the Christianity imposed by the whites was a religion of meekness and submission. Genovese contends, however, that it was the reality in which these transplanted people found themselves that prevented their developing the sense of national mission that elsewhere made the Protestant faith a fighting ideology:

The black preachers saw Africa in America as it was, not as they may have wished it. Their realism reflected that of the masses they sought to sway. . . . The slave communities, embedded as they were among numerically preponderant and militarily powerful whites, counseled a strategy of patience, of acceptance of what could not be helped, of dogged effort to keep the black community alive and healthy—a strategy of survival that, like its African prototype, above all said yes to life in this world.

Marxist dogma still defines blacks as a nation within the nation, subject to imperialist exploitation by the white majority, and in the thirties the American Communist party line called for creation of a separate black soviet in the South. This, like the non-Marxist separatist movements that have sprung up from time to time, has so far had little lasting appeal for the rank and file, whose ambition has been to join, not overturn, the middle class. "Whatever later ideologues might say," Genovese wrote, "the slaves and freedmen knew that their lives had grown intertwined with those of the whites; that in some ways and to some extent no divorce would ever be possible because it would rob them of the only history they had."

4

The Great Fratricide

At an early age I acquired a voracious and largely indiscriminate reading habit. One of my numerous aunts maintained a collection of printed matter that could loosely be called a library, and when my mother hauled me along for a visit I happily found my way to the shelves. Aunt Mamie Anderson, an admirer of Robert Browning, had a sign on her porch: PIPPA PASSES, and her collection was long on poetry. But it also contained a number of memoirs by Confederate generals, all of which, as I recall, wound up explaining that things would have been different had the author had one more regiment at Shiloh.

If this martial prose had any lasting effect it was to cure me of any weakness for the romantic version of the Civil War that prompted many of my contemporaries to join round tables and pursue the exploits of dead generals and forgotten privates. I think I knew by instinct what I would learn in practice when I became an infantry officer myself—that war is basically a dull business, with any moments of glory offset by great stretches of tedium and discomfort broken by flashes of sheer horror. And I began to wonder why my relatives of the appropriate age, unanimously as family legend had it, went off to fight for a cause most of them didn't really believe in.

Aunt Mamie's collection also included the works of Sir Walter Scott, whose tales of the age of chivalry were said to have aroused a response transmitted through Scotch-Irish genes that made *Ivanhoe* more responsible for the outbreak of civil war than *Uncle Tom's Cabin*. Certainly there was no excess of rationality among leaders who elected to launch a war when they didn't have a cannon factory—and even less among those who thought they could bluff the North into letting the South go peaceably. These were the men who responded to the impassioned rebuttal to the abolitionists by South Carolina's rhetorical fusileers, notably Robert Barnwell Rhett, his son and namesake, who edited the *Charleston Mercury*, and William Lowndes Yancey, who moved on to Alabama and headed the radical faction there. But these were low-countrymen, long-standing political antagonists of my grandparents and their kind, who made the upcountry a unionist stronghold.

After the 1830s there was no open antislavery movement in the South; the issue, as the politicians tried to frame it, was preservation of the nation. In South Carolina the political infighting was sharpened by the upcountry-lowcountry cleavage, but not confined to it. Men of standing took issue with the "ultra" followers of Calhoun. They argued that holding the union together was essential to maintaining order, which, as the lowcountry planter, Sen. James H. Hammond, wrote, "is a prime necessity in every community, especially an agricultural one, and most especially a slaveholding one."

In South Carolina the unionists functioned as a faction within the Democratic Party. "Take my word for it, conservatism, in name at least, will not do for a pressing, impetuous people like our own," William Gilmore Simms wrote to Hammond in 1841. "It must be *ultraism, in profession at least*, if not altogether in practice." Elsewhere the unionists moved into the Whig Party when it emerged in the 1840s to carry the conservative banner in national politics. By 1850 the owners of three-fourths of all the slaves in the South were counted as Whigs. Frederick Merk found this entirely natural:

They were Whigs in outlook when the party was formed. On such economic issues as banking and currency, and internal improvement, they accepted the leadership of Henry Clay. On the tariff issue the planters favored protection at a high level, at least on sugar and molasses. . . . They were compromisers with regard to slavery and its extension, as exhibited in the issues of annexation of Texas and the Mexican War. They wished to remain in harmony with the northern wing of the party, realizing that in a violent clash over slavery large property owners in the South would have the most to lose.

How, then, did these powerful men lose control of the situation in both North and South? The moralists seemed to cancel each other as their exchange of polemics flew back and forth across the Mason-Dixon line. When Garrison placed the mark of Cain upon the slaveholder, distinguished Southern divines sprang forward to reply in kind. In 1850 the eminent Presbyterian, Dr. J. H. Thornwell, president of South Carolina College, separated the sheep and goats: "The parties to this conflict are not merely abolitionists and slaveholders—they are atheists, socialists, communists, red republicans, jacobins on the one side, and the friends of order and regulated freedom on the other. In one word, the world is the battleground— Christianity and atheism the combatants; and the progress of humanity the stake." I find it hard to believe that the Whig gentry could have taken this kind of thing at face value, but they did come to believe that the relentless abolitionist campaign was producing a tangible threat to their own safety. "Many men of the South," Ulrich Bonnell Phillips wrote, "thought of themselves and their neighbors as living above a loaded mine, in which the Negro slaves were the powder, the abolitionists the spark, and the free Negroes the fuse."

ALMOST without exception the planters who left behind diaries and correspondence incorporating their private views expressed full confidence in the loyalty of their own slaves. Living in isolation as they did, a handful of whites in the midst of what amounted to a sizable black village, they were certainly vulnerable to the disaffected, who had ready access to firearms used for hunting, assorted sharp and blunt instruments, and the torch that might incinerate a sleeping family. Yet, except for the Nat Turner rising in Virginia in 1831, there were no major incidents of organized insurrection, and few of individual violence.

But the same men who had confidence in their own slaves believed that collectively the black population could be incited to wage what Andrew Jackson termed "servile war" against their masters, and this prospect came to provide the ultimate argument against emancipation. It was taken seriously by that perceptive French observer, Alexis de Tocqueville, who wrote in 1835: "The Negroes may long remain slaves without complaining; but if they are once raised to the level of freemen, they will soon revolt at being deprived of almost all their civil rights; and as they cannot become the equal of the whites, they will speedily show themselves as enemies." Tocqueville could see no alternative to slavery but "the most horrible of civil wars, and perhaps . . . the extirpation of one or the other of the two races."

Accepting this thesis, as most of them did, the Southerners could only assume that the immediate, unconditional emancipation demanded by militant abolitionists would leave those in the plantation belt vastly outnumbered by incipiently hostile freedmen. All the states attempted to close their borders to antislavery agitators and the mails to their literature. And some enacted laws requiring the expulsion of all free blacks, responding to the view expressed in an 1858 circular signed by leading citizens of Arkansas: "Even if they do nothing actively, their very existence here, and their condition as free men, make them constant, though silent preachers to the slave, of notions that are dangerous in the last degree to us, and injurious to him."

In the famous 1820 letter in which he cited the debate over the Missouri Compromise as a firebell in the night, Thomas Jefferson deplored the limitation of slavery to the southern tier of new states, calling for maximum dispersal as essential to providing a black-white ratio that would allay fears of insurrection or domination by freed blacks. "Of one thing I am certain," he wrote, ". . . their diffusion over a greater surface would make them individually happier, and proportionately facilitate the accomplishment of their emancipation by dividing the burden on a greater number of coadjutors." But the idea of domestic diffusion proved no more practical than the scheme for African repatriation; there was no effective support for it on the receiving end.

In the states and territories designated as free under the Missouri Compromise, the popular opposition was not merely to slavery but to the presence of blacks under any circumstance. The dedicated abolitionists who operated the underground railway to assist runaway slaves were heavily outnumbered by Northern whites whose racist views were, if anything, harsher than those of the Southerners. When Arkansas and Mississippi ordered the expatriation of freedmen, Illinois and Indiana responded with exclusion laws forbidding dark-skinned refugees from settling within their borders. Abraham Lincoln, perhaps as expert in divining public opinion as any politician of his day, summed up the prevailing view in his 1854 debates with Stephen Douglas. Citing the failure of the Liberian repatriation scheme, Lincoln posed and answered the burning question: "What next? Free them and make them politically and socially our equals? My own feelings will not admit of this, and if mine would, we well know that the great mass of white people's will not."

History has proved the fear of slave insurrection largely groundless. There were cases of whites murdered by their retainers, but these were usually individual acts. I never heard any such incident mentioned by anyone I knew who had lived through the war and its aftermath, and no such atrocities crop up in the family legends. The devotion of the blacks who kept the plantations going under the direction of white mistresses after the able-bodied men went off to the war is no invention of Southern propagandists. In 1861 Mrs. Chesnut noted in her diary: "A genuine slave-owner, born and bred, will not be afraid of Negroes. Here we are, mild as the moonbeams and as serene; nothing but Negroes around us, white men all gone to the army."

The majority of blacks continued their fealty even after invading Union soldiers had arrived to guarantee protection to those who chose to strike out for freedom. And all but a small minority maintained an amiable relationship with the whites after emancipation, when abolitionist agitators were actually within the gates and backed by an army of occupation. I have always regarded as the most splendid of the ironies of the great fratricide the evident fact that the success of Confederate arms was dependent upon the reservoir of goodwill among the slaves. This permitted white men to head for the front in wholesale lots, confident that their womenfolk would be protected by loyal blacks, who also would bring in the crops required to keep the armies in the field.

"Secession was the product of logical reasoning within a framework of irrational perception," Steven A. Channing wrote in *Crisis of Fear*. So it was that Congressman Lawrence Keitt of South Carolina saw in the rise of the Republican Party the advent of a new social order: "The concentration of absolute power in the hands of the North will develop the wildest democracy ever seen on this earth—unless it shall have been matched in Paris in 1789. . . ." The fact—as Abraham Lincoln was to demonstrate—was that the militant abolitionists who might fit this description constituted a small minority in a political party whose leaders were moderate, compromising men. These, surely, accepted the proposition that "immediate, absolute abolition" as demanded by Garrison's Anti-Slavery Society was an impossibility in the face of the situation described by Senator Hammond:

Here we have in charge the solution of the greatest problem of the ages. We are here two races—white and black—now both equally American, holding each other in the closest embrace and utterly unable to extricate ourselves from it. A problem so difficult, so complicated, and so momentous never was in charge of any portion of Mankind. And on its solution rests our all.

Summing up his study of the changing political climate in South Carolina after 1836, Channing wrote: "The nation was led into war in 1861 by secession of the lower South, not by the desire of the Northern people either to end slavery or bring equality to the Negro." For the majority of Southerners the secession sentiment fanned by the ultras grew out of frustration; after the abandonment of the African repatriation scheme the leadership never came forward with any alternative of phased emancipation to provide an answer to the moral issue, which many Southerners certainly perceived, even if they no longer said so out loud. When they marched off in what they considered the defense of their homeland, Mrs. Chesnut estimated that "not one-third of our volunteer army are slaveowners," and that "not one-third of the third fail to dislike slavery as much as Mrs. Stowe or Horace Greeley."

The legal and philosophical niceties of the debate over states' rights were never impressed very deeply on the public consciousness. Declaring that the South faced a threat of invasion from the North, Rhett's *Mercury* simply dismissed the constitutional issue and proclaimed an absolute, prior right of secession: "Defense of home is a matter that takes precedence of every other consideration and is antecedent in men's minds to the formality and technicality of law."

William Lloyd Garrison insisted that he was committed to the use of moral, not military force to achieve his ends. But he spoke the language of Armageddon, and a Southerner would not have to be a hysteric to connect the launching of *The Liberator* in January 1831 with the bloody uprising in Virginia led by Nat Turner in August of that year. It is virtually certain that the voice Nat Turner heard inciting him to wreak vengeance was not Garrison's. But a man on a remote plantation, seeing a sullen black watching him out of the corner of his eyes, could hardly be expected to assume that the fulminations of the abolitionists would continue to be without effect—particularly since these were usually relayed to him by his local press stripped of temporizing qualifications.

Finally, there was John Brown. In 1855 the wanderer who would be called "God's angry man" arrived in Kansas territory with his five sons and a wagon load of guns and ammunition paid for by wealthy Bostonian supporters of the antislavery cause. As guerrilla leader of Free-Soilers against pro-slavery settlers he launched a raid in the Osawatomie district in which five men were hacked to death. This made the old man with the burning eyes a hero to the more exalted of the abolitionists, including Henry David Thoreau, who saw Brown's willingness to lay his own and his sons' lives on the line as a reproach to those who inveighed against slavery from the safety of Puritan New England.

Then, on October 16, 1859, Old Osawatomie led sixteen whites and five blacks across the border of Virginia to seize the arsenal in the little town of Harpers Ferry. Taking sixty hostages, he held out for two days against the local militia before the United States Marines arrived to take him prisoner. This abortive foray confounded the abolitionists; some, including the leading antislavery newspaper editors, disavowed Brown's violence, but others, torn by conscience, thought they must stand by him as he went to trial, and, inevitably, to the gallows. To the Southern ultras, Old Osawatomie was a godsend. Now a real live abolitionist, weapons in hand and black men at his side, had actually set foot on the sacred soil of Virginia to demonstrate his intention of arming the slaves against their masters. To Barnwell Rhett, the raid on Harpers Ferry was simply "fact coming to the aid of logic"—logic, of course, dictating the secession for which he had been agitating for thirty years.

THE ultras now concentrated on splitting the Democratic Party, which had become a haven for Northern and Southern unionists as the Whig Party disintegrated, its Free-Soil wing providing the basis for the new Republican Party. In South Carolina they had largely succeeded by the time the Thirty-sixth Congress convened early in 1860. In that star-crossed session a cousin of my grandfather held the upcountry seat in the terminal South Carolina delegation. John Durant Ashmore was the last of the state's Democrats left standing in the wake of a deadlock over the speakership. After a series of Southern candidates failed to obtain a majority in the Democratic caucus, he cast his vote for Congressman McClernand of Illinois, an unswerving states' righter on the slavery issue. McClernand received the unanimous vote of the Southern Democrats, except, as Ashmore noted, "four gentlemen from Alabama and my five colleagues, who do not claim to be within the organization of that party." The *Mercury* wheeled out its editorial artillery:

We know very little of Mr. Ashmore's political principles. He comes from the old Whig Federal district of the state . . . In his canvass for the seat in Congress he occupies he professed, we are informed, the strongest States-rights and Southern-rights views . . .

Yet, for some reason or other, he seems to glory in a [Democratic] banner which has inscribed upon it: "Exclusion of the South from our territories by squatter sovereignty; no more slave States; and the plunder of the Federal Treasury for internal improvements." He says that if "stricken down" it will "cover" him. *It was stricken down, and we think it will cover him, politically, as effectually as six feet of earth.*

The South Carolina unionists were on the run. The 1860 presidential contest was looming, and Stephen Douglas of Illinois was the leading contender for the Democratic nomination. That, as Ashmore saw it, posed a profound dilemma for those who believed that only a unified Democratic party could head off the secession movement. The unionists must do their best to secure the Democratic nomination for a "Southern man with true States' Rights principles" the lonely congressman wrote to the South Carolina faction's leader, Benjamin F. Perry of Greenville, but he obviously thought the prospects were dim.

On December 21, 1860, John Ashmore formally tendered his resignation from Congress in response to South Carolina's ordinance of secession. But he had delivered his valedictory ten months before when he arose to defend himself against the *Mercury*'s onslaught. "I am not surprised that certain disunionists in the South should excite that feeling as readily in the bosoms of Northern men, as disunionists of the Garrison school of the North excite the same feeling in Southern men," he said. But he reminded his colleagues that he spoke not for the Southern ultras, but as their victim—a lifelong nationalist representing pro-union constituents:

They are a people domestic in their habits, quiet in their deportment, raised to habits of toil and industry, and who daily labor by the side of the slaves whom they have raised, and whom they treat more as companions—as they are—than as the miserable, down-trodden servile creatures your fruitful imaginations have depicted them . . . These men, with souls as independent as the bird that cleaves the air of heaven, as free as the wild deer that grazes amid their own beautiful valleys and mountains, when excited to action under a sense of wrong and aggression, will rouse as the lion from his lair or the fierce tiger from the jungle.

And so they did. But by August 1863, Col. John Ashmore, functioning as Confederate enrolling officer for the Fifth Congressional District, reported confidentially to Col. James Chesnut and President Jefferson Davis that the mountain counties were "infested" with deserters:

They are, unfortunately, sustained in their conduct by many persons who have heretofore been regarded as good and loyal citizens, and who, if they do not proclaim hostility to our cause, urge that it is lost because of the extortions and speculations so rampant through the land. . . . This argument is unfortunately too true, and cannot be met by denial. They swear by all they hold sacred that they will die at home before they will ever be dragged forth again to do battle for such a cause.

The time came when slavery was abolished, immediately and unconditionally. It could be argued that the ultras were finally responsible, for in defeat their uncompromising doctrine still dominated the reactions of the ex-Confederates who briefly returned to power in the period of mild, Presidential Reconstruction initiated by Abraham Lincoln and carried forward after his assassination by Andrew Johnson. South Carolina's provisional governor was the Greenville unionist, Ben Perry, who had opposed secession to the end and then declared, "You are all going to the devil, and I'll go with you." But the emancipation provided under the "black codes" adopted in South Carolina and other Southern states was so limited as to be properly construed by the Radical Republicans as a continuation of the essentials of slavery. So came Congressional Reconstruction, with Yankee military commanders charged with enforcing the enfranchisement of blacks and the disenfranchisement of all those who had supported the Confederacy— that is, the great majority of whites. The record of the Reconstruction era has been a source of primary interest, and of controversy, among succeeding generations of historians, a whole new school having sprung up in recent years under the impetus of the civil rights movement.

Harvard seemed to be an ideal place to pursue my own interest in the period, and in many ways it turned out to be. I had begun to find many of the standard sources suspect. As an undergraduate at Clemson, where the ghost of Calhoun still walked, I heard a professor suggest, more or less seriously, that the nation would be well served by a good, objective history of the Civil War written from the Confederate point of view. There were those on the distinguished faculty of the old Abolitionist seat who might have been said to have made the case in reverse. Another Nieman Fellow, the Mississippi editor, Hodding Carter, came away "convinced that it has been almost as unfortunate for our nation that the North has remembered so little of Reconstruction as that the South has remembered so much."

I was aware that waves of revisionism had been washing over historiography for a good many decades, and that the tide was by no means receding. Prior to 1900 the textbooks used in Northern schools treated the South pretty much as the foreign nation it finally sought to become. The Confederacy was referred to as "the slave power," the war was "the great rebellion," and white Southerners were considered to have gotten their just deserts in the course of Reconstruction. Then, in the 1890s, Prof. William A. Dunning of Columbia University launched a revisionist school that effectively reversed the punitive view. Frances FitzGerald wrote in *America Revised*, her study of the textbooks of the period, "The intellectual heirs of Charles Sumner and Henry Adams gushed sentimentally about the decline of the great plantations and the trials of Southern womanhood."

Ms. FitzGerald gave special attention to Dunning's Columbia colleague, David Saville Muzzey, whose *An American History* became a national best seller among school texts when it was published in 1911 and remained in print for sixty-five years. Muzzey, she found,

. . . looked upon Reconstruction from the perspective of the white Southern gentry. President Andrew Johnson was "coarse, violent, egotistical, obstinate and vindictive," but the Radical Republicans (including the "unspeakable demagogue" Butler) were a good deal worse. Indeed, there was nothing good about Reconstruction—not even the Fourteenth and Fifteenth Amendments, since the enfranchisement of the freedmen "set the ignorant, superstitious, gullible slave in power over his former master." Muzzey moderated his language a bit in later editions, but he continued to insist that the situation in the South improved only in 1887, when "the Southern people were given charge of their own government." Not until the 1961 edition did the book suggest that blacks might be numbered among the "Southern people."

In the 1930s Francis Butler Simkins and others began to challenge the Dunning school, presenting evidence that Reconstruction had not been terminated because the victorious North had come to recognize the excesses of the Radical Republicans, but because the dominant business interests of the nation had seen the wisdom of making a deal with the conservative white leadership. The revisionist tide continued to rise. In the 1950s C. Vann Woodward gave the title *Reunion & Reaction* to an account of the Compromise of 1877, concluding that the end product was an enduring North-South coalition of like-minded conservative politicians. Kenneth Stampp discovered overlooked positive goods in the programs promulgated by the carpetbaggers and freedmen, and by the 1960s Staunton Lynd and his New Left confreres were arguing that the real tragedy was that the Radical Republicans hadn't gone far enough.

These essentially political reinterpretations reflected shifting ideological currents. Swinging from Left to Right to Left again, the primary revision was in the attributed motives of the actors, rather than in the result of their action. The only constant was that blacks remained victims, although in the Dunning view whites were, to some extent, victims too.

WHEN Simkins and Robert H. Woody wrote their generally acclaimed *South Carolina During Reconstruction* they noted the limitations of the usual sources: the historical narratives were narrowly political, the journalistic accounts sensational, the memoirs of natives "dominated by the Southern sense of reticence," and the accounts of outside observers usually clouded by preconceptions. The most notable exception I have found is a contemporary account fortuitously focused directly on my home county, written by a Union army officer who headed the Bureau of Refugees, Freedmen and Abandoned Lands in three counties of Cousin John Ashmore's old congressional district. I can recognize every name and every ascribed characteristic in John William De Forest's *A Union Officer in the Reconstruction*, and I find nothing that jars my inherited sense of that time and place.

Invalided after three strenuous years of combat with the 12th Connecticut Volunteers, Major De Forest was adjutant general of the Veteran Reserve Corps in Washington, D.C., when he was posted to South Carolina. At Greenville, where he took over the bureau in October 1866, he had no assistant and the nearest Union garrison was forty miles away. His lot was a lonely one. "To my native infamy as a Yankee I added the turpitude of being a United States military officer and the misdemeanor of being sub-assistant commissioner of the Freedman's Bureau," he wrote. So, although he dealt with all classes of white and black Southerners in his official capacity, he remained at a social distance. A successful author, with prewar novels and essays to his credit, he improved his free time by maintaining the detailed journal that provided the basis for a series of articles published, beginning in 1868, in *Harper's*, *Atlantic Monthly*, and *Putnam's*.

Before his death De Forest collected and augmented these

articles for book publication as a companion to a similar volume
of his wartime writing. But neither saw print in hardcover until
the Yale University Press brought them out after World War II.
James H. Croushore and David Morris Potter, who edited and
annotated the second volume, wrote of De Forest:

Scorning a politic reticence, he stated his individualistic conclusions
with a vigor that probably offended both Northern and Southern
readers in the 'sixties, and may retain this double effectiveness even
today. . . . He was a man of markedly superior intellectual talent,
and one of the salient features of his literary skill was his impatience
with stereotypes and his readiness to acknowledge, without regard for
current intellectual fashions, the merits of the individual man or the
individual situation.

De Forest had moved in the highest strata of antebellum
Southern society. His wife was the daughter of a professor of
natural history simultaneously on the faculties of Amherst and
the South Carolina Medical College at Charleston, where De
Forest spent considerable time after 1855 in the course of his
courtship and early married years. He admired the qualities of
dignified self-respect he saw in the best of the lowcountry
aristocrats, and also saw how these qualities were often pervert-
ed into arrogance and pugnacity. He needled a Charleston
friend who was discoursing on the special, high qualities of the
"true Southern gentleman" by remarking, "Oh! you mean
Texans and Arkansans, I suppose." His friend laughed and
dismissed the notion. "Not in the least. When *we* speak of the
Southern gentleman we mean the product of our city and of
the region immediately around it. All else is more or less
spurious—a base imitation."

In the upcountry, De Forest found this kind of ingrained
pride of place less ostentatious but no less pronounced. "I'll
give you my notion of things," a sturdy old planter told his
recent enemy. "I go first for Greenville, then for Greenville
District, then for the upcountry, then for South Carolina, then
for the South, then for the United States; and after that I don't
go for anything. I've no use for Englishmen, Turks, and
Chinese." Yet De Forest sensed how this powerful identification
with the environs had been accentuated by the lost war and the
humiliating situation created by military occupation. A part of
his duty was to arbitrate grievances of newly liberated black

servants against their former masters, and he speculated on the result had the tables been turned and his neighbors in Connecticut faced with a comparable change in relationship with their Irish retainers: "Just imagine the North conquered by the South, Confederate officers stationed in every community as agents of the 'Copperhead Bureau,' and all the Bridgets of the land flowing to them with complaints against their masters and mistresses."

The major found the eighty thousand whites and thirty thousand blacks in his district gripped by poverty and faced with the necessity of piecing together a new economic system to replace the slave-based agriculture that had provided such prosperity as they had known in the past. He had government rations to issue, and destitute poor whites were his clients as well as blacks. His observations stress the threeway stratification of Southern whites, with a middle class—"semi-chivalrous Southrons," he called them, in derisive reference to Sir Walter Scott—between the aristocrats and the poor whites. In the foothills and mountains he found a bountiful supply of the latter—"the dull, unlettered, hopeless English farm laborer grown wild, indolent, and nomadic on new land and under the discouraging competition of slavery . . ."

De Forest thought the blacks in danger of suffering a similar fate in the absence of the discipline imposed by slavery. The problem, as he saw it, was that both whites and blacks were "tyros in the mystery of free labor." When the former masters complained to him that they could not handle their workers without some sort of contract that bound them to the land and authorized punishment for the shiftless, he could only inform them that this was no longer possible, and advise them to pay weekly wages and discharge any man who was not earning his pay. "But," he added, "this policy was above the general reach of Southern capital and beyond the usual circle of Southern ideas."

Yet the acculturation of the blacks was so complete they shared the prevailing sense of dread at being publicly branded as paupers. They insisted on their government-issue rations as a matter of right, and when the major suggested that some might be better off in the county poorhouse, the reaction was one of horror:

. . . the mere word was sufficient to frighten off all but the most hopeful claimants; gaunt, filthy, bare-footed women would answer, "Lord's sake! Don't send us to the poorhouse." They would accept beggary from door to door, wintry life in a house of pine boughs, prostitution, and thieving rather than sleep under the roof of public charity. It was a shadow which blighted self-respect and tortured the sensibilities of the meanest white and the most shiftless Negro.

De Forest discovered that alms offered on a personal basis, however, carried no stigma, and he came to consider this a prime cause of the continuing economic stagnation:

. . . the habit of private charity is widely diffused in the South; the "high-toned gentleman" gives as of old, and much more than he can now afford. The better classes despise and almost detest the "low-down people," but rarely have the heart to refuse them . . . . I learned during my stay in Greenville that many men whose incomes were little more than nominal constantly contributed to the support of their absolutely indigent neighbors, whether worthy or unworthy.

. . . Oh! but that slavery was costly, with its breed of parasite poor whites and its remaining dross of decrepit old Negroes! I do not think I exaggerate greatly when I declare that two-thirds of the people in my Bureau district were burdened with the support of the other third. A Greenville merchant assured me that what with gifts outright and credits to people who, as he knew, could never pay, it cost him five times as much for the living of other people as for his own.

What is most striking about De Forest's firsthand account is that he found so little evidence of racial tension above the level of petty disputes over wages and shares as deposed masters and emancipated slaves struggled with a rudimentary free market for labor. Among the burdens of his army paperwork was a monthly report with one column headed "Outrages of Whites Against Freedmen" paired with "Outrages of Freedmen Against Whites." The first generally, and the second almost invariably, had a line in red ink drawn diagonally across it showing that there were no outrages to report. De Forest was the final local authority in any racial altercation, but it was his practice to refer complaints to the local courts:

. . . the civil authorities were disposed, as I soon learned, to treat Negroes fairly . . . Of the 50 or 60 magistrates in my district I had occasion to indicate but one as being unfit for office by reason of political partialities and prejudices of race. New York City would be fortunate if it could have justice dealt out to it as honestly and fairly as it was dealt out by the plain homespun farmers who filled the squire-archates of Greenville, Pickens and Anderson.

The prospect of race mixing, which would continue to be the stock in trade of Southern demagogues for a century to come, appeared to this clear-eyed Yankee to be nonexistent. Miscegenation, he found, was already diminishing now that emancipation had ended the close family contact of slavery and imposed financial burdens upon any white who sired a mulatto child. "There will be no amalgamation, no merging and disappearance of the black in the white, except at a period so far distant that it is not worth while now to speculate upon it," he wrote. He had no such certainty about the future of the separate black race now being pushed into competition with whites for a place in the larger society:

. . . the higher civilization of the Caucasion is gripping the race in many ways and bringing it to sharp trial before its time. This new, varied costly life of freedom, this struggle to be at once like a race which had passed through a two-thousand year growth in civilization, will probably diminish the productiveness of the Negro and will terribly test his vitality. . . . What judgment shall we pass upon abrupt emancipation, considered merely with reference to the Negro? It was a mighty experiment, fraught with as much menace as hope. To the white race alone it was a certain and precious boon.

5

Liberalism,
Southern Style

*T*he most extreme manifestations of abrupt abolition, and of Southern reaction to it, emerged after
John William De Forest ended his tour of duty, and occurred in
places other than the Carolina upcountry. Still, as he said, he
had based his judgment of the native whites and blacks on
"fifteen months of intercourse with the most unfair and discon-
tented of both parties," and I don't think his conclusions can be
faulted. He could foresee that men of his own enlightened view
would not remain on the scene long; in the way of all military
occupations, line officers would be replaced by opportunists
looking for the main chance among the ruins of Southern
society or, even worse, dissolute incompetents on the order of a
revenue officer sent into the Greenville district—"a fair speci-
men of a New York City Johnson man, who stayed drunk from
morning till night, falsified his returns, and solicited bribes."

It was De Forest's view, as it had been Lincoln's, that it was
not practically possible to impose upon the prostrate region a
radical transfer of political power to blacks and poor whites.
"Notwithstanding its military and financial overthrow, the old
planter class, with its superior education, its experience in
politics, and its habit of authority was still the most potent
moral force in the South," he wrote. These were conservative
men, but they were also the most open of all Southerners to
granting the rights of citizenship to freedmen. My grandfather's wartime cavalry commander, Wade Hampton, led the
Red Shirts, South Carolina's unmasked version of the Ku Klux
Klan, in a campaign to intimidate black supporters of the
carpetbag regime, but when he ran for governor he circulated
a campaign brochure titled, *Free Men! Free Ballots!! Free
Schools!!! The Pledges of Gen. Wade Hampton . . . to the Colored
People of South Carolina, 1865–1876.*

There was no hypocrisy in this. In an 1879 symposium in the *North American Review*, Hampton, L.Q.C. Lamar of Mississippi, and Alexander Stephens of Georgia agreed that disfranchisement of the freedmen was not only impossible but undesirable. Hampton said he believed "a large majority of the intelligent and reflecting whites" shared his view that "as the Negro becomes more intelligent, he naturally allies himself with the more conservative of the whites." Under his leadership there was no effort to impose demeaning segregation of public facilities.

In 1885, T. McCants Stewart, a black journalist who located to New England after emancipation, was sent back to his native South Carolina by the *New York Freeman*; the newspaper opposed the election of Grover Cleveland and Stewart's mission was to find evidence that return of Democrats to power would mean the end of freedmen's rights. But from Columbia he reported:

I feel about as safe here as in Providence, R.I. I can ride on first-class cars on the railroads and in the streets. I can go into saloons and get refreshments even as in New York, I can stop in and drink a glass of soda and be more politely waited on than in some parts of New England. . . . For the life of me I can't "raise a row" in these letters. Things seem (remember I write seem) to move along as smoothly as in New York or Boston. . . . If you should ask me, "Watchman, tell us of the night" . . . I would say, "The morning light is breaking."

In *The Strange Career of Jim Crow*, C. Vann Woodward cited this evidence to support his thesis that alternatives to segregation were seriously considered, and to some extent put into effect, in the decade after the Redeemers took over from the Republicans, only to disappear in a rising tide of racism after the old Confederates lost the support of the poor whites. "The better class of whites certainly want to conserve the Negro," Hampton said, and added, "The lower whites are less favorable." Woodward defined the attitude as one in which "the conservatives acknowledged that the Negroes belonged in a subordinate role, but denied that subordinates had to be ostracized; they believed that the Negro was inferior, but denied that it followed that inferiors must be segregated or publicly humilated. Negro degradation was not a necessary corollary of white supremacy in the conservative philosophy."

That, of course, was noblesse oblige—"paternalism" as it would later be called, and condemned. Yet it was, at least in the case of many blacks, open-ended, permitting, and within the limits of a socially stratified society, encouraging self-improvement. Woodward makes the point that no trial was ever given to a truly liberal and fully democratic alternative such as that proposed by George Washington Cable of Louisiana, who challenged the Redeemers' insistence that there had to be "honest" government before there could be "free" government. What came to be called "liberalism" in the South was in fact the old, paternalistic concept inherited from the days of transition from Reconstruction to home rule. Even that was dormant through the first third of the twentieth century until it was revived with the coming of the New Deal.

ALTHOUGH the Roosevelt regime initially introduced no reforms bearing directly upon racial segregation, the political ferment of the 1930s served to focus attention upon the evident deficiencies of slavery's successor institution—still peculiar to the region, still dominating its culture, and now clearly inhibiting its economic growth. Those called "Southern liberals," some of them functioning as agents of the Roosevelt administration, gave new life to the tentative interracial organizations that had emerged after the First World War to deal with the more obvious problems besetting the minority race.

In the late thirties white Southerners of standing were emboldened to speak out against the poll tax, which did not necessarily certify them as pro-Negro, since the price tag on the vote disfranchised whites as well as blacks. There had always been those who, as a matter of conscience, denounced overt brutality, particularly in its manifestation by white mobs, and some of these publicly defied the states' rights tradition to support federal antilynching legislation. It had become possible to gain respectable white support for a black cause that could be argued in terms of justice, provided the proposed remedy stopped short of anything that could be construed as "social" equality, defined as the actual or potential intermingling of the two races.

This was the situation when I departed for Cambridge in

the fall of 1941. When I returned to the South four years later there were no visible signs of institutional change, but it was evident that the attitudes that sustained the segregated society had been profoundly affected by the great war that engulfed my generation. At Clemson I had enrolled in the Reserve Officers' Training Corps primarily because the minuscule cash uniform allowance was important to a chronically broke student, and when Pearl Harbor brought on full mobilization I was already in possession of a second lieutenant's commission. Within a few weeks I was being pounded into shape for combat at Fort Benning's Infantry School.

The military services were then as thoroughly segregated as any organization could be; the two races were not only consigned to separate units and kept as far apart as possible, but most blacks were allowed to serve only as supporting service troops. The prevailing view of the military high command was that they were collectively unfit for front-line duty, and thus to all the other degradations was added denial of that traditional rite of manhood, the test of arms. With the greatest reluctance the army yielded to political pressure to provide a few token combat units—an air corps fighter group, a half dozen detached battalions, and a single infantry division. Even here the senior command positions were reserved for whites.

I ran into two of these Jim Crow units in the course of my service and found that the expectation that they were inherently unready for combat was wholly unfounded, except to the extent that it turned out to be a self-fulfilling prophecy. When my own Ninety-fifth Infantry Division was training in the California desert, the black division was camped next to us —next being some fifty miles down the road. As an operations officer I had business with my opposite number and flew over in a liaison plane to spend the better part of a day at the division headquarters. Every white officer I encountered was overflowing with self-pity. They considered their assignment a rejection by their peers, and all were actively trying to end their disgrace by arranging a transfer. They expressed these feelings openly in the presence of blacks, which surely must have been a more effective means of lowering morale than anything ever devised by Axis propagandists. I came away feeling that it was absurd to expect soldiers training under such circumstances to fight well; it would be a miracle if they were willing to fight at all.

In the European theater, where the Ninety-fifth served in Gen. George S. Patton's Third Army, I had a more sustained contact with the ETO's only black tank battalion. After the Battle of the Bulge we received word that we were to be reassigned to the new Ninth Army being assembled in Holland for the final assault across the Rhine. In the course of the transfer we would pick up replacements for nonorganic supporting units. When the order assigning a new tank battalion came through, its numerical designation meant nothing to me, but it did to the division commander. Maj. Gen. Harry L. Twaddle erupted when I showed him the message: "The hell they will! That's the colored outfit! They've been trying to get rid of it, and now they're going to saddle it on me to take along to Ninth Army." His protest was in vain, and next day a black liaison officer reported to me at the operations section—and sent a ripple through the lily-white ranks when I took him over to the headquarters mess.

A good soldier and a decent man, General Twaddle saw to it that the black troopers got proper treatment, and he went out of his way to explain his initial reaction to me. An upstate New Yorker who had spent much of his service career abroad, he considered himself free of racial prejudice, but he knew that such a "reject" outfit would come with low morale and poor equipment. He was right about the equipment, but the white Virginian who commanded the battalion had passed from despair to outrage at the way his men were being treated, and his anger was communicated to his tank crews. In the battles they fought under our command, the black men in those battered old Shermans performed as well as any armored troopers we saw in action in the bloody campaigns that took us from Normandy to the Ruhr.

In World War I blacks had accepted assignment to all-black units as an unavoidable extension of the segregated society in which the great majority still lived. The contrasting reaction of blacks to the summons to service in World War II marked the real beginning of the civil rights movement. By the time Adolf Hitler launched his xenophobic crusade in Europe there were sizable black enclaves in the cities of the North, and these had produced a new generation of leaders free of traditional racial inhibitions. In July 1941, with the draft in effect and war mobilization well under way, A. Philip Randolph, president of the Pullman porters union, announced that he would lead a mass march on Washington to demand equal treatment for blacks in the armed services and open employment in war industries. "Though I have found no Negroes who want to see the United Nations lose this war, I have found many who, before the war ends, want to see the stuffing knocked out of white supremacy and of empire over subject peoples," he said, and went on to ask the unanswerable question: "Why has a man got to be Jim Crowed to die for democracy?"

President Roosevelt received Randolph at the White House and made concessions sufficient to head off the projected march. Although black draftees were to remain segregated, the way for advancement of black officers was opened, and, most important of all, the president issued the first Fair Employment Practices order, directing all industries under government contract to end discrimination in hiring and promotion. This famous victory did not persuade Randolph that the ranks necessarily should stay closed. In 1942, noting that "both management and labor unions in too many places and too many ways are still drawing the color line," he called a series of mass meetings. Twenty thousand blacks turned out at Madison Square Garden, sixteen thousand in Chicago, nine thousand in St. Louis—as Randolph described them, "businessmen, teachers, laundry workers, Pullman porters, waiters and red caps; preachers, crap-shooters and social workers; jitterbugs and Ph.Ds."

Here, for the first time, blacks were acting wholly on their own to challenge the white leadership. Randolph identified the largely spontaneous movement as "all-Negro and pro-Negro but not for that reason anti-white . . . a non-violent demonstration of Negro mass power." And he cited the motivation in terms that would take on profound significance in the decades to come: "By fighting for their rights now, American Negroes are helping to make America a moral and spiritual arsenal of democracy."

Sealed away in remote training camps until shipped overseas, I had no real sense of the effect of these new racial dispensations until the war ended in Europe and I was ordered to Washington for assignment to the War Department General Staff, where I would serve until after V-J Day. The Operations

Division at the Pentagon was wired into the White House at the highest policy level, and the capital was full of newspaper colleagues who could fill me in on accumulated news and gossip from the home front. I was soon convinced that the geographic and psychological dislocations of the war years had brought on a new era in race relations—one in which it would no longer be possible to separate the so-called social issue from the effort to obtain full civil rights for blacks. This would rule out the rationale employed by the white liberals and black leaders who first established interracial organizations in the South to deal with lynching, the poll tax, exclusion of blacks from juries, and discriminatory allocation of public services. The theory had been that extension of political rights to blacks really had nothing to do with social equality, and in any case would provide for only a gradual lowering of the traditional barriers.

Within the limits imposed by the region's peculiar history and restricted resources, the pre-World War II reformers had been trying to bring the South's racial practices into conformity with the nation's. If, for tactical reasons, they usually didn't say so publicly, they had to accept the fact that the right to full political participation by blacks was an inescapable if not immediate goal. Unrestricted black voting provided the most significant difference between the de facto segregation of the North, and the formal legal segregation of the South. Yet, as the Southerners were acutely aware, meeting the ideal of universal suffrage would produce entirely different results in their home precincts.

Before World War II touched off a resurgence of black migration to the cities of the North and West, the black vote posed no threat to entrenched Northern politicians; only a single Chicago congressional district had a sufficient concentration of minority population to defy gerrymandering and send a black representative to Washington. In the South, however, an untrammeled black vote had the potential of dominating a number of congressional districts and local governments, and everywhere it raised the possibility of a new power balance that would threaten existing political arrangements. For obvious reasons, entrenched white Southern politicians could not be expected to ally themselves with the movement to broaden the franchise.

The overwhelming majority of Southerners, black as well as white, accepted the political *status quo* as a given. It was the belief, or at least the hope, of the reformers that this was a passive attitude on the part of most whites, and there could be little doubt that it cloaked deep resentment on the part of blacks. It might, therefore, be possible to bring about change through moral suasion, the only means available to them. But the defenders of the *status quo* not only had inertia on their side, but the powerful arguments perfected by Henry Grady in his "New South" campaign to heal the wounds of Civil War and Reconstruction by promoting a new unity of economic interest between North and South.

In a famous address to the Boston Merchants Association in 1890 the *Atlanta Constitution*'s editor offered no apologies for the South's denial of "this vast, ignorant and purchasable vote—clannish, credulous, impulsive and passionate— tempting every art of the demagogue, but insensible to the appeal of the statesman." Grady then went on the offensive, and drew no significant dissent from the Boston Brahmans when he answered the unspoken question he assumed his audience had brought to the hall:

When will the black cast a free ballot? When ignorance anywhere is not dominated by the will of the intelligent; when the laborer anywhere casts a vote unhindered by his boss; when the vote of the poor anywhere is not influenced by the power of the rich; when the strong and steadfast do not everywhere control the suffrage of the weak and shiftless—then and not till then will the ballot of the Negro be free.

Henry Grady's doctrine left white supremacy intact, but tempered it to the Northern taste by rejecting the harsh strictures of the racist demagogues and affirming a paternalistic concern for improvement in the condition of the blacks. For Southerners it combined a sentimental exaltation of the mythic Old South with the promise of economic improvement to be found in the New, giving it an appeal to the upward-striving entrepreneurs who were beginning to replace the plantation gentry in the places of power. If these men had no pronounced impulse toward social reform, they did have an immediate concern for promoting orderly economic development, and they could recognize racial strife as a threat to their own interests. It is not surprising that the first significant Southern entry in the field of race relations, the Commission on Interracial Cooperation, received some of its initial funding from the American Cast Iron Pipe Company of Atlanta.

THE Interracial Commission's organizer, like many of those who staffed the movement in the early days, came of a religious background. Will W. Alexander, beginning his Methodist ministry in Nashville, became convinced that racism and poverty were the besetting twin evils of the South, and dedicated a long and fruitful career to their eradication. He was able to recruit prominent supporters among his fellow men of the cloth—the Episcopal bishop of Mississippi, the presidents of Baptist Wake Forest University and Methodist Randolph-Macon—and the appeal to the Christian conscience was emphasized in every public utterance. Allied with the religious leaders were three of the South's leading sociologists, Howard W. Odum, Thomas J. Woofter, Jr. and Arthur F. Raper, and with their university colleagues they provided studies circulated under the commission's imprimatur.

The commission, with headquarters in Atlanta and chapters in thirteen Southern states, attained a membership of seven thousand, but it never attempted anything that could be deemed direct action. Organizationally, it was hardly more than a loose coalition of moderates united primarily by their abhorrence of the brutality represented by lynching. It at least can be said that during its twenty-four years of existence the annual total of deaths from mob violence dropped from seventy-six to three, and would never be reckoned in double digits again. But, in his *In Search of the Silent South*, Morton Sosna pronounced it counterproductive:

In attempting to soften and humanize segregation as it was practiced in the South in the 1920s and 1930s, the commission in effect sanctioned the idea of the Southern Negro as a second-class citizen. All the good will and sensitivity to the problem of blacks shared by white Southern liberals did not obviate this fact. When in time the caste structure of the South came under direct attack by blacks and Northern whites, Alexander's organization began to look more like an obstacle than a stimulus to progress.

The new surge of liberal activism inspired by the New Deal sent the commission into eclipse. In 1935 its prime mover, Will

Alexander, was drafted into service as assistant to Rexford Guy Tugwell in the new Resettlement Administration, which was intended to lead the way out of the South's moribund share-cropping system. Alexander raided his former staff in Atlanta to bring up Clark Howell Foreman, grandson of the publisher of the *Atlanta Constitution*, who became advisor on racial matters to Interior Secretary Harold Ickes, and a confidant of Eleanor Roosevelt credited with inspiring her special interest in the plight of Southern blacks.

Foreman was a moving spirit behind a great gathering intended to unite and inspire Southern liberals to move to a new plateau in their search for social justice. The political clout of the Roosevelt administration brought a set of authentic shakers and movers to Birmingham in November 1938, to join with the veterans of the commission movement. Gov. Bibb Graves agreed to greet the delegates; the speakers included Associate Justice Hugo Black of the Supreme Court; Senators Claude Pepper of Florida and Lister Hill of Alabama; Mary McLeod Bethune, director of the Division of Negro Affairs of the National Youth Administration; and Pres. Frank P. Graham of the University of North Carolina. Listed among the organizers were such journalistic heavyweights as Ralph McGill of the *Atlanta Constitution*, John Temple Graves of the *Birmingham Age-Herald*, and Mark Ethridge and Barry Bingham of the *Louisville Courier-Journal*. Others of similar standing had initially signed on when it was understood that there would be twelve hundred invited delegates, about one-fifth of them black, but had hastily withdrawn when they found that six Communist party members were included on the list.

The delegates convened in good order on a Sunday, and blacks and whites mingled freely in defiance of Birmingham's segregation ordinance, which it was assumed could be safely ignored in such prestigious circumstances. The next day, however, Police Commissioner Theophilus Eugene Connor made his first appearance in the national media, arriving at Municipal Auditorium with fifteen policemen under orders to start making arrests unless whites and blacks regrouped into separate seating. There followed one of those combinations of low comedy and high tragedy that marked so many such confrontations during the Jim Crow era. This one wound up with the delegates "voluntarily" agreeing to sit on opposite sides of the hall, while Mrs. Roosevelt occupied a chair in the middle of the aisle by way of protest. The Southern Conference on Human Welfare resolved never to hold a segregated meeting again, but "Bull" Connor had made his point, creating the headlines that forced upon the organization a race-mixing image that, combined with its tolerance of the Communist delegates, would scare off respectable support. Even so unintimidated an editor as Jonathan Daniels of the *Raleigh News and Observer* lamented that SCHW "began in tragic mistake when action was taken which resulted in placing emphasis upon the one thing certain angrily to divide the South."

The Southern liberal best equipped to weather the storm stepped in to salvage the fledgling venture by accepting the chairmanship. Frank Porter Graham, a remarkable combination of Christian charity, old shoe back-country charm, sheer guts, and unswerving devotion to academic excellence, had been conditioned by long experience in beating back North Carolina's Bourbon leadership in defense of the South's least inhibited and most distinguished university faculty. Graham stuck to the traditional Southern liberal line on segregation, asserting that SCHW's purpose was to promote social justice for blacks, not social equality. Under his somewhat distracted leadership, the organization brought suffrage completely out of the closet, putting poll-tax repeal at the top of its agenda, and launched a Southwide lobbying and publicity effort. This politicized the organization in a fashion the Interracial Commission had managed to avoid. Steadily more and more isolated. SCHW hung on for another ten years, but it never recovered from its early wounds and in the end it served only as a refuge for the few genuine radicals visible on the Southern scene.

DESPITE its militant rhetoric, and its constant involvement in abrasive political controversy, SCHW was as much a paternalistic product of the South's middle-class white community as was the Interracial Commission. This is often cited as having guaranteed the ultimate futility of both organizations. By consigning blacks to a secondary, largely window-dressing role, the argument goes, white liberals sealed off any driving force for social justice, using the movement to salve their own consciences while effectively preserving the discriminatory advantages whites had reinstated at the end of Reconstruction. Yet anyone who lived through the period between the wars must find it difficult to see how the outcome could have been any different. Going back over the record with the benefit of hindsight I find nothing to sustain the notion that these movements failed as a result of moral obtuseness or lack of courage on the part of their white leaders and black followers.

I would agree that white paternalism inevitably had a stultifying effect upon the development of black leadership. But the truth of the matter is that respectable whites had to take the lead if there was to be any betterment of the condition of the mass of Southern blacks. The minority had no capacity of its own to force open the closed channels of material and social advancement in the white society, and no means to create a tolerable domain of its own beyond the walls of segregation.

In later years many blacks would come to believe that the first leader of their race to rise to national prominence in the post-Reconstruction era sold out their interests to the whites. But, again, I find it difficult to see what option was available to Booker T. Washington when, as president of white-supported Tuskegee Institute, he appeared before the Cotton States and International Exposition in Atlanta in 1895, the first black man in history to address such an audience. Jim Crow was now firmly in place, and he was recognizing reality when he conceded that the advancement of his people, and perhaps their survival, depended upon "making friends, in every manly way, of the people of all races by whom we are surrounded. . . . The wisest among my race understand that the agitation of questions of social equality is the extremest folly." The further reality was that "it is at the bottom of life we must begin," which meant the mastery of agricultural and mechanical skills, concentrating the educational drive on vocational training.

Like Henry Grady, he invoked the mythic South when he promised that whites who supported these efforts could be

. . . sure in the future, as in the past, that you and your people will be surrounded by the most patient, faithful, law-abiding and unresentful people that the world has seen. As we have proved our loyalty to you in the past, in nursing your children, watching by the sickbed of your mothers and fathers, and often following them with tear-dimmed eyes to their graves, so in the future, in our humble way, we will stand by you with a devotion no foreigner can approach, ready to lay down our lives, if need be, in defense of yours; interlacing our industrial, commercial, civic and religious life with yours in a way that shall make the interests of both races one. In all things that are purely social we can be as separate as the fingers, yet one as the hand in all things essential to mutual progress.

The speech created a sensation, dovetailing as it did with Grady's New South doctrine. At a stroke it made Washington, in the acid phrase of his great black adversary, W.E.B. Du Bois, "the most distinguished Southerner since Jefferson Davis, and the one with the largest personal following. . . . It startled the nation to hear a Negro advocate such a program after many decades of bitter complaint; it startled and won the applause of the South, it interested and won the admiration of the North; and after a confused murmur of protest, it silenced if it did not convert the Negroes themselves."

New England born, Du Bois was the intellectual successor to the eloquent freedman, Frederick Douglass, who had been the most conspicuous black in the abolitionist movement. In 1908 he would be among the founders of the National Association for the Advancement of Colored People, along with such notable white heirs of the abolitionist tradition as Jane Addams, Oswald Garrison Villard, John Dewey, and William Dean Howells, and all his long life he would serve as an often scathing voice of conscience for those, black or white, North or South, he considered guilty of yielding on the central moral issue.

In *Souls of Black Folk*, published eight years after Booker T. Washington came to fame, Du Bois broadened his indictment of the Alabama educator to condemn his espousal of the materialistic "gospel of Work and Money," terming him

the leader, not of one race but of two, a compromiser between the South, the North and the Negro. Naturally, the Negroes resented, at first bitterly, signs of compromise which surrendered their civil and political rights, even though this was to be exchanged for larger chances of economic development. The rich and dominating North, however, was not only weary of the race problem but was investing largely in Southern enterprises and welcomed any method of peaceful cooperation. . . . Mr. Washington represents in Negro thought the old attitude of adjustment and submission.

Du Bois and Washington stood at the poles of Negro political thought during the first third of the twentieth century. When Du Bois spoke of "the Negroes" as embittered by Washington's compromising stand, he did not speak for the mass of blacks, certainly not in the beginning. But he did speak for the small group of black intellectuals who were growing in prominence and influence outside the South, gaining significant allies among white liberals in such key centers as New York, Boston, and Chicago.

Originally, blacks who were free to vote had been ordained Republican by their devotion to the Great Emancipator, Abraham Lincoln, but with the coming of the New Deal they flocked to the Democratic fold, lining up philosophically with the more progressive union leaders and agrarian populists, and practically with the big city Democratic machines. These voting blocs gave militants of the Du Bois school leverage to bolster the influence of those in the Roosevelt hierarchy who, like the president's wife, had begun to condemn segregation as inherently unjust.

In 1944 Gunnar Myrdal wrote in *An American Dilemma*, "The Negro protest is bound to rise even higher. But the influence of the protest motive is limited mainly to the propagation of certain ideas about how things *should* be." There could be no doubt that Southern blacks shared the goals proclaimed by their Northern brethren, but their own local leaders were in no position to act upon them. Myrdal found most of these embittered over the contemptuous "Uncle Tom" label applied to them by Northern black intellectuals:

In a sense, every ambitious and successful Negro is more dependent upon the whites than is his caste fellow in the lower class. He is more conspicuous. He had more to lose and he has more to gain. If he becomes aggressive he is adding to all the odds he labors under the risk of losing the good will and protection of the influential whites. The Southern whites have many ways of keeping this prospect constantly before his mind. He knows he has to "go slow."

The Southern white reformers were almost as vulnerable. As had been the case with the antebellum unionists the rhetorical attack by latter-day abolitionists, and the counterfire from embattled white supremacists, began to cut the ground from under Southern-based New Dealers.

IT was not only elected officials who were affected by the steadily increasing exacerbation of Southern white sensitivity. While they had more latitude than the officeholders, other key opinion leaders—educators, ministers, newspaper editors— enjoyed no real immunity, and the pressures upon them mounted with the revival of the more or less dormant North-South polarization of professed attitudes on race. The new black militancy dramatized by Randolph's movement aroused apprehensions of racial violence throughout the South, and if these fears were fed by ancient prejudices they could not be dismissed out of hand. The ethnocentric horrors perpetrated by Adolf Hitler gave the moral issue a new edge, raising the consciousness of sensitive Americans, opening the eyes of the complacent to the racism practiced everywhere in their own country. White Southerners were not immune to these feelings of guilt, but for most the reaction was defensive; there was understandable resentment of the equation of their discriminatory practices with the genocide epitomized by Hitler's concentration camps and gas ovens, and this gave new force to the old complaint that people who had no race problem of their own had no right to criticize those who did.

Newspapermen who had been using their editorial pulpits to argue the case for social justice now found themselves, as I would soon discover in my own right, cast in an entirely different and sometimes contradictory role—trying to preserve order at an incipient riot. The case of Virginius Dabney is particularly poignant. The editor of the *Richmond Times-Dispatch* presided over a humane, highly civilized editorial page in the former Confederate capital, a post of high symbolic importance inside and outside the region. V. Dabney was not only perfectly named but perfectly cast; a descendant of First Families of Virginia on both sides, reared on the campus of Thomas Jefferson's university, where his father taught history, he exemplified the best qualities of the legendary Southern gentleman. In 1932 the University of North Carolina Press tapped him as spokesman for the breed, commissioning the book he titled *Liberalism in the South*. Dabney dismissed the racist demagogues who tarnished the image of his beloved region; he considered it an obligation of his class, and of his profession, to assume the burden of protecting blacks against oppression, and to nurture their advancement within the framework of a segregated society.

As a Jeffersonian defender of individual liberties, he often found himself out on a lonely limb, as when he was one of only two Southern editors to speak out in defense of a nineteen-year-old black Communist organizer of an Atlanta protest march who was given an outrageous sentence under a preposterous Georgia law against insurrection. On key racial issues he went as far as any of his contemporaries and considerably farther than most. In 1936 he came out against the poll tax, a particularly noteworthy stand for the leading newspaper in the state dominated by Harry Byrd's archconservative political machine. In 1937 he endorsed a federal antilynching bill sponsored by the NAACP; Walter White was so impressed he began actively lobbying for a Pulitzer Prize for Dabney, citing his stand as "one of the most significant positions taken by an American newspaper since the Civil War." In 1941 Dabney called upon defense industries to hire blacks and give them the same pay as whites. In 1943 he urged the end of Jim Crow seating on buses and other common carriers—a stand that drew a letter of appreciation from Roy Wilkins of the NAACP, but was greeted with what Dabney called a "thunderous silence" by his friends and colleagues on Southern newspapers.

Dabney had now pressed his public argumentation to the outer limits of his concept of justice within a segregated society, only to see demands for redress by Northern blacks and their white supporters continue unabated in, as he sensed it, the face of mounting danger of racial violence. In January 1943 he put his national reputation as a liberal on the line in what he considered an appeal to reason published in *Atlantic Monthly* under the alarmist title "Nearer and Nearer the Precipice," contending that "a small group of Negro agitators and another small group of white rabble-rousers are pushing this country closer and closer to an interracial explosion. . . ." The black response was fairly restrained, but Dabney drew a sharp rejoinder from another white Southerner, Thomas Sancton, a Louisiana journalist who had been in my class of Nieman

Fellows at Harvard. Sancton, now living in New York, wrote a series in the *New Republic* in which he charged that "understandably rebellious" blacks were again being subjected to the "same old rationalized prejudices and selfishness." In a letter to Dabney, he wrote:

I think someone has got to drive it into the heads of well-to-do housewives who sit around talking their snide talk about Mrs. Roosevelt and the beastly servant problem that the New Deal is causing by paying Negro husbands such wages and sending the mothers of Negro soldiers all that money—I think someone has got to tell these people straight to their faces even though it means insulting them that . . . a change of attitude is damn well demanded of them by virtue of every soldier who is risking and giving his life to keep this country worth living in.

Those who adopted a similar stance necessarily wrote off the entire list of Southerners accorded places on the honor roll of courageous American journalists. "What's Happened to the Southern Liberals?," demanded the *New Leader*, citing the likes of Dabney, John Temple Graves, Mark Ethridge, Jonathan Daniels, and Jennings Perry as "caught woefully off guard, unprepared to measure the impact of the war . . . and unable to channel their general humanitarian impulses into the stream of rapid social and economic change." The author of the article, Cy Record, added the usual radical charge that wounded ego was a large element in the default of these displaced elitists, who found assumption of leadership by blacks in their own right "shocking to the liberal temperament, not to say terrifying."

The suggestion that failed nerve, excessive prudence, or personal pique motivated these men is, I believe, nonsense, but then I am a prejudiced party since most were then, or later became, my friends. To be understood they must be seen in the context of their time and place. "It should never be forgotten that white Southerners who became identified as racial liberals in the period between the 1920s and the 1940s grew up precisely when racism in the South was most bitter, violent and blatant," Morton Sosna wrote in his throughgoing and unsparing study of key figures in the emerging interracial movement. "To a large extent, Southern liberalism is a history of how these people each arrived at an island of tolerance in a sea of hate."

6

The Literary View

My role as a military combatant rendered me a political noncombatant in the early phase of the struggle over civil rights that began amidst the tensions and dislocations of World War II, but that immunity ended with the Japanese surrender. As state capital correspondent for the *Greenville News* I had also written on politics for the *Charlotte News* in North Carolina, which had a considerable circulation across the state line, and the end of hostilities brought an offer to join the Charlotte paper as editor of the editorial page. It seemed a natural and perhaps necessary move; in the year before my departure for Cambridge my irreverent view of the reigning Bourbons had begun to strain the tolerance of the proprietors of the conservative *Greenville News*. So, in October 1945, I settled in at the feisty afternoon newspaper in the city that considered itself the hub of the Carolina piedmont.

The family-owned *News* was run by J. E. and Carey Dowd, amiable, civilized members of the local establishment who accepted, and sometimes enjoyed, the fact that their competitive position dictated a lively, more or less liberal policy. The morning *Observer* had the largest circulation between Richmond and Atlanta, and dominated the territory with solid, dull news coverage and a mossback editorial page. The *News* fought back with the brash, literate output of a remarkable assemblage of talented transients; in the newsroom the saying was that management would give you anything but money, the compensation for low pay being frequent bylines and considerable freedom of action. In those days the *News* attracted some of the brightest journalists in the region.

My place on the editorial page had been left vacant early in the war by the departure of the newspaper's most distinguished alumnus, Wilbur Joseph Cash. He had distilled a lifetime of acute observation of his native region into a remarkable book, *The Mind of the South*, and when its critical success earned him a grant to write another he had gone off to Mexico, where his deteriorating mental health drove him to suicide. That single work was all he left behind between hard covers, but it is a major legacy. Joseph L. Morrison opened his biography, *W. J. Cash: Southern Prophet*, with this appraisal:

> . . . in 1941 he achieved no more than a mild *success d'estime* that was swallowed up by his own death and by World War II. At the war's end, with a new generation of American whites and Negroes confronting one another, Cash's prophetic work gradually came into its own as obligatory reading. During the second half of the twentieth century, it has been accepted by virtually everyone that studies of the South—and, by extension, of the Negro revolution—must begin where Cash left off.

Where Cash left off is summarized in a closing passage of *The Mind of the South* in which he noted a great falling away of the traditional virtues, and in a typically rolling sentence set forth a catalogue of the Southerner's enduring vices: "violence, intolerance, aversions and suspicions toward new ideas, an incapacity for analysis, an inclination to act from feeling rather than thought, an exaggerated individualism and a too narrow concept of social responsibility, attachment to fictions and false values, above all too great attachment to racial values and a tendency to justify cruelty and injustice in the name of these values, sentimentality and a lack of realism . . ."

The fact that Cash mentioned race only toward the end of his list was revealing. He recognized the presence of blacks as central to the development of the complex of attitudes he identified with the Southern mind, and he did not blink at the palpable injustice of their treatment, but he saw their plight as incidental to the larger tragedy that had befallen the South as a result of its hubris. He had a profound distrust of the New South's leaders, often expressed in terms of savage contempt, but his social conscience was primarily stirred by the exploitation of white "lintheads" in the cotton mill villages where he grew up.

"Cash was ashamed—for he was no hypocrite—at the way

the local Negroes idolized him as their champion when his book came out," Morrison wrote. "He knew only too well that he was no activist; more than that, he was thoroughly pessimistic about the chances for racial progress in the then-current atmosphere of adamant and unyielding white supremacy." When Walter White thanked Cash on behalf of the NAACP, the author insisted he had done nothing to deserve such gratitude. Morrison summarized his attitude:

He had simply concluded that Southern white men, rich and poor, had always yoked together in their common and enforced ascendancy over the Negro, first in the days of slavery and then later in legal and extralegal white supremacy. Cash referred to this brotherhood of white men by the high-flown expression "proto-Dorian convention" (in which the common white was elevated into a position comparable to the Doric knight of ancient Sparta), but this did not in the least becloud his point that the rich white man often paid off his poorer brother in white-supremacy status instead of the coin of the realm.

Cash's was essentially a literary view, reflecting aesthetic outrage more consistently than social concern. A loner by temperament, rebelling early against his family's solid, middle-class Baptist respectability, he created a bohemian world of his own in the forbidding environs of Charlotte, where he fed his iconoclastic bent with prodigious reading. After graduation from Wake Forest University, he apprenticed on the *News*, returning as book page editor after a starveling period of world travel and free-lance writing. He never found a real home in the bustling, commercial-minded city he once described in the *American Mercury* as a "Calvinist Lhasa," hopelessly isolated from high culture by its impenetrable bigotry and obscurantism, a natural haven for the poisonous Babbittry he saw as the predominant characteristic that set the New South apart from the Old.

Cash's main thrust was aimed at the sentimental mythology he believed had beclouded the Southern mind and left it prey to the false prophets of the new age of progress. He calculated the number of families with a valid claim to Cavalier antecedents to be so small as to provide only a negligible influence on the slavocracy that emerged as the Cotton Kingdom spread to the Mississippi valley. The few planters who did hold to the aristocratic ideal of honor and magnanimity had long since been pushed aside by tough minded upward-strivers, "horse-trading men" Cash called them.

If Cash was a demolisher of other men's stereotypes, his method was to replace them with a set of his own. He fashioned these in an ornate literary style, as when he wrote:

Typically he spent his money with a childlike simplicity of improvidence and abandon, which was the perfectly natural issue of his long training in irresponsibility and his romantic-hedonist tradition— almost entirely for things which tickled his love of pleasure and of show.

This was not, as might be expected, a rendering of the standard literary Black Sambo, but Cash's view of the white linthead. Many of the mill hands were descendants of the poor whites who had subsisted on the margin of the agrarian society, and he found them blighted by the proto-Dorian bond offered them by their superiors in lieu of economic advancement:

. . . however much the blacks in the "Big House" might sneer at him, and however much their masters might privately agree with them, he . . . would always be a white man. And before that vast and capacious distinction, all others were foreshortened, dwarfed, and all but obliterated. The grand outcome was the almost complete disappearance of economic and social focus on the part of the masses.

So the poor white, whether running a still on the isolated slopes of the high mountains, prowling the lowland swamps with fishing pole and shotgun, or laboring at the looms in a textile mill's company town, was left enthralled by the corrupted romantic-hedonist ideal—"to stand on his head in a bar, to toss down a pint of raw whiskey at a gulp, to fiddle and dance all night, to bite off the nose or gouge out the eye of a favorite enemy, to fight harder and love harder than the next man, and to be known eventually far and wide as a hell of a fellow—such would be his focus."

At the other end of the scale Cash saw the new masters of the industrializing South as typified by the "bastard barons" who had taken the helm of the cotton mills. The original factories, almost entirely financed through local stock subscriptions, had been brought into being under Bourbon leadership late in the nineteenth century as self-professed civic enterprises aimed at salvaging the decaying community. But Cash saw the result as an extension of the plantation ethos in the name of "progress." He conceded an element of noblesse oblige in the founding of the mill villages but voiced the dark suspicion that the real motive of the master class had been to keep the poor whites from sinking to such a level they would accept social equality with blacks, thereby severing the proto-Dorian bond and creating a new class consciousness that would rend the very fabric of the prevailing order.

Cash had been fascinated by European culture in the course of his threadbare wanderjahr, and his wide reading gave him an affinity with the New York intellectual community. H. L. Mencken welcomed him to the scattered company of literary rebels the "Bad Boy of Baltimore" managed to unearth in the Sahara of the Bozart. Yet the North was also anathema to Cash, for he saw it as the source of the crass materialism being forced upon his own exploited province. He called Reconstruction "the frontier the Yankee made," and the acerbic Mencken's influence could be seen in the most outrageous caricature in *The Mind of the South*, that of the Yankee school ma'am come down to educate the freed blacks:

Generally horsefaced, bespectacled, and spare of frame, she was, of course, no proper intellectual, but at best a comic character, at worst a dangerous fool, playing with explosive forces which she did not understand. She had no little part in developing Southern bitterness as a whole, and along with the peripatetic Yankee journalist, contributed much to the growth of hysterical sensibility to criticism.

In its mordant way this indictment of Reconstruction's female outrider, and the baleful impact upon the Southern mind attributed to the brief presence of a few thousand of her kind, seems to me to be as romantic, and as blindly defensive, as any of the mythic Southern stereotypes Cash so assiduously attacked. His deeply pessimistic view provided him with no heroes—not, at any rate, in the living present or the recent past—so he populated the Southern landscape with villains, and, where conscious evil did not apply, with those who, as in the case of the denizens of Erskine Caldwell's Tobacco Road, could be described as afflicted with a "peculiar and grotesque and malignant innocence."

CASH's scorn for the go-getting disciples of Henry Grady was shared by most of the writers who came to prominence in the course of the remarkable renascence of Southern letters that began in the twenties. The self-appointed bellwethers were poets clustered around Vanderbilt University who called themselves "Fugitives." They were appalled as they saw Zenith City being replicated in Atlanta and Birmingham and Memphis with the full panoply of Chamber of Commerce promoters, smug Rotarians, and hustling Elmer Gantrys. The greatest of the Southern artists, William Faulkner, also deplored these modernist phenomena, but he treated them as an emerging element in the regional backdrop against which he developed individual character in universal terms of tragedy and comedy. The Fugitives opted for direct literary attack; augmenting their ranks and calling themselves "Agrarians," they mounted an organized effort to preserve the traditions of the Old South against the depredations of progress.

In 1930 the Agrarians issued a manifesto, *I'll Take My Stand*, which declared holy war on the clamorous advance of industrialism. In their exaltation of nineteenth-century Southern values they parted company with Cash, who thought that little worth preserving had survived the cultural erosion of the last hundred years. And they also parted company with the liberal reformers who considered modernization and growth of the Southern economy essential to improvement in the social condition of Southerners—most particularly to that of the submerged black population. Seen in retrospect, the Agrarian movement was little more than a heartfelt cry of anguish. It gained recognition from the character of its adherents: six of the twelve who signed the manifesto were, or were to become, literary figures of commanding national reputation, and the others were accorded high standing in the scholarly disciplines.

The founding poets, John Crowe Ransom, Donald Davidson, Allen Tate, and Robert Penn Warren, were first moved to action by the Scopes "monkey trial" in their native Cumberland region. That famous test of the Tennessee law forbidding the teaching of evolution in the public schools attracted a coterie of Yankee journalists who found the trial a hilarious example of what their leader, H. L. Mencken, called "boobocracy." The running caricature of the hill people sent north over the news wires moved Davidson to observe that religious fundamentalism, although representing at its worst a "belligerent ignorance," also embodied a "fierce clinging to poetic supernaturalism against the encroachments of cold logic," and reflected a moral seriousness that deserved something more than scorn. Tate saw the issue raised by the fundamentalists as reflecting the deeper question of the rights of science in conflict with those of religion, in which he found that science had very little to say for itself. "The church these days of course is decayed," he wrote, "but the attack on it should be ethical, not scientific."

The Agrarian manifesto foreshadowed the conservationist campaign mounted forty years later against runaway technology and the doctrine of progress. The contributors to *I'll Take My Stand* also thought that small was beautiful, and that civilization could not survive the continued exploitation of irreplaceable natural resources. Andrew Nelson Lytle saw "a war to the death between technology and the ordinary functions of living." Progressivism to John Crowe Ransom was "a principle of boundless aggression against nature," and industrialism a "program under which men, using the latest scientific paraphernalia, sacrificed comfort, leisure and the enjoyment of life to win Pyrrhic victories from Nature at points of no strategic importance." And, as the New Leftists were to do, the Agrarians simply dismissed the constraints of economic theory and practice. Donald Davidson wrote:

We came at last to economics, and so found ourselves at odds with the prevailing schools of economic thought. These held that economics determines life and set up an abstract economic existence as the goal of man's effort. We believed that life determines economics, or ought to do so, and that economics is no more than an instrument, around the use of which should gather many more motives than economic ones.

There was a nobility about this futile effort to stay, and even roll back, the tide of history. But there was a fatal flaw in the humanist doctrine these sensitive men attempted to propound as salvation for their beloved region: to halt progress was to freeze into place a system that denied elementary social justice to the black population. Davidson, having no answer of his own to the problem, could only attack those who claimed they did:

For better or worse, the sociologist has become the chief expert consultant on the Negro problem, at least to that part of the American public which believe that the problem can be solved by legislative means. The reasoning of this public can be briefly stated as follows: The cause of the problem is race prejudice, which is a kind of social disease afflicting white folks, especially in the South; the sociologist is a kind of doctor, who isolates and describes the disease, and then designates remedy and treatment; apply remedy and treatment through Federal legislation, and you have the cure . . . The sociologists, some quite unwillingly, others with obvious unction and high hope, have inherited the leadership formerly held by William Lloyd Garrison, Wendell Phillips, Charles Sumner, Thad Stevens and Company.

What, then, could the Agrarians say to the blacks who were inescapably a part of the South they sought to preserve? Davidson said it in verse:

> Black man, when you and I were young together,
> We knew each other's hearts. Though I am no longer
> A child, and you perhaps unfortunately
> Are no longer a child, we still understand
> Better maybe than others. There is a wall
> Between us, anciently erected. Once
> It might have been crossed, men say. But now I cannot
> Forget that I was master, and you can hardly
> Forget that you were slave. We did not build
> The ancient wall, but there it painfully is.
> Let us not bruise our foreheads on the wall.

THE Agrarian movement was a not insignificant manifestation of the Southern literary renascence, but it did not embrace some of the most notable of the regional authors who came to national prominence in the years between the wars. Only two of these, the Pulitzer Prize-winning Arkansas poet, John Gould Fletcher, and the Mississippi novelist, Stark Young, joined the founding Fugitives as contributors to *I'll Take My Stand*. Some became apostates, in the Agrarian view, by relocating in enemy territory and looking homeward from afar; Davidson dismissed the most prominent of these, Thomas Wolfe, with a sideswipe at the movement's academic adversaries: "I suggest that his trouble was that he had been taught to misunderstand with his head what he understood with his heart. Thomas Wolfe had a divided sensibility which very likely resulted from his education at Mr. Howard Odum's progressive University of North Carolina, and from his subsequent unfortunate experience at Harvard." But most of the others certainly understood the South with their hearts, and if they stopped short of the defensive polemics of the Agrarians, they were left no less bereft by the decay of the pastoral society that had shaped their values.

At Stockholm, accepting the Nobel Prize, William Faulkner set forth his belief that the artist must leave "no room in his workshop for anything but the old verities and truths of the heart, the universal truths lacking which any story is ephemeral and doomed—love, and honor and pity and pride and compassion and sacrifice. Until he does so he labors under a curse. He writes not of love, but of lust, of defeats in which nobody loses anything of value, of victories without hope, and, worst of all, without pity and compassion. His grief grieves on no universal bones, leaving no scars. He writes not of the heart but of the glands."

Faulkner created his literary site, Yoknapatawpha County and its seat, Jefferson, as a far place, not limited by the lineaments of his own Oxford, Mississippi, and its inhabitants, although not false to them either. Thus, as John Maclachlan wrote in *Southern Renascence*, "there is no segmentation, segregation, of caste, class, sex, of age from youth or male from female or white from black to prevent a whole view of life as a whole. . . . It is a community of no secrets. Each knows all that is true, and much that is not, about each. Not a man's own life alone is known, but the life of the father and the grandfather as well, and that of the son." One who wrote in this mode in the South would have to populate the landscape with blacks. He might keep them in the background, with no effort to portray them in the round or to deal with the intractable issue of race relations, but the effect of their presence was an inescapable element of characterization and plot.

None of the treatment of blacks by Southern novelists entirely satisfied the critics. It took Faulkner half a lifetime to gain recognition from the reviewers who dominated literary criticism in New York; six years before he received the Nobel Prize, all seventeen of his extant works were out of print. He was charged with stereotypical Samboism, and Maxwell Geismar even accused him of hating the Negro. Irene C. Edmonds, a black poet, dismissed this as palpable nonsense, but added: "On the other hand, neither can one agree with those who claim that he loves the Negro, unless they are referring to the Dilsey-type Negro servant." Ms. Edmonds thought that an essential ambivalence—"his thinking about the problem is unsettled and inconclusive"—tended to limit Faulkner to stereotypes. But Ralph Ellison, the black novelist, credited him with an "impulse that made Faulkner more willing perhaps than any other artist to start with the stereotype of the Negro, accept it as true, and then seek out the human truth which it hides."

Faulkner thought it was not the artist's function to preach, and he usually resisted the impulse. But he did not share the Agrarians' illusion that the segregated Southern community could, or should, hold against the pressures mounting against it. His concern was that admission of blacks to the larger society would expose them, unprepared, to the shoddy values he saw pervading the country as the old regional isolation was broken down by the communications revolution. In 1948, when the civil rights issue was beginning to come to a head in Washington, he spoke through the lawyer, Gavin Stevens, in *Intruder in the Dust.* Stevens is defending Lucas Beauchamp, a stubborn, proud old black who "refused to mean mister to white folks even when he said it." In a long speech in which one generation is self-consciously addressing the next, the lawyer tells his young nephew that what he is really defending is the white South's privilege of setting its own people free, fully understanding that this means that

Lucas Beauchamp can shoot a white man in the back with the same impunity to lynch-rope or gasoline as a white man; in time he will vote anywhen and anywhere a white man can and send his children to the same school anywhere the white man's children go and travel anywhere the white man travels as the white man does it.

This, he tells his nephew, is his black client's earned right, but to try to secure it for him he is also defending Lucas Beauchamp

from the North and East and West—the outlanders who will fling him decades back not merely into injustice but into grief and agony and violence too by forcing on us laws based on the idea that man's injustice to man can be abolished overnight by police.

Gavin Stevens appears again in *Requiem for a Nun*, published in 1951, speaking of a black nurse who has confessed to the murder of the white child in her charge, and is now awaiting execution:

We're not concerned with death. That's nothing: any handful of petty facts and sworn documents can cope with that. That's all finished now; we can forget it. What we are trying to deal with now is injustice. Only truth can cope with that. Or love.

THE immediate impact of the literary view of the South was confined to those who read serious novels, short stories, poetry and belles lettres—not a large company in the region, and not much larger elsewhere. Unreconstructed Southerners were repelled by the brutality and decadence necessarily revealed by those who tried to see the region whole. The less curious left the original works unread and accepted the generally unfavorable characterization that filtered through the popular press; when Faulkner's Nobel Prize was announced Major Frederick Sullens of the *Jackson Daily News* averred that his state's most famous son was "a propagandist for degradation and properly belongs to the privy school of literature."

I had the good fortune to be exposed early to the outpouring of regional literature by an extraordinary high school teacher, Dorothy Zirkle, a Virginian gifted with sound taste and a total lack of inhibition in contemplating the seamiest and saltiest aspects of the Southern scene. She was safe enough, I suppose, in exposing those of her students she deemed at least incipiently literate to the mannered novels of Ellen Glasgow, but she must have run some risk when she included in her list James Branch Cabell's mildly scandalous *Jurgen*. In any case, she pointed me in the right direction, and at Clemson a beloved English professor, John Lane, kept me on track. I would continue to read them all as they came into view—Tennessee Williams, Truman Capote, Walker Percy, the intricately talented ladies, Carson McCullers, Flannery O'Connor, and Eudora Welty, and the only black Southerners who may properly be counted as figures in the renascence, Richard Wright and Ralph Ellison. These two provided an insight into black consciousness that often eluded the most sensitive white, the dimension beyond the immediate brute impact of the scorn, cruelty, and deprivation against which the black had no effective defense.

Ellison made an indelible imprint upon me with his evocation of the condition cited in the title of his fine novel, *Invisible Man*. Segregation denied opportunity and, for most blacks, imposed poverty, but its great blight was denial of identity—and this could not be cured even if all the other wrongs were redressed within the framework of separate but equal. "Hence the predicament of the poor after their self-preservation has been assured," Hannah Arendt wrote in *On Revolution*, "is that their lives are almost without consequence, and that they remain excluded from the light of the public realm where their excellence can shine; they stand in darkness wherever they go." For the mass of blacks there was the added burden of their unique heritage for, Ms. Arendt contended, "the institution of slavery carries an obscurity even blacker than the institution of poverty."

Cash's *The Mind of the South* deserves its special place in the literature of the period, but I doubt that he is entitled to the designation "prophet" his biographer bestowed upon him. Cash understood that time was running out for the Old South, but he neither mourned nor celebrated the passing. Barely able to tolerate the crass present in which he found himself, his pessimism was such that, out of sheer dread I suspect, he largely avoided looking to the future. His most profound insights were derived from the vanishing, not the emerging South.

Central to Cash's appraisal of the Southern mind was the universal acceptance of what he called "the savage ideal . . . whereunder dissent and variety are completely supressed and men become in all their attitudes, professions, and action, virtual replicas of one another." He traced this, correctly I think, to the 1830s, when the Southern leadership united in defense of slavery and the dissenting voices began to fall silent. Insofar as racial attitudes were concerned, he certainly had been, as had I, subjected to a stifling conformity. But it seemed to me that he gave his thesis far more weight than it could bear when he depicted the savage ideal as virtually undiminished since it had been reinforced by Reconstruction to a point "unknown by any Western people since the decay of medieval feudalism, and almost as truly as it is established today in Fascist Italy, in Nazi Germany, in Soviet Russia . . ."

Ironically, the reception given *The Mind of the South* refuted the savage ideal in spectacular fashion. Since, in its most salient features, it conformed to the prevailing national literary view of the region, the praise it drew from leading critics was not surprising. But the book fared even better with reviewers in Southern newspapers, and drew additional applause on the editorial pages. One of the wealthiest textile barons came forward to thank Cash for "a cool breeze blowing through our land," and *Mind* rose to number one on the Atlanta best-seller list. Morrison, reviewing returns from throughout the region, found that Cash's "dissent was met not with savage intolerance but with respectful—even prideful—attention."

The fact that Cash was so patently Southern in all his insights and humors—writing, as one reviewer put it, "in bitter truthfulness and love"—no doubt helped overcome the automatic rejection that greeted similar appraisals by outlanders. But there had to be more to it than that. The rising racial tensions touched off by the wartime black protest against discrimination presumably resulted in large part from the reflexive reaction of Southern leaders, and the response of poor whites still bound by the proto-Dorian bond. But there was reason to wonder how this really affected white middle-class citizens in the Southern cities and towns. The weight of conformity was still such as to prevent many of these from speaking out, even privately, if the issue involved social equality. But the concessions made to blacks by the Roosevelt administration in the name of national necessity were generally as well accepted in the South as they were elsewhere. Mark Ethridge suffered no loss of status when he took leave from the *Louisville Courier-Journal* to serve as chairman of the first Fair Employment Practices Commission.

Even in the most extreme case, that of Lillian Smith, who became an outright evangelist for the black cause, the novelist retained her social standing as an authentic Southern lady. Settling down in the twenties at Old Screamer Mountain in north Georgia, where she had inherited the fashionable girl's camp that provided her a living, she began a writing career that

found its first outlet in her own periodical, ultimately titled
North Georgia Review. In her writing, and in frequent speeches
to religious and school groups, she denounced white racial
chauvinism as a sickness. Yet the proper young ladies from
leading families continued to spend their summers at Old
Screamer, and the mountain folk in nearby Clayton continued
to treat her with affection and respect.

Miss Lillian's status survived even the test of Southern
tolerance posed by publication in 1944 of her first novel,
Strange Fruit, which treated frankly and sympathetically the
ultimate taboo, miscegenation. She had assumed that as her
writing attracted widespread attention it would mean the ruin
of her summer camp: ". . . I draw my children from the
South's wealthiest and most conservative families. God knows
they've taken plenty from me already. My camp patrons and I
are friends, and our warm personal feelings have made it
possible for me to get away with almost the impossible in social
philosophy, sex education and religious skepticism. But I have
had good luck so far. As everyone tells me, the time will
come . . ." Instead *Strange Fruit* made her a national celebrity,
and gave her added immunity. Laurel Falls Camp continued
to prosper until she decided on her own motion to close it in
1948.

Georgia's red-gallused Governor, Eugene Talmadge,
called her novel "a literary corncob," but this may have helped
sales, which continued to flourish across the South without any
of the difficulties that beset *Strange Fruit* in the North, where it
was banned in Boston because of its explicit sex. It was also
declared obscene by the U.S. Post Office in an order promptly
rescinded by Franklin Roosevelt at the behest of his wife
Eleanor. Miss Lillian, like Cash, was astonished that there was
no resurgence of the savage ideal, not even in the Georgia hill
country where, instead, her neighbors turned out to honor her
at a party she gave for her New York editor: "They all wept a
little, kissed me and embraced me, ate my chicken sandwiches
and little cakes and went down the hill feeling that each of them
had written at least one chapter of it. Bless them . . . as far as I
know, things are going to be all right."

By the time she published her hortatory *Killers of the Dream*
in 1949, Lillian Smith had concluded that her fellow Southern-

ers no longer had the option of temporizing on racial matters. She rejected the arguments for gradual change; for her, segregation posed a moral choice between good and evil, life and death of the spirit. She thus publicly parted company with virtually all her peers, refusing to join the moderate Southern Regional Council, lending her name instead to the more militant black organizations as they came into being. But the parting was her choice; Miss Lillian was never an outcast. When she died in 1966 many Southerners acknowledged the region's debt to this indomitable woman, and included among them were some of those who had tried, and failed, to kill her dream.

7

The Gathering Forces
of Change

*T*he American racial dilemma, the black poet, James Weldon Johnson, wrote, "is not a static condition; rather it is, and always has been, a series of shifting interracial situations, never precisely the same for any two generations." This was profoundly true for my contemporaries. The society into which we were admitted as adults was beginning to mobilize for what still stands as the most extensive collective undertaking in human history: the creation and simultaneous deployment of massive armed forces across two oceans, with enough materiel left over to sustain our battered allies. To those caught up in that mighty effort—and to some extent all of us were—neither the exterior world, nor our interior view of each man's place in it, would ever be the same again. This had special implications for Southerners, white and black.

I do not intend to suggest that my generation came home from the war imbued with a passion for racial justice. The civil rights movement would come later, in stages, and would enlist the active support of only a small minority of whites. But I thought I could detect among my contemporaries a new permissiveness; they seemed to me no longer prepared, as their fathers had been, to sacrifice their self-interest on the altar of white supremacy. When the frontal assault on Jim Crow began in the 1950s, C. Vann Woodward wrote: "Behind these conscious agencies of change were such great, impersonal forces of history as lay behind Emancipation, the First Reconstruction, and Redemption. They included economic revolution, rapid urbanization and war—war in a somewhat new dimension called total war."

My own relocation in Charlotte involved no significant change of geography; I had only moved a hundred miles up the Southern Railway's main line between Washington and Atlanta, and I was still in the piedmont domain of the Scotch-Irish. But if there was little surface difference between Greenville and Charlotte, a political sea change was involved in the transition from one Carolina to the other. In Columbia the politicians still labored under the stultifying heritage from the antebellum plantation culture; in Raleigh the primary influence had always come from the western reaches of the state, and this area had produced the industrial growth that had moved North Carolina ahead of its Southern neighbors in every significant economic category.

The incursion of seaboard culture from Tidewater Virginia and Charleston had been confined to the isolated eastern counties ranged behind the Outer Banks that deprived North Carolina of a major port of its own. West of Raleigh growing cities challenged Charlotte's population lead—Durham, Greensboro, Winston-Salem, High Point, Asheville—and in their satellite towns factories were turning out textiles, tobacco products, and furniture at a rate that made them prime suppliers of national markets. North Carolina provided the closest approximation of Henry Grady's New South the region had yet produced.

Because the state had pioneered in public education early in the century, and had created at Chapel Hill a university recognized as the region's most distinguished, North Carolina was generally considered liberal, by Southern standards at least. It was in fact a stronghold of classic conservatism. If respect for learning produced a certain tolerance for scholars and an unusual incidence of newspapers of high quality, the state was still a bastion of religious fundamentalism. Related to that, as is usually the case, was the widespread commitment to individual material advancement that provided the motive power for the great industrial leap forward.

No one understood this better than a poker-playing companion I encountered on the fringe of the newspaper fraternity. This gifted newcomer provided a particularly discerning view of Charlotte, appraising the city in the unique perspective he would later bring to the South as a whole. Born in a Galician *shtetl*, brought up by a scholar father in the dense Yiddish culture of New York's Lower East Side, educated in that stronghold of the Young People's Socialist League, the College of the City of New York, made prosperous by a boomtime career in Wall Street, married into a solid middle-class Irish-Catholic family and happily adapted to a commuter's life in suburban Larchmont, Harry Goldhurst had put an abrupt end to his American success story by becoming involved in a mail-order stock fraud that sent him to federal prison for almost four years. Starting a new life under a new name, Harry Golden in his middle years had become, and would remain, a Tarheel tried and true. Earning his living with a jackleg advertising agency, he had begun to crank out his then-obscure *Carolina Israelite* as an outlet for an irrepressibly witty running commentary on the contemporary scene.

Arriving in Charlotte during the war years, Golden discovered that he had chosen as his new home the only American city he ever heard of where the natives had been able to hold out against the merchandising genius of his fellow Jews. Charlotte's leading department stores, all of which operated chain outlets throughout piedmont Carolina, bore the names of staunchly Protestant proprietors. Belks were Presbyterian, Efirds were Baptist, and Iveys were Methodist, so much so the patriarch, old George Ivey, ordered the shades drawn on his display windows on Sunday, and refused to stock playing cards, poker chips, or cocktail glasses—prompting Golden to inquire in the *Israelite*, "Why beds?" "What had always fascinated me about Charlotte," he wrote, "was that I was able to turn the stereotype inside out. I have been enthralled as I watched the Presbyterians, Methodists and Baptists chase the buck. The Protestants *do* have all the money, and they go at it with an intensity unknown anywhere else in the civilized world."

Another aspect of everyday life in this Southern city also fascinated Golden: "Almost half the Charlotte population, the colored half, was invisible." Out of curiosity, and the special sensitivity to oppression born of his Jewish heritage, Harry Golden made it his business to know what was going on in the submerged black community. And, when the personal journalism he practiced in the *Israelite* was incorporated in best-selling books that made him a national celebrity, he became an unconventional and highly effective civil rights advocate. As a rising star on the civic club and religious fellowship lecture circuit his indestructible good humor allowed him to maintain rapport with the white audiences who flocked to hear him satirize their shibboleths.

Even when Southerners became increasingly thin-skinned under the pressure of federal court decisions pushing inexorably toward desegregation, Golden was able to continue his gentle ridicule of the more preposterous manifestations of white supremacy. Sympathetic laughter greeted his Vertical Integration Plan; since no white Southerner objected to standing by a black, while many objected to sitting by one, he proposed that conventional schoolroom furniture be replaced by old-fashioned bookkeeper's desks so that the rising generation could be educated standing up. And when a professor's wife at black Johnson C. Smith University in Charlotte wanted to see a filmed Shakespearean drama available only at a theater without a segregated "nigger heaven" balcony, Golden borrowed a white child so the lady could be admitted on the assumption that she was a nursemaid—thus giving rise to his widely publicized Rent-a-Child scheme. Here was tangible evidence of a growth in sophistication that in time would undermine the last-ditch resistance to desegregation advocated by the South's political leaders.

Even in the early days, when the *Israelite* subsisted as a sort of house organ for the small, scattered Jewish communities of the Carolinas, Golden found himself welcome as he traveled through the little towns peddling advertising and subscriptions, usually lecturing for his supper. We often discussed the ironic fact that, in his paunchy, rumpled, horn-rimmed, cigar-chomping, conspicuously Jewish person, he was demonstrating that the South, which deserved its reputation as the nation's preeminent citadel of race prejudice, was, despite an occasional outbreak of Kluckery, largely free of the kind of routine anti-Semitism Golden had known all his life in New York.

In the Southern cities there were old Jewish families whose roots went back to antebellum days, and in the seaports to colonial times. Usually of Sephardic or German lineage, these were accorded all the marks of status except such rarefied tokens as membership in the most exalted social clubs. Golden was amused to find that some of these, and not necessarily as protective coloration, assumed the most patrician of Southern attitudes, including devotion to the doctrine of white supremacy. He wrote of a visit to Hobcaw Barony, the aptly named plantation retreat in the South Carolina lowcountry maintained by Bernard Baruch, whose father had been a Confederate surgeon:

He told me he was "bone-of-the-bone and blood-of-the-blood" of old South Carolina. I asked Mr. Baruch about Israel bonds, and he replied, "I buy American bonds." I asked him about Father Coughlin calling him the head of the Sanhedrin, and Baruch replied, "My wife tells me, 'Bernie, don't get into politics.' " Finally, I asked, since he had advised so many Presidents, how about advising Jews? and he replied, "I do best in the high grass."

But the lesson, of course, was not that white Southerners seemed to be less anti-Semitic than white Northerners, or that Jews could be as snobbish as anyone else. The point, which applied in reverse to blacks, was the equation between numerical proportion and the overt manifestation of prejudice. The Jews in the South were few and prosperous; the blacks in the South were numerous and poor. "No hotel boasts of a restricted clientele," Golden wrote, "because there simply are not enough Jews to go around."

IN the mid-forties there was still no effective challenge to the famous dictum of the historian of slavery, Ulrich B. Phillips, who found Southerners irrevocably committed to the proposition that their region "shall be and remain a white man's country . . . [This] whether expressed with the frenzy of a demagogue or maintained with a patrician's quietude, is the cardinal test of a Southerner, and the central theme of Southern history." When Phillips rendered this verdict in 1928 there could be no doubt that Southerners, and for that matter Northerners too, universally accepted it as a statement of fact. But with the coming of the New Deal there began to surface a division between those who recognized, and deplored, the social and economic consequences of the traditional devotion to white supremacy, and those who exalted it as the ultimate test of the frayed aristocratic faith of the Bourbons. That dogma was never set forth more candidly than in a 1937 editorial in the *Charleston News & Courier*:

Again, let it be said and clearly understood that were the *News & Courier* a democratic newspaper, if it believed in democracy as President Roosevelt believes in it . . . it would demand that every white man and woman and every black man and woman in the South be protected in the right to vote. It would demand the abolition of all "Jim Crow" laws, of all drawing of the color line by law. That is democracy. But the *News & Courier* is not a democrat. It fears and hates democratic government. The *News & Courier* believes in Democratic government—Democratic with a big "D," and that is another word for a measure of aristocratic government that ought to be more aristocratic than it is.

Ten years later not even the doughty old Charleston thunderer would have stated its doubtless unshaken conviction in these terms. White veterans returning to the South believed, most of them, that they had been fighting for little "d" democracy, and if they were not yet willing to extend it fully to their black neighbors, many were prepared to go part of the way. At the *News* I aroused no great outcry when I argued editorially for full political rights for blacks, and some of the leading newspapers in the upper South took the same position.

The rock of white supremacy still stood, but the new latitude in public discussion of its consequences was sufficient to bring to office a new breed of forward-looking politicians— men like Ellis Arnall of Georgia, Estes Kefauver of Tennessee, Lister Hill and John Sparkman of Alabama, Claude Pepper of Florida, J. William Fulbright of Arkansas, and Lyndon Johnson of Texas. Except for issues directly related to segregation they approached the national Democratic norm, strongly internationalist in foreign policy, generally liberal in social and economic matters. They cemented the fealty of their business-oriented constituents by crusading for amendment of freight rate and tariff schedules that gave non-Southern manufactured products a market advantage over those produced in the region. And they sought benefits for all Southerners by pushing for federal development of the region's neglected natural resources, including the great, multipurpose projects of the Tennessee Valley Authority.

The ideological framework within which these progressive

Southerners worked had been fashioned over three decades by
Howard W. Odum, who identified himself professionally as a
sociologist but served as a sort of all-purpose intellectual
resource for those who were trying to chart patterns of politico-
economic change. Born in Georgia in 1884, educated at Emory,
Clark, and Columbia, he settled in at Chapel Hill, where he
organized the department of sociology, edited the *Journal of
Social Forces*, and founded the Institute for Research in Social
Science.

Odum professed a commitment to the rigid application of
the scientific method to social problems, but he also had a
tendency to break into poetry. At one point he turned away
from his charts and graphs and sometimes turgid sociological
exposition to write a fictional trilogy depicting the adventures
of a "Black Ulyssess"—an itinerant construction worker whose
life and times he sought to recount in a form he described as "a
sort of unretouched photograph, nevertheless presented with
the idea that the Negro after all is a human being, with a sort of
timeless and spaceless folk urge." But Odum's masterwork was
the more conventionally sociological *Southern Regions of the
United States*, published in 1936; it became basic fare in Southern college social science courses, where I first encountered it,
and it had a marked effect in reshaping the thinking of my
generation of students.

Odum's great contribution was to replace the traditional
magnolia-scented view of a monolithic South with a much more
diverse regional concept. Lopping off Texas and adding Kentucky to the old Confederacy, he labeled this the Southeast—
one of six cohesive regions of the United States that could be
transformed through application of the new planning tools
coming into use by the New Deal agencies. Within this Southeast region, he wrote, "there were many Souths, yet *the* South.
It was preeminently national in backgrounds, yet provincial in
its processes." Odum did not flatly reject the Phillips dictum.
"The story of the Negro in the South becomes from the
moment of his coming to complicate the picture, the most
decisive factor in the architecture of Southern culture . . . ," he
wrote. "Whatever else may be true, it must be clear that this is
what makes the South distinctive from other regions." But his
concern was less with the moral problem of achieving racial

justice than with freeing both blacks and whites from the debilitating restraints of their heritage.

Odum thought Southerners would begin to recognize new possibilities for the future once they appreciated the distinct differences among his many Souths: those of the black belt, the piedmont, the river delta, the mountains, the piney woods. In most of these the plantation system had only peripheral economic importance; in none did it represent the way of life of the majority of whites.

In 1947, in *The Way of the South*, Odum proclaimed that the time had come to lay the old ghosts and recognize the past significance and future potential of the white middle class:

Among the important neglected factors in the interpretation of the agrarian South is that of the large number of upper middle class, non-slaveholding white folk who constituted the backbone of reconstruction and recovery. Their contributions were definitive in the regional culture. It was upon their sturdy character and persistent work that the "New South" was largely built. . . . This group stands out in contrast to the "planter class" to which so much attention has been given, who numbered in the Southern states less than 200,000 as compared to no less than a million and a half of these farm folk corresponding to the upper farmer class in the earlier East and Middle West.

Odum had no illusion that the substantial citizens descended from the yeoman farmers and small holders were free of race prejudice. But he believed that when put to the test theirs would be less virulent than that of the other two classes—the planters, who had a vested interest in maintaining a pool of cheap black labor, and the poor whites, whose pigmentation provided their only mark of status.

His institute carried on what Odum called a sort of informal, hidden poll of Southern folk and in *Race and Rumors of Race*, published in 1943, he acknowledged a "Southern credo" which still held that "the Negro was a Negro and would always be that and nothing more." In the fifties, when he had accepted the inevitability of federal sponsored desegregation, he insisted that "it was of the first importance that Southerners face the plain assumption that they did not appraise the Negro as the same sort of human being they themselves are."

This kind of pragmatism was highly offensive to the

romantic Southern intellectuals of the Agrarian movement, and no less so to Northern radicals committed to a concept of class revolt that would bring blacks and poor whites together to overthrow the oppressive ruling class. Like most of the South's native reformers Odum sometimes found it difficult to conceal his irritation with those who crusaded for change on uncompromising moral grounds. He dismissed the NAACP as a "well-meaning but unscientific agitation agency that did more harm than good." These occasional flashes of resentment no doubt reflected his own frustration with the intractable nature of the deeply emotional issue that affected, usually adversely, his grand design for regional progress. In the course of the rising black protest during the war years he commiserated with the embattled Virginius Dabney, saying that one necessarily had to "feel inadequate in a situation which has no satisfactory solution in the sense of here and now, yes or no, white or black, North or South, you or me." Anyone who attempted to deal with interracial matters could feel some sympathy with Odum's plaint in *An American Epoch*:

The appeal of many liberal Southerners was that they be not asked to accomplish the impossible, or that they be urged with undue pressure to hasten issues which in another generation would probably not exist. They wanted to meet whatever issues came in the day's work but they regretted the tendency to search out issues of conflict in which to test the strength, will and endurance of those who were to carry the load.

He voiced that appeal in 1930. Two decades later, when I came to know him, he had long since recognized its futility. The issues that now tested the strength, will, and endurance of Southern liberals were inescapable, and the aging scholar, as always, was carrying more than his share of the load.

As president of the Commission on Interracial Cooperation after 1937, Howard Odum sought without success to reshape that mild, religiously oriented organization into an effective instrument to further his concept of regionalism. The commission's undeviating adherence to the separate-but-equal principle, and the token role assigned its black members, left the organization increasingly vulnerable to the kind of attack made by W. E. B. Du Bois in 1939: "It does not reduce Negro ignorance or poverty by calling the plight regional and proceeding to give the whites better schools and higher wages." By 1942 the commission was coming to the end of its road, and one of the surviving staff members, Jessie Daniel Ames, launched a behind-the-scenes effort to found a successor institution that would provide a more prominent place for black leaders. The result was an all-black conference at Durham to draft a "new charter on race relations."

The assemblage came forth with a statement signed by the South's leading black educators that managed to neither affirm nor deny segregation while demanding equal pay and equal opportunity for blacks, antilynching legislation, equality in public services, appointment of black policemen, and abolition of the poll tax and the white primary. It was forthright enough to draw the praise of the normally skeptical Thomas Sancton, who found it "a far cry from the Booker T. Washington line." Mrs. Ames followed up with an all-white conference in Atlanta to respond to the Durham statement, with Ralph McGill in the chair.

The effort to distinguish social segregation from all the lesser forms of discrimination almost scuttled the movement when the two groups came together in Richmond in June 1943. Odum finally got through a saving resolution that declared that American Negroes were "entitled to and should have every guarantee of equal opportunity that every other citizen of the United States has within the framework of the American democratic system of government." Out of the Richmond meeting came a new interracial organization with Howard Odum as its first president. It was called, not surprisingly, the Southern Regional Council, and it was soon alone in the field. In October 1943, the Interracial Commission formally disbanded, and the Southern Conference on Human Welfare was already incapacitated by the factional infighting that would lead to its dissolution in 1948.

The black leaders at Durham had declared: "We are fundamentally opposed to the principle and practice of compulsory segregation in our American society." But they sought to make room on their platform for their white opposite numbers by adding: "We regard it as both sensible and timely to address ourselves to the current problems of racial discrimination and neglect and to ways in which we may cooperate in the advancement of programs aimed at the sound improvement of race relations within the democratic framework." The first executive director of SRC, Odum's colleague at the Institute for Research in Social Science, Guy B. Johnson, thought it imperative to avoid an uncompromising antisegregation stand so that members of the white establishment could be enlisted to provide financial support and political influence. The issue, however, would not down. In the spring of 1944, Lillian Smith joined the black historian, J. Saunders Redding, in publicly charging that SRC's straddling policy made the organization "potentially more harmful than beneficial." Johnson replied with some heat that it was unrealistic to adopt a policy that would restrict SRC's membership to those who were willing to denounce segregation but were powerless to do anything about it.

The pragmatic position was initially accepted by the Northern philanthropists, whose financial support was critical. Will Alexander, now director of race relations for the Rosenwald Fund, endorsed a favorable recommendation by Stetson Kennedy, who thought the SRC board had correctly concluded that "the best way to rid the South of segregation is to set out to rid the segregation of discrimination." But Guy Johnson found himself caught in the middle of SRC's internal black-white division. At the December 1944 board meeting Virginius Dabney introduced a resolution declaring that segregation was "the law of the land" and therefore must be supported; Benjamin Mays, president of black Morehouse College, countered with a clear-cut antisegregation motion. It took all of Odum's prestige to put down both proposals, and in the wake of the stormy session Johnson told him, "We've got to dispose of this segregation dilemma as soon as possible or it will keep blocking the future of the Council." It wasn't disposed of, and by mid-1947 Guy Johnson had gone back to Chapel Hill.

Johnson's successor was another Southern intellectual with long experience on the racial front—the economist, George S. Mitchell. He had been brought into the Roosevelt administration by Will Alexander, and had earned a reverse accolade as one of the New Dealers the *Memphis Commercial Appeal* included in its "galaxy of bleeding hearts produced by the Rexford Guy Tugwell school of screwball planners and uplifters." He headed

SRC during the years when the organization moved step by painful step toward open endorsement of desegregation.

There wasn't, in fact, any real choice after President Truman's Commission on Civil Rights published its historic report, *To Secure These Rights*, in October 1947. The fifteen distinguished signatories recommended all the items that would make up the civil rights agenda in the years ahead: urging federal action across the board to root out Jim Crow wherever it existed, using the leverage of a cut-off of federal funds to force compliance. Walter White was not indulging in hyperbole when he called the report "the most uncompromising and specific pronouncement by a government agency on the explosive issue of racial and religious bigotry." And the tone of the report was perhaps as significant as the content, for it made no concession to the plea of the two Southern members —Frank Graham and Mrs. Dorothy M. Tilly of SRC—that the language be tempered to minimize exacerbation of white sensibilities.

A turbulent decade would pass before the civil rights agenda began to be implemented, and it would require action by the Supreme Court to overcome the hesitance of Congress and the executive to move into the most critical areas. But as a general statement of principle, *To Secure These Rights* had wide public acceptance in the North, and in the South it served to finally cut the ground from under the gradualists. No black leader could now temporize on the ultimate goal of ending segregation and maintain his standing in the black community. And no white leader could propose concessions in the less sensitive areas of discrimination without facing the charge that he was a closet integrationist.

In May 1947, the SRC's *New South* published a declaration by the black veteran of interracial cooperation, President Charles S. Johnson of Fisk: "For the Negro to accept segregation and all of its implications as an ultimate solution would be to accept for all time a definition of himself as something less than his fellow man." In 1948, when President Truman sent his civil rights package to Congress, Ralph McGill said in a national radio interview that both the white and black leaders of SRC opposed this kind of federal legislation. Challenged by Walter White, the SRC executive committee denied that McGill had represented its views; the weaseling now came down to a suggestion that the members would have preferred to see the Southern states themselves guarantee the rights of all citizens, but they affirmed that the council would not oppose federal civil rights legislation. Albert W. Dent, president of black Dillard University and vice-president of SRC, continued to press the issue, and in 1951 the board approved a policy statement drafted by Harold C. Fleming, the young Georgian who was to succeed Mitchell as executive director. The separate-but-equal doctrine was forthrightly declared an anachronism: "It is neither reasonable nor right that colored citizens of the United States should be subjected to the humiliation of being segregated by law. . . ."

THE personal views of Southern liberals generally followed the course of painful adjustment reflected in the actions of the council, although few of those beholden to a popular constituency stepped forward to identify themselves with the embattled interracial organization. The newspaper editors who had cooperated in the founding of SRC largely disappeared from the ranks of active supporters; Odum plaintively wondered what had happened to "that brilliant coterie of liberals that we had counted on." The new permissiveness I had noted in the World War II veterans who were assuming positions of prominence was still there, but its public display brought them under direct attack from old guard defenders of the status quo, reluctant to yield their places of power and newly armed by public reaction against the report of the Civil Rights Commission and President Truman's effort to translate some of its recommendations into law.

As a matter of logic it could be argued that federal action was justified to guarantee constitutional rights the state governments were clearly unwilling to support—notably voting rights and service on juries—and that this had nothing to do with the bugaboo of social equality. In the *News* I pointed out that a white wouldn't even have to stand beside a black in the polling place, and, indeed, that any form of intercourse would be barred within a hundred feet of the voting booth. And I made as much as I could of the fact that the proposals of the commission were thoroughly in accord with the tenets of free enterprise, as attested by the wholehearted endorsement of its chairman, that staunch defender of the conservative faith, Charles E. Wilson, president of General Electric.

The few Southern newspaper editors who did not reject out of hand the agenda set forth in *To Secure These Rights* generally followed a similar tactical line as we toe-danced through our commentary on the North-South rift now reopening in the Democratic party. Privately, we all recognized that the civil rights proposals recommended by President Truman to Congress, limited as they were and certain to be watered down in the legislative process, would lend new impetus to the drive for ultimate desegregation of the public schools—and we knew that when that item reached the top of the agenda the social question could no longer be side-stepped. But for the time being there seemed to be no option except to stay within the limits of separate-but-equal if we were to be heard at all as we argued the case for what now was being denounced, in immemorial states' rights fashion, as "outside interference."

What our moral critics saw as default, and most politicians recognized as prudence, was summed up by Marion A. Wright, a remarkable South Carolina lawyer whose enlightenment had begun when he served as a youthful house-sitter and read widely in the extensive library of a neighbor frequently absent in Washington, Pitchfork Ben Tillman. In March 1949, Wright, who would later serve as president of SRC, warned in *New South* that those who were committed to the immediate end of Jim Crow could expect no effective support below the Mason-Dixon line:

Local newspapers, with exceptions so small as to be negligible, are owned, published and edited by Southern whites. Their subscribers are white; their advertisers are white. Is it not going a little far to expect complete objectivity and candor of a white Southern editor in discussing the duty of his subscribers and advertisers to members of a race that brings him no bread and butter? The politicians are probably no more practical fellows than the editors, and they are hardly examples of courageous leadership in this ticklish field. Ellis Arnall ventured to run a little ahead of the pack in Georgia, and Herman Talmadge took over.

This sardonic appraisal hardly pleasured me and my fellow editors, but we would have been hard pressed to challenge its accuracy.

8

The Dixicrat Rebellion

Early in 1947 an ebullient New Englander, Thomas L. Robinson, used his Ivy League connections
with some of North Carolina's reigning textile and tobacco
families to put together sufficient financing to purchase the
News. This, as *Time* magazine noted, aroused speculation as to
whether "the new owners would turn out to be too fat to fight."
Robinson sought to allay these apprehensions by conferring
upon me the title of editor previously retained by J. E. Dowd.
The new publisher did, as he promised, hold to the *News*'s
traditional policies, including parsimony; my elevation in rank
carried with it no increase in pay.

There were, however, other emoluments, soothing to the
ego and useful to the professional reputation. *Time* cited me as
"one of the South's most realistic and readable editorial writers," and sought to place me in the political spectrum:

His campaigns (for two-party politics, racial and religious tolerance,
votes for Negroes, higher pay for teachers) have established him as
neither a Yankee-lover nor a deep-dyed Southerner. Ashmore . . .
tempers his enthusiasm for reform with consideration of the facts of
Southern life. Says he: "We hope to avoid the usual Southernisms
[such as] undue sensitivity to outside criticism . . . I am a Southerner
by inclination as well as by virtue of two Confederate grandfathers,
but it is high time we rejoined the union."

I was now beginning to attract inquiries from publishers
who figured, correctly, that I might be interested in an editorial
position that afforded a wider audience, and a higher salary,
than the *News* could provide. *Time* sent an emissary with an
invitation to discuss the possibilities with Henry Luce, whose
expanding newsmagazine empire had attracted some of the
ablest young journalists in the country. I declined virtually by

reflex since I had a deep distaste for *Time*'s assembly-line journalism, and an even deeper distaste for New York's abrasive life-style. I recognized that the metropolis was the capital of my trade, but my reaction was then, and has remained, that ascribed to his Virginian father by William Styron: "He detested New York only for what he called its 'barbarity,' its lack of courtesy, its total bankruptcy in the estimable domain of public manners. The snarling command of the traffic cop, the blaring insult of horns, all the needlessly raised voices of the night-denizens of Manhattan ravaged his nerves, acidified his duodenum, unhelmed his composure and his will. . . ."

Expatriation had been the usual answer for generations of Southerners with literary or journalistic ambition, but I had decided to pursue my career within the region. If I read the signs correctly, I was situated in the middle of the most significant politico-socioeconomic development to be found anywhere in the United States, and I had been consciously preparing myself to deal with it. In December 1944, writing from a forward command post under the guns of the Siegfried line, I had included a sententious passage in a letter replying to J. E. Dowd's offer of a postwar place on the *News:* "Some day, when the weariness has passed, I will want to get back into the old fight, of which this war is a military phase. I've come to believe that the important things, the essential freedoms, the democratic processes, are luxuries, not inalienable rights, and the price we must pay for them is high. Sometimes we fight to preserve them with guns, sometimes with typewriters, but always we must stand ready to fight." Whatever else may be said of it, this was a sentiment that would serve to winnow prospective employers.

Before the change in management at the *News* I had been asked by Virginius Dabney to come to Richmond to discuss the opening on the *News Leader* left by retirement of Douglas Southall Freeman. I was flattered, but convinced in advance that this would turn out to be a clear case of incompatibility. My instinct was confirmed in the course of a pleasant luncheon with D. Tennant Bryan, publisher of the Richmond newspapers, and his general manager, John Dana Wise. After an exchange of views on the issues of the day had established a yawning void, Wise, a native South Carolinian, shook his head and said, "I thought so—we've never had any luck with these Tarheels."

I headed back to Charlotte reminded of the old saw that characterized North Carolina as a vale of humility between two mountains of arrogance. The *News Leader*'s editorial pulpit went to James Jackson Kilpatrick, who in the years to come would employ it to urge defiance of the United States Supreme Court in his anointed role as the father of interposition. In his autobiography, *Across the Years*, Dabney told of a bitterly personal running campaign waged by Wise to force his resignation. Bryan refused to go along, and tolerated the divergent editorial views of his morning and afternoon newspapers until the Supreme Court's school desegregation ruling forced a showdown on the racial issue. At that point the publisher exercised his prerogative as the final authority on policy. "The *Richmond News Leader*, under the same management as the *Times-Dispatch*, and edited by James J. Kilpatrick, carried the ball, as it were, for massive resistance," Dabney wrote. "The *Times-Dispatch*, under my editorship, did not attack massive resistance, although it would liked to have done so. Neither did we espouse it actively. . . . Most of the time we simply acquiesced in it silently, without making overtures on its behalf."

I was now firmly emplaced among those Southern editors usually called "liberal," although, as evidenced by *Time*'s cursory treatment of my views, the designation was subject to a regional discount. "There are relatively few liberals in the South," Gunnar Myrdal wrote in *American Dilemma*, "and practically no radicals." Since no more than a dozen major Southern newspapers openly supported the positions on racial matters I advanced in the *News*, the limited range of employment possibilities for one of my persuasion was another of the facts of Southern life I was constrained to give due consideration. An editor might defy his newspaper's owners on occasion, particularly on issues where his dismissal would create a public scandal and divide the staff, but a continuing standoff would soon become intolerable. A sensible owner would not expect slavish agreement on all details of policy, but he could hardly be expected to entrust his property to the ministrations of an editor who didn't share his general philosophy.

It followed that if I were to move on from Charlotte I

would have to find an opening on one of the family-owned newspapers that took its institutional obligations seriously. The trouble was that the appropriate editorial chairs were already occupied, often by a member of the owning family, and when a vacancy did occur the proprietors functioned under tacit agreement not to lure away an editor employed by a contemporary who was also a close friend.

This clubby arrangement also had advantages for the editors. When I went to Raleigh to look in on the state legislature, old Josephus Daniels and his son Jonathan, editor of the *News & Observer*, extended the hospitality of the newsroom, which included their own invaluable advice and counsel. So it was in Atlanta, when I went down to write firsthand commentary on the most bizarre event of the 1946 political season—the forcible eviction of Ellis Arnall from the state capitol by Herman Talmadge, who had the state legislature designate him his father's successor after old Gene dropped dead between election and inauguration. There in the crumbling Victorian edifice that housed the Constitution I first encountered in the abundant flesh my most illustrious peer, Ralph McGill, initiating a close personal relationship that continued until the sad day in 1969 when I came back to Atlanta to serve as his pallbearer.

In the spring of 1947 I took part in a panel discussion at the annual Washington convention of the American Society of Newspaper Editors, which was as much an old boys' reunion as a professional meeting. A few weeks later I received a telephone call from a member of the audience, John Netherland Heiskell, the principal owner of the *Arkansas Gazette,* who for more than forty years had served as his own editor and, at age seventy-five, thought perhaps he deserved relief. He invited me to fly out to Little Rock and discuss the possibilities.

I went home in some trepidation to relay this latest feeler to my wife, Barbara, who was just settling into a house of her own with our year-old daughter Anne, after arduous service as one of the peripatetic homemakers of the era—having carried our household in suitcases and cardboard cartons as we moved from Greenville to Cambridge, and thence by order of the U.S. Army to Georgia, Texas, Louisiana, California, Pennsylvania, and Virginia. I had met my Boston-born, Swampscott-reared bride when she came south to teach at Furman University and, while she bore no resemblance to W. J. Cash's libelous portrait of the carpetbagging Yankee school ma'am, she did retain traces of the parochial New England view of the hinterland. She responded to my report on the call from Heiskell after a long pause: "Little Rock? Little Rock? Why, it's not even on the way to anywhere."

A WEEKEND visit with J. N. Heiskell and his son-in-law, Hugh B. Patterson, Jr., who was destined to become publisher, convinced me that there would be no problem of compatibility with the venerable *Gazette*.

In August I set forth on the trail so many of my forebears had followed, circling the base of the Appalachians and heading west for the Mississippi valley. The landscape was familiar enough as I drove through the northern hill country of Georgia, Alabama, and Mississippi, but I came upon a land new to me when I reached the alluvial plain of west Tennessee, crossed the great river at Memphis, and entered upon the Arkansas delta. This was the classic plantation country that marked the western reaches of the Cotton Kingdom, and of the ill-starred Confederacy. The prospect of getting to know this river-valley South at first hand had given J. N. Heiskell's offer a special attraction.

I came equipped with an inherited folk wisdom. The look and the sound of the people would not be strange to me, and I knew that given time I could strike up cousinhood with many. I shared the feeling of Hodding Carter, editor and publisher of the spirited *Delta Democrat-Times* in another Greenville, the one in Mississippi, who had written: "I cannot travel through the Valley of Virginia nor along the Mississippi without experiencing a quickening of the blood; if my sons or even strangers are with me, my tongue loosens and I want to tell them of the people who settled and fought and clung there, for they were my people; and if the allegiance is sentimental it is not shallow. I understand the forces that fashioned these men. I am at home with their spirits." And I knew exactly what he meant when he added, ". . . defiant and resentful of the alien critic, they are even more enraged by the native censor, stigmatizing him as a nest-fouler and suggesting that he go elsewhere if he is not satisfied with what he finds." My status as a newcomer would enhance the hospitality of the Arkansans, but I would always be something of an interloper to those who got there first.

The Arkansas River bisects the state from northwest to southeast, and the metropolitan complex that surrounds the capitol straddles the stream at midpoint; Little Rock is on one bank, the separate municipality of North Little Rock on the other. Upstream the river valley cuts through the steep, regular ridges of the Ozarks, and the modern residential sections of the two cities reach into wooded foothills; downstream the land abruptly flattens, and there are major plantations within the county limits. In no other Southern city is the upland and lowland culture so directly joined, and the geographic conjunction is enhanced by the fact that the capital is the only major city in the state. The morning *Gazette*, circulating statewide, had twice as many subscribers outside the home county as within.

I found the *Gazette* unique in other important ways, with a remarkable continuity of ownership that had shaped the commitment of those who set its policies. As the oldest newspaper west of the Mississippi it actually predated its place of publication. On November 20, 1819, Volume One, Number One came off a wooden hand press at Arkansas Post, the now vanished territorial capital the United States had acquired from France in the Louisiana Purchase. In 1821 the newspaper accompanied the new government as it relocated a hundred miles upstream at the river bank landmark that gave the present city its name. The only lapse in more than a century and a half of publication came with the Yankee occupation of the capital in 1863, when the proprietor, Capt. C. C. Danley, declined to take a loyalty oath on the ground that he would make a better federal prisoner than federal editor. The newspaper reappeared as a daily when the war ended, and had never missed an issue since.

In 1902 the *Gazette* came under the control of a single family, and for the next sixty-eight years J. N. Heiskell bore the titles of president and editor. An erudite patrician who by choice kept his distance from officeholders and office-seekers, he did not hesitate to practice what is now called "adversary journalism." At the beginning of his long tenure he found himself arrayed in editorial battle with Jeff Davis, a free-swinging demagogue who rode to power on the wave of populist protest at the end of the last century. In rallying the "one-gallus boys" against the "high-collared city crowd" Davis employed the state's leading newspaper as his whipping boy. "I see an agent out there in the audience giving out that old red harlot, the *Arkansas Gazette*," he would proclaim. "I would rather be caught with a dead buzzard under my arm, or a dead polecat."

In 1913, in his first and last personal appearance in the political arena, Heiskell as a matter of poetic justice accepted appointment to serve out the deceased Davis's unexpired term in the United States Senate. He was there only twenty-four days, and his maiden speech was also his valedictory. He took the occasion to reassure those who feared that the spreading direct primary movement might give undue power to voters "dubbed with the uncouth terms 'redneck' and 'hillbilly.'" These, he said, "were the very foundation course of the strength of human society, who work at the trades of the countryside or cultivate small farms," and if they are misled "the fault is not so much with them as with him who perverts his talents and abuses his powers to play upon their honest hearts and open minds."

In his memoir, *James Street's South*, the Mississippi-born novelist fondly recalled his apprenticeship on the *Gazette*, which impressed him as "a Southern lady from any angle, her Confederate limbs hidden under a Victorian petticoat and seen only in stormy weather when she kicks up her heels in an eye-catching crusade for her principles." He described one of those occasions in 1927, Little Rock's last lynching, in which a mob killed a black man and dragged his burned body through the streets. The *Gazette* reported the outrage, and fixed the blame, under a rare front-page banner headline: WITH OFFI-CERS MAKING NO ATTEMPT AT RESTRAINT, MOB BURNS NEGRO'S BODY AND CREATES REIGN OF TERROR. A front-page editorial, written by J. N. Heiskell, declared: "The city of Little Rock suffered last night the shame of being delivered over to anarchy. Little Rock and Pulaski County must demand an accounting from the officers who have failed us." Expanding his metaphor, Street wrote:

Her tenets have made her one of the most successful journals in the world and yet her tenets are simple: What is best for humanity as the

Gazette sees it, an honest profit is not evil, change is not always progress but never fear change, and lay not a greedy hand, sir, on the fair breast of Arkansas, point not a dirty finger.

At the end of the war Heiskell found his newspaper weakened by dispersal of its staff, beset by newsprint and equipment shortage, and bereft of the top management he had counted on to carry forward the family tradition. On the business side he brought in his son-in-law, returned from service as an air force major, and with previous managerial experience in commercial printing. On the editorial side, however, the succession had been tragically disrupted by the loss of his only son, Carrick, one of the pilots killed flying the airlift across the Himalayan Hump. My role, as executive editor, would be to work in close collaboration with Hugh Patterson as he prepared himself to assume the office of publisher, left vacant for more than forty years until the Heiskells were satisfied that they had turned up one of their own with proper qualifications. Patterson soon demonstrated that he had not only the requisite skills, but the stubbornness required to modernize a business operation encrusted with quill-pen tradition. He was able to ease the suspicion of modernist heresy with his ultimate Southern credentials —descent from a long line of Scotch-Irish Presbyterian ministers, teachers and lawyers, and a birth certificate that identified him as a native of Cotton Plant, Mississippi.

I HAD hardly found my way around the Gazette Building before I was initiated into political combat, Arkansas style. In those waning months of Harry Truman's first term, a formidable effort was under way to deny the feisty Missourian nomination at the coming Democratic National Convention. The president's proposed civil rights program provided the primary ammunition for the Southern wing of the Stop Truman movement, and in Arkansas this produced a coalition of the red-necked heirs of Jeff Davis's one-gallus boys with the high-collared conservatives. By the time I arrived one of the latter, Gov. Benjamin Travis Laney, had become a leader of the States' Rights Jeffersonian Democratic faction, whose resounding title would soon shrink to Dixiecrat.

The civil rights package President Truman sent to Congress in February 1948, actually stopped far short of direct intervention into the sensitive areas of so-called social equality. It proposed creation of a continuing Commission on Civil Rights, and continuation of the wartime Fair Employment Practices Commission, with the only specific extension of federal authority limited to protection of individuals against lynching and discrimination in interstate travel, and a guarantee of the right to vote. Moreover, no one in Washington believed that there was any chance of getting the package through Congress without drastic revision. Its introduction was a symbolic gesture geared to the political strategy devised by Harry Truman's astute counsel, Clark Clifford, who considered it necessary to bolster the president's waning support among restive Northern liberals and moderates, without whose backing the nomination was clearly out of reach.

The Dixiecrats countered with the open threat of a bolt unless the national party repudiated both the president and the civil rights program. Their theoreticians resurrected the old scenario of a third party ticket that would siphon off enough electoral votes to deny either major candidate a majority; this would throw the election of president into the House of Representatives where the popular choice could be nullified, allowing the wily Southern members to make a deal that would elevate one of their own to the White House. I doubt that any sensible politician took this fanciful scheme seriously, but it provided bait for voters who could be incited to join a crusade on behalf of white supremacy—thus providing a bloc of votes essential to political strategists whose real objective was to divert enough Democrats to insure the election of a conservative Republican.

I rolled out the *Gazette*'s heavy editorial artillery to take on the Dixiecrats, bearing down on the issue of party loyalty. It was a campaign that came naturally to the venerable newspaper; its founder, William E. Woodruff, had nailed the Democratic banner to the masthead when he brought forth the first edition in 1819, and his Confederate son, who served as editor during Reconstruction, had been a key figure in the effort of the Redeemers to bring an end to carpetbag Republican rule. At our morning editorial conference, after prudently apologizing for my ignorance, I asked Mr. J. N. if the *Gazette* had ever been other than Democratic. Peering out his open office door to be sure he couldn't be overheard, he leaned across his desk and confided, "I don't like to talk about this, but the fact is we went Whig twice."

In the spring the Dixiecrats gathered at Jackson and agreed to reconvene at Birmingham to field a ticket of their own if the Democratic Convention did not accept their version of the true faith: "We hereby declare that the president of the United States has by his acts and declarations repudiated the principles of the Democratic Party, threatened to disturb the constitutional division and balance of the powers of government, and has thereby forfeited all claims of allegiance from members of the party who adhere to its principles." Ben Laney emerged as chairman of the movement, but as a result began to lose control of the party machinery in his own state. Arkansas's patronage-minded federal officeholders were acutely sensitive to the party loyalty issue, and some of these began responding to the *Gazette*'s demand that delegates to the national nominating convention be required to affirm in advance that they would support the party ticket. Sen. J. William Fulbright squared off with the governor, although his own differences with Truman were such that the president had publicly branded him an "overeducated sonofabitch." This internal division made it impossible for Laney to handpick the delegation, and it was a divided, squabbling lot that finally went with him to Philadelphia.

In May Laney and I debated the civil rights issue at a town hall meeting in Little Rock broadcast over a statewide radio network. Played back thirty years later, the transcription of that confrontation has a disembodied quality, as it must have had for most listeners at the time.

If the governor and I did not exactly remain on high ground there was a minimum of what might properly be called racist invective. Laney ignored the actual content of the civil rights legislation President Truman had sent to Congress, and instead read out of context the most stringent passages from the report of the now disbanded Civil Rights Commission. I, in my turn, made a states'-rights-cum-responsibilities pitch— arguing that the only answer to federal antilynching, antipoll tax, and antidiscrimination legislation was to demonstrate that it wasn't necessary, which could be done simply by carrying out in good faith the provisions of Arkansas's own constitution. The governor's wrath, predictably, was directed primarily at the Fair Employment Practices Commission (FEPC)—"it is the heart of the program and they know it"—"they" being meddling outsiders dedicated to the destruction of states' rights, the regulation of business, and ultimately to the Communist ideal of total regimentation of people of all races and creeds. I replied that "they" must also include the leaders of the Republican Party, who would be the primary beneficiaries of the Dixiecrats' threatened secession from the Democratic Party. "I came down here to talk about civil rights," Governor Laney complained, "and all Mr. Ashmore wants to talk about is party loyalty." He was absolutely right.

THE national political conventions in Philadelphia that July were the first I had attended, but with my ingrained taste for political comedy I found myself perfectly at home. The Dixiecrats arrived with bands playing and Confederate flags flying, joining other elements of the Stop Truman movement converging on the City of Brotherly Love from all parts of the country and all points on the political compass. The result was the most disparate set of bedfellows in the annals of American politics, joining the Southern firebrands with the New Dealing Americans for Democratic Action, such big city bosses as Jacob Arvey of Chicago, Ed Flynn of the Bronx, and Frank Hague of Jersey City, and an assortment of free-floating leftist intellectuals. All these were united in the effort to draft Dwight D. Eisenhower, some not knowing, others not caring that the general was a classic Republican conservative—as he would demonstrate four years later when another draft summoned him to his rightful home. Eisenhower's declination collapsed the Stop Truman movement.

The Dixiecrat bolt was touched off by an obscure young delegate, Mayor Hubert Humphrey of Minneapolis, who challenged the bland rewrite of the 1944 civil rights plank recommended by the platform committee, offering as a substitute a resolution unequivocally rejecting all forms of racial discrimination. Humphrey was allotted ten minutes to make his case, and in that brief compass he delivered what he always considered the best of the tens of thousands of speeches he uttered in the course of his long and loquacious career. The convention erupted when he shouted his famous peroration: "The time has arrived for the Democratic Party to get out of the shadow of states' rights and walk in the bright sunshine of human rights!"

The Humphrey substitute was adopted 651½ to 582½. Gov. J. Strom Thurmond of South Carolina stalked up the center aisle on his way to launch a third party, taking with him his own delegation, Mississippi's, and half of Alabama's, thirty-five delegates in all. Locked in by a unit rule adopted at Fulbright's behest, Ben Laney stayed in the hall with the Arkansas delegation, thereby waiving his presumed place at the head of the Dixiecrat ticket—which I suggested in the *Gazette* was probably the best thing that had happened to him since he arrived in Philadelphia.

DESPITE the ironic overtones, this was the partisan political process working at its best—stripping away obfuscation and forcing genuine divisions over policy to the surface, testing the limits of compromise, and ultimately eliminating those who might seek to sabotage the election campaign from within. And if it seems an ultimate irony that blacks were virtually invisible at the convention, and were not much more evident in the behind-the-scenes maneuvering, that too was a reflection of contemporary political reality. A party preparing for an election campaign is necessarily a mosaic of voting blocs, and black Americans were not yet situated, and organized, to exert leverage in their own right.

The commitment against discrimination embodied in Hubert Humphrey's platform plank was not soon to be fulfilled, but neither was it to be abandoned, and it had more than symbolic importance. By forcing the Dixiecrat bolt it separated the Deep from the Upper South, and in November Harry Truman demonstrated that he could win without the electoral votes that went to Thurmond in South Carolina, Alabama, Mississippi, and Louisiana. Throughout the region the hands of loyalist Democrats were strengthened, and they were certified as moderate. And now the Democratic stand on civil rights contrasted unmistakably with the weaseling approach of the Republicans.

Truman's election demonstrated not only that the Democratic Party could win without the Dixiecrats, but that it could survive the simultaneous defection of its extreme left wing. The party bolt on the right was matched on the other flank by the movement that grew up around the candidacy of Henry Wallace of Iowa, the prairie populist of mystic bent who in 1944 had been displaced as Franklin Roosevelt's vice-president by Harry Truman. It was evident from the outset that the Wallace "Progressives," as they called themselves, were being used as a front by the Communist Party. The prime motive of the Progressive strategists was to arouse popular opposition to the anti-Soviet Cold War policies of the Truman administration, but the popular appeal was to the downtrodden proletariat—and as a means of dramatizing it Wallace was induced to undertake a head-on personal challenge to Jim Crow in the South. Black leaders were appalled by the unreality of the Wallace strategy, and none to the right of Paul Robeson could be persuaded to join what he called "Gideon's Army."

THE two side shows of the 1948 presidential election were played out primarily in the South. When the votes were counted in November the rump candidates had attracted an almost identical level of popular support: 1,169,021 voters turned out for Strom Thurmond, almost all within the region, and 1,157,172 voted for Henry Wallace, almost all outside the South. The rhetorical centerpiece for both campaigns was white supremacy—Thurmond proclaiming it a God-given states' right, Wallace attacking it as an immoral manifestation of capitalist exploitation. Temperamentally, the two men were much alike. Each wore the blinders of the true believer, convinced that his own rectitude guaranteed the purity of his cause; each ignored the dubious company in which he found himself, simply refusing to entertain any suggestion that he was being used by strategists whose motives were somewhat different from his own.

Strom Thurmond was a figure out of my past. As a young reporter I had covered his court when he served as a circuit judge in South Carolina, and our paths had crossed in the army. When he plunged into state politics, riding the wave of sentiment aroused by returning veterans, he considered himself a liberal reformer—and at least it could be said that he was an outsider to the political establishment, cast in the maverick role he was to play throughout his remarkable career. It can be assumed that in the beginning he had no intention of exploiting the race issue, since he suggested that I resign my post at the *News* and join him as campaign manager. I don't think he ever understood why I rejected what he regarded as a golden opportunity, and, of course, politeness prevented my stating the real reason—that the humorless, stiff-necked probity that made him an honest if uncompassionate judge seemed to me to render him unfit for the give and take of political office.

The qualities that appalled me made Thurmond an ideal instrument for those who sought to divert Southern votes from Harry Truman. He laced his oratory with biblical quotations, and the text he hurled at those Democrats who placed party loyalty above his version of revealed truth was the judgment of the church in Laodicea, as set forth in the Book of Revelation: "I know thy works; thou art neither cold nor hot; I would thou wert cold or hot. So then because thou art lukewarm, and neither cold nor hot, I will spew thee from my mouth." That was the stuff to feed the embittered populists in the four states he carried. Robert Sherrill, the *Nation*'s caustic political writer, described the Dixiecrat constituency:

They are the super-South, the nerve strand that has been peeled slick, stretched taut between the poles of Black and White, and twanged . . . Thurmond once proclaimed that "Mississippi and South Carolina are the two most democratic states in the nation," and while this at first appears to be a prima facie absurdity, it gathers sense when one realizes what he means by democracy: namely, that the lowliest individual in the community has the same right as the highest to pursue his personal sonofabitchery to the point of rebellion, so long as he does not violate the traditions of the state.

In Arkansas the Dixiecrats had at their disposal the political organization assembled by Governor Laney, but the Wallace Progressives were hard pressed to find enough supporters to fill the list of electors on the state ballot. In the industrial cities of the North the Communist Party was a going concern with a substantial complement of fellow travelers, but out in the Southern hinterland the faithful were few, and understandably reluctant to appear aboveground. The Arkansas Communist Party had its headquarters in Oklahoma City, where the chairman also exercised jurisdiction over party affairs in the neighboring state. Under these circumstances it should have been a fairly easy matter to rig the qualifications to keep the Wallace electors from even being listed on the general election ballot—but the *Gazette* was able to frustrate the effort, largely by ridiculing the hanky-panky being devised in the statehouse to eliminate an electoral threat that so far was virtually invisible.

The matter became more serious when Wallace scheduled Little Rock as the last stop on the Southern swing designed to dramatize his opposition to Jim Crow. To that end he announced that he would not speak in any hall that required a segregated audience. In Little Rock this would have caused no difficulty, since the traditional site for campaign speeches was an outdoor bandshell at a downtown park where segregation had never been required. Faced with loss of the issue, the Wallace advance man applied for a municipal auditorium that operated under an ordinance requiring separate seating, but this was waived. He finally succeeded in getting a flat turndown when he tried to rent a hotel ballroom.

These absurdities outraged J. N. Heiskell's libertarian sensibilities, and one morning he announced that any qualified candidate for president had a right to speak in Arkansas, and the people had a right to decide whether or not they wanted to hear him. To guarantee that this was the case, he said, he would provide Wallace free air time on the *Gazette's* powerful radio station. The station manager greeted this edict with alarm, and sought to head it off by pointing out that he would have to provide equal access to all other candidates. This would not be the case if the appearance were treated as a news event, Mr. J. N. replied, so Wallace would be presented in an interview. When the manager continued to object, Mr. J. N. cut him off by saying he needn't have anything to do with the broadcast except to clear the air time. Mr. Ashmore, he announced to my surprise, would do the interviewing.

Wallace arrived in Little Rock in a near-paranoid state. Bully boys had turned up at his campaign rallies as he swung across North Carolina and Tennessee, hurling invective and sometimes eggs and vegetables. There had been sufficient police protection to prevent any actual violence, but the local lawmen treated Wallace and his aides with a cold-eyed hostility that was hardly conducive to a good night's sleep. The candidate roared up to the Gazette Building for the radio broadcast in an ancient limousine provided by a Negro funeral home, flanked by police motorcycles with sirens in full cry. He emerged from the car to be surrounded by a flying wedge of bodyguards who headed him at a high lope squarely in the wrong direction, across the street to the local branch of the Federal Reserve Bank, where they were greeted by startled guards with unholstered pistols.

By the time the Wallace phalanx shouldered its way into the third-floor studios, the candidate was so visibly shaken I felt it incumbent to open the broadcast by assuring him that if he wasn't among friends he at least could be sure that he was safe from harassment—that, indeed, the whole purpose of the interview was to make sure that he had a full opportunity to state his position on the issues. Once his standard strictures against Truman's anti-Communist foreign policy and the South's segregationist practices were out of the way, I encouraged him to discuss the real revolution that was transforming the South under New Deal policies formulated during his tenure as Roosevelt's Secretary of Agriculture. On that familiar ground he relaxed and began responding with an ease and eloquence the correspondents traveling with him said they hadn't encountered since he crossed the Mason-Dixon line. The broadcast had been scheduled for a half hour, but it went so well the station manager passed in a note suggesting we stay on the air for another thirty minutes.

Wallace's departure was marked by another low comedy scene. When his bodyguards rushed him into the limousine, the motorcycle escort took off with sirens screaming but the candidate's car remained at the curb. The waiting driver had turned on the radio to listen to the broadcast and the battery was dead. The last I saw of Wallace he was helping the trailing press photographers push off the shiny old Cadillac. It may have been, as he said, the century of the common man, but he was himself so uncommon a campaigner as to function beyond the ken of those who were the object of his concern. His doctrinaire handlers had him expounding the sulphurous pomposities of radical cant, which did not come naturally to him, and when he followed his own bent he floated off into opaque mysticism. So far as ordinary blacks were concerned, and working-class whites for that matter, he was speaking in an unknown tongue.

A few weeks later Strom Thurmond came to town and, as the station manager had predicted, his handlers demanded equal time. I tried, as I had with Wallace, to steer him into discussion of issues outside his narrow campaign litany, but to no avail. It was a civil enough exchange, but it was clear that he saw me as one of the lukewarm souls he had spewed out of the company of loyal Southerners. As we came out of the studio, the station manager apologetically informed us that lightning had struck the transmitter tower and that the station had been off the air during about a third of our interview. Some of the local Dixiecrats charged that I had used the accident to deny their candidate a full hearing, but Thurmond never joined in the complaint. It would, after all, have been unbecoming to even discuss the possibility that God might have hurled a thunderbolt that worked in favor of the infidels.

9

Of Liberties and Rights

*U*nder the new political configuration emerging in the wake of World War II it became increasingly difficult to maintain the traditional distinction between civil liberties and civil rights. Classic libertarian doctrine, exalting the individual and demanding immunity from interference in the exercise of conscience, was at the heart of the concept espoused by the founding fathers—buttressing the insistence that government be limited to providing, in Abraham Lincoln's oft-quoted formulation, only those services the individual cannot provide as well or better for himself. In the case of governmental action necessary to insure ordered liberty—that required to protect person and property, to mediate disputes, provide a medium of exchange, guarantee the common defense, and the like—the rights of the individual would be protected by guaranteeing his ability to participate in governance as, at a minimum, voter, juror, and petitioner. Neither as slaves nor as segregated second-class citizens could blacks be said to have been included, even potentially, in this dispensation. So it was that high-minded whites, often conservative in all other matters, could and did take up the cause of blacks as an obligation of their libertarian commitment.

The Great Depression had demonstrated that this concept of civil liberties no longer had broad application in modern industrial America. If it was to apply to those outside the financially secure upper class, whose position largely precluded unwelcome intrusions by government, it would have to be extended to provide similar immunities to citizens unendowed with the status that comes with affluence. Thus liberties came to be paralleled by rights, and these required not less, but more government—imposing public authority in areas previously considered private under the principles of free enterprise. The idea of meritocracy, the libertarian answer to the egalitarian demands of social levelers, came to require not only equality before the law, but equality of opportunity for social and economic advancement. Somewhere along this progression those loosely identified as liberal and conservative parted company, but for men of philosophical bent in either camp the unassimilated black minority continued to provide a test of simple justice the evolving American system of government could not meet.

In the standard shorthand version of American history the Civil War is held not only to have terminated slavery, but, by incapacitating the Southern white supremacists, to have cleared the way for the national government to confer upon the freedmen all the rights and immunities embraced by the libertarian concept of citizenship—only to have these effectively rescinded by the Redeemers when they restored native white rule to the Confederate states. It didn't work out quite that way.

The Thirteenth Amendment, submitted by Congress in 1865, provided that "neither slavery nor involuntary servitude, except as a punishment for crime whereof the party shall have been duly convicted, shall exist within the United States . . ." However, the former Confederates who dominated the state governments that came to power in the brief period of Presidential Reconstruction soon demonstrated that they intended to undo even the most limited interpretation of the amendment —contriving labor codes that by contract bound freedmen to their employers almost as tightly as before its adoption. This intransigence prompted Congress to submit the Fourteenth Amendment, the first section of which provides:

All persons born or naturalized in the United States, and subject to the jurisdiction thereof, are citizens of the United States and of the State wherein they reside. No State shall make or enforce any law which shall abridge the privileges or immunities of citizens of the United States; nor shall any State deprive any person of life, liberty or property, without due process of law; nor deny to any persons within its jurisdiction the equal protection of the laws.

Embodied here are provisions that have become famous in the course of a hundred years of litigation aimed at securing full citizenship for blacks, most notably the "due process" and "equal protection" clauses. The Fourteenth Amendment could be interpreted as guaranteeing the vote to Southern blacks, and it also included a section which denied all persons who had joined or supported the Southern rebellion from holding office until at some future date Congress chose to lift the ban by a two-thirds vote. This ushered in the period of Congressional Reconstruction, during which a majority of white Southerners were effectively disenfranchised at the same time blacks achieved voting rights. Thus the Fourteenth Amendment, as implemented under the First Reconstruction Act, created a situation that could not endure; it lasted only until the Compromise of 1877 signaled, in C. Vann Woodward's telling phrase, "the abandonment of principles and force and a return to the traditional ways of expediency and concession."

The votes of these newly enfranchised blacks not only created Republican carpetbag rule in the defeated Southern states, but provided Republican majorities in the electoral college and the Congress. Here the business interests of the North had an obvious stake in using the new balance to perpetuate the party's conservative economic policies. In *Simple Justice,* his massive history of the black struggle for equality under law, Richard Kluger noted that the Republican majority looked upon the civil rights amendments as "more of a political and economic device, and a punitive slap at the South, than the culminating ritual in the anointment of the Negro as citizen. . . ."

The Fifteenth Amendment contained language intended to remove any doubt that the franchise was extended to blacks: "The right of citizens of the United States to vote shall not be abridged by the United States or by any state on account of race, color or previous condition of servitude." This represented the high water mark of the Radical Republican effort to guarantee the rights of black citizens. Its effect was limited to the defeated South, for the franchise extended to blacks elsewhere was practically meaningless. They were too few and too scattered to elect members of their own race, or to exert pressure on white officials charged with guaranteeing them equal protection under law. If they did not usually suffer the organized brutality sometimes employed in the South to keep blacks in their ordained place at the bottom of society, more genteel forms of discrimination served the same purpose for all but an extraordinarily gifted few. Because blacks were powerless, indeed effectively invisible, the whites who conducted national affairs were under no compulsion to construe the libertarian doctrine in their favor. In the decades after the Civil War the United States Supreme Court, now dominated by non-Southern appointees of Republican presidents, interpreted the Reconstruction era amendments under a concept of limited government so narrow it legitimatized the discriminatory practices enacted into law in the South, and encouraged their de facto application in any Northern city where blacks gathered in significant number.

In the post Civil War period the learned justices did not openly reiterate the doctrine of white supremacy as it was unflinchingly delineated by Chief Justice Roger Taney in the 1857 *Dred Scott* decision. Taney justified the finding that blacks could properly be treated as property by contending that the Declaration of Independence's proclamation of the equality of all men obviously excluded slaves; thus, he reasoned, it was evident that the signers were in general agreement that blacks were "beings of an inferior order, and altogether unfit to associate with the white race, either in social or political relations; and so far inferior that they had no rights which the white man was bound to respect." So inhumane a view could hardly be ascribed to Associate Justice Samuel F. Miller of Iowa, a certified abolitionist appointed by Abraham Lincoln. Race, in fact, was not an issue in the 1869 state licensing case in which Miller wrote the opinion holding that it was not the Fourteenth Amendment's purpose "to transfer the security and protection . . . of civil rights . . . from the states to the federal government." That language, however, established a precedent that virtually reinstated the states' rights doctrine of John C. Calhoun in litigation affecting blacks.

In an era of increasingly narrow construction, the Court held that manipulation of the poll tax to deny a black Kentuckian registration as a voter did not violate the Fourteenth Amendment since the state was not required to grant such a right—only not to deny it on the basis of race. When a white mob broke up a black political rally in Louisiana the majority found that this was private, not state action, and it was not the federal government's business if the state failed to protect its black citizens' right of peaceful assembly. The Court specifically enjoined the states from excluding blacks from jury service, but its ruling provided that the only way black defendants could insure that they not be tried by an all-white judicial system was to bring an individual challenge in each case—a practical impossibility in most instances.

What came to be called the "Civil Rights Cases" arose from actions brought by the federal government on behalf of blacks who had been arbitrarily denied service in places of public accommodation. The Supreme Court agreed that such denial was specifically prohibited by the 1875 act of Congress, but held that federal enforcement exceeded the authority granted under the Fourteenth Amendment. These were private, not state acts, Justice Joseph P. Bradley of New Jersey held on behalf of the majority, following this line of reasoning to bring into jurisprudence the theory that three generations later would be called "reverse discrimination":

It would be running the slavery argument into the ground to make it apply to every act of discrimination which a person may see fit to make as to the guests he will entertain, or as to the people he will admit into his coach or cab or car, or admit to his concert or theatre, or deal with in other matters . . . There must be some stage in the progress of [the freedman's] elevation when he takes the rank of mere citizen, and ceases to be the special favorite of the laws, and when his rights, as a citizen or a man, are to be protected by the ordinary modes by which other men's rights are protected.

The opinion was endorsed by an eight-to-one majority of a Court whose members were all Republicans, and, with one exception, Northerners. "The legalized degradation of the Negro in the form of a state-mandated caste system had begun," Richard Kluger wrote. The capstone was applied in the *Plessy* decision, handed down in 1896. The case at issue involved a Louisiana law requiring segregation on railways—an incontestable matter of state, rather than private action. To clear that hurdle the Court came up with the separate-but-equal doctrine. The majority opinion turned on this interpretation of the Fourteenth Amendment:

The object of the Amendment was undoubtedly to enforce the absolute equality of the two races before the law, but in the nature of things it could not have been intended to abolish distinctions based upon color, or to enforce social, as distinguished from political equality, or a commingling of the two races upon terms unsatisfactory to either.

If the result of the decision was to lend constitutional sanction to white supremacy, it could plausibly be argued that this was a by-product of the application of libertarian doctrine —protecting the individual's right to avoid commingling with members of another race, and impartially extending the protection to any citizen, black or white, who might find such commingling unsatisfactory. It seems fair to assume that this was the reasoning of Justice Henry Billings Brown, who wrote the opinion. Massachusetts born and reared, he practiced law in Michigan before he moved up through the ranks of the federal judiciary. Kluger found him "relatively free of ideological ballast. His guy wires fastened to unadorned, conservative, Anglo-Saxon, Protestant, white middle-class values that were probably as close to the national consensus as a computer might have determined it."

It apparently was Justice Brown's desire to disassociate himself from the blatant white supremacist dogma common in the South that led him to establish precedents that reached far beyond the matter of providing separate-but-equal railway cars and waiting rooms. In a fateful dictum intended to demonstrate that segregation was not a peculiarly Southern institution, he brought public education under the separate-but-equal dispensation: "The most common instance of this is connected with the establishment of separate schools for white and colored children, which has been held to be a valid exercise of the legislative power even by the courts of States where the political rights of the colored race have been longest and most earnestly enforced."

If it is conceded that the eight justices who concurred in *Plessy* were not guilty of conscious hypocrisy, it must be assumed that they acted in ignorance of the reality of the black man's condition in the more or less isolated region where most members of the minority race still lived. This may be borne out by the fact that the sole dissent came from the only member of the Court who could not claim such innocence. John Marshall

Harlan of Kentucky, who also was the lone dissenter in the Civil Rights Cases, came of a slaveholding family, and had supported the peculiar institution and opposed the Thirteenth Amendment. But he also was a Unionist who opposed secession, served as colonel of a federal regiment, and earned appointment to the Court with his support of the Republican nominee in the Hayes-Tilden election contest. The record of his thirty-four years on the bench, during which he heard 14,226 cases and filed only 316 dissents, indicates that his guy wires were as firmly fixed in conservative values as were those of Justice Brown. It was, indeed, on libertarian ground that Harlan cited the fallacy of the majority ruling, and correctly predicted its consequences:

The white race deems itself to be the dominate race in this country. And so it is, in prestige, in achievements, in education, in wealth, and in power. . . . But in the view of the Constitution, in the eye of the law, there is in this country no superior, dominant ruling class of citizens. There is no caste here. Our Constitution is color blind, and neither knows nor tolerates classes among its citizens. . . .

Sixty millions of whites are in no danger from the presence here of eight millions of blacks. The destinies of the two races in this country are indissolubly linked together, and the interests of both require that the common government of all shall not permit the seeds of race hate to be planted under the sanction of law. . . .

[Under the majority ruling] there would remain a power in the States, by sinister legislation, to interfere with the full enjoyment of the blessings of liberty; to regulate civil rights, common to all citizens, upon the basis of race; and to place in a condition of legal inferiority a large body of American citizens. . . .

For the next half century Justice Harlan's colleagues and their successors reversed the implication of his contention that the Constitution is color blind—using it to justify the Court's refusal to apply quantitative tests that would have invalidated *Plessy* by demonstrating the gross inequality it permitted the white majority to impose upon a black minority rendered powerless by legalized segregation.

IN recent years leftist revisionists have produced a considerable literature intended to prove that Radical Reconstruction was not inherently flawed, as previous historians had generally found it. Their thesis is that the constitutional amendments intended to secure citizenship for freedmen, as implemented by the Civil Rights Acts of 1866 and 1875, could have guaranteed justice for blacks had they not been undone by the nation's ruling class; in this view the Compromise of 1877 is seen as a deal under which the rights of blacks were sacrificed in order to advance the special interests of the small body of white elitists who have always controlled the national government. It is a plausible, if tendentious interpretation of the facts, and it has the virtue of running counter to the simplistic notion that injustice to blacks is simply a manifestation of rampant racism, a finding that ignores the fact that exploitation of the powerless poor is not an experience unique to Americans with dark skins. Moreover, the theory spreads the guilt instead of, as in the popular view prevalent until recently, assigning it exclusively to Southern whites.

In my reading of the history of the period the radical theory breaks down at its core. I find it unlikely that a ruling class capable of exercising firm control over the course of events in the years after the Civil War would have arranged to have things turn out as they did. To the Southern wing of the political coalition the Compromise of 1877 was the only available way out of what had become an intolerable situation. Many of these would have supported a phased transition of blacks from slavery to citizenship, as moderate Republicans in Congress seemed to favor when they contended that the Thirteenth Amendment abolishing slavery did not, and should not, automatically guarantee the franchise to all freedmen. The moderates were soon disarmed by the retributive passion of the Radical Republicans on one side, and the recalcitrance of the Confederate leaders on the other. The leaders of the Northern financial establishment rode the tiger unleashed by Congressional Reconstruction and, as is usually the case, came out reasonably well. But I find it beyond my capacity to imagine the side-whiskered, beaver-hatted gentry of the Gilded Age deliberately fostering a policy which, as Richard Kluger described it, conferred upon a propertyless, almost totally illiterate mass of blacks the power to vote

at the very same time the best elements of the community—the great landowners and statesmen and captains of the Confederacy—had been denied the vote. The freedman's vote, moreover, was cast under the gaze of federal troops. It was coercive democracy. And it had patently been jammed down the South's gullet as a punitive measure, intended to humiliate the proud white man who had climbed so high on the black man's back.

Congressional Reconstruction has to be seen, I think, as an abortive revolution, one which would have uprooted the old Southern society and turned it upside down had it succeeded in the terms its sponsors proclaimed. As an exercise in what Kluger called "coercive democracy" it was doomed by its own contradictions; the coercion undertaken in the name of providing democratic rule employed a conquering army to restrict participation by the majority. It was a design that could only have been conceived by men whose moral fervor left them indifferent to the immediate consequences of their action.

Racism was certainly a factor in the national reaction that terminated Reconstruction. The concept of white supremacy had been exalted in the South in defense of slavery, but it was by no means confined to the region. Belief that whites were inherently superior to colored people was embedded in the precepts of the European nations that provided the original American settlers, and the immigrants who came later. The reluctant white majority that supported Abraham Lincoln's prosecution of the Civil War was concerned with preserving the union, not with guaranteeing full rights of citizenship for blacks. To the extent that there could be said to have been popular support in the North for the extreme measures of Congressional Reconstruction, it was rooted in an understandable but hardly noble desire for revenge against the trouble-making rebels. It soon became evident that a crusade for black rights not only ran counter to the interests of the business establishment, but to the prejudices of the rank-and-file voters who elected the national legislature.

By the end of President U.S. Grant's second term, William Gillette wrote in *Retreat From Reconstruction*,

white supremacy, the political slogan of Southern conservatives, was reasserted as the prevailing belief of the majority of Northern whites, whose view was that "the races are presumed to be equal—only they are not. There are two races—an inferior race and a superior race—and the superior race is not willing to accord the inferior race exact justice"— not even, one might add, a fair chance.

The quotation is from an 1874 edition of the *Cincinnati Commercial* and might be discounted as tainted by left-over Copperhead sentiment. But by 1877 the *Springfield Republican* in abolitionist Massachusetts had dismissed the moral issue with unabashed pragmatism: ". . . federal protection of the Negro is a delusion . . . No remedy whatever exists against moral intimidation and race prejudices."

But it does not follow that racist attitudes alone ordained the fate of the failed experiment. It is reasonable to assume that the reaction would not have been different had the Revolution been mounted in the name of bringing justice to an exploited white minority. The revolutionary tradition endemic in Europe is rooted in a class consciousness that never took hold in America. The idea that real power is covertly exercised, virtually without restraint, by a small, self-perpetuating ruling class has been largely confined to the radical intellectual community and proved to have no staying power when it briefly motivated activist protest by agrarian populists in the 1890s and youthful New Leftists in the 1960s. The historical context has been sketched by the journalist and political theorist William Pfaff:

This has never been a country of fixed classes, in the European sense, but there were nonetheless hierarchies that outlasted the first century and a half of our existence. The most ignoble was racial, with the black man scarcely educated, largely confined to menial work, segregated even while waging war for his country—the object of systematic legal discrimination.

Another lasting hierarchy was of values, in which a certain conventional system—of Protestant religious and British legal and social origin—dominated public life and education. Americans who did not accept the system of general beliefs at least paid it the tribute of hypocrisy. The United States was a puritan, entrepreneurial, unintellectual, middle-class nation, and those who did not belong to the white Protestant ascendancy but wanted to succeed made themselves as much like it as they could—Booker T. Washingtons of every race.

It was a nation set in this mold that in the middle of the twentieth century came under increasing pressure to recognize, and deal with, the fact that the hierarchy of caste that trapped its black citizens was aberrant to its hierarchy of values. This meant that the concept of civil liberty, to which all Americans paid homage, would have to be extended to mandate federal action to secure rights still denied blacks not only by recalcitrant Southern state governments, but by property owners, employers, labor unions, and public and private institutions everywhere in the nation. As the reach broadened it would become evident that abrogation of discriminatory practices previously sanctioned by the United States Supreme Court would raise issues that went far beyond those involved in guaranteeing impartial treatment for blacks. But, at the beginning of the series of historic court actions through which a new generation of black lawyers began chipping away at restrictive Supreme Court precedents, it was still generally assumed that the impact would be confined primarily to the South.

THE delusion that segregation was a peculiarly Southern institution blinded most Americans to the fact that the United States as a whole was, by any institutional test, a racist society. At the beginning of the 1950s the black protest movement produced hardly a ripple on a national consciousness bemused by a compelling urge to return to what Warren Harding in another postwar era had called "normalcy"—a yearning now frustrated by a hot war in Korea and a cold war with the Soviet Union. The side effect was a resurgent anti-Communist witch hunt that demoralized New Deal Democrats still in office and rejuvenated Republican conservatives, who saw in it the means of ending their long political exile.

The sound and fury was provided by Red-baiting demagogues who achieved instant fame, or at least notoriety, as they exploited the unprecedented emotional impact of television, now rapidly replacing the print media as the primary means of mass communication. Political leftists, who had always listed racial discrimination in their bill of indictment against the middle-class majority, were divided among themselves; those who refused to abandon Marxism in the face of Soviet realpolitik, and some of those who did, were occupied with their own survival in the face of the free-swinging onslaught led by the blue-jowled bullyboy from Wisconsin, Joe McCarthy.

Yet, if one looked beneath the roiled political surface, there were signs that racial attitudes were changing significantly. For the rising generation the experience of depression and war, and what had seemed to be a final victory over both, had restored a measure of idealism; the melting pot scenario, subordinating religious and ethnic differences to a common, uniquely American faith, had entered a new phase in the vast suburban tracts that began encircling the major cities. It was not only physical differences that set these new neighborhoods apart from the congested urban districts that supplied most of their residents. In providing a more open environment they encouraged, indeed required, tolerance. Standardized pricing of mass-produced housing provided a natural selection process to the extent that income determines class, but even so, William Manchester, looking back on the phenomenon in *The Glory and the Dream*, found the suburbs "free, unstructured, and genuinely hospitable to anyone from any background, except blacks, whose time had not yet come." William Whyte, a social critic who made his reputation deploring the bland conformity of the new life-style, conceded that the new suburbanites had achieved "a pretty high quotient of kindliness and fundamental decency."

Suburbia was only the most conspicuous manifestation of an unprecedented rate of change that affected the whole of American society. The Levittowns and Elysian Heights and Willowbrooks were monuments to the shift of the nation's population from predominantly rural to predominantly urban. In the span of a generation the sectional interests that had always shaped national politics were fundamentally altered, recasting the traditional power bases. A technological revolution had created a new demography as it mechanized agriculture, ending the age-old dependence on animal power and hand labor; now engineering advances were rendering whole industries obsolete, bringing forth radically new forms of communication, manufacture, and distribution. The great internal migration of the war years did not lapse, but gained momentum; the sparsely settled West began to take on the growth patterns that had characterized the densely populated Northeast and Midwest.

The South's primary role was to feed the migratory streams with workers made surplus by the transformation of the farm economy. The region's isolation from the mainstream had not yet ended, but it was breaking down—and with this came a proportionate reduction and internal redistribution of black population that invalidated the basic assumptions upon which the institutional patterns of race relations had been based. From 1940 to 1950 all the Southern states except Florida and Texas showed population gains below the national average, and the two lowest in per capita income, Arkansas and Mississippi, had a net loss. However, the South's gain in white population was 16.5 percent, against 13.4 percent for the rest of the nation. This was in dramatic contrast to an increase in black population in the South of only 1.5 percent against a black increase of 55.6 percent in the non-South. These figures foreshadowed the relocation of the national socioeconomic problem Franklin Roosevelt had rated number one back in 1937. With no means of absorbing millions of workers displaced by the changing farm economy, the South had begun to export its historic racial dilemma to the great cities of the North and West.

In retrospect it seems astonishing that what can only be described as a demographic convulsion attracted so little attention until, in the last third of the century, its predictable results began to be seen as a full-blown national urban crisis. The migration of upwardly mobile whites to suburbia had been universally applauded as a fulfillment of the American Dream and was actively encouraged by government at all levels— through federally insured mortgages, subsidies to encourage developers, and the provision of necessary facilities and services at public expense. At first the urban planners, now coming into their own as technicians indispensable to such explosive growth, seemed oblivious to what was happening to inner city neighborhoods being vacated by the new suburbanites. The poorest and most dilapidated of these were filling with black, and to a lesser extent poor white, migrants from the South conditioned by a generations-old rural heritage that hardly fitted them for city life.

I suppose loyal disciples of Adam Smith considered this the normal working of the free enterprise system: The market for labor had shrunk in the South, therefore the surplus workers would seek out and, if necessary, create new markets by making their services available at wages competitive enough to attract entrepreneurs. But even if such brutal social Darwinism could be considered acceptable, it soon became evident that the system wasn't balancing supply with demand—and had no prospect of automatically doing so under conditions that were fundamentally different from those encountered by earlier immigrants.

The newcomers who made the melting pot scenario a success story had been brought from abroad to meet a chronic labor shortage created by an expanding, labor-intensive economy; if, handicapped by language and alien customs, these newcomers had to start with the most menial jobs, they had reason to believe that as they improved their skills they could gain a higher living standard and at least a tolerable degree of acceptance by the established community. It was a system that could, and usually did, reward conformity to the Protestant ethic requiring hard work and orderly personal conduct. And, of course, all except a handful of Oriental immigrants had white skins, and their children could, if they chose, dispense with Old World customs and language and find at least a contingent place in the larger society at whatever level their income indicated.

The America of the 1950s was a different place. If the economy, as measured by gross national product, was still growing, the rate was beginning to slow, and the infrastructure was beset by contradictions. The emergency expansion of the job market in World War II, which had given blacks a toehold in high wage industrial employment, was over—and in critical areas contraction would begin as the fighting in Korea wound down. The industries born of the new technology were, for the most part, not labor intensive; the primary purpose of the new phase of automation introduced by computers was to replace human workers, and the few new jobs it created generally called for relatively high skills. Where there was expansion, in merchandising, white collar clerical work, and public service, there was little room for semiliterate country folk. Even the demand for domestic servants, traditionally extended to blacks, was declining with the spread of mechanical home appliances and packaged prepared foods. The well-to-do matron could, and usually preferred to, run her household without the full-time services of a houseman, cook, or maid.

It seemed to me, viewing these trends from my Southern

perspective, that we were, for better and worse, moving toward a national norm in racial attitudes. Prior to the great influx of lower-class blacks, the manifestations of racism in the North had been essentially negative. The typical white living above the Mason-Dixon line could see no practical need to invoke government sanctions to keep blacks in their place, but neither was he disposed to support affirmative action to improve their lot. In the rare instances when the occasion arose, he usually practiced social segregation just as his Southern counterpart did. Under real or perceived pressure, Americans generally have adopted exclusionary practices against any identifiable group seen to be markedly different; marriage outside the faith was forbidden to Catholics and Jews and frowned on by the Protestant sects, and no matter what theological niceties were invoked this implied inferiority on the part of the unchosen.

Even when no doctrinal conflict was involved, and no visible ethnic difference, the bosom of the family usually remained closed to those who came of a different cultural heritage. Albert Eisele, in a biography of the era's leading advocate of civil rights, found that when Hubert Humphrey's father was married to Christine Sannes in Lily, South Dakota, the bride's father was "the happiest man in Codington County, relatives said, because most Norwegian girls in the area married Swedes, whom he considered second-rate citizens."

There was, of course, a significant difference between maintaining segregation largely by custom, as a matter of individual choice, and imposing it by law as a matter of presumed social necessity. The rationale for the Southern practice was that the proportion of blacks to whites was such as to require caste stratification to insure that "responsible and accomplished" citizens remained in control—a system within which, on a master-servant basis, the two races could work together and live in harmony. In a physical, if not a psychological sense, segregation in the North, as reflected in residential patterns, was more complete than in the South. Blacks had their own description of the regional difference: "In the North they don't care how high you get as long as you don't get too close; in the South they don't care how close you get as long as you don't get too high."

Except in a relatively few Southern counties the new

demography had removed any possibility that blacks could take over the political process by sheer weight of numbers; the fear of black rule, which had seemed real enough in Reconstruction, was now without substance. By midcentury there was concrete evidence that this was so. In 1944 the United States Supreme Court invalidated the white primary in Texas, holding that party nomination was an integral part of the election process and therefore involved state action, a precedent that permitted NAACP lawyers to systematically knock down restrictions on the franchise in all the Southern states. Blacks qualified to vote in increasing numbers—up from 250,000 in 1940 to 750,000 in 1948—without significantly changing the complexion of state and local officeholders although the new black voters in the cities, where most were concentrated, constituted special interest blocs sizable enough to prompt municipal officials to moderate the cavalier treatment long accorded the minority.

To the most ambitious blacks—and these were the first to migrate—the North and West still seemed to offer greater opportunity for economic advancement and, of equal importance, greater immunity to the personal degradation implicit in the South's rigid caste system. But as their numbers grew in the great cities, both prospects diminished; when the migratory stream began to scoop up those at the very bottom of Southern society the change of scene produced no effective change in condition. They were surplus population in the cities as they had been on the land, and the term *underclass* came into fashion, with the adjective "permanent" usually appended.

10

The Anatomy of Racism

*T*here were significant changes within the closed black society in the years after the Civil War. The freedmen had placed education first among their demands, and, if it was never fully met, a rudimentary school system came into being in the cities and towns and slowly expanded across the rural South. By mid-century, anyone who looked closely could see that, despite all the obstacles put in their way by custom and law, blacks had produced a growing middle class beyond the wall of segregation—solid, religious, respectable, committed to the Protestant ethic. By any rational test the qualifications of this black bourgeoisie to exercise the duties and meet the obligations of citizenship was above the average of the white electorate.

Although it had produced the few crusaders for racial equality, and in its next generation would reject segregation on principle, the property-owning, taxpaying black middle class was still conspicuously conservative—so much so it was scorned by radicals for social pretensions that were seen as a caricature of white snobbery. In 1955 the black scholar, E. Franklin Frazier, aroused much resentment within the ranks of the black middle class when he charged in *Black Bourgeoisie* that protection of its special status gave this class a vested interest in maintaining the segregated society:

Its behavior as well as its mentality is a reflection of American modes of behavior and American values. . . . They wanted to forget the Negro's past, and they have attempted to conform to the behavior and values of the white community in the most minute details. Therefore they have often become . . . "exaggerated" Americans.

The trouble was that few Southern whites chose to look beyond the pale. There was nothing that required them to do so, and much in their tradition and, in the case of the more sensitive their unspoken sense of guilt, that prompted them not to. The media largely ignored the black community except to occasionally trot out one of the three standard stereotypes: the grinning, heel-flinging comic figure of Sambo and his female counterpart; Uncle Tom, the faithful old body servant and his handkerchief-headed mate; or, in crime reports, the Bad Nigger who deserved the harsh treatment meted out by a repressive, all-white criminal justice system. Complacency had more to do with maintaining the status quo than the fulminations of the pathological white supremacists whose rhetoric was colored by outright race hatred, and whose treatment of blacks, when they could get away with it, was deliberately sadistic.

The more rabid racists still held sway out in the far reaches of the plantation country, and in the crossroads trading centers whose lifeblood was being drained away as the automobile brought within reach the superior merchandising and service facilities of the towns and cities. Here, poverty spread a pall over white and black alike, and the most ambitious younger members of both races put their feet in the big road, leaving behind those least equipped by temperament and education to challenge the embittered whites who used blacks as scapegoats to relieve their own frustration. Any journalist looking for a racist horror story could still find one in the emptying hinterland of any Southern state.

But in the urban places, where the whites who dominated the economy and controlled the political process were now concentrated, overt racists were not conspicuous, and those who made a career of bigotry were consigned to the crackpot status of streetcorner orators. In *The South and the Southerner* Ralph McGill included this sketch of old "Doc" Simmons, who emerged in Atlanta as a latter-day reviver of the Ku Klux Klan:

. . . Doc was, they said, a pious, prissy-walking big man. Lodge badges and charms were heavy upon him, and he carried his burden joyously. Their weight was well-distributed on lapel, vest, fingers and hung pendant-fashion from the heavy gold watch chain, which was the hallmark of the salesman, or confidence man, of the times. His britches were rump-sprung . . . from much sitting in the wooden chairs of lodge rooms, rural church pews, offices of county and municipal politicians, and the severe, high-backed chairs found behind pulpits. Mints and cloves wrestled with the bourbon on his breath, deceiving the good ladies of the WCTU, but causing the knowing to speak of him with the half-condemning, half-affectionate, sometimes profane, phrases reserved for the amiably fraudulent who manage to be equally at home leading prayer, preaching, taking a dram, or making a fourth at poker.

There was no way of determining the extent to which the rising level of sophistication had undermined the average white Southerner's devotion to the outward manifestations of white supremacy. In the absence of some startling local outbreak of racial protest—and these were still rare in the first half of the 1950s—the matter was rarely discussed, and when it was, candor could not be expected from those who privately dissented from what they believed to be the prevailing view. To do so publicly, as I was often reminded, was to forfeit a degree of respectability. However, I found in my own experience that under close scrutiny the white stereotypes were losing substance along with the black. I can think of a dozen or more lawmen I knew who had all the visible characteristics of the pussle-gutted, broad-brimmed, strictly-from-Dixie sheriff of present-day television drama, but who in fact were effective protectors of the blacks who came within their charge. The problem, as I began to appraise it, now lay not with the fire-breathing Dixiecrats and their racist acolytes, but with the considerable majority of basically decent white Southerners who treated blacks with a reflexive paternalism, degrading the minority race without conscious intent—indeed, without even realizing they were doing so.

ONE of the most persistent complaints of blacks in those days was raised against the gratuitous denial of common courtesy titles—a trivial matter, surely, in comparison to the far more serious grievances suffered by most members of the race, and yet one that proud men and women found peculiarly lacerating. The practice went back to antebellum days, when it would not have occurred to the most sympathetic master to address a slave as Mr., Mrs., or Miss. Instead, blacks were referred to, as were whites short of their majority, as "boy" or "girl," and in intimate address by their first names until their age was too advanced to be ignored; then they were accorded the affectionate titles of "uncle" and "aunt." Whites usually recognized the status of the few black professionals by calling preachers "Reverend," physicians "Doctor," and lawyers "Attorney," but the ordinary prefixes accorded most white men and maidens, and all white married women, were withheld from even eminently proper and respectable blacks. What had started out as a mere convention, not essentially different from that followed by white masters in dealing with white servants, had become a deliberate mark of contempt as white supremacy was politicized in the years after the Civil War. This was now seen by blacks as a denial of human dignity, with the same connotation as that invoked by the term "nigger."

When I joined the *Gazette* the style sheet followed the usual practice of most Southern newspapers, and my suggestion that it ought to be changed was the occasion of my first discussion of a specific racial matter with J. N. Heiskell. He listened thoughtfully when I pointed out that, aside from the resentment it aroused among blacks, the practice was illogical and awkward. By refusing to use Miss or Mrs. we had no way of indicating a black woman's marital status, which often was relevant, and in a second reference had to resort to something like "the Jones woman" even when we were referring to a respected black schoolteacher. In the case of Mr. my proposal was that we minimize the problem by dropping it entirely, except for such special cases as the president, the governor, the clergy, and the deceased. He readily agreed—not, I think, primarily as a matter of correcting an injustice, but because he was a meticulous grammarian who could see that the style forced clumsy convolutions in the use of his beloved English language.

In his personal dealings Mr. J. N., I am sure, had never failed to treat a black with the courtesy ingrained in his formal, old-fashioned style. It simply had not occurred to him that the conventional address he had used all his life was offensive, and no one had ever called the matter to his attention. This reflected the insulation from the inner life of the black community that had become the normal lot of the urban white. Mr. J. N.'s only contact across the color bar was with the servants who maintained the household where he reigned as a Victorian paterfamilias, the waiters at the private clubs and restaurants where he occasionally dined, and the janitors at the Gazette building who were at the far end of the pecking order he headed. Even if one of these had happened to have a white skin, I cannot imagine his approaching the elegant patrician with the suggestion that he ought to alter the accepted social forms.

An ascetic who limited his alcoholic indulgence to a pre-prandial glass of sherry, never used profanity or obscenity in even the most private conversation, and made a hobby of collecting rare books rather than the usual hunting and fishing, Mr. J. N. reversed the country squire image of the traditional Southern gentleman. Yet the same gene pool and family environment had produced his brother Fred, a roistering, quick-tempered gallant, who as managing editor until his death in 1931 presided over a city room equipped, *Front Page* style, with green-eyeshaded deskmen, ribald reporters, battered typewriters, a sea of crumpled paper, and a permanent pall of tobacco smoke laced with the fumes of corn whiskey. Although Fred Heiskell, as one of the sporting gentry, was fully exposed to the ordinary, even the seamy side of Arkansas life, there is no indication that he departed in any significant way from the essentially libertarian views of his older brother.

The temperamental contrast between the two was dramatically demonstrated on the night in 1927 when Mr. J. N.'s front-page editorial denounced the peace officers who stood aside and permitted a lynching, thereby challenging the mob that perpetrated it. James Street recalled that when rumors spread that a march was planned on the Gazette Building, Fred Heiskell armed himself and then

called the staff together and said it was a management fight and that the *Gazette* would allow no employee to jeopardize life and limb for her honor. Who was he kidding? That night the boys fortified themselves with .45s and a little moonshine and strutted around like heroes. . . . At the height of the to-do, while a few hoodlums milled outside the *Gazette*'s office, somebody propped a shotgun close to Mr. J. N., against his head-high stack of back issues of the *New York Times* and the *Kansas City Star*. "Why, gentlemen"—his eyes moved from the blunderbuss to his staff—"I am not acquainted with firearms. I couldn't hit the side of a barn." It was a unique admission from a man born in the Tennessee mountains during the trigger days of Reconstruction.

I was constantly reminded of the long span of history imprinted on the memory of the aging editor. The first half of his life, when values are shaped and tend to become fixed, had been spent in a South I could know only by hearsay. He was, as James Street's memoir indicated, a mild man, one not disposed to crusade for change but fully prepared to display the courage of his convictions in defense of the humane principles he believed in. He described the *Gazette* as a conservative newspaper that usually disappointed conservatives.

The office day began with an informal conference between the two of us, and while there was rarely serious disagreement on editorial policy, it was evident that a generational difference colored our perception of the issues. I recall the morning after Joe McCarthy took the floor of the Senate to imply that Gen. George C. Marshall was guilty of treason. Mr. J. N. was profoundly shocked by this attack on the integrity of a Southerner who epitomized what Stephen Vincent Benet called the "broadsword virtues" of an older America. "I have always opposed dueling," he said, "but I have begun to wonder if there is any other answer in the face of this kind of cowardly attack upon a man's honor."

This was an idea that could not possibly have occurred to me, who thought of the *code duello* as a romantic absurdity of the buried past. But it was hardly that to Mr. J. N., who had begun his newspaper practice at a time when editors could expect a demand for personal satisfaction if they traduced a thin-skinned, hot-blooded subscriber. Long after the formalities of the dawn meeting under the oaks had been dispensed with, the substitute advance notice that the offender would be shot on sight was common. A nephew of Pitchfork Ben Tillman responded to editorial criticism by shooting the editor of the *Columbia State* on the steps of the capitol, and in Mr. J. N.'s day the nearby *Vicksburg Journal* lost five editors in thirteen years.

He was not an unduly modest man but he did not indulge in the ego gratification offered by the civic organizations that sought out newspaper executives to serve on their boards and committees, rejecting these overtures, I suspected, because he found the usual run of boosters boring. Total commitment to his newspaper was his excuse for noninvolvement, and he used it even to justify his absence from church, finding it necessary to spend the hours of the Presbyterian service at the office, where, he claimed, the Sunday morning quiet of the empty building enabled him to catch up on his handwritten personal correspondence. The sole exception to his noninvolvement was the Little Rock Public Library, which he served for many years as board chairman.

When the matter of admitting blacks to the main library arose, he expressed the view that they were more conveniently served at the separate branch maintained in one of the black neighborhoods. But when a younger board member persuaded him to visit the colored branch and Mr. J. N. saw its gross inequality he readily reversed himself. Any man of any color who wanted to read a book should be encouraged to do so, he said; but he had a nagging concern that shiftless black street idlers might lie around at the main branch—an apprehension I managed to ease by pointing out that the gelid stillness of the reading room was hardly likely to lure many triflers away from the pool hall and beer joint.

I was convinced that desegregation was inevitable, and saw the *Gazette*'s mission as alerting the community to the necessity of preparing for what was bound to be a difficult transition. He did not demur, but he continued to hope that no fundamental change in racial relationships would be involved and that those that could not be avoided would proceed at a pace determined by their voluntary acceptance in the white community. His faith in gradualism was sustained by his wishful belief that all blacks except an uppity few were satisfied with their lot—the assumption that had eased the conscience of his generation. It was shared by the most sophisticated and uninhibited civil libertarian of the first half of the twentieth century, H. L. Mencken, who wrote approvingly of the admission of a single black student to the University of Maryland Law School under state court order, but added, "I am not arguing here for mixing races in the public schools. . . . In the present state of public opinion in Maryland it probably would be most unwise, no matter what may be said for it in the abstract." Segregation in the public schools, the Sage of Baltimore went on, was resented only "by a small faction of colored people, and inasmuch as virtually all the whites of the state are in favor of it, it is not likely to be abandoned in the near future."

THE dilemma Gunnar Myrdal cited in the title of his massive study of American race relations, was a moral one.

Moreover, it had become truly national in character; the surface differences in attitude between Northerners and Southerners had little practical effect on the plight of blacks, although they continued to color the rhetoric produced by the clash of regional interests. The real conflict of values had not yet surfaced; it still centered, as Myrdal defined it, in the hearts of white Americans:

The American dilemma is the ever-raging conflict between the values which we shall call the "American creed," where the American thinks, talks and acts under the influence of high national and Christian morals, and on the other hand, the values of individual and group living, where personal and local interests; economic, social and sexual jealousies; considerations of community prestige and conformity; group prejudice against particular persons or types of people; and all sorts of miscellaneous wants, impulses and habits dominate his outlook.

The essential moral argument, that simple justice required an end to segregation, was still without practical force; most of the whites who recognized the inequity of the treatment accorded blacks still believed that redress could be obtained under the separate-but-equal dispensation certified by the Supreme Court not only as permissible but as socially desirable. If the new, increasingly militant black leaders emerging in the wake of World War II personally rejected the view, they had no tactical choice but to seek redress within the limits of institutional segregation. There was as yet no popular support, black or white, for a head-on attack on the color bar.

The two national organizations devoted to improving the condition of blacks had been dependent upon white financial support ever since their founding, and were still interracial at the level of policy making. The more conservative of the two, the National Urban League, worked through local chapters in the larger cities, usually carrying on social work as a member agency of the Community Chest. "As an interracial, dependent organization it can never develop a program which will spur the Negro masses and win their confidence," Ralph Bunche wrote. "It operates strictly on the periphery of the Negro problem and never comes to grips with the fundamentals in American racial conflict." Myrdal found that the more activist

NAACP had "nowhere been able to build up a real mass following among Negroes. The membership is still confined to the upper classes." Thurgood Marshall was to recall that in his youth "we used to say that NAACP stood for the National Association for the Advancement of Certain People."

Beginning in the thirties the NAACP had initiated lawsuits aimed at equalizing public services and institutions provided for blacks, and it had some success in matters such as bringing teachers' pay up to par with whites. Then, in the forties, it succeeded in restoring to blacks the franchise effectively denied by the white primary; aside from the practical significance of providing Southern blacks leverage on the political process, this marked a significant departure from the Court's prior reluctance to supersede the policy-making authority of state and local governments by mandating action under the equal protection clause of the Fourteenth Amendment.

The Court was still a long way from reversing the *Plessy* separate-but-equal precedent when it finally conferred the franchise on blacks, but, as Richard Kluger wrote, in broadening its definition of equal protection it had "decided, by a narrow margin, that the twentieth century was constitutional."

At this critical juncture Thurgood Marshall was the black movement's legal point man, and Walter White, the debonair executive secretary of the NAACP, was its energetic and highly skilled publicist. A native of Atlanta, White had joined the struggling organization in its formative years when his fair skin, blue eyes, and stylish manner were an indispensable asset, enabling him to pass for white as he undertook spot investigations of racial outrages. A pragmatist by nature as well as necessity, he had been largely responsible for easing the uncompromising Du Bois out of the association when his ideological views began to strain relations with white financial supporters and Northern political leaders. Walter White nevertheless was regarded by white supremacists as the radical race-mixer incarnate; it is a measure of his effusive charm that he still managed to keep his lines open to politicians who accepted the fact that no man in his position could be expected to compromise his pro forma objection to segregation in any way.

I first met White in late November 1948 when Hodding Carter and I journeyed to New York to defend the honor of the South at Town Hall. We were opposed by White and Ray Sprigle, a white *Pittsburgh Post-Gazette* reporter who had published a sensational series of articles after he darkened his skin and traveled "underground" through the South disguised as a Negro. The debate, broadcast nationally by radio and on the rudimentary television network, addressed the subject, "What Should We Do About Race Segregation?" We had several relaxed hours together before we went on stage, including the time used to plaster on the heavy theatrical makeup required by the embryonic TV cameras. There was, we agreed, a particular problem in this case, since the pink-cheeked, white-haired Negro representative seemed the most conspicuous Aryan among us, while the swarthy Carter's skin was dark enough to prompt a Mississippi theater usher to direct him to the balcony. The makeup man was instructed to darken down Walter and lighten up Hodding.

The exchange on stage was necessarily limited by format and time. Sprigle led off by proclaiming that in four weeks as a pseudo-Negro he had found that "wanton, inexcusable, capricious murder walks the streets and highways of the Southland, dogging the heels of ten million black men—women, too—and pouncing whimsically, with or without provocation." White was far too seasoned a hand to indulge in such vulnerable oversimplification. He took to the highest ground, citing his recent experience in Paris, where as a consultant to the United Nations General Assembly he had heard Germans, Poles, and Russians defend tyranny by challenging Eleanor Roosevelt because of the second-class citizenship imposed upon Negroes in the United States. And he set forth the NAACP line in terms impossible for Carter and me to refute:

There are two major aspects of this question of racial segregation. The first is its effect upon those segregated and those who do the segregating. There can never be any equality within the framework of segregation. Denial of equal educational and economic opportunity, disfranchisement, the ghetto, and the humiliation of the human spirit are the inescapable consequences of segregation. At the same time, a false sense of racial superiority is bred among those who do the segregating. The second consequence of segregation and the evils which grow out of it is the steadily lowered prestige of the United States among the two-thirds of the people of this earth who are colored, and also among many white peoples.

Hodding Carter took advantage of Sprigle's hyperbole to assert that Mississippi would take care of its murder problem when "the State of New York stops having more murders, interracial and otherwise, in one month than we have down there in a year." Both of us contended that there had been a steady improvement in race relations in the South, and that continued progress was threatened by undue pressure from without. "The so-called civil rights program does not put first things first," Carter argued. "It is a windmill attack upon certain diminishing results of racial antipathies rather than upon the causes." I rested my case by pointing to the results of the recent election, in which the Dixiecrats had been routed and Harry Truman reelected. I indulged in a little hyperbole of my own when I proclaimed:

With their ballots the voters of the South declared race a dead issue in the great majority of Southern states. . . . Seven hundred thousand Negroes were qualified to vote in the South last Tuesday, and so far as I know, most of them did vote. . . . In eighty years, only a moment in the sweep of history, the Negro has moved within sight of his traditional goal of proper civil rights. Tolerance, it has always seemed to me, is a considerable virtue, and I suggest to you that the Southern white man, who also finds himself in a political minority, has earned a full measure of it.

Offstage our exchanges were a good deal more candid. In conversation with Walter White I conceded that no white man had a right to ask a black man to wait any longer for rights that presumably had been guaranteed him eighty years ago, but pointed out that under a democratic system of majority rule there was no way to force whites to yield except by armed intervention—and that had been counterproductive the last time it was tried. I could, I said, understand why White rejected gradualism, since it was often used as a transparent excuse for inaction. Yet, I insisted, he must recognize that the alternative of immediate, total dismantlement of institutional segregation was a practical impossibility.

There was a touch of standard Southern sophistry in my implication that there was no tenable middle ground. I knew very well that the NAACP's legal strategy was to proceed case by case to secure court-ordered desegregation in limited areas where it was impractical to meet the test of equality with separate facilities, and where only a few educated and respectable blacks would be forced into the company of whites. Thus Thurgood Marshall and his legal team had moved to breach the educational structure at the very top, winning a Supreme Court ruling that opened the way for admission of blacks to the graduate and professional schools of Southern universities— including, as White had reminded the audience during the debate, the medical and law schools of the University of Arkansas, which had recently enrolled their first black students without setting off any pronounced public reaction.

White's response to my temporizing was a personal challenge. "You know segregation is morally indefensible and has to go," he said. "There you are, six feet tall, blond, blue-eyed, a certified Confederate WASP. You've been a colonel in the army, you've been in combat. What are *you* afraid of?" It was calculated, skillful needling. White knew that physical courage was essential to a proud Southerner's self-image. And he knew that I knew that he had earned the right to ask the question.

In 1919 one of his many trips to high-tension scenes of racial violence brought the young journalist to Elaine, Arkansas, where black tenant farmers tried to organize the first union ever heard of in the remote plantation country that stretches back from the banks of the Mississippi. A white deputy had been shot by a black man, and that touched off rioting which ultimately brought in the governor of Arkansas at the head of five hundred federal troops. When trouble broke out again the soldiers moved through the countryside, taking into "protective custody" every black they could find, except those who were shot for resisting, or seeming to.

The *Gazette* reported that twenty-five blacks and five whites were killed at Elaine. On the basis of his undercover investigation, White published reports that set the black death toll nearer to two hundred. Twenty-five years later James Street wrote, "No one knows to this day just how many folks were killed." But one thing is certain: no representative of the *Gazette*, in that day or in my own, was ever subject to personal danger as intense and protracted as that faced by the young investigative reporter from the NAACP during the weeks he spent among the inflamed citizens of that God-forsaken back-water.

It is a sad fact that in those critical years raw courage was more important to the progress of blacks than the moral cogency of their demand for justice. With the odds what they were, no one is entitled to place undue blame on the ordinary men and women of both races who took refuge in Jim Crow conformity, but that made the extraordinary few even more conspicuous. Those who served as the advance guard of black protest had to take their stand in the knowledge that the admiration they aroused among their own people would remain sub rosa; they were without prospect of rallying the kind of mass demonstrations that would spread the risk among those of the next generation when they marched for freedom.

The fact that they survived is testimony that they were not candidates for martyrdom, and this provided an additional test of will, for they were often scorned by radical members of their own race as compromisers willing to sacrifice principle in order to work within the system. In the NAACP's internal power struggles Walter White, who married a sophisticated white New Yorker, was accused of being a closet white himself, engaged in a self-serving effort to exploit the black cause to gain personal celebrity. And Thurgood Marshall, who used his disarming manner and self-deprecating humor to ease his way through Southern courthouses and improve his clients' chances of success, was given the Uncle Tom label by some of his detractors.

This seemed a supreme irony to those of us who saw the vanguard in action in the Jim Crow South. Their very presence probably had as much to do with their ultimate success as the considerable skills they brought to their self-assigned tasks, for it invoked the broadsword heritage which, at the same time it increased their hazard, commanded respect for their sheer guts—and with respect began to come a grudging sympathy for their cause. It is often assumed that this reaction was confined to high-born whites, and was another manifestation of noblesse oblige. But it was by no means unusual to hear a flint-eyed redneck, relaxing in the company of his neighbors, say of a defiant black, "Hell, if I was a nigger I wouldn't have took that either."

11

On the Flanks
of Segregation

*T*he first black militant to gain national prominence, Frederick Douglass, took his cue from the
New England abolitionists who became his sponsors. "Those
who profess to favor freedom, and yet disparage agitation," he
said, "are men who want crops without plowing up the ground.
Power concedes nothing without a demand. It never did and
never will." But this was a non sequitur to Southern blacks, who
had no semblance of power of their own to support a demand
based on the claim Booker T. Washington incorporated in his
Atlanta supplication: "It is important and right that all privileges of the law be ours. . . ."

"To expect the Negroes of Georgia to produce a great
general like Napoleon when they are not even allowed to carry
arms, or to deride them for not providing schools like those of
the Renaissance when a few years ago they were forbidden the
use of letters, verges very closely on the outer rim of absurdity,"
the black scholar, Kelly Miller, wrote in 1908. But by 1927
Miller, now dean of Howard University in Washington, was
urging young blacks assembled in the federal enclave between
North and South to face up to the consequences of the
condition he had so pointedly described: "The white race has
furnished leaders for us. No man of one group can ever
furnish leadership to people of another group, unless he is
willing to become naturalized into the group he seeks to lead."
And that was hardly likely to happen in a society still committed
to the doctrine of white supremacy.

Here was the black side of the American dilemma. Segregation trapped the minority race in a vicious circle: the deficient social background used to justify exclusion of blacks from
the larger community created an environment which perpetu-
ated the deficient social background. The separate black society

had few resources to encourage the creation of facilities that might have provided an effective degree of internal self-sufficiency. Blacks had begun life as freedmen without property or access to credit. In a remarkable demonstration of innate capacity, a fourth of all black farm families by 1900 had employed their agricultural skills to acquire land of their own and escape the fate of those trapped in the sharecropping system, but these were subsistence operations for the most part. Those who left the land found no openings except in menial jobs. The few trained as craftsmen under slavery had to hire out to whites to obtain employment; as slaves or freedmen they had not been allowed to occupy positions where they might perfect the managerial skills required of independent businessmen.

The black community remained almost entirely dependent upon the white for employment, for housing, and for mercantile supplies and professional services. When they crowded into Northern slums blacks did not duplicate the patterns of the foreign immigrants who preceded them; earlier newcomers, without proficiency in English, were constrained to establish neighborhood businesses to serve those who needed to speak their native language as they shopped for essential goods. That was not a requirement for immigrants whose English might be regarded as quaint, but was nevertheless serviceable. In Harlem at mid-century, after an estimated four hundred thousand blacks had been wedged into a neighborhood built to accommodate perhaps seventy-five thousand people, most of the shops and service facilities were still owned and operated by Jews. Nationwide, sales of black-owned businesses accounted for only two-tenths of one percent of the total volume.

The families that made up the black bourgeoisie first attained the minimum economic base necessary to provide stability by working in the service trades. In the South, domestic service was an exclusive province of blacks; if the pay was low it provided additional income in kind—in the best situations, housing, food, and clothing. By extension, blacks usually provided personal service in places of public accommodation, and here there were opportunities to acquire skills that assured a degree of independence and an income sufficient to maintain dignity and respectability.

In my youth the kitchens and dining rooms of the best Southern hotels, clubs, and restaurants were manned by blacks, as were the leading barber shops. In token recognition of the federal government's obligation to the freedmen blacks could qualify as mailmen and postal clerks. Jobs which required a strong back along with a measure of skill and responsibility were reserved for them on the railroads, notably those of locomotive fireman, dining car chef and waiter, and porter. In time the railroad operating unions tried to freeze black firemen out of these relatively well-paying jobs to make way for whites, and black barbers disappeared from Southern shops. The Pullman porters and dining car attendants survived in the Jim Crow era by organizing their own union to protect jobs in which their members often performed the functions of white crewmen in addition to more menial chores.

This kind of employment, along with teaching and preaching, produced the black middle class. Its members worked in close proximity to whites, absorbing at least a truncated version of their aspirations and life-style—including a commitment to advance their children's education at all costs. Living in the towns and cities, they had access to the best of the unequal educational facilities, including the black denominational and state colleges. If this upward striving produced what E. Franklin Frazier and others derided as an Amos and Andy caricature of white society, it also produced some of the most dedicated and effective leaders to grace the modern American scene.

Considering the obstacles they had to overcome, and the white role models they necessarily chose to emulate, it was inevitable that the founding members of the black middle class should be exemplars of the Protestant ethic. A. Philip Randolph, born in Florida to a circuit-riding AME (African Methodist Episcopal) minister and the mulatto daughter of a lumber dealer, gave his parents credit for instilling in him the discipline and self-confidence that undergirded his unshakable commitment to racial justice: "My home was almost Calvinistic. It was rigidly moralistic, and rigidly supervised. I never saw a bottle of whiskey, nobody used profanity, and there was no playing on Sunday." When he began his career in the labor movement by taking a job with a New York union of black headwaiters, Randolph described his haughty employers with awe: "They were real aristocrats."

The grandiose term was not misplaced. The attributes of aristocracy, if not the usual trappings, were visible in the upper reaches of the black middle class. The parents of Thurgood Marshall brought him up in a proper Baltimore neighborhood where it was said that he was about as well protected against the world's cruelties as an urban black child could be. His mother, a schoolteacher who had done graduate work at Columbia University, had him christened in St. James Episcopal Church. His father, Will, who had worked on dining cars before he became head steward of an exclusive Chesapeake Bay boat club, was a man of imposing presence. The Marshalls, each half-white and perhaps more, were eminently qualified for membership in what Richard Kluger described as the cautious, color-conscious mulatto aristocracy of Black Baltimore:

But their direction, while upward-mobile, was not toward the showy status of the black bourgeoisie with its implied defensiveness. The Will Marshalls were transitional figures in the history of the American Negro, for they would not settle for what modest comforts they could accumulate within a ghetto culture. They were proud of who and what they were, yet they became, in their fashion, race-conscious rebels against the cold grip of white supremacy.

Middle-class blacks like the Marshalls saw enough of their white contemporaries at close range to conclude that they were themselves as good as, if not superior to, the average run of the other race. Their self-confidence was such that they had no doubt they could compete with whites on even terms if given a chance, so they rejected the counsel of timorous black leaders who argued that segregation provided a necessary protection— at least until the black rank and file had attained higher levels of education and higher standards of personal conduct. Nor were they responsive to radical insistence that blacks must merge their interests with the white proletariat and work for a revolution that would turn the capitalist system upside down. Their ambition was not to destroy middle-class America, but to gain unrestricted admission to it. By any ideological test applicable in twentieth-century America the demand for a racially integrated society was conservative, although it was hardly so regarded by a complacent white majority that saw it only as a threat to the status quo.

INTEGRATION became the primary objective of the NAACP when the well-educated sons and daughters of the black middle class began to dominate its inner councils. By 1934 this had led to the departure of the proud old Brown Brahman, W.E.B. Du Bois, increasingly alienated from the American system and contemptuous of those who sought to work within it. As he moved closer to the Marxist view that American blacks must see themselves as an exploited nation held subject by a corrupt, imperialist power, Du Bois began to endorse separatism as essential to black revolution: ". . . twelve million American Negroes have the inborn capacity to accomplish just as much as any nation of twelve million anywhere in the world ever accomplished." Now teaching at Atlanta University, he argued in the *Journal of Negro Education* that blacks who believed that they could obtain a good education only through admission to white schools accepted the stigma of racial inferiority, rejecting the possibility that blacks were capable of creating first-rate institutions of their own:

I know that this article will forthwith be interpreted by certain illiterate "nitwits" as a plea for segregated Negro schools and colleges. It is not. . . . It is saying in plain English: that a separate Negro school, where children were treated like human beings, trained by teachers of their own race, who know what it means to be black in the year of salvation 1935, is infinitely better than making our boys and girls doormats to be spit upon and lied to by ignorant social climbers, whose sole claim to superiority is ability to kick "niggers" when they are down.

The Du Bois thesis was anathema to the remarkable coterie of young black lawyers who began to take over the NAACP's court business. They were determined to force the central issue that segregation, per se, was incompatible with simple justice, and they convinced themselves that they could prevail against their white adversaries in a forum where they could get a fair hearing—which they now believed might be the long-time repository of broken black dreams, the Supreme Court of the United States.

The senior black lawyers who launched this largely Southern company on its way were educated in the North, and in the
course of their own practice had relied on sympathetic white
colleagues for leadership in pressing the line of NAACP cases
demanding equal treatment for blacks. The organization's legal
career began in 1910 when Joel Elias Spingarn, a wealthy
Jewish intellectual who would devote most of his own time and
energy to the cause, brought in his lawyer brother Arthur to
defend blacks against police brutality and discrimination in
New York. Simply providing a legal defense for individual
blacks was, of course, an endless task. One of the NAACP's
white founders, the eminent Boston lawyer and past president
of the American Bar Association, Moorfield Storey, began
looking around for "class-action" suits, those where a ruling in
favor of an individual plaintiff would affect all blacks "similarly
situated." In 1915 he wrote an amicus curiae brief in an
Oklahoma voting rights case, and in its first entry at this exalted
level the NAACP was on the winning side of a unanimous
decision—which also marked the first time the high court had
used the Fifteenth Amendment to overturn a state law.

In 1917, Walter White's articles on the Elaine race riots
touched off a national protest that brought $50,000 pouring
into a defense fund for the twelve men an Arkansas court
condemned to death, and the sixty-seven given life terms; on
appeal to the Supreme Court Storey won an order for a new
trial from a bench that, under Chief Justice William Howard
Taft, had lapsed into its most conservative period—demonstrating that when mistreatment of blacks on a wholesale basis
was palpably outrageous even an ossified judicial system would
not tolerate it. Moreover, with a skilled publicist like Walter
White at work, this kind of litigation could, even in the South,
generate a political response. Under pressure the state of
Arkansas ultimately freed all the Elaine defendants.

But there were no further victories on the class-action
front. The Oklahoma authorities devised a substitute for the
outlawed statute and continued to keep the state's primaries
white. And when Storey, accompanied for the first time by two
black NAACP lawyers, came before the Court in 1926 to
challenge the convenants written into Washington real estate
deeds prohibiting sale of property to blacks, the justices ruled

unanimously against him—falling back on the proposition that the arrangement was a private contractual agreement that did not constitute state action.

IN those years the nation's capital was as thoroughly segregated as any Southern city, but there was one important distinction: the practice of opening federal employment to blacks at the lower levels provided only a limited number of jobs elsewhere, but in the Washington bureaus, with their thousands of employees, a token percentage created a sizable body of black residents enjoying the income level, and to an extent the protected job tenure, of middle-class whites. Moreover, the public services in the District of Columbia, which had no elected government, were directly financed by federal appropriation, with the result that the segregated public schools were more nearly equal than those anywhere else. All of this made Washington a magnet for ambitious blacks seeking opportunities denied them in the South.

One of these was Thomas Jefferson Houston, a former Kentucky slave who practiced as a Baptist preacher and earned his living as a cabinet maker. With an income bolstered by his wife's skills as a hairdresser, he provided an educational opportunity for his son William that took him all the way through the Howard University Law School. Hanging out his shingle in the 1890s, when there were only twenty-five black lawyers in Washington and no more than seven hundred in the country as a whole, William Houston began a legal career that would culminate in his appointment by Franklin Roosevelt as assistant attorney general, while his cousin and law partner, William Hastie, became the first black federal district judge— prudently stashed away by FDR among the black U.S. citizens of the Virgin Islands.

Like most successful men, William Houston hoped his son, Charles, would follow in his footsteps. The boy excelled at the high school, later renamed Dunbar, that sent forth well-prepared and highly motivated black students to leading white colleges and universities. Charles Houston's choice was Amherst, where he made Phi Beta Kappa and graduated near the top of his class. In 1919 he entered Harvard Law School, where he served on the *Law Review* and became a special protégé of perhaps the most brilliant, and certainly the most energetic member of the faculty, Felix Frankfurter. Graduating in the top 5 percent of his class, he stayed on another year to work under Frankfurter for the degree of Doctor of Juridical Science, and won a traveling fellowship which enabled him to acquire still another diploma as Doctor of Civil Law at the University of Madrid. When Charles Houston came home in 1924 to join his father's law firm he was as well educated as any beginning lawyer in the United States, white or black.

This progression across three generations parallels that of most of the leading white families of the period. The Houstons demonstrated that blacks, too, were capable of climbing rung by rung up the ladder of success as measured by prevailing American standards. Under the widely accepted theory of social Darwinism, those blacks who survived the grueling ascent could only be reckoned as even more fit than their white counterparts. The incentives and opportunities available to them were much more limited, they were uniquely subject to rebuffs that could sap the ambition of lesser men, and even when they arrived at the top they were still barred from critical areas of professional and business life open to whites of demonstrably less ability. The emergence and steady growth of the black middle class gave the lie to the doctrine of white supremacy, and at the same time pointed the way out of the American dilemma—as the members of Charles Houston's generation would demonstrate when they began to displace white patrons in key positions of leadership in the civil rights movement.

IN the thirties Washington became the field headquarters of the movement for racial equality. The main office of the NAACP remained in New York, where it drew inspiration from the Harlem renaissance in literature and the arts, and financial sustenance from the wealthy white philanthropists who were its principal source of income. But what was needed now was legal and political talent—and that was made available in high quality and growing quantity by an institution that had served for three-quarters of a century as a bedraggled monument to governmental guilt. Howard University was founded in 1867 by the Freedmen's Bureau as a training school for blacks, and acquired its title by virtue of the affiliated Freedmen's Hospital and its makeshift medical school. Financially malnourished by Congress, Howard's standards remained deplorably low, but it stood as the closest approximation to a full-fledged university, complete with graduate and professional schools, available to blacks other than the outstanding few who could hurdle the entrance requirements and quota restrictions of Northern institutions.

In 1926 Howard underwent a rebirth under its first black president, Mortecai W. Johnson, who went to the top of the Washington establishment for advice and support. In the case of the law school, principally a night operation where part-time students received routine instruction from a part-time faculty, his advisor was Justice Louis Brandeis, whose recommendation was blunt: "I can tell most of the time when I am reading a brief by a Negro attorney. You've got to get yourself a real faculty out there or you're always going to have a fifth-rate law school. And it's got to be full-time, and a day school." The challenge was not merely to provide an academic ornament for Howard, but to meet a critical national need; there were still only some eleven hundred black attorneys serving twelve million black Americans, and no more than a hundred of these had been trained at ranking law schools.

The man best qualified by education and temperament to undertake the formidable task of reconstructing the Howard law faculty was at hand. In 1929 Charles Houston accepted appointment as dean, and promptly cleaned house. Despite the low salaries permitted by his limited budget (his own was only $4,500) he was able to recruit top men from the tiny reservoir of qualified black practitioners—among them his cousin, William Henry Hastie, also an Amherst Phi Beta Kappa and graduate of Harvard Law; Leon A. Ransom, who graduated first in his law class at Ohio State; and James Nabrit, trained at Northwestern. He augmented the black faculty with a roster of visiting white lecturers that included such outstanding teachers and practitioners as Dean Roscoe Pound of Harvard and the great advocate, Clarence Darrow.

Before Houston's advent the law school had been conferring degrees annually upon some two dozen graduates. Under the standards he imposed the thirty members of the class entering in 1930 had dwindled to eleven by graduation time. The man who finished number one in 1933, Thurgood Marshall, recalled that Dean Houston never stopped hammering home the reminder that they were preparing themselves to compete head to head with white lawyers trained in the very best law schools, and he permitted no crying in their beer because they were Negroes. By 1931 the Howard law school for the first time was fully accredited, and had begun to attract bright young blacks who might well have been admitted to prestigious white institutions.

In 1929, armed with a $100,000 grant from the Garland Fund, the NAACP launched a coordinated legal attack on the flagrant inequality of the public schools of the South. The strategy was to avoid a direct challenge to the right of the states to segregate the races while forcing improvement of the facilities available to blacks by demonstrating a degree of inequality that clearly violated *Plessy*. Indisputable evidence was readily available; in 1930 the records kept in their own education departments showed a white to black ratio of per capita expenditure in the dual school systems ranging from ten to one in the Deep South to two to one in the border states. In cases where it was impossible, or inordinately expensive, to duplicate facilities for a small number of black students, equalization orders would force consideration of integration as the only economical alternative.

In 1935 Charles Houston, who had represented the NAACP in various court actions and had been serving informally as a personal legal and political advisor to Walter White, accepted appointment as full-time special counsel to implement this strategy. He established legal outposts in the Jim Crow states, signing up black lawyers on a case-by-case basis, and in key areas squeezing out a sum sufficient for a full-time retainer—a matter of $2,400 plus expenses for his star Howard graduate, Thurgood Marshall, who in 1936 was assigned to cover Maryland and Virginia from his Baltimore law office.

Houston himself was all over the region, lending his impressive presence and high legal skills to the presentation of NAACP cases in Southern courtrooms, and in the process providing invaluable inspiration and on-the-job training for his young black associates. By the time he turned over direction of what was to become the largely autonomous NAACP Legal Defense and Education Fund to Marshall in 1938 he had won some notable cases, including the landmark decision of a Maryland court that ordered admission of the first black student to a previously segregated law school. But perhaps his most prophetic statement was made while arguing a Tennessee graduate school admission case he lost:

This case may mean nothing in 1937, but in A.D. 2000 somebody will look back on the record and wonder why the South spent so much money in keeping rights from Negroes rather than granting them. . . . We'll all be better off when, instead of spending money on lawsuits, we spend it on social advancement. . . .

Remarkably, the NAACP's continuing successes in the courts made little impression on the white community. Despite the alarums and excurions of the Dixiecrat rebellion, I could detect little reaction among the *Gazette*'s readers as we faithfully reported the developing trend in the federal courts and discussed the open strategy of the NAACP. There was no great outcry when Supreme Court orders in cases arising in neighboring Oklahoma and Missouri opened their state universities' law schools to blacks, prompting the new president of the University of Arkansas, Lewis Webster Jones, to recommend a voluntary change in admission policies. The Board of Trustees agreed, Governor Laney and the legislature went along, and in 1947 there was one black student in the law school at Fayetteville, and one, who was almost as distinctive because she was female, in the medical school at Little Rock.

The calm acceptance of this token integration seemed to me a hopeful sign, although anyone who kept an eye on national political developments would have to conclude that it was rooted in the kind of pervasive unreality that had always characterized the white community's approach to any consideration of race relations. If the number of blacks involved was small, and the situation remote, the tendency was to shrug it off. In *American Dilemma*, Gunnar Myrdal, sensing the prospect of the same kind of blind reaction to the impending enfranchisement of blacks as that which had prevented orderly transition from slavery to citizenship in Reconstruction days, warned that

it is urgent, from a conservative point of view, to begin allowing the higher strata of the Negro population to participate in the political process as soon as possible, and to push the movement down to the lower groups gradually. It is also urgent to speed up the civic education of these masses who are bound to have votes in the future.

But the great majority of Southern conservative white people do not see the handwriting on the wall. They do not study the impending changes; they live in the pathetic illusion that the matter is settled. They do not care to have any constructive policies to meet the trends. They think no adjustments are called for. The chances that the future development will be planned and led intelligently—and that, consequently, it will take the form of cautious, foresighted reforms instead of unexpected, tumultuous, haphazard breaks, with mounting discords and anxieties in its wake—are indeed small.

Seven years after Myrdal published his gloomy prognosis I had occasion to put it to a most practical test.

In the course of the 1948 campaign in which the Truman ticket carried Arkansas, a progressive young World War II veteran, Sid McMath, was elected governor. Nominated in the summer Democratic primaries, he was waiting for the usual pro forma certification in the general election when Dixiecrat leaders came to him with the demand that he agree to an electoral college slate including Thurmond supporters who would cast their votes against the Democratic candidate regardless of the popular vote. If he refused to go along with this unprecedented but technically feasible scheme, he was warned, the Dixiecrats had waiting in the wings a veteran demagogue who would be endowed with a bottomless fund to wage a race-baiting independent campaign against McMath in the November election. As he would demonstrate in his subsequent career, the former marine colonel was about as intimidation-proof as a politician can be; he rejected the proposition in barracks-room language, and nothing came of it. Three years later, when it was his turn to serve as host at the annual Southern Governors Conference, the attempted blackmail still rankled. He had discovered, he told me, that in the entire history of that organization race relations had never been on the agenda, and he thought perhaps I might like to address the governors on the subject.

There was, of course, more to it than that. McMath had become a protégé of Harry Truman, and as an unusually handsome and persuasive representative of the emerging postwar generation of political leaders had gained a place in the inner circles of the Democratic Party. There it was assumed that dissident Southerners would try again to split the party in 1952, and a new and more formidable set of strategists was now maneuvering for position from which they could avoid the third party stigma and lead their followers directly into the Republican fold. Unlike the frenetic ad hoc movement headed by the maverick Strom Thurmond, this effort was led by a man of vast experience and high prestige—James F. Byrnes, who had returned from Olympus embittered at Harry Truman, and, as an elder statesman of seventy-one, had been elected governor of South Carolina virtually by acclamation.

The last gathering of the Southern governors before the 1952 presidential election was of critical tactical importance to the Democratic high command. A previous conference in Charleston had been rigged as an anti-Truman extravaganza; at Hot Springs, in November 1951, McMath was out to reverse the scenario, and the National Committee sent down a team of heavyweights headed by a prime exemplar of loyalty to the party of his fathers, Speaker Sam Rayburn. The national political correspondents, attracted by the possibility of partisan mayhem, turned out in force.

All the governors from the Southern and border states assembled in the old resort town were at least nominal Democrats except Theodore McKeldin of Maryland. I was scheduled to speak at a luncheon session on the opening day. Looking over the text from which I read, I found among the handwritten emendations a change in the acknowledgment of my introduction; I had assumed I would be introduced by McMath, but it turned out that the presiding officer was Gov. Fielding Wright of Mississippi, who had shared the Dixiecrat ticket with Thurmond three years before. At the head table there was no danger of the ice cream melting.

Read thirty years after its delivery the speech comes

through as a dispassionate appeal for moderation, and, indeed, it was so intended. It fairly represented my personal convictions, and was tempered for the occasion only to the extent that I made a conscious effort to avoid gratuitous offense to those in the audience whom I had subjected to caustic editorial comment. I could not, given my assigned topic, ignore the political tension of the divided conference; it necessarily came into the open with my first mention of the issues underlying President Truman's civil rights programs:

We went through a tragic and divisive internal political struggle in 1948. . . . The makings of another great political rebellion are here in this room, and again it is the peculiar institution of the one-party South—with its roots in the basic problem of race relations—that is its cause. I am not personally involved in these matters. I bring them up only to illustrate my major point—that it is vital for Southerners of all political persuasions to develop a positive course for dealing with the peculiar circumstances out of which our peculiar institutions have grown.

Blacks, I pointed out, now had the franchise under federal guarantee, and most Southerners had accepted this as an inevitable and not entirely unwelcome development. The same reaction could be expected in the case of the other true civil rights, which I contended the federal government had no choice but to enforce if the states continued to default on their clear obligation to provide equal protection under law. The only item on the president's agenda to which I conceded legitimate objection was FEPC; I agreed that civil rights did not include the guarantee of the right to a job, which the opponents insisted would be the import of outlawing denial of employment on the basis of race. Still, Southerners had to concede that the Negro had never had, and still did not have, equality of economic opportunity, and it followed that this contributed greatly to general levels of poverty that affected the whole community. We could, therefore, "agree with the stated objective of FEPC while still arguing in good conscience that the method it envisions is both impractical and wrong in principle." I concluded with a warning:

By and large the relationship between the races has been good, but if it is to continue so . . . we cannot turn our backs upon injustice simply because a black man is its victim, nor can we find a safe retreat in the sort of legalistic buck passing that recognizes the existence of an evil but insists it is somebody else's responsibility.

When I finished, the only applause came from the lone Republican, Governor McKeldin; the Democratic loyalists grouped around Sid McMath, and my colleagues at the press table, where the Georgia-bred Washington columnist, Thomas Stokes, shouted "Bravo!" Another Georgian, Herman Talmadge, stalked out at mid-passage. And when John Popham of the *New York Times* asked Governor Byrnes for comment all he got was the shocked response, "Why, I believe I know that boy's family!"

I had no illusion that I was likely to make any public converts. In the presence of the country's leading political writers, no elected official could be expected to indicate approbation of views that not only ran counter to those of his most impassioned and vocal constituents, but were implicitly critical of his own conduct. In private conversation in the course of the social round that followed at least half of the governors conceded that I had correctly analyzed the situation they faced, but even these tended to resent McMath's putting the subject, and me, on the agenda of a gathering which rarely allowed anything of a genuinely controversial nature to openly intrude upon its boozy good fellowship.

The real significance lay in the fact that reaction for the record was so restrained; I was dismissed without comment more often than denounced. And the speech did serve to force the issue of a party bolt to the surface in a fashion that disrupted the behind-the-scenes maneuver planned by Byrnes and Allan Shivers of Texas, who was riding shotgun on the attempted roundup of Republican converts. A year later the South Carolinian and the Texan were the only two Democratic governors to openly declare for the Republican nominee, and Byrnes was unable to carry his own state. The landslide precipitated by the nomination of the wartime hero, Dwight Eisenhower, stopped short of the Southern heartland, reaching only to Florida, Tennessee, Texas, and Virginia.

12

Into the Breach

"*I*t is not easy to draw up a balance sheet on race relations," *The Crisis* noted in summing up the decade of the 1940s. "Yet we feel that Negroes reaped more wheat than tares." The Nobel Peace Prize awarded Ralph Bunche for service in the United Nations was cited as an important symbol, "a personal achievement which redounds to our credit and which racial barriers would have denied Negroes fifteen years ago." Census statistics documented progress on the economic front: the black wage earner received only 52 percent of the white average in 1950, but that was up from less than 40 percent in 1940. Life expectancy for a black male had increased by twelve years during the decade. And of great significance for the future, blacks were staying in school longer; the average was still three years less than that for whites, but increasing numbers were going all the way through the system, with 15 percent of the eighteen-to-twenty-four age group enrolled in college, against 9 percent in 1940.

Black leadership was now solidly lodged in the NAACP, with the middle class beginning to rally to its program of lobbying and court action. In January 1950, when 4,000 delegates from thirty-three states convened in Washington for an emergency mobilization in support of President Truman's civil rights program, almost 3,000 represented NAACP chapters; the CIO sent 383, the AFL 119, B'nai B'rith 350, the American Jewish Congress 185, Americans for Democratic Action 60, and some 200 represented a variety of interracial church groups. The white supporters were still important, but the black leaders were out in front—most notably the mobilization's principal organizer, Roy Wilkins, the soft-spoken Kansas City newspaperman who had succeeded Du Bois as editor of

The Crisis and was now acting secretary during a year-long leave of absence for Walter White.

Wilkins, who was to become the movement's leading political strategist, insisted that the lobbying effort must be concentrated on a single piece of legislation and persuaded the other participating organizations to endorse FEPC as "the most fundamental of all pending civil rights bills." The permanent Leadership Conference on Civil Rights that emerged from the mobilization made a valiant effort to push a mandatory FEPC bill through both houses, but the drive was stymied by the hoary committee system designed to bottle up or denature controversial legislation. The iron-tongued Southern orators in the Senate did not need to carry on a protracted filibuster, only to indicate that they stood ready with a full supply of Thomas Jefferson quotations and potlicker recipes; every test showed that the votes to cut off debate by cloture were not to be had.

"Most of the principals in the parliamentary farce now going on want to keep the FEPC issue alive for campaign purposes in the congressional elections," Arthur Krock wrote in the *New York Times,* suggesting that even President Truman could be counted among the farceurs. *The Crisis* parceled out condemnation with an even hand: ". . . neither the Republicans nor the northern Democrats can blame the Dixiecrats. Cloture on FEPC was blocked by northern and western senators of both parties, nine Republicans and twelve Democrats." That pattern was to prevail until 1957, when an FEPC bill finally made it out of committee and had to be done to death in open voting.

There was not yet enough black political clout to carry the day in the legislative branch, and the growing white liberal support for the civil rights cause was too diffuse to be effectively concentrated on the pressure points that galvanize elected representatives. Roy Wilkins and his fellow lobbyists did better with the executive branch. As the Korean War brought on partial remobilization, President Truman moved to strengthen enforcement of antidiscrimination clauses in government contracts, replacing the World War II machinery with a high-level President's Committee on Government Contract Compliance. And the doughty ex–National Guard captain began pushing the star-spangled commanders of the armed services to get on with the integration he had mandated in a 1948 executive order. In Korea black faces began to appear among the white in combat units all the way down to squad level.

To my considerable surprise, and discomfiture, I was afforded an inside look at the transformation of the Jim Crow army. Upon relief from active duty at the Pentagon after V-J Day I had been automatically reassigned to the army reserve, with my lieutenant colonel's commission transferred from the infantry to the general staff corps. Since I was strictly a wintertime soldier with no interest in maintaining standing in the peacetime army, I paid no attention to the occasional communications from reserve headquarters until one arrived during the Korean buildup ordering me to report to Headquarters, Camp Chaffee, Arkansas, for two weeks' active duty. The reservation near the old frontier post that is now the city of Fort Smith is situated in true redneck country, sprawling across the Arkansas River valley where it separates the Ozark and Ouachita mountains. It occurred to me that if an experiment in mass integration could find acceptance there, it ought to work anywhere.

And it was working, on the post at least. A weekly shipment of a thousand or so raw draftees was received directly from induction stations, mostly in the South and Southwest, and put on a treadmill that would take them through thirteen weeks of rigorous basic training. Since no one at headquarters had any idea what to do with a temporary, supernumerary operations officer, I was turned loose on my own to look over the entire process and see if I could suggest any way to improve it. For one interested in determining how racial intermingling was working out in the military, it was an ideal situation: all doors were open and so far as the officers and men were concerned they were discussing their situation with one of their own, not with a nosy newspaperman.

Upon arrival at Chaffee the draftees were mixed together without racial distinction. A white boy from backcountry Mississippi would find himself in a training battery where a black boy slept in the next bed, bathed under the next shower head, and ate at his elbow in the messhall. Even more shocking, he would not only find himself taking orders from black officers and noncoms, but, in the hard-nosed army way, being dressed down by them. So far as I could see, the racial mixture caused no special tension; at least there was no more evidence of disciplinary problems than I had encountered as we put an all-white infantry division through the same kind of basic training in World War II.

It was, of course, an inherently abnormal situation. All sorts of unpleasant things began happening to these young men as soon as they drew their uniforms, and the sudden absence of the color bar was only one more manifestation of an abruptly changed life-style. Moreover, they had to assume that in this, as in most things that now affected them directly, they had no choice. Once the top military brass had reached a similar conclusion the hierarchical command structure no longer tolerated the foot-dragging subterfuge that had been common when the integration order was first issued.

Off duty there was not much fraternization. In the post exchanges and noncom and officers clubs blacks and whites usually grouped separately—although those who chose to mingle over drinks or meals attracted no special attention. An army post in those days was still a man's world; except for those who arrived with escorts to dine and dance at the clubs there were no women around to complicate social relationships. Off base the two races normally went their separate ways, but in some of Fort Smith's bars and restaurants segregation was waived in the case of men in uniform. According to military police records disturbances there, and in the small towns in the area, were less numerous and less severe than they had been in World War II when Chaffee was all white.

At the bar in the headquarters club I had a chance to check my impressions with the career officers and reserve retreads who clustered there when the sun passed the yardarm. One of the regulars was a Louisiana-bred major who spoke out of his experience as a battalion executive in the lone World War II black division. "This is the only way to handle the problem," he said. "Trying to make a fighting force out of Nigra troops under white officers no longer gets the job done. And if you're going to draft white kids for combat you sure as hell can't let the black ones stay home."

Did he mind living with blacks as equals? "It took a little

getting used to," he said, "but now I hardly notice it. It works that way for most everybody." He doubted that the experience would change a man who really hated blacks, and he didn't think it was going to produce many "nigger-lovers" either. "It seems to me the white kids we're getting now don't have the kind of deep prejudice we grew up with. At least I haven't run into any that had serious difficulty making the adjustment. It shakes them up at first, but they begin to realize that they can work and fight alongside a Nigra, and even under one, without having any close personal contact if that's the way they want it.

"But the main thing is what it does for the Nigras. It gives them the kind of self-confidence a soldier has got to have if he's going to put his ass on the line. And once they get it they average out about like whites—about the same percentage of yardbirds, ordinary joes, brown-noses, and beavers who are going to work hard to go up through the ranks. There're some problems, of course. A commander who wants to discriminate can still get away with it to some extent—and the other side is that Nigras are likely to holler discrimination any time they fall short. But, hell, that's the way it is with whites, too. If your superior officers have got it in for you for whatever reason you're liable to grow old in grade, like I'm doing—and it just ain't human nature for anyone to admit he was passed over for cause."

There were still some who bitched about the new dispensation, talked fondly of the good old days of Jim Crow, and occasionally let their prejudice show in their dealings with blacks. But even these tended to agree with the major that if the army had to accept blacks, desegregation represented the only way to handle the problem. And none expected to see the clock turned back. "The army is slow to change, but it changes," an aging regular colonel said. "I would never have believed I'd live long enough to see the cavalry give up its horses. Letting Negroes come in through the front door is nothing compared to dismounting George Patton."

By 1950 Thurgood Marshall had put in ten years as head of NAACP's Legal Defense and Educational Fund, now maintained in offices apart from those of the main headquarters in New York. This was done ostensibly to establish a separate identity that would qualify the fund for tax-exempt grants, but it was generally believed that it was also intended to protect Walter White from being eclipsed by the tall young lawyer who was beginning to acquire a constituency of his own. White had reason to be concerned. "Before he came along," Charles Thompson, editor of the *Journal of Negro Education* observed, "the principal black leaders—men like Du Bois and James Weldon Johnson and Charles Houston—didn't talk the language of the people. They were upper-class and upper-middle-class Negroes. Thurgood Marshall was *of* the people."

He wasn't, really. What he brought to his leadership role was the kind of classic Southern charm old Cotton Ed Smith used to rouse the common folk. He had had a chance to study the master at close range, for Cotton Ed was a member and regular patron of the Chesapeake Bay Club where the elder Marshall was chief steward and young Thurgood worked as a waiter during college vacations. However, his appeal was neither consciously imitative nor superimposed, but was the natural outgrowth of a gregarious nature. When he was thirty-four a profile in the *Afro-American* described him as a man "who is liked by other men and probably adored by women. He carries himself with an inoffensive self-confidence, and seems to like the life he lives. He wears and looks especially well in tweed suits." And one of his long-time colleagues said: "He loves to have a drink, to tell a story, to pat asses, to be hearty company."

But Thurgood Marshall took with him more than an easy manner and a considerable forensic talent when he traveled the South in the waning years of Jim Crow to fight legal battles, large and small, on behalf of black clients. He won some, and lost some, but in the process he was reminding whites and blacks alike that a Negro had appeared on the scene who could not be fitted into any of the familiar stereotypes. Herbert Hill, the NAACP's white labor affairs expert, noted the symbolic importance: "He was a very courageous figure. He would travel to the courthouses of the South, and folks would come for miles, some of them on muleback or horseback, to see 'the nigger lawyer' who stood up in white men's courtrooms."

If he was anything but a conventional administrator, Marshall nevertheless managed to hold together in working

relationship the feisty young lawyers who manned his headquarters staff, and the distinguished white legal experts who
served as advisors and sometimes co-litigants—as when Prof.
Thomas I. Emerson of the Yale Law School put together a
187-member Committee of Law Teachers Against Segregation
in Legal Education to file an amicus curiae brief in the case that
opened Southern law schools to blacks. In June 1950, forty-
three of these legal counselors joined with fourteen NAACP
state and branch presidents to consider whether to continue the
successful line of cases brought under the separate-but-equal
doctrine, or to move head on against *Plessy.*

There were a good many cautionary voices, including that
of Louis Pollack, later to become dean of the Yale Law School,
who recalled, "I would not have had the courage to go after
segregation per se—and certainly not at the public school
level." Thurgood Marshall had the courage, although he was to
have a good many second thoughts, and he came out of the
planning session with a resolution providing that all future
litigation would "be aimed at obtaining education on a nonseg-
regated basis and that no relief other than that will be
acceptable. . . ." Marshall spelled it out in a public statement:
"We are going to insist on nonsegregation in American education from top to bottom—from law school to kindergarten."

By the end of the year the NAACP was moving ahead with
five public school cases covering the range of segregation laws
still in force in the eighteen jurisdictions where separate schools
were required or permitted. All were to make their way to the
United States Supreme Court, where they would be combined
to provide the basis for the historic ruling that took its shorthand name, *Brown,* from the case that arose in Topeka, Kansas,
and was the first to be filed on appeal.

BRIGGS, originating in Clarendon County, South Carolina,
provided the most striking example of the inherent injustice of
institutional segregation, and of the simple-minded prejudice
that sustained it throughout the rural South. Clarendon, in the
lowcountry midway between Charleston and Columbia, had
been preserved in amber after the end of Reconstruction—a
literal backwater of the Santee River delta where seven out of
ten of the thirty-two thousand residents were black. The

thousand persons who lived in Summerton and the three thousand in Manning could be called urban only by courtesy; the county was dependent on the income from 4,000 farms, of which less than a quarter were owned by those who worked them. The average income for the 4,590 black households recorded in the 1950 census was less than $1,500; only 280 reported $2,000 or more.

It is one of the many ironies of the Clarendon case that it arose initially out of busing—the issue that a quarter century later would provide the code word for white residents of major American cities who, for whatever reason, chose to resist desegregation of the public schools. Here, as in all the rural areas of the nation, buses provided the means by which farm children escaped the limitations of the traditional one-teacher country school. In 1947 there were thirty buses to serve the 2,375 whites who attended twelve consolidated schools, but none for the 6,531 blacks, most of whom were consigned to sixty-one dilapidated one- and two-room shacks scattered along the back roads. The sawmill operator who served as school board chairman responded to a request for transportation of blacks with a clear-cut statement of policy: "We ain't got no money to buy a bus for your nigger children." That attitude prevailed even after black parents scraped together enough to buy a secondhand bus on their own; the school board refused to pay for gasoline to keep it running.

Word of the black crusade for legal redress had spread even to Summerton, however, and Albert DeLaine, a school-teacher and AME minister, organized a NAACP chapter and began looking for a black man who could qualify as parent and taxpayer to support a formal demand for bus service. Harold R. Boulware of Columbia, one of the new breed of black lawyers being turned out at Howard, went into federal court in March 1948, seeking an order limited to equalizing transportation—only to have the case thrown out on a technicality involving the plaintiff's eligibility to bring the case.

But Clarendon was now on the NAACP's agenda, and a year later Thurgood Marshall told DeLaine and his followers that he would himself go back to court on their behalf—but only if they were willing to seek an order equalizing the system from top to bottom, not only buses but buildings, teachers' salaries, and teaching materials. Moreover, he would need not one, but at least twenty plaintiffs, for he had learned by experience that it would require that many to offset the attrition he could expect in the face of the intimidation blacks would be subject to once they were identified with such a lawsuit. The Clarendon group knew what he was talking about; the original plaintiff, a farmer, had had his credit cut off by the local banks and his suppliers, and some of his known supporters had had similar treatment, or had been fired by white employers. Such economic reprisal was to become widespread across the South in the coming era of the Citizens Councils, whose members professed to be squeamish about the kind of physical brutality employed for the same purpose by the Ku Klux Klan.

If the Clarendon suit had remained confined to equalization it probably would have gone into the records as another in the string of NAACP actions that were forcing change upon South Carolina. The school district spent $179 per white child in 1949–50, against $43 per black, and there was an even greater disparity in physical facilities. Stiff-necked school officials had finally recognized that such blatant discrimination was legally indefensible; federal court orders had already resulted in equalizing teachers' salaries in urban districts, and the state was moving to plug the gaps left in the impoverished and recalcitrant rural jurisdictions. In his 1951 inaugural address, Governor Byrnes had declared, "It must be our goal to provide for every child in this state, white or colored, at least a grade school education." He pushed through a 3 percent sales tax to underwrite a $75 million bond issue to equalize facilities, and defended it by saying, "We should do it because it is right. For me that is sufficient reason."

But by the time *Briggs* came to trial in federal court at Charleston, the NAACP had adopted its new policy of going head on against *Plessy*. For that purpose, Clarendon County with its three-to-one black population, pervasive poverty, and general backwardness was hardly the ideal place to launch an experiment in wholesale desegregation. A prudent strategist would have selected a district with a small minority of blacks in an urban area where the doctrine of white supremacy did not have the unusually deep roots it had acquired in the course of

South Carolina's traditional defiance of federal authority. Thurgood Marshall, of course, realized this, and sought to straddle by drafting his pleading so as to emphasize inequality in such a way the court could order equalization even if it rejected the muted argument that segregation was unconstitutional on its face.

But, in another of the splendid ironies that abounded in South Carolina, the state's eastern district was the seat of the federal judge who was the most likely of any in the South to rule against *Plessy,* and was itching to do so. Marshall had won a famous victory in that court in 1948, when the then governor, Olin Johnston, attempted to offset the Supreme Court ruling against the white primary by repealing all state election laws. Judge J. Waties Waring rejected that absurdity, and used the occasion to lecture the state's highest officials: "It is time for South Carolina to rejoin the union. It is time to fall in step with the other states and to adopt the American way of conducting elections. . . ."

THERE is a considerable literature dealing with the manner in which Waties Waring arrived at his racial views, most of it speculating on the psychological aspects of his conversion from the white supremacist faith in which he was born and bred. He was the quintessential Charleston aristocrat of his day, by inheritance a member of the Charleston Light Dragoons, the military company organized before the Revolution, and of the St. Cecilia Society, from which it was said that one could be removed only by death or adultery proved in court. In the eyes of his peers Judge Waring qualified on the second count when late in life he divorced his Charleston-bred Episcopalian wife and became the third husband of a spirited outlander from Detroit. His critics charged that his desegregation rulings were intended to punish the proper Charlestonians who ostracized his new bride. He insisted that prior to the social commotion, as far back as 1945, he had begun to face up to the palpable injustice implicit in the cases of racial discrimination coming before him. As a Southerner of the broadsword persuasion, his duty was clear: ". . . I knew the thing was coming to a showdown someday—and probably was coming in my state. The question arose as to whether I should dodge it or meet it."

Certainly no disposition toward heresy was evident in his career before he ascended the bench in 1941 at the age of sixty-one. He was active in politics as corporation counsel to Burnet Maybank in his days as mayor and political boss of Charleston, and had served as campaign manager for Cotton Ed Smith; the judgeship was his reward when Maybank joined Smith in the Senate. Whether he rose, or was thrust above prevailing racial attitudes, his ascent was rapid once he and his outspoken new wife began to attract the attention of the national media. I did not know him personally, but his nephew, Thomas Waring, editor of that unreconstructed defender of the faith, the *News & Courier,* was an old friend who once remarked to me plaintively, "I wish to God somebody in the United States knew there was a Waring in Charleston besides Uncle Waties."

At a preliminary hearing on the Clarendon case Judge Waring told Thurgood Marshall he would dismiss the present action without prejudice if Marshall would refile so as to directly attack the constitutionality of South Carolina's segregation laws. Marshall could hardly decline. Under federal court procedure the effect of the shift in constitutional emphasis was to require trial by a three-judge panel. Now Waring would share the bench with George Bell Timmerman, whom he privately described as a "rigid segregationist," characterizing himself as an "equally rigid antisegregationist." The man in the middle was John J. Parker, chief judge of the Fourth Circuit Court of Appeals. I knew Judge Parker from my days in Charlotte, where he lived, and I think Waring fairly described him as "an extremely able judge who knows the law, and follows the law, but quite unwillingly in the Southern country." However unwillingly, Judge Parker maintained his reputation for unshakable integrity in handling the critical cases that passed before his court in the years that followed his decision in *Briggs.*

Thurgood Marshall won what he had started out to achieve for his Clarendon clients—an order requiring school officials to equalize the dual system promptly, and to report back to the court within six months on progress toward compliance. But Judge Parker, with Judge Timmerman concurring, cited all the separate-but-equal precedents from *Plessy* forward and held that "it is a late day to say that such

segregation is violative of fundamental constitutional rights.
. . . If conditions have changed so that segregation is no longer
wise, this is a matter for the legislatures and not the courts." In
his dissent, Waties Waring anticipated and summarily rejected
most of the arguments that would occupy the federal courts for
the next three years:

Segregation in education can never produce equality and . . . is an
evil that must be eradicated . . . all the legal guideposts, expert
testimony, common sense and reason point unerringly to the conclusion that the system of segregation in education adopted and practiced in the state of South Carolina must go and must go now.
  Segregation is per se inequality.

FRANKLIN ROOSEVELT stayed in office long enough to make
appointments that changed the character of the Supreme
Court that had frustrated his early New Deal reforms. His first
appointment was a Southerner who, like John Marshall Harlan,
approached the race problem in human terms that led him to
reject the legal abstractions employed by his Yankee colleagues
to condone palpable injustice in the name of judicial restraint.
Hugo Black, briefly and expediently a member of the Ku Klux
Klan at the beginning of his political career as a police judge in
Alabama, had matured into a notably liberal and humane
United States senator. Since joining the Court in 1938 he had
built a reputation as a legal scholar, by his own definition a strict
constructionist who held that the Constitution meant precisely
what it said, which he construed as authorizing the Court to
restrain state action that denied individual rights or permitted
unequal treatment under law. It could be assumed that Justice
Black's view of *Plessy* paralleled that of Judge Waring.

This was also true of William O. Douglas, a congenital
maverick who was to become my close friend. But beyond these
two, the reaction of the justices to the school desegregation
issue was far more difficult to predict. When the five cases
came before the divided and fractious court in June 1952,
their import was unmistakable. The constitutional issue now
was drawn so sharply that a decision by the Supreme Court
upholding the majority finding in *Briggs* would have the effect
of reinvigorating *Plessy* just at the point when segregation was
beginning to yield in the upper reaches of the educational

structure under pressure toward equalization. At the same time, the complacency with which the Southern leaders had greeted the initial school cases had been shattered by the militant stance the NAACP assumed in *Briggs,* and by the psychological and sociological evidence introduced to support the argument that segregated schools diminished the learning ability of black children by branding them with a badge of inferiority.

This kind of thing had been dismissed as egghead sophistry back in the days when I covered the South Carolina legislature. As the ripple effect of the Maryland decision opening that state's law school to a black student reached Columbia, the veteran speaker of the House, Sol Blatt, announced that he was prepared to put through legislation establishing a law school at the black state college in Orangeburg—the device actually carried out in Texas. I asked if that wouldn't be a pretty expensive way of taking care of a few black students. Blatt replied, "Not at all. We'll just hire a nigra lawyer for a faculty and give them a Sears Roebuck catalogue for a library."

A decade later Jimmy Byrnes took the prospect of desegregation far more seriously—so much so, he sent his former colleagues on the Court a characteristically South Carolinian message of warning and defiance. After pushing through his school-equalization bond issue he felt he had done his duty, and if the federal courts now chose to outlaw segregation, he announced, he would order the schools closed. A few months later a referendum on the issue carried by two to one, giving the legislature standby power to take such action. This time, Jonathan Daniels observed in the *Raleigh News & Observer,* South Carolina was not merely threatening to secede from the union, but from civilization.

To argue his state's case before the Supreme Court, Byrnes hired the best lawyer he could find—John W. Davis, senior partner of the Wall Street firm of Davis, Polk, Wardwell, Sunderland & Krindl, formerly Woodrow Wilson's solicitor general and ambassador to the Court of St. James's, and 1924 Democratic presidential nominee. There would be other counsel arguing the case on behalf of the several states involved, but it was a foregone conclusion that South Carolina's advocate would take the lead.

Davis entertained no doubt that *Plessy* would be upheld. Never, he told his colleagues, had he taken a case to the Supreme Court with precedent so heavily stacked on his side. Segregation had been "so often and so pointedly declared by the highest authorities it should no longer be regarded as open to debate," he wrote. "Only an excess of zeal can explain the present challenge." And he dismissed the evidence presented in the court below: "I have never read a drearier lot of testimony than that furnished by the so-called psychological and educational experts." But it was precisely this esoteric documentation of the psychic damage done by segregation that weighed heaviest with the Court as it wrestled with the five consolidated cases for more than two years before it could pull itself together and render a verdict.

IN so portentous a ruling it was essential to have as nearly unanimous a court as possible, but when the justices assembled for their first conference after the oral arguments it was clear that there was no majority on either side. The count, as best it could be reconstructed on the basis of the fragmentary evidence that escaped the Court's traditional confidentiality, indicated that four justices—Black, Douglas, Burton, and Minton—were prepared to overturn *Plessy*. One, Stanley Reed of Kentucky, was prepared to uphold. The others were uncommitted and deeply troubled.

The jurisprudential problem of upsetting a long-settled precedent vexed the scholars among the brethren, and sharpened the issue of judicial restraint that by 1952 left the Court divided in 82 percent of its opinions. But far more compelling was the question of how the Court could implement a desegregation decree in the face of the resistance it could expect. That was a matter no one on either side of the argument had yet faced. Elected officials in the Southern states simply rejected the possibility and saw political hazard in its mere discussion. On the other side, the legal crusaders of the NAACP were carried away by the righteousness of their cause. Robert Carter, who helped argue *Briggs* before Judge Waring, recalled the mood as the young black lawyers girded for battle:

We really had the feeling that segregation itself was the evil—and not a symptom of the deeper evil of racism. Thus, we attached no importance then to the ratio of blacks to whites in the Clarendon schools. It wasn't our concern to figure out how integration would work. We minimized the social consequences in the immediate environment—that wasn't the issue for us. The box we thought we were in was integration itself, and most of the nation saw it that way, too.

At a rehearing on *Briggs* Judge Timmerman asked Marshall what he thought would happen if the Court followed his suggestion that desegregation be ordered as the only means of obtaining equality. Did he actually propose that twenty-five hundred black children be moved into schools occupied by three hundred whites? "If they were already filled up, wouldn't there be a problem of sitting somebody on somebody else's lap?" The best answer Marshall could offer was that some of the white children might be shifted, "mixing them, or sharing the school equally." The implications of that vague response were, of course, the heart of the matter so far as the resistant Southern leaders were concerned—and they could no longer be blinked by those who agreed that justice required an end to segregated public schools.

Largely at the insistence of Justice Frankfurter the Supreme Court decided to buy time by calling for additional briefs. The matter of implementation was becoming more disturbing to the justices the more they examined it. Philip Elman, the assistant solicitor general who prepared the government's brief for the rehearing, was a former clerk to Justice Frankfurter, and his pipeline into the Court's inner chambers was about as reliable as any in Washington. Here is his graphic reconstruction of what went on there as Hugo Black insisted that his brethren not only must overturn *Plessy,* but must face up to the consequences:

Hugo was telling the brethren that you cannot constitutionally defend *Plessy,* but if and when they overruled it would mean the end of Southern liberalism for the time being. The Bilbos and Talmadges would come even more to the fore, overshadowing the John Sparkmans and Lister Hills. The guys who talked nigger would be in charge, there would be riots, and the army might have to be called out—He was scaring the shit out of the Justices, especially Frankfurter and Jackson, who didn't know how the Court could enforce a ruling against *Plessy.*

Elman's brief sought to ease these fears by providing those who wanted to rule for the black plaintiffs a means of withholding immediate relief in cases that might precipitate an epidemic of civil disobedience. He devised the concept of "deliberate speed," noting that "a reasonable period of time will obviously be required to permit formulation of new provisions [for] orderly and progressive transition." Twenty-five years later he looked back upon his handiwork as the proudest accomplishment of his legal career, but noted ruefully that "when we filed our brief in early December, I went on the NAACP's shit list as a gradualist. . . ."

He was not alone in that distinction. I earned a place on the list at a conference at Howard University where the split between black militants and accommodationists came into the open. The title of the three-day colloquium treated the pending Supreme Court decision as foregone: "The Courts and Racial Integration in Education." I opened my address at a crowded evening session by acknowledging that "a new generation of Negro leaders, far more militant than their predecessors, could not be faulted for seizing upon the school issue as an opportunity to exploit the whole of their racial grievances." But, as the only white Southerner on the program, I felt obliged to challenge the proposition set forth in the colloquium's prospectus: "Negroes are determined, and all but the most reactionary whites are resigned to the fact, that enforced segregated schools must go in the very near future." On the contrary, I said, "a large majority of Southern whites are far from resigned to the prospect of terminating the dual school system, and blacks delude themselves if they think Jimmy Byrnes was not speaking for his constituency when he threatened last-ditch resistance." Worse still, they might undercut their prospect of winning their case in the Supreme Court if they did not recognize that the justices were wrestling with the "eternal problem of every jurist—should a court hand down a decision that may very well be, in view of popular opinion, unenforceable?"

There were a few other cautionary voices, mostly among the minority of white participants. John P. Frank of Yale Law School noted that "a judge cannot be blamed if he shrinks from precipitating a race riot." Will Maslow, general counsel of the

American Jewish Congress, suggested that it might be better to ease off on the confrontation in the Deep South and continue to chip away at segregation in the border states.

But Thurgood Marshall and his men were committed, and they had powerful support among the black leadership. A ringing reply to the moderates was given by James Nabrit of Howard Law School:

Shall the Negro child be required to wait for his constitutional rights until the white South is educated, industrialized, and ready to confer these rights on his children's children? . . . Wherever the Negro is laboring under constitutional disabilities in the South, there is the best place to attack. The attack should be waged with the most devastating forces at hand. . . . The Supreme Court will have to worry over community attitudes. Let us worry about the problem of pressing for our civil rights. . . . Let the Supreme Court take the blame if it dares to say to the entire world, "Yes, democracy rests on a legalized caste system. Segregation of races is legal." Make the Court choose. . . .

The Court would choose, but it would take a while to get rid of the problem of community attitudes.

13

⚘

On the Political Front

*R*obert McCormick Figg, Jr., the Charleston lawyer who defended South Carolina in the Claren-
don County suit, noted that his distinguished associate, John
W. Davis, always thought the case would be viewed as a strictly
legal matter. "I don't think he ever realized the swirl of social
and political events affecting it," Figg said. This was true of
most of the nation's leaders, public and private, despite the fact
that the Court had signaled its intention to reexamine the basic
issue of segregation when it set oral argument for the month
following the 1952 general election. In the presidential contest
that was to have a profound bearing on its outcome the
NAACP's frontal assault on *Plessy* didn't draw even a passing
mention.

Despite the best efforts of Adlai Stevenson, perhaps the
most eloquent and thoughtful presidential candidate ever
fielded by the Democrats, the soporific campaign of his
Republican opponent, Dwight D. Eisenhower, not only
carried the day but swept the boards. In his biography of
Stevenson, *A Prophet in His Own Country*, Kenneth S. Davis
included a brief chapter entitled "The Issues of the '52 Campaign." He could identify only three differences in the stated
positions of the candidates that could be defined with any
clarity: foreign policy, state versus federal ownership of tide-
land oil lands, and the use of humor in politics, a hallmark of
the Stevenson effort the GOP managers deplored as unseemly.
"Republican strategists transformed the contest largely into one
of synthetic personalities: Eisenhower as hero, Truman as
villain, Stevenson as 'eggheaded' clown," Davis wrote. "To do so
they employed public relations techniques on an unprecedented scale." Thus politics entered fully into the electronic age,

with television now sufficiently advanced to augment radio —and to impress the demands and possibilities of the visual medium upon a new breed of professional campaign tacticians.

There was nothing in the scenario that required Eisenhower even to take notice of the black minority. Its limited vote had long since been written off by the Republican strategists, who had discovered that by handing it over to the New Dealers they created a divisive internal issue for the political enemy. This was demonstrated again at the Democratic National Convention in Chicago in July. By the time the Democrats convened, the Stevenson bandwagon was rolling—despite his insistence that, as a declared candidate for reelection as governor of Illinois, he was not in the running. This seeming coyness irritated President Truman, who had offered Stevenson his blessing, and brought in contenders from both flanks—Alben Barkley and Richard Russell on the Right, and Averell Harriman and Estes Kefauver on the Left. But the center was wide open, and by the time I arrived in Chicago to cover the convention it seemed virtually certain that Stevenson would get the draft he was generally believed to be seeking.

The North-South skirmishing began, as usual, at the preconvention meeting of the Platform Committee. The Democratic national chairman, Frank McKinney, announced wistfully that the primary purpose of the platform would be to "remove the disunity that existed in 1948." But Francis Biddle, chairman of Americans for Democratic Action, claimed he had 654 delegates lined up to support a civil rights plank at least as strong as the one that prompted the Dixiecrat bolt. The showdown shaped up in the Credentials Committee, where Govs. Allan Shivers of Texas and J. P. Coleman of Mississippi were something less than forthright in responding to demands for an advance pledge of support for the nominees of the convention. Although the "loyalty oath" carryover from the Dixiecrat debacle did not directly involve Stevenson, the credentials fight had become the principal weapon of those who were trying to head off his nomination.

A measure of the mounting tension came when Eleanor Roosevelt appeared at a ceremonial session. She received a standing ovation, with two conspicuous exceptions: Governor Shivers's Texas delegation remained seated, and Sen. Harry F.

Byrd of Virginia stalked out of the hall. On Thursday, when the roll call for nominations was due, a challenge from the floor produced a ruling by Speaker Sam Rayburn that the South Carolina, Virginia, and Louisiana delegations had not yet satisfied the convention's rule calling for an unconditional pledge of support for the ticket. I watched the confused skirmishing that followed with particular interest, for Jimmy Byrnes had now assumed a leading role, and I could see reemerging here the strategy of the Hot Springs governors' conference.

As the evening wore on, Byrnes took up his microphone to assure the delegates that in his state, as in the others whose standing was at issue, the convention's nominees would be on the ballot—but, as had Governor Battle of Virginia, he refused under protracted cross-examination to say whether they would appear as nominees of the state Democratic Party. Just at the point where Byrnes testily announced that he would not answer any further questions, a fire broke out in the paper-strewn aisle beside the South Carolina standard. When the blaze was safely extinguished, and the momentary panic had subsided, the little South Carolinian arose to the last point of personal privilege he would ever claim at a Democratic conclave: "Mr. Chairman, I want to announce that I did not set the place on fire."

In the early skirmishing the Illinois delegation voted 45 to 15 against seating Virginia. But the Pennsylvania delegation, also supporting Stevenson, voted 57 to 13 in Virginia's favor. The Harriman and Kefauver floor managers, now united in support of the Tennessean, began to work both sides of the issue—using the Illinois vote to inflame the Southerners, pointing to Pennsylvania as a warning to those who feared a sellout on civil rights. "It suddenly dawned on us what was happening," Jack Arvey said later. The only chance of nominating Kefauver was to reduce the total of convention votes by making demands on pro-Stevenson Southern delegations that would force a wholesale walkout.

At 8:50 P.M. Arvey reversed the Illinois vote to 52 to 8 in favor of seating Virginia, declaring that Stevenson's home state "had confidence in Governor Battle." This was the signal to the party regulars, and for more than an hour the loudspeakers boomed out notices of delegate switches. At 9:55 P.M. the recording clerk announced 615 votes in favor of seating Virginia, 529 against, 86 not voting. The regulars had prevailed, and the indefatigable Estes Kefauver's run for the presidency was postponed for another four years.

As in 1948, there were few black faces to be seen among the sweating wheelhorses who wrestled for delegates on the crowded convention floor. The race issue was still only a symbolic device for rallying the party's opposing factions.

FIVE years and more of wooing by leaders of both parties preceded the nomination of Dwight Eisenhower at the 1952 Republican convention. Yet I find little in the voluminous literature produced by those involved in that unprecedented political courtship to indicate that anyone seriously sought to sound out the potential candidate's attitude toward the black minority. In the course of the campaign the token black in the entourage, E. Frederick Morrow, discussed with him the problem he faced with black voters because of his congressional testimony against integration of the armed forces, in which he had declared the services unready "spiritually, philosophically, or mentally to absorb blacks and whites together." He told Morrow he had been influenced in that judgment by his field commanders, most of whom were Southern, but confessed that his own view had been shaped by assignment to command black National Guard troops as a fledgling second lieutenant: "I'm afraid that association with colored troops early in my career may have unconsciously obscured any positive thinking on the matters for years." Morrow's sad chronicle of his own subsequent service as the first black to hold an administrative position in the White House, *Forty Years a Guinea Pig*, indicates that after the general left the sheltered life of the professional soldier nothing happened to raise his consciousness in racial matters above the level of a kind of petulant neutrality.

After the election was over a sympathetic Eisenhower biographer, Robert J. Donovan, wrote: "When the administration took office it was plunged into the whirlpool of Korea, China, the budget, etc. . . . Somehow no one gave much thought to the special problem of the Negro, and practically nothing was done about this politically very sensitive matter." Subsequent events were to demonstrate that it probably would have made little difference had someone in the inner circle raised the question. An unsympathetic biographer, Marquis Childs, recalled that the general had reacted to the 1948 overtures of the Democratic liberals with a combination of amusement and annoyance, telling a reporter that he was "a strong believer in states' rights, and if he had to name any single individual with whose outlook he agreed it would probably be Senator Harry F. Byrd of Virginia."

For obvious reasons Adlai Stevenson had no disposition to smoke out his opponent in the course of the campaign, since his own overriding problem was to minimize an issue that could unglue the uneasy Democratic coalition. Stevenson's personal record was as pro-Negro as that of any major figure in contemporary political life. As far back as 1939 he had served as the first chairman of the Civil Rights Committee of the Chicago Bar Association. He had participated in the fight for a strong civil rights plank at the 1948 Democratic convention, and had worked hard for a state FEPC bill. But he maintained an accommodating approach to the Southern wing of the party. His choice of Sen. John Sparkman of Alabama as his running mate salted the wounds of doctrinaire New Dealers, already lacerated by the skirmishing over the nomination. Distress was particularly acute among the party intellectuals, who were at once attracted by Stevenson's highly literate style and sophisticated approach to the issues, and repelled by his patrician manner, which they suspected bespoke an innate conservatism. This mixed reaction was prevalent among the bright young men who flocked, by invitation or on their own motion, to Springfield, where the presidential campaign headquarters was spread around in makeshift office space in the vicinity of the governor's mansion.

The Republicans, with a popular hero to carry their banner, plus the traditional affinity of the wealthy for their party, could count on unlimited campaign funds and the active support of what Stevenson called "the one-party press." The primary Stevensonian weapon, of necessity, would be his oratory—the eloquence that had attracted the literate public's attention when the national audience was first treated to his evocative phrasing in the course of his televised acceptance speech, with its pledge to "talk sense to the American people."

He had some help with that speech, but mostly it was his—bearing the unmistakable imprint of one who cherished his own special way with words. This would be the case with many of the utterances for which he is remembered, but no man could possibly compose the torrent of oratory he would have to spout as he barnstormed the country. Stevenson never was reconciled to the evident necessity of ghost-written campaign material. "For the first time I am suddenly confronted with the ugly reality that I cannot hope to do my writing in toto myself any longer, and I shudder at what it means, psychologically for me, and publicly for the record," he wrote to his Princeton classmate, T. S. Matthews, editor of *Time*. Reluctantly he agreed to the recruitment of a small corps of speech writers who, out of deference, called themselves "researchers." They were given working quarters in, of all unlikely places, the Springfield Elks Club.

John Bartlow Martin, the most discerning of Stevenson's biographers, was in the group that came to be called "The Elks" after their habitat. Prominent among them were John Kenneth Galbraith, the Harvard economist; John Fischer, editor of *Harper's*; Bernard De Voto, the historian; David Cohn, the Mississippi essayist; Willard Wirtz, then a law professor at Northwestern; Robert Tufts, on leave from the policy-planning staff at the State Department; Herbert Agar of the *Louisville Courier-Journal*; and Eric Hodgins of *Fortune*.

The most productive Elk was Arthur Schlesinger, Jr., the brilliant young Harvard historian who played a key role in the founding of Americans for Democratic Action. His energy and drive made him de facto straw boss of the wordsmiths, and he directed his effort toward weaning Stevenson away from the complex, philosophical style he favored. This was more than a matter of semantics. Schlesinger shared the conviction of many liberals that the Democrats could win only by declaring unstinting support for the positions staked out under the New and Fair Deals. It followed that he considered Stevenson too pro-Southern and insufficiently committed to civil rights and the interests of organized labor.

Schlesinger wrote in a memorandum to his brother Elks: "What Adlai must understand is that the central domestic issue is still the fight between the business community and the rest of the country. . . . All of us will have to do a lot of work on him in the next few months." If he was not entirely successful in reorienting the candidate's moderate approach, it was not for lack of trying. Among Stevenson's published papers is a dispatch from the campaign trail dated September 25: "Mr. Schlesinger—For Pete's sake please tell the writers to cut down on the *attack* stuff."

A North-South split among the "researchers" was inevitable; it came when Cohn withdrew from the Elks Club and established a redoubt at the St. Nicholas Hotel where he was joined by Agar and Hodgins on what the others called "the moonlight and magnolia team." When the first swing through the South was scheduled, Cohn asked me to come to Springfield for a few days and help out with the writing chores. I had planned to join the campaign press corps for the pass through Louisiana, Florida, and Tennessee, and agreed to spend a few days at headquarters before picking up the caravan at St. Louis.

My first personal encounter with Stevenson, over a ritual toddy at the fusty old governor's mansion, confirmed the favorable impression I had taken away from the Chicago convention. He was one of the great conversationalists of the day—witty, perceptive, often ironic at his own expense—the style of his private discourse echoing that of his public address. But there was also a winning, unbuttoned informality about him, and a curiosity and willingness to listen rare among politicians of his stature.

He emphasized in that first conversation that he would take no position on civil rights before any audience that he wasn't prepared to take before all, and warned that it would be a waste of time to try to shape a policy statement to fit any set of regional prejudices. His greatest campaign asset, he felt, was the fact that the convention draft strategy had gained the nomination without burdening him with obligations to any political leader or special interest. This was true enough, but it did not insulate him against the pulling and hauling of the contending factions now represented within his entourage, nor did it help in his dealings with politicians whose support he needed. His own deeply held view on racial matters was not satisfactory to either side. The eastern leaders were hardly pleased when he appeared before their followers to deplore what he called the coercive "sledgehammer approach" to civil rights, contending that in the end it would be harmful to both races. And his Confederate antecedents, which permitted him to turn up kinfolk everywhere he went in the South, did not allay the suspicions of such political satraps as his cousin, Richard Russell of Georgia, who remained convinced that there must have been some kind of civil rights deal between Stevenson and Harry Truman.

He had found the national black leaders who came to call at Springfield surprisingly restrained in their views, he said, most of them privately rejecting the militancy that characterized much of the civil rights rhetoric in the North. They, as did I, came away from one of these soul-searching sessions with the candidate convinced that his purpose was, as Martin described it, "above all, to try to serve as a bridge between what was at that time presented as a question not of black versus white, but of North versus South, to use the political process to resolve what he already recognized as the most divisive issue in modern political life." Here the high road of conscience coincided with the low road of practical politics, for if that bridge could not be maintained there was no chance that a Democrat could be elected president.

I STAYED in Springfield a few days to work with Cohn on the speeches scheduled for Florida and Tennessee, and then moved over to St. Louis to sign on the press plane for the trip South. There I joined Ralph McGill, and in the course of the evening we ran into James Hicks of Harlem's *Amsterdam News*, one of only two black reporters among the scores following the candidate. Hicks had just discovered that New Orleans's segregation laws had prevented the campaign's advance man from booking him into the Roosevelt Hotel, where the party was to stay the next night. Arrangements had been made to put him up at the home of a black college professor—and the more Hicks thought about this the angrier he became.

Next morning, on the flight to Oklahoma City for a luncheon speech, McGill and I sat with Hicks. He had by then made up his mind that he would not accept the separate accommodation, but would make a public issue of it and withdraw from the campaign entourage. When we landed I warned Arthur Schlesinger, who was on the candidate's plane, that there was trouble ahead, and found a private telephone where I could call a fellow Greenvillian, George Chaplin, who had been my city editor on the *Piedmont* and was now editor of the *New Orleans Item*. I urged George to call the hotel manager and persuade him to simply ignore the local Jim Crow law— assuring him that two black reporters would never be noticed in the confusion that would attend the arrival of two planeloads of bedraggled journalists and politicians. George sighed, and said yes, under almost any other circumstances that could be done—but the owner of the Roosevelt was a dedicated Dixiecrat who would be delighted with the opportunity to embarrass Stevenson.

On the flight to New Orleans McGill made his last, best effort to placate Jimmy Hicks. How would it be, he asked, if he and Ashmore stayed with him at the professor's house? It didn't work, and when the press room was established at the hotel, Hicks went there to announce his protest departure. William Flanagan, Stevenson's press secretary, took the rap—saying that he was responsible for the arrangement and that the candidate knew nothing of it. Before any of the reporters could get to Stevenson we were all on our way to a rally in Beauregard Square. The subject of the speech was foreign trade, encapsulated in some of Dave Cohn's lacy rhetoric. It included the mandatory bow to the platform in this fashion: "As you know, I stand on the Democratic Party platform with reference to minority rights. I have only one observation to make on this subject; one that must sadden you as it saddens me. It is that, after two thousand years of Christianity, we need discuss it at all." Most of the correspondents wound up in the Latin Quarter after the speech, and Jimmy Hicks's protest got little more than a paragraph or two in the national press.

Next day there were two stops in Florida, and a major evening address in Nashville, to which I was the principal contributor. I have always appreciated Martin's appraisal; he managed to approve my effort even while reflecting the Elks's bias against moonlight and magnolias: "Like all Southern speeches it was very long and contained a recitation of Stevenson's Southern ancestry; the crowd expected and liked it . . . it was a skillful speech."

I left the campaign party at Nashville, and had no more to do with the 1952 effort except to send along an occasional suggested speech passage by mail. In retrospect, I doubt that Stevenson's position on civil rights helped or hurt. If he did not emphasize it, he certainly did not conceal it, and those on both sides who were sensitive to the subject surely knew where he stood. As on other issues where passionate advocates were pressing him to take positions that offended his essentially moderate nature, his reaction was to stubbornly insist on saying what he had been warned his audience didn't want to hear. "I should justly earn your contempt if I talked one way in the South and another elsewhere," he said in endorsing the civil rights platform before a segregated audience in Richmond. So he went out of his way to praise his running mate, John Sparkman, when he addressed Averell Harriman's followers at the Democratic State Convention in New York. He spoke his true feeling, I think, at Richmond: "I do not attempt to justify the unjustifiable, whether it is anti-Negroism in one place, anti-Semitism in another—or, for that matter, anti-Southernism in many places. And neither can I justify self-righteousness anywhere."

He was correctly identified in the title of a critical biography by Bert Cochran, *Adlai Stevenson: Patrician Among the Politicians*. In his rigidly class-conscious study, Cochran wrote: "For Stevenson, as for Lincoln, the question was to maintain the unity of White America; justice for the Negro was a matter of *noblesse oblige*." He was correct, I think, in the first part of his appraisal, but was led astray in the second by his antielitist bias. Martin was much closer to the mark when he wrote that Stevenson "did have a deep private commitment to civil liberties, but a much shallower one to civil rights. . . . As the years passed, Stevenson's positions became increasingly liberal. But he was never a dedicated—or even a convinced—liberal ideologue. He remained skeptical."

IN the early months of 1953 the *Brown* case remained in suspense before the Supreme Court and finally was put over for another year as Chief Justice Vinson issued a call for additional briefs as a means of assuring that the views of the new administration would be heard. It seems probable that Vinson was disposed to uphold *Plessy*, but death intervened, on September 8, before his position ever became a matter of record. President Eisenhower had pledged the first vacancy on the Court to a senior Republican who had withdrawn his own presidential bid to make way for the general's unanimous nomination. Earl Warren resigned his office as governor of California and on October 5 was sworn in as the fourteenth chief justice of the United States.

The appointment met with general approval, but aroused little enthusiasm. "Court observers," the Associated Press reported, "voiced doubt that Warren's ascent to the bench will change the balance of that body—now considered generally conservative." The liberal California journal, *Frontier*, expressed the hope that the mild-mannered career politician "may become, if not a great Chief Justice, a good Chief Justice who will serve as a moderating influence on the rampant reactionary trend of the times." No one—certainly not the man who appointed him—would have dared predict that the advent of the tall, bulky Californian would change the course of the Court's snarled deliberations, and of the nation's history.

It was becoming evident, however, that the ruling on *Brown* would have a momentous effect on the dual school system of seventeen states whether or not *Plessy* survived. On the basis of argument already heard, it could be assumed that at the minimum, the Court would require absolute equalization of school facilities at all levels and would instruct the lower courts to retain jurisdiction to see that the requirement was carried out in good faith. This would suddenly impose upon segregated school districts heavy financial and administrative burdens they had previously avoided and were ill-prepared to handle. If the decision went the other way, and the Court required outright merger of the separate systems, the emotionally loaded problems confronting responsible school officials would be without precedent in the history of public education.

Early in the year the possible consequences of the pending ruling became the subject of exploration by officers and staff of the Fund for the Advancement of Education, the agency created by the Ford Foundation to dispense the millions it had earmarked for conventional educational institutions. They found, not surprisingly, that there was little, if any, reliable information on the actual disparities within the dual systems.

Statistics on black schools had been neglected, and often doctored, for so many years the public records provided no basis for an accurate estimate of the costs of equalization.

The board of directors of the Fund, chaired by retired Supreme Court Justice Owen J. Roberts, concluded at its spring meeting that the need for a new, comprehensive look at the structure of biracial education was urgent and, in view of the apparent paralysis of public agencies, a proper object of private philanthropy. The Fund's president, Clarence H. Faust, and vice-president, Alvin C. Eurich, were authorized to offer a blank check to any appropriate institution in the South that would undertake the assignment on the crash basis required to produce results by the time the Court made its ruling—now anticipated at the end of the 1953–54 term. It was soon evident that the project was too politically charged to obtain the sanction of any university administration in the region, although there were a number of competent scholars who were willing and anxious to participate as individuals.

I had come to know Faust and Eurich during their visits to Arkansas, where they had enlisted the support of Lewis Webster Jones, the state university president, for a somewhat less explosive experiment in teacher education. I saw them again when they were making the rounds seeking a home for the dual school project, and I agreed that it deserved the Fund's highest priority. In June, vacationing in Canada with my wife and daughter, I received a phone call from Faust asking me to come to New York as soon as possible to discuss the latest development on the school front.

I arrived at Fund headquarters to find that the development was an urgent request that I sign on as director of the project, which would dispense with the usual institutional base and be sustained directly by the foundation. My lack of scholarly credentials was brushed aside; all the experts I could possibly use were available and would be recruited and retained by the Fund; Philip Coombs, the secretary-treasurer, would be delegated to act on the Fund's behalf; a coordinating staff would be provided. I had, it seemed, become a volunteer for hazardous academic duty, not by stepping forward three paces, but by standing still while everyone else stepped back three.

Back in Little Rock I laid the proposition before J. N. Heiskell and Hugh Patterson. I had warned the Fund that our staff situation was such that I could not take a leave of absence without dumping an undue burden of editorial policy making back on Mr. J. N., and that if I took on the assignment I would have to handle it with one hand. Even so, it would entail a substantial diversion of time and energy. Moreover, the project was highly controversial and was bound to increase the disaffection of *Gazette* subscribers and advertisers already upset by our moderate racial stance and recurring bouts with the Dixiecrats.

Put that way, Mr. J. N. said, with one of his patented sly grins, it was not a matter of principle but of business, and he would defer to the publisher. "Of course it is," Patterson replied. "It would be an act of fiscal imprudence if we didn't insist that Ashmore accept. When that Supreme Court decision comes down every newspaper in the South is going to have to deal with the consequences, and we'll have the best-informed editor available—at Ford Foundation expense."

THERE was now something less than twelve months in which to complete the massive survey and prepare a report on the findings—a prospect that alarmed academics almost as much as the certainty of political fall-out. Nevertheless, we were able to locate some forty men and women on various campuses who were qualified to sift through the available data and extract additional facts from those who processed the scanty public records in the state departments of education and key local school districts. Most of these were rounded up by Philip Hammer, who took leave from his post as executive officer of the National Planning Association's Committee of the South to head up the coordinating staff established in Atlanta. Serving with him were Harold Fleming of the Southern Regional Council; John A. Griffin, then on the faculty at Emory University; Mozell Hill, a black sociologist at Atlanta University; and Ruth A. Morton of the American Friends Service Committee.

Field studies of non-Southern schools that had recently experienced transition to integration were assigned to Robin Williams of Cornell; an appraisal of the integration experience in Southern universities to Guy B. Johnson of the University of North Carolina; legal research to Dean Robert Leflar of the

University of Arkansas Law School; demographic and economic studies to Ernst Swanson and John Griffin of Emory and
John Maclachlan of the University of Florida; and an examination of public school administration to Truman Pierce of the
George Peabody College for Teachers. Each was authorized to
sign on as many assistants as he could use.

The charge to all of these was clear enough: "The Fund
will not undertake to argue the case for or against segregation
in public education, and in no sense will it become involved as
an advocate on either side of the issues now pending before the
Supreme Court." But it was, of course, impossible to insulate
the project against the qualms of the nervous school officials
with whom we dealt. When I explained to a veteran Arkansas
politician what I was up to, he replied, "Son, it sounds to me
like you have got yourself in the position of a man running for
sonofabitch without opposition." Toward the close of the project we invited the chief state school officers to meet with us in
Atlanta to review the summary statistics we had compiled from
their own records. In order to obtain their acceptance we had
to hold the meeting in an isolated suburban resort and guarantee that the session would not only be secret, but that in case of
a leak we would deny it had ever taken place.

I had begun the project assuming that my principal
obligation would be to edit the several volumes scheduled to be
published by the University of North Carolina Press. But it
soon became evident that my scholarly colleagues were never
going to get their material in shape for publication in time to be
of use to those who would be immediately affected by the Court
decision. So I found myself functioning as a rewrite man, with
Harold Fleming providing invaluable assistance in ferreting
through the voluminous research to extract portions I could
condense, put into lay language, and arrange in a coherent
summation. The result was a three hundred-page volume, *The
Negro and the Schools,* published the day before the Supreme
Court handed down *Brown* on May 17, 1954. To make that
deadline UNC Press established, and I suspect still holds, the
course record for breakneck scholarly publication.

We did manage to hold to the neutral role enjoined by the
Fund, and the summary volume was accepted as authoritative
even by so jaundiced a reader as Tom Waring of the *Charleston*

News & Courier. But it seemed to me that anyone who read my account of the path the South had followed since the beginning of public education late in the last century, and considered the implications of the changing demographic patterns revealed by the pages of tables and graphs, could not doubt that time was running out on the rigidly segregated society hammered into place eighty years before. In the concluding paragraph of *The Negro and the Schools,* I wrote:

In the long sweep of history the public school cases before the Supreme Court may be written down as the point at which the South cleared the last turning in the road to reunion—the point at which finally, and under protest, the region gave up its peculiar institutions and accepted the prevailing standards of the nation at large as the legal basis for its relationship with its minority race. This would not in itself bring about any great shift in Southern attitudes, nor even any far-reaching immediate changes in the pattern of bi-racial education. But it would re-define the goal the Southern people, white and Negro, are committed to seek in the way of democracy.

What the Fund chose to call the "Ashmore Project" probably had little, if any, effect in shaping the initial opinion of the Court, although Justice Roberts, who wrote the foreword, told me he wouldn't be surprised if copies of the galley proofs wound up on the bedside tables of his former colleagues. It did, however, come to play a significant role in the jockeying for position that followed after the Court postponed issuing implementing orders for another year and called for new briefs from the parties. In the relative calm that followed, the question of how, and how soon, the schools would be desegregated was finally, and unavoidably, open for discussion. We had provided the only available handbook.

14

The Great Default

*T*he second chief justice of the United States, John Marshall, established the right of judicial review, giving the Supreme Court final word in defining and limiting the constitutional powers of the other branches of the federal government and the states. He promptly ran afoul President Andrew Jackson when the Court ruled that Georgia had no right to remove the Cherokee nation from ancestral lands guaranteed by treaty. The old Indian fighter sat on his hands, refusing to use the powers of his office to exact compliance from the resistant Georgians. "John Marshall has rendered his decision," Old Hickory is reputed to have said. "Now let him enforce it." More than a century later, President Dwight Eisenhower, aghast at the *Brown* decision, said privately that the worst damnfool mistake he ever made was putting Earl Warren in charge of the Supreme Court. And he too sat on his hands as long as he could.

The president's chagrin at the position taken by the chief justice was a measure of the political naiveté produced by a lifetime spent in the insular confines of the military. Having discovered that Warren was a Mason and a Moose, a faithful husband and devoted father, a baseball and football fan, a hunter and fisherman, Eisenhower assumed that his appointee shared his complacent devotion to the status quo. What he did not understand was that Warren also was one of the last of the old Bull Moose Progressive breed. He exemplified the tradition bequeathed to California by Hiram Johnson, who had so successfully melded fiscal prudence with political reform that he had virtually wiped out party lines. Cross-filing in both primaries, Warren won nomination by the Democrats as well as the Republicans when he was elected to the second of his three terms as governor.

A politician practical enough to spend all but three years of his working life in public office, Warren's career as prosecuting attorney, state attorney general, and governor had never been tainted by even a passing hint of corruption, and his respect for the civil rights of defendants was attested by the fact that not one of his convictions was reversed on appeal. The one putative racist lapse on his record was his uncritical support of the incarceration of Japanese-Americans in the tense days after Pearl Harbor—and that, after all, was an action ordered by President Roosevelt, carried out by the Justice Department, and upheld as a proper exercise of war powers in a 6–3 Supreme Court opinion written by Hugo Black.

Few who have served on the Supreme Court were less doctrinaire than Earl Warren. In the view of his most obstreperous colleague, Justice Douglas, it was this quality that enabled him to expand the 5-to-4 majority against *Plessy*, which Warren's arrival assured. Douglas wrote in *The Court Years:*

As the days passed, Warren's position immediately impressed Frankfurter. The essence of Frankfurter's position seemed to be that if a practical politician like Warren . . . thought we should overrule the 1896 opinion, why should a Professor object? [There was] a like influence on Reed and Clark. . . . Jackson had had a heart attack and was convalescing in the hospital, where Warren went to see him. I don't know what happened in the hospital room, but Warren returned to the Court triumphant. Jackson had said to count him in, which made the opinion unanimous. We could present a solid front to the country.

The school desegregation edict the chief justice fashioned, and persuaded his contentious brethren to join, was an exercise in moderation. It could only be judged radical by those who held extreme opinions of their own or, as in the case of Eisenhower, were far removed from the reality of race relations as they existed at midcentury. There was, of course, a profound moral component, an affirmation of the requirements of simple justice. But the chief justice was determined to avoid the moralism that sometimes affected his more eloquent colleagues; he instructed his clerks that draft decrees offered for consideration should be "short, readable by the lay public, nonrhetorical, unemotional, and, above all, nonaccusatory."

And that was how *Brown* came down. In simple, straightforward sentences the opinion first pointed out that in determining whether *Plessy* was still applicable the Court had found it necessary to consider public education in terms of its full development from its rudimentary state in 1868, when the Fourteenth Amendment was adopted:

Today [education] is a principal instrument in awakening a child to cultural values, in preparing him for later professional training, and in helping him to adjust normally to his environment. In these days, it is doubtful that any child may reasonably be expected to succeed in life if he is denied the opportunity of an education. Such an opportunity, where the state has undertaken to provide it, must be made available to all on equal terms.

Then followed the central question: "Does the segregation of children in the public schools solely on the basis of race . . . deprive the children of the minority group of equal educational opportunities?" And the unequivocal answer: "We believe it does." The opinion went on to endorse the psychological contentions offered in the lower courts by Kenneth Clark, holding that the arbitrary separation of black children generated "a feeling of inferiority as to their status in the community that may affect their hearts and minds in a way unlikely ever to be undone." Finally came the two sentences that by implication were to provide the basis for reversing public policy in all areas where segregation had enjoyed constitutional sanction: "We conclude, unanimously, that in the field of public education the doctrine of 'separate but equal' has no place. Separate educational facilities are inherently unequal."

THE eight associate justices who joined Warren in *Brown* were appointees of Franklin Roosevelt and Harry Truman, replacements for the "nine old men" who had occupied the bench as a heritage from the previous Republican era. But if the pragmatic Californian was able to bring about what his biographer, John D. Weaver, called "a triumph of justice over geriatrics," he still had to face the practicalities of implementing a desegregation decree in the face of certain resistance in many Southern communities. He was able to obtain the unanimous vote for *Brown* only by adopting the Justice Department's "deliberate speed" formula in setting forth guidelines for implementation. To bring in the reluctant Stanley Reed, he offered assurance that the prescribed process for merging the separate school systems would be gradual. The pledge was not only compatible with Warren's equable nature but with the political strategy he deemed necessary to bring some, at least, of the Southern leadership into active support of the desegregation process.

When the chief justice departed for California for the 1954 summer recess, he took with him a copy of *The Negro and the Schools,* and some years later, when I came to know him, he told me that he had found it useful. So, with opposite results, did most of the Southern attorneys general who were invited to submit briefs setting forth their views on the means of compliance. These made a tendentious selection of the findings and offered them in support of proposed schedules so limited and protracted they could not possibly have been taken seriously by the Court and were, on their face, monuments to recalcitrance.

The niceties of constitutional theory now gave way to questions of community attitudes—how adamant they were in the affected districts and the extent to which they might be modified. "It is axiomatic that separate schools can be merged only with great difficulty, if at all, when a great majority of the citizens who support them are actively opposed to the move," I had written. "No other public activity is so closely identified with local mores." That assertion of the obvious was extrapolated in the Southern briefs to support the contention that it would be impossible to comply with a segregation order until a great majority of the citizenry agreed that the move was desirable. This, in effect, would make compliance voluntary, and postpone it for, as the Virginia brief put it, "a now indeterminable period."

The Southern advocates, including Attorney General Richard W. Ervin of Florida, who retained me as a consultant, chose to ignore the passages in the book reporting on findings we had made in school districts that had recently desegregated: "One thing that stands out in these case histories is the frequency with which those who have had experience with integration—professional educators and laymen alike—have steeled themselves for a far more severe public reaction than they actually encountered." I had further noted that there was no indication that a gradual approach to desegregation smoothed the transition, and that some of those interviewed thought the reverse was true—that a markedly gradual program which allowed continuation of some segregated schools for an indefinite period invited opposition and allowed time for it to be organized.

My own conclusion, reinforced by private conversations with a wide variety of Southern leaders, was that a formula which allowed reasonable latitude to those responsible for working out feasible means of merging the separate systems would be acceptable in the border and upper Southern states. Experience there would demonstrate that the patterns of social segregation would not be drastically altered by the proximity of the two races in the classroom, and this in time would reduce the legal foot-dragging in the Deep South, where lawyers were already forecasting a generation of litigation.

After meeting with Attorney General Ervin in Tallahassee in September, I sent him a memorandum setting forth an argument for a decree that would leave it up to each school district to draw up a plan for compliance in accordance with local conditions. The elongated state of Florida provided a sampling of the variety of community attitudes, and of proportion of white and black population, that could be found across the whole region—ranging from those of the Deep South in the upper tier of cracker counties to those of the New York Jewish ghetto in resort and retirement communities farther down the peninsula. It was, therefore, unrealistic to assume that such diverse communities could proceed toward the goal at the same rate. The test to be applied in federal district court by a judge familiar with local conditions should not turn on the degree of desegregation achieved at any given point, but whether the district was proceeding in good faith. The memorandum concluded:

In its decision of May 17 the Supreme Court has put to a new test the essential machinery of democracy, which must protect the rights of the minority while recognizing the desires of the controlling majority. With the patience and forebearance of the Courts, we believe the State of Florida can meet the test here posed. We plead only for a chance to work out our own solutions under the terms of legal precedents and decrees that recognize the realities before us.

My draft brief, it turned out, was exactly the kind of response Chief Justice Warren had hoped to get from the Southern attorneys general—a response that would accept the principle set forth in *Brown* and plead only for concessions of time, thereby committing local officials to work out their own methods of compliance and relieve the federal district courts of the necessity of assuming the assignment powers of local school boards. The conditions I set forth were fully met in the implementation decree that came down on May 31, 1955, the last day of the term. I cannot, however, claim that my pleading had any bearing on the Court's unanimous decision, for it never found its way into the proceedings.

Attorney General Ervin, a courtly man who later served as his state's chief justice, thanked me kindly and wrote that "we were able to work in some of the material in your memorandum at the last minute." The few phrases that did survive were totally out of context, embedded in a turgid, contentious disquisition intended to demonstrate that the Supreme Court had projected "an immediate inrush of turbulent ideas" that might cause "a tornado which would devastate the entire school system." The Florida brief proposed a legal obstacle course that would have put the entire burden of obtaining compliance on individual black plaintiffs, while arming local and state school officials with a set of vaguely defined legal standards that could be used to wear out the most determined litigant. My good faith test was reduced to caricature when this exercise in duplicity concluded: "The Court stands not in the need of the whip and the scourge of compulsion to drive our people to obedience. . . ."

ON the day of jubilo celebrated by the black community on May 17, 1954, Thurgood Marshall told the *New York Times* he expected school segregation to be totally eliminated within five years. But the Supreme Court had already built in at least a year's delay, and its call for additional briefs reopened the argument over community attitudes the NAACP's lawyers had tried to dismiss as irrelevant. The key question among the five posed by the Court asked whether schools might not be required to integrate through "an effective gradual adjustment."

While the task force for the Ashmore Project was putting together its findings, Kenneth Clark mobilized a select group of social scientists to make a similar examination on behalf of the NAACP. Their report filled an entire issue of the *Journal of Social Issues,* a publication of the American Psychological Association, and in sum agreed with our conclusion that there existed little affirmative support for desegregation among white patrons of the schools affected by *Brown.* But Clark contended that, faced with the absence of any effective alternative, people could be expected to change the way they acted before they changed the way they thought—and that actual experience would serve to allay unrealistic fears rooted in prejudice.

This was, as I have indicated, pretty much in line with my own view. But, for tactical reasons, the NAACP lawyers elected to ignore a key point when they adopted the Clark thesis as the basis of their brief: such changes in the hearts and minds of men could take place only after they had been persuaded to accept the conditions that would make them possible. Clark cited the necessity for a combination of "clear and unequivocal statement of policy by leaders with prestige"; firm enforcement of the new policy in the face of initial resistance; and refusal of local authorities to "resort to, engage in, or tolerate subterfuge, gerrymandering or other devices for evading the principles and the fact of desegregation." The central question was whether the Court could devise a decree that would invoke such a response from federal, state, and local officials.

The tactical issue remained in suspense after circumstances forced postponement of the reargument originally set for October. Shortly after the Court convened in the fall Robert Jackson suffered a fatal heart attack. President Eisenhower chose as his successor a distinguished New Jersey jurist from the Second Circuit Court of Appeals whose qualifications could not be challenged, but whose very name aroused apprehension among Southern senators. The record of John Marshall Harlan, fifty-five-year-old grandson of the lone dissenter in *Plessy,* made it clear that he was as strict a constructionist as conservatives could wish for, but the echoes of Reconstruction invoked by his lineage delayed his confirmation until March. Final oral arguments began on April 11, 1955, and continued for more than thirteen hours spread over four days.

The position of plaintiffs and defendants hadn't really been modified since they first appeared to argue the cases on principle. The star of the first round, John W. Davis, was conspicuous by his absence. "We have met the enemy and we are theirs," he informed his client, Jimmy Brynes, and he was too sound a constitutional lawyer to lend himself to the kind of double-talk embodied in the Southern briefs. So he gracefully bowed out, declining the $25,000 fee proffered by the state, accepting a silver tea service instead. He was dead, at eighty-one, before what the lawyers called *Brown II* became the law of the land.

In the end, the NAACP lawyers found themselves unable to stomach the cautionary advice of those who thought prudence demanded concessions on the time scale. They insisted that segregation be ordered at the beginning of the fall school term and be completed within a year. After eighty years of separate-but-unequal treatment under *Plessy,* they argued, further delay was justice denied. "There is nothing before this Court that can show any justification for giving this interminable, gradual adjustment," Thurgood Marshall asserted. The constitutional authority of the federal government to enforce compliance had been proclaimed in *Brown,* and the plaintiffs thought it ought to be exercised.

From the beginning the justices had been looking for a way to, as Earl Warren put it, "give the district courts as much latitude as we can, and as much support as we can." When they convened for their final conference after oral argument they were all, including the new member, Justice Harlan, firmly united in their determination to make *Brown II* unanimous if they could. In his summary of discussion at the key court conference Richard Kluger demonstrated how the chief justice made that possible:

Earl Warren, presiding, showed in his opening remarks that he had picked and chosen eclectically from the blended caution and resoluteness of the Justice Department brief . . . from the canny ruminations of Felix Frankfurter, from the fervent fears of the Court's Southern contingent—Black, Reed and Clark—and from the most astute outside commentators on the problem, such as Harry Ashmore. His suggestions, as recorded in the notes of Burton and Frankfurter, leave little doubt that he was the Court's driving force in resolving the *Brown* decree.

The order that came down on May 31, 1955, again the last day of the term, contained only seven paragraphs, and its language was deliberately prosaic. It began with a reaffirmation of the "fundamental principle that racial discrimination in public education is unconstitutional," and pointed out that all contrary federal and state law must yield. Federal district judges, sitting as courts of equity, would have the responsibility for fashioning orders recognizing that desegregation must overcome "certain obstacles" in a systematic and effective manner. That was as close as the Court came to specifically identifying resistant community attitudes as the central problem, and it tempered that concession with the assertion that "it should go without saying that the vitality of these constitutional principles cannot be allowed to yield simply because of disagreement with them."

In its nature the decision was a disappointment to the more emotional partisans on both sides. Some of the NAACP lawyers thought they had suffered a defeat of such magnitude as to undo the famous victory they had won a year before. Thurgood Marshall, as I expected him to be, was far more philosophical. He had used all his eloquence and force to argue for a rigid time scale for compliance, but he hadn't really expected to get one. He was too experienced, and too pragmatic, to assume that white public opinion in the South was going to yield automatically to what Justice Frankfurter referred to as "the mere imposition of a distant will." There was going to be plenty of litigation ahead, but now he had precedent on his side, and, presumably, the full weight of the federal government. "Those white crackers are going to get tired of having Negro lawyers beating 'em every day in court," he predicted. "They're going to get tired of it. . . ."

I had my first extended conversation with Marshall in the interim between *Brown I* and *Brown II*, when he and his colleagues were still trying to determine how they should deal with the Court's implementation query. This came about in the wake of the annual *New York Herald Tribune* Forum in the fall of 1954. While winding up the Ashmore Project I had helped the officers of the Fund for the Advancement of Education set up an agency to monitor, and report, the progress of desegregation in the region—the Southern Education Reporting Service established at Nashville under an interracial board made up of six leading newspaper editors and six educators, including the presidents of Vanderbilt, Fisk, and Peabody. I had persuaded my former Charlotte colleague, C. A. McKnight, to leave his post as editor of the *News* to organize the fledgling project. He joined me in New York to discuss the implications of *Brown* on a program that included Marshall and other black leaders.

During the year in which the Supreme Court deliberately left the implications of *Brown* in suspense there was widespread euphoria among the kind of neo-abolitionists who turned out at the Hunter College auditorium in response to the invitation of the high-minded *Herald Tribune*. My own optimism was real, but limited, and in my offstage conversations with Marshall I found myself in the cautionary role that seemed to be becoming habitual. After the platform guests repaired to the elegant Fifth Avenue apartment of the newspaper's proprietor, Mrs. Helen Reid, the evening grew more relaxed and increasingly bibulous. With a heavy leaven of down-home kidding, Marshall and I kept coming back to the implementation question.

We wound up at one end of the long drawing room leaning against Mrs. Reid's grand piano, where McKnight, an accomplished amateur jazz musician, had been persuaded to the keyboard. Marshall invoked Ken Clark's experts to support his argument for an uncompromising, coercive Court order. I countered with the testimony of the Ashmore Project team that white resistance could be pushed to the point of no return, and that this prospect would be enhanced if all the pressure came from outside.

Several drinks later Marshall grinned and said, "Oh, the hell with this. We're never goin' to get this settled this way. I tell you what—we'll Indian-wrestle two out of three, and I'll go with the winner." By this time the distinguished assemblage had gathered around the piano, and McKnight announced that he would accompany our historic encounter with an original composition entitled "Nigger-Loving Boogie." It was no contest. With McKnight's jazz aria thumping in the background, the big lawyer put my forearm down with dispatch, and I cheerfully conceded the logic of his position. He didn't, of course, make out as well with the Court.

IN the immediate aftermath of *Brown I* there had been an automatic roar of defiance from the Deep South, but across most of the Jim Crow states responsible political leaders held their tongues, and not a few indicated that they felt sure that the law would be obeyed. In bellwether Virginia, Gov. Thomas B. Stanley announced that he would convene a meeting of local and state officials "to work toward a plan which shall be acceptable to our citizens and in keeping with the edict of the Court. Views of leaders of both races will be invited. . . ." Most Southern newspapers deplored the decision as premature but counseled calm and some predicted ultimate acceptance. Leading churchmen spoke out approvingly, and the organized denominations endorsed the ruling as morally correct.

In Little Rock, the school board, with the evident approbation of the local establishment, announced within a week of *Brown I*: "It is our responsibility to comply with federal constitutional requirements and we intend to do so when the Supreme Court of the United States outlines the methods to be followed." In the border states, and some areas in the Upper South where the proportion of black students to white was small, voluntary desegregation began on a scale that ultimately eliminated Jim Crow in seven hundred and fifty districts without intervention by the courts.

This reaction involved a mixture of conscience and pragmatism. The fact of the Court order stiffened the resolve of those whose moral convictions had already begun to move them toward recognition of the inherent injustices of the segregated society; they now had a practical reason to break through the stifling conformity imposed by local mores. And the industrializing South had begun to create a business community with leadership sophisticated enough to recognize the adverse economic consequences of an outbreak of racial strife.

Toward the close of the Ashmore Project I had visited a number of leading industrial managers and promoters to discuss privately their reaction to the possibility that the Court might order an end to segregated schools. My conversation with C. Hamilton Moses, the evangelical president of Arkansas Power and Light, was typical. Moses, who employed a gaudy country-preacher manner on behalf of the parent Dixon-Yates combine's crusade against TVA's "creeping socialism," reacted with genuine shock when I told him I believed the Court would overturn *Plessy*. "They can't do that," he said. "Why the folks in the country won't stand for it." But suppose they do order desegregation, and there is widespread racial trouble? "Oh my God, no!" Moses cried. "If the Klan starts riding again we'll never sell another bond issue on Wall Street." Would he, then, be prepared to speak out publicly on behalf of law and order? Neither he nor any of the others I talked with were willing to go that far—but there could be little doubt that they would be using their influence behind the scenes, at least so far as it didn't involve undue political risk.

There was, then, if I read the signs correctly, considerable latent support for an orderly adjustment. What was missing was effective local leadership, and in the volatile, uncertain atmosphere that could not be expected to emerge of its own volition. But there would be, I was convinced, an affirmative response to a summons to civic duty from the president of the United States. A pillar of the Southern establishment could hardly reject a moral appeal from a certified conservative who was also a war hero with popular support so widespread it had elevated him above partisan politics.

There is no way to know whether that judgment was correct, for Dwight Eisenhower simply rejected any and all suggestions that he speak out in support of the Supreme Court and *Brown*. There is evidence that he tried to persuade the justices not to abandon outright the separate-but-equal doctrine. In 1958, sitting beside Virginius Dabney at a Washington banquet, he deplored the decision and confided, "I went as far as I could, but was unsuccessful." Anthony Lewis, then Supreme Court correspondent for the *New York Times*, saw a draft of the Justice Department pleading with emendations in Eisenhower's handwriting which added up to insistence that the Court go easy on the South. But his subsequent course indicates that the president had nothing to do with, and indeed must not have read, the concluding passage:

The responsibility for achieving compliance with the Court's decision in these cases does not rest on the judiciary alone. Every officer and agency of the government, federal, state and local, is likewise charged with the duty of enforcing the Constitution and the rights guaranteed under it.

The president's voice was missing from the national chorus that greeted *Brown* as an act of judicial statesmanship. He simply refused to offer any substantive judgment on the merits, limiting himself to the assertion that he accepted the Supreme Court ruling as the law of the land. In 1956, when resistance in the Deep South had become virtually universal and the threat of violence was growing, he refused to go beyond this negative position, saying in response to a question as to whether he agreed with the decision, "I think it makes no difference whether or not I endorse it. The Constitution is as the Supreme Court interprets it; and I must conform to that and do my very best to see that it is carried out in this country."

In response to entreaties that he make a public statement that would provide moral support for Southern leaders who could be persuaded to speak out for law and order, the president fell back on some version of his reiterated view that the law could not change the hearts and minds of men. He blamed the rising unrest in the South on "extremists on both sides," thus equating blacks, who were peacefully seeking their legal rights, with whites who were threatening, and soon would be committing violence to obstruct duly entered Court orders.

The ostentatious neutrality of the executive branch encouraged denigration of the Court, which now began to come under direct fire from right wing organizations that identified minority rights with Communist conspiracy. In Congress, liberals of both parties were disarmed by the silence from the White House, while the powerful Southern bloc was soon in full cry. As the opening of the next school term approached, moderate leaders in the Upper South fell silent. Governor Stanley of Virginia reversed himself, announcing: "I shall use every legal means at my command to continue segregated schools in Virginia." He did so at the direction of the state's venerated political boss, Harry Flood Byrd, the very model of a righteous conservative, who sent a signal to neo-Confederates everywhere when he proclaimed, "We have a right to resist. . . ."

The cumulative effect of all this was to rob moderate Southerners not only of effective political support, but of respectability. Genteel Virginians now joined red-necked nigger-baiters of the Deep South in calling for massive resistance. James Jackson Kilpatrick, editor of the *Richmond News Leader*, resurrected a pre-Civil War doctrine to proclaim a state's constitutional right to interpose its police powers between the federal government and a local school district on the ground that court-ordered desegregation was a threat to domestic tranquility. His publisher assembled Kilpatrick's inflammatory editorials in a pamphlet circulated to key officials across the South.

Virginius Dabney, editor of the *Richmond Times-Dispatch*, consulted leading local lawyers—including Lewis F. Powell, Jr., later to occupy a seat on the Supreme Court—who told him the interposition theory had long since been discredited and could not possibly stand up. In the *Arkansas Gazette* I condemned Kilpatrick's latter-day nullification doctrine as an invitation to disaster for any Southern governor foolish enough to invoke it. V. Dabney didn't even have that consolation; the *Times-Dispatch* was silenced by order of the publisher. And that, too, was a signal from the capital of the late Confederacy that would not be ignored by the newspaper fraternity; most of those who could not stomach the crudities of massive resistance did not find it prudent to denounce it.

Earl Warren, respecting the separation of powers, never made any public complaint about the manner in which the Court was left twisting in the wind, and I never heard him discuss the matter privately, although he could be quite sulphurous on the conduct of one of Eisenhower's successors, Richard Nixon. After both principals were dead, one of the last survivors of the Warren Court, Justice Tom Clark, said, "If Mr. Eisenhower had come through, it would have changed things a lot." In his posthumous memoir Justice Douglas was more outspoken: ". . . if he had gone to the nation on television and radio telling the people to obey the law and fall into line, the cause of desegregation would have been accelerated. Ike was a hero and he was worshiped. Some of his political capital spent on the racial cause would have brought the nation closer to the constitutional standards. Ike's ominous silence on our 1954 decision gave courage to the racists who decided to resist the decision ward by ward, precinct by precinct, town by town and county by county." Such default at the highest level of political leadership was bound to produce a domino effect among those who were most immediately exposed to the harsh winds of public disapproval.

15

The Southern Way

*I*n the spring of 1955 a bright young Mississippian, whose father had sent him off to the University of Texas with the idea of ventilating the parochialism of his Yazoo City upbringing, decided to run for editor of the student newspaper. At an election rally he was asked how he stood on school desegregation. "There's an inner turmoil in the United States; there's an inner turmoil in me," Willie Morris replied. "The Supreme Court decision was inevitable, but I don't think any universal rule can be applied to the entire nation when the time for integration comes. I don't think Ole Miss is ready for integration, I think the University of Texas is."

It was a prescient appraisal. The movement for voluntary desegregation in the border states had begun to spill over into the Upper South, where Texas was usually counted despite the geographic discrepancy. But in Mississippi and the rest of the Deep South the Supreme Court decision had been condemned· out of hand, and organization had begun for massive resistance.

At Indianola, not far from Morris's home town, fourteen leading citizens "met and counseled together on the terrible crisis precipitated on Black Monday"—that being the day the high court handed down *Brown*. Thus was born the White Citizens Councils, the loose confederation of segregationist organizations that soon spread across the South with varying degrees of local support. The first chairman, Robert P. Patterson, a Leflore County planter, condemned the traditional night-riding violence of the past and pledged that opposition to school desegregation would be carried out by lawful means. The founders' legal expert, Judge Thomas Pickens Brady, specifically disavowed the Ku Klux Klan. "They hide their face," he told the council membership, "because they do things you and I wouldn't approve of."

What the councils would approve of was spelled out for Willie Morris shortly after he came home from Austin for summer vacation. Yazoo City was one of five Mississippi towns selected by the NAACP for a test of *Brown,* and fifty-three black parents submitted a petition to the school board asking for an immediate end to segregation. In response, a mass meeting of whites was called at the high school auditorium, and out of curiosity young Morris wandered into the back of the jam-packed hall. There, for the first time, he encountered "the pent-up hysteria of organized crowds . . . a kind of claustrophobic terror." More than a dozen prominent men sat on the stage. "I knew them all," Morris wrote. "Some of them were fathers of my best friends, men I had known and admired and could talk to on a first-name basis." In the audience he saw his own father, sitting with a neighbor. And from the back of the hall he heard rebel yells and shouts of, "Let's get the niggers!"

The chairman quickly stilled the clamor. The white citizens of Yazoo City, he said firmly, would neither commit nor condone violence. He then outlined the procedure to be followed in preserving the Southern way of life: employers of blacks who signed the petition would fire them. If they were tenants their landlords would evict them. Wholesalers would cut off supplies and credit to the black retailers who had signed. And white merchants would refuse to sell their goods to the petitioners. The chairman, obviously on advice of counsel, noted that this action was not being undertaken by the Citizens Council, but represented the spontaneous reaction of the white community as a whole. The combination of outrage to his sense of justice and insult to his intelligence marked the end of innocence for Willie Morris, who, like many a sensitive Southerner before him, was launched on the road that would take him, as he was to title his memoir, *North Toward Home.*

On the legal front, the federal district courts were still in a holding pattern. In three of the cases on which the Supreme Court had ruled—those that came up from Kansas, Delaware, and the District of Columbia—the affected school districts moved promptly toward compliance, so there was no need for further action. In Virginia the judge sitting on the Prince Edward County case refused to set a time limit on the ground that "apparent inaction on the part of the defendants does not necessarily show noncompliance." And in the South Carolina case the three-judge court presided over by Judge Parker provided an interpretation of *Brown II* that would set the pattern for pleading in the hundreds of cases to come:

What has been decided, and all that has been decided, is that a state may not deny to any person on account of race the right to attend any school that it maintains. . . . The Constitution, in other words, does not require integration. It merely forbids discrimination. It does not forbid such segregation as occurs as a result of voluntary action. It merely forbids the use of governmental powers to enforce segregation.

This meant that segregated schools could continue in any district where black citizens did not challenge the practice in the federal courts. This circumstance should, it seemed to me, take the heat off those areas where white resistance was strongest— for these usually were also the areas where blacks were effectively leaderless and least likely to press for their newly declared rights. If the process were allowed to run its natural course for a few years, with prodding from the NAACP limited to strategically determined sites, I thought it likely that patterns of compliance would begin to spread southward from the border states, bypassing depressed rural areas with high proportions of blacks while the separate school systems in the more sophisticated and permissive larger cities were being merged.

But this presupposed effective support and encouragement from Washington for local leaders who were disposed to work out desegregation patterns that would unite, rather than polarize, the affected white and black communities. In the quiet time between *Brown I* and *Brown II* a good many of these came forward. In Arkansas, two school districts with small black population voluntarily desegregated without arousing concerted local opposition.

At the Ozark town of Charleston the young lawyer then serving as school board chairman convinced his fellow-townsmen that it made no sense to continue sending a handful of local blacks over the mountains to Fayetteville since that district, which included the University of Arkansas, had already announced its intention of desegregating its high school. His name was Dale Bumpers, and sixteen years later his election as governor would end the protracted tenure his Madison County neighbor, Orval Faubus, gained by taking the opposite tack and defying the United States Supreme Court.

At Hoxie, by unanimous vote of the school board, twenty-five black students joined the thousand whites in the local high school, ending the awkward and expensive practice of shipping resident blacks to another district in order to comply with the compulsory attendance law. But here the local people were not allowed to work out their own solution. An obscure Little Rock lawyer, Amis Guthridge, came to town with bundles of Citizens Council literature and began urging that the school patrons had an obligation to God, their country, and the white race to resist the actions of their own elected officials. As demonstrations and threats of physical reprisal mounted, the school board initiated legal action that brought the federal courts into the controversy by the back door.

A district judge issued a landmark injunction against those attempting to interfere with desegregation of the Hoxie schools. The Eighth Circuit Court of Appeals, affirming the order, held that federal courts have jurisdiction in equity to deal with attempted deprivations of constitutional rights, and that the First Amendment does not protect free speech employed to incite disobedience to the law. This injunctive power would increasingly be called upon as segregationist demonstrators became more and more aggressive. At Clinton, Tennessee, in the first significant incident of mass violence, a roving agitator named John Kaspar wound up in jail for contempt of federal court.

Precluded from inciting their followers to physically bar admission of blacks, the Citizens Council leaders turned to a campaign of harassment against whites who supported desegregation. At Hoxie this included a suit in state court charging school officials with financial misconduct, and anonymous threats against the school superintendent concerted enough to cause his resignation. The militant segregationists were not content to hold the line in communities where they might well arouse majority popular support; they now made it clear that they would use whatever weapons came to hand against those whites who, in their favorite derogation, bowed the neck and bent the knee before federal authority.

Sen. James Eastland of Mississippi emerged as the principal spokesman for the resistance movement, calling for "all patriotic organizations . . . to cooperate in a united movement for the preservation of America under a constitutional form of government"—which he claimed had been abandoned when the Court bowed to "pressure groups bent upon the destruction of the American system of government, and the mongrelization of the white race. . . . The Court has responded to a radical, pro-Communist political movement in this country. . . . We in the South cannot stay longer on the defensive. This is the road to destruction and death. We must take the offense."

In their effort to keep the movement respectable, the Citizens Council leaders continued to disavow violence. But they found it impossible to draw a clear moral distinction between old-fashioned night-riding and the kind of brutal economic reprisal they advocated against black or white dissidents. And by their own nature, and that of the crowds they attracted to their public meetings, Council orators could not tone down the inflammatory rhetoric that could only be heard as a battle cry. At a rally in Alabama, Jim Eastland stayed on what in that league could be called high ground, but neither he nor any other speaker disavowed the unsigned handbill circulating through the audience, a parody of the Declaration of Independence that began: "When in the course of human events it becomes necessary to abolish the Negro race, proper methods should be used. Among these are guns, bow and arrows, sling shots, and knives. . . ."

The council movement was never to attract a mass membership. By its own claim, active supporters at the high point ranged from one hundred thousand in Alabama downward to only twenty thousand in Texas. The failure of whites to flock to the activist banner did not, of course, mean that there were not many more who shared the desire to maintain the segregated school system, even though they could not stomach the Council's methods. It was to these the organization addressed its relentless propaganda campaign, aimed not so much at making converts as at silencing any who dared dissent from its insistence that the Southern political leadership must present a solid front against the federal courts.

"There are only two sides in the Southern fight—those who want to maintain the Southern way of life and those who want to mix the races," a red-and-black full-page ad in the *Montgomery Advertiser* proclaimed over the signature of state senator Sam Englehardt, executive secretary of the Citizens Councils of Alabama. "There is no middle ground for moderation . . . that middle ground has been washed away by the actions of the NAACP in seeking to destroy the freedoms of the Southern white man." Senator Englehardt ended his broadside with assurance that "there is no hate or animosity in this organization," but this was of doubtful comfort to the few Alabama moderates who remained outside the closet.

B<small>Y</small> the summer of 1955 it was evident that President Eisenhower was not going to abandon his role of personal neutrality on the school desegregation issue. The deteriorating situation in the South, it seemed to me, cried out for a national leader who would assume the role Eisenhower rejected, that of a conciliator who could use the great moral prestige of the office to encourage white and black leaders to work within the area of practical compromise left open by the Supreme Court. The man best equipped by temperament and political connection for that role, I concluded, was the most likely Democratic candidate, Adlai Stevenson.

In May I sent him an editorial from the *Gazette* in which I argued that he was the best possible choice for the Democrats in 1956, and urged that he abandon his Hamlet posture and make it clear that he expected to be nominated again. This stung him, as I knew it would. "Does it strike you that 'coyness' is what the other fellow does while you yourself are engaged in the honorable pastime of 'playing them close to your chest?' " he replied, adding a hand-written postscript that left little doubt that his mind, in fact, was made up.

The exchange continued into the summer, culminating when I charged that he had a moral obligation to the Democratic Party, and to the country, to declare his intention of standing for renomination before the field became cluttered with other hopefuls. If he was willing to do his duty as I saw it, he replied, what was I willing to do in return? When I paid him an overnight visit at Libertyville in August he told me he was beginning to assemble a small personal staff to plan for the campaign, and asked me to join him as soon as I could arrange to take leave from the *Gazette.*

In September, committed to serve at least until the next summer's Democratic convention, I moved my wife and grade-school daughter to a tall, gloomy Victorian house near the University of Chicago campus. My title was personal assistant to the unannounced candidate, and at a press conference Stevenson defined my role as providing advice on "substance, issues, and problems." Speech writing was one of my obligations, a critical one as far as the acutely word-conscious candidate was concerned, but I was also expected to establish a better relationship with the media and provide a conspicuously non-Ivy League persona in Stevenson's immediate entourage.

At a press conference in Chicago on November 16 which attracted a full turnout of national political correspondents, Stevenson publicly launched his second run for the presidency, announcing that he would enter the Minnesota primary and others to be designated later. He was his usual jaunty self, but in fact was deeply disappointed, for he had made his original commitment on the assumption that he could avoid the grueling state-by-state popular contest for delegates, and instead devote the months before the national nominating convention to staking out positions on the issues he deemed to be of urgent importance.

He had been anticipating a rematch on his own terms, this time with a presidential record to run against, rather than the smiling image of an apolitical hero who seemed all things to all men. Then in late September Eisenhower suffered a heart attack, casting doubt on his ability to stand for reelection. The Democratic nomination suddenly became a real prize. Estes Kefauver put on his coonskin cap and announced that he would be back on the primary trail come spring. The Democrats' putative elder statesman, Harry Truman, never reconciled to what he regarded as Stevenson's toplofty approach to practical politics, announced his neutrality in such a way as to encourage Averell Harriman, who again stood by waiting for a deadlock to develop.

The effect of this was to accentuate the North-South division in the party and move the race issue to the top of the

Democratic agenda. This time it would have to be dealt with in terms of the specifics raised by *Brown*. The shape of things to come emerged at the press conference in a question by Edward P. Morgan of ABC-TV, who suggested that the apparent support of the Stevenson candidacy by many Southern leaders indicated that he had compromised his views on civil rights. Stevenson responded with a short, flat denial. Served up a creampuff in the form of a request for his reaction to a statement by Lyndon Johnson that the Supreme Court decision had removed civil rights from the political arena, he said this ought to be the case and hoped it would be. To my considerable relief a question that referred to the most recent atrocity in Mississippi beginning, "Governor, on the Emmett Till case, could you tell us how you—" got cut off in the shuffle at the close of the conference.

I would later be credited—or charged—with selling Stevenson the moderate position on school desegregation he adopted and saw interpreted by his critics as the kind of gradualism that could no longer be supported, on the record at least, by black leaders. In fact, before we ever discussed the specific points that had to be dealt with in the wake of *Brown,* he had plucked sensitive nerves by announcing his opposition to legislation sponsored by Harlem's Rep. Adam Clayton Powell to withhold federal aid from school districts that did not desegregate forthwith. The measure carried little practical weight since there was then no significant federal funding for the public schools, but most Democratic liberals supported federal aid for education and the potential for carrot-and-stick pressure gave the black congressman's bill high symbolic importance.

In July, speaking to the National Education Association, Stevenson endorsed both federal aid and the desegregation requirements of *Brown II,* adding: "And I hope that what is good for all will not be lost to all by any linking together of the school aid and desegregation issues, which would delay realization of our hopes and expectations on either or both these vital fronts. In the long run segregation and discrimination, like other obsolete heritages, will yield quickly to the general advance of education." Hubert Humphrey, the Senate's leading advocate of both federal aid and civil rights, wrote to praise the NEA speech, and pointed to the political reality: there was no way to get an education aid bill out of committee without the Powell amendment, and no way to get it past the Senate with the Powell amendment. But the emotinal quotient on both sides of the race issue had now reached the point where this kind of standoff no longer was seen as a signal that compromise was in order. Stiff red-necks were being matched by stiff black ones—and white liberals removed from the scene of actual collision in the South tended to be even more adamant than the blacks. The dilemma would dog the Stevenson campaign all the way to November.

THE Minnesota primary looked like a setup, so much so it encouraged our fond belief that a solid victory over Kefauver would relieve the candidate of more than token participation in the other contests to follow. He had the formal endorsement of the Democratic Farmer Labor organization and the active support of its leaders. And Minnesota, with only a small black population concentrated in Minneapolis and St. Paul, hardly seemed a place where the race issue should have high priority. I still remember the only black I ever saw at a rally outside the Twin Cities. A February blizzard was tugging at his Russian-style fur cap when I encountered him at the entrance to a snow-banked town hall up in the Iron Range country. "Man," he said, taking note of my accent, "we sure a long way from home."

But the mere presence on the stump of the tall, shambling Kefauver raised the issue. He was a living symbol of populism, casting himself in the role of David eternally arrayed against an establishmentarian Goliath, and in Minnesota this invoked the kind of glandular, sentimental devotion to civil rights that had helped make Hubert Humphrey the state's leading political figure. So, as these disparate figures barnstormed across the frozen countryside, the soft-spoken man from Andrew Jackson's segregated home town, with no more than a passing mention of race, turned the issue against the unhappy warrior from Abraham Lincoln country, who saw no reason to mention it at all. When the votes were counted on March 20, Kefauver had won handily, and now the contest would go down to the wire with the decision turning on the June primaries in California and Florida.

On our first swing down the west coast I was quickly reminded that the civil rights issue was indigenous and inescapable in those parts. I was greeted at San Francisco by Franklin Williams, a brilliant black lawyer who had been sent out from New York as the NAACP's west coast representative. We were destined to become friends, but in that first encounter Williams seemed to view me as though I were a lineal descendant of Simon Legree. In Oregon a few days before, Stevenson had tempered his unconditional support for *Brown* by suggesting that those who were untouched by the Supreme Court order should not be overzealous in condemning the South, which was now faced with recasting its long-standing social order. His key point, which he would reiterate throughout the campaign, was that the hope for progress lay in promoting interracial understanding, not in the use of force. Williams made it clear that this kind of conciliatory talk was unacceptable. At a minimum he wanted endorsement of the Powell amendment, and a pledge to use any other means necessary to root out Jim Crow. Otherwise, he warned, the black vote in the primary would go solidly for Kefauver.

Blacks were not yet numerous enough in California to constitute a major bloc vote, and they did not have the tight political organization this threat implied. Kefauver, after all, also had a problem with his civil rights stand if he was to stay in the running in Florida, and he had been no more outspoken than Stevenson on the specifics of desegregation. The fact was that Williams's influence was greater with the reflexive white liberals who were then riding high in the California Democratic Party than it was in the black wards of San Francisco, Oakland, and Los Angeles. But, as we were to discover at the California Democratic Council convention in Fresno, this only made the issue even more acute.

Before that volatile audience, which would also be addressed by Kefauver, Stevenson elected to take the high ground. John Bartlow Martin, who had joined the entourage, described the Fresno address as a political disaster: "It was lofty, thoughtful, and almost nobody in California liked it." Kefauver, coming on with his standard denunciation of fat cats and special interests, rang all the right bells, and Martin noted that Stevenson buttons were falling like autumn leaves. Growing increasingly testy under the pressures of nonstop campaigning, Stevenson gave his own verdict on the speech, which was largely his handiwork: "Here among the intense young liberals it missed its mark. Evidently what they want to hear about is civil rights, minorities, and Israel and little else, and certainly no vague futures."

A worse blow fell in Los Angeles. Before a sweating black audience jammed into a low-ceilinged room, the candidate not only used the dread word *gradual* but went out of his way to emphasize it. The acoustics were so poor I doubt that anybody heard all he actually said in response to vaguely worded questions from a black preacher, but the fragments that reached the correspondents ranged around the room created a furore when their dispatches were published in the East. Stevenson voiced his standard objection to the Powell amendment, and in the confused babble that followed, his final words came through clearly to me, and to William Lawrence of the *New York Times* who was standing at my side in the rear: "I will do everything I can to bring about national unity even if I have to ask some of you to come about it gradually." As the crowd broke and the entourage headed for the cars, Bill Lawrence said, "He's blown it," and I knew that interpretation would lead his report, and provide the emphasis for next day's network broadcasts.

There was also trouble on the other flank. In March I received word that Strom Thurmond was circulating what came to be called the "Southern Manifesto" among the Southern congressmen, and that most were likely to sign it. I flew to Washington to see if anything could be done to at least keep Stevenson's most conspicuous supporters off the list. The statement, I found, had little real substance, denouncing *Brown* as an abuse of judicial power that substituted the justices' "personal and political and social ideas for the established law of the land" and pledging that the 101 senators and representatives from the eleven Confederate states who finally signed would "use all lawful means to bring about a reversal of this decision which is contrary to the Constitution." Lyndon Johnson and Sam Rayburn were not asked to sign on the ground that they held national office as majority leader and Speaker. The only other prominent Southerners missing from the list were Estes Kefauver and his colleague from Tennessee, Albert Gore.

It was clear that the manifesto would be a body blow to Stevenson, but his supporters on the Hill offered nothing more tangible than expressions of regret. After our skirmishes in the Dixiecrat campaign I figured there was no point in discussing the matter with Thurmond, so I tried a flanking movement with his South Carolina colleague, Olin Johnson. Couldn't he, I asked, at least persuade Thurmond to hold off until after the primaries? "It's no use trying to talk to Strom," Johnson said. "He believes that shit." On March 9 I was tipped that the *New York Times* would break the story next morning, and I had to pass on a warning to Stevenson in Detroit, where he was sharing a platform with the most outspoken of Democratic civil libertarians, Gov. Mennen Williams.

AFTER the debacle in Minnesota it was necessary to revamp our campaign strategy. I had been trying, with a total lack of success, to wean Stevenson away from his dependence upon written speech texts for even the most informal of whistle-stop appearances. He could be, I knew, a brilliant ad-libber, and no one really expected substantive remarks in those brief personal appearances. My dissatisfaction with the candidate's stump speaking was matched by his resentment of my failure to produce the endless flow of deathless prose he thought he needed. The real trouble was that the primaries required a candidate to run as though he were standing for county sheriff; the voters wanted to look their man in the eye and press the flesh, and what he said didn't matter half as much as the fact that he was present and available in their home town. Stevenson understood this, but he resented the necessity. "I have never enjoyed slapstick politics or extemporaneous speaking, and that seems to be all that is contemplated," he wrote, giving me my comeuppance.

The irony was that he was really very good at it, sustained, I think, by his own amusement at the very absurdity of much of what he was required to do. Once when we were hop-scotching from town to town down the spine of Florida, he asked me how he had done at the last supermarket stop. "Well,

Governor," I replied, "when a little girl in a starched white dress suddenly steps out of a crowd and hands you a stuffed alligator, what you say is, 'I've always wanted one of these to go on the mantlepiece at Libertyville.' What you don't say is what you did say, 'For Christ's sake, what's this?' " He was delighted, and repeated the conversation in his remarks at every stop for the rest of the day, in the process no doubt losing votes to Estes Kefauver, who was born knowing what to do with a stuffed alligator.

As we came near the end of the primary trail, the Florida race took on critical importance. A good many of our people were convinced that Kefauver was making promises to black leaders in private that went far beyond his public position on civil rights, and those in his camp circulated the same charge against Stevenson. In our case it certainly was not true, and I never believed it was in Kefauver's. But neither candidate had any real control over what was being said on his behalf by local supporters in the redneck counties along the Georgia border. "On the word-of-mouth level, Kefauver's people are undoubtedly making hay with the ain't-nobody-here-but-us-Confederates approach to segregation," I wrote in a report to Jim Finnegan, the campaign manager. "In the cracker country the standard technique is a broad wink and the question: Who do you think can handle them niggers better, a city fellow from Illinois or a country boy from Tennessee?"

At the end of March I sent a memorandum to Stevenson appraising the deteriorating situation in the South, and the special problem we now faced in Florida. When we had first visited the state the previous November, LeRoy Collins, the most conspicuously moderate governor in the region, was talking openly of finding means to comply with *Brown.* Now, five months later, he had found the position untenable and his race for reelection against a nondescript field was uncomfortably close. Attorney General Ervin, trying to offset the racist attack on Collins, proposed an amendment to the state constitution which would vest sole power of pupil assignment in the governor on the theory that he had immunity from federal legal action. An absurdity, of course, and privately Ervin told me he agreed with the characterization of the proposal by Nelson Poynter, publisher of the *St. Petersburg Times,* who said there were only three things wrong with it—it was bad morally, legally, and politically. But the attorney general insisted that the amendment was a necessary survival measure.

As a conciliator Stevenson could not expect to appease the irreconcilables—and these now included the latter-day Confederates, some of the black leaders, and those I called "Madison Avenue Abolitionists." My advice was that he support his moderate public stand by driving home two essential points in his personal contacts with influential politicos: "(1) To the Southern leaders: You can stand anything but a party bolt, and the only man who can head it off is Adlai Stevenson; (2) To the Negro and liberal leadership: The worst thing that can happen to the American Negro in 1956 is a Southern bolt which, regardless of the outcome of the presidential election, will bring racists to power in many of the Southern states and keep them there for years to come. . . ."

AFTER the calamitous exchange with the black preachers in Los Angeles, Stevenson wrote me a tart note: "I think the time has come to try to get some of this stuff straight and I wish you would put in my hands as promptly as possible a draft statement with respect to (1) desegregation (2) voting, and (3) violence." Well, I tried, and so did almost every other member of his personal staff, with voluminous input from such advisors as Arthur Schlesinger. Now, in April, he was due back in Los Angeles for a major speech, and there was no question that civil rights had to be revisited. "He could not forget that what he said in California would be read in Florida," Martin wrote. "It was the most dangerous issue of all, the one that could defeat Stevenson in the primaries. It was at the same time the issue that could rescue him, for it might appear to the Democratic managers at convention time that only Stevenson could prevent the party from being torn apart by the race issue."

Martin, Bill Wirtz, and I all wrote drafts. I don't know how much of mine actually survived in the reading copy, but the position I had advocated from the beginning was spelled out in the clearest terms yet. "For my part," Stevenson said, "like most Northerners, I feel that the Supreme Court has decreed what our reason told us was inevitable, and our conscience told us was right."

The Supreme Court said *what* is to be done. The question of *how* we will effect this transition in an orderly, peaceful way remains to be settled. The question is not going to settle itself. And the longer we drift the greater the danger—the danger from those who would violate the spirit of the Court decision by either lawless resistance or by undue provocation.

Here, for the first time, he took the issue directly to Eisenhower, urging that the president immediately call together white and black leaders for a full and open discussion of the means by which compliance with the Court decision could be furthered. At the end of April, in New York, he took trenchant notice of the president's failure to respond:

The presidency is, above all, a place of moral leadership. Yet in these months of crucial importance no leadership has been provided. The immense prestige and influence of the office has been withheld from those who honestly seek to carry out the law in a gathering storm and against rising resistance. Refusing to rise to this great moral and constitutional crisis, the administration has hardly acknowledged its gravity.

We squeaked by in California and Florida, and Stevenson went on to win the nomination and share the ticket with Estes Kefauver as his running mate. But both he and the party had suffered heavy damage, so much so his valiant effort to push Eisenhower toward dealing effectively with the race issue has been overlooked or dismissed by many chroniclers of the civil rights movement. Bert Cochran, in his radical critique, wrote: "In the circumstances, with one candidate espousing gradualism and moderation, and the other taking refuge in surly silence, civil rights passed into the background of the presidential campaign." In a history of the movement written from the black perspective, *Walls Come Tumbling Down,* Thomas Brooks reached the remarkable conclusion that "by comparison . . . with the waffling of the Democratic Party candidate, Adlai Stevenson, Eisenhower's posture seemed to be one of commitment."

The Democratic platform dealt forthrightly with civil rights, and was generally praised at the time of its adoption. Walter Lippmann saw it as an unequivocal declaration in favor of using persuasion to bring about compliance. The Democratic leaders, Governor Stevenson himself, Mrs. Roosevelt, who is the keeper of the party's conscience on this issue, were wise enough not to force the hands of the Southern leaders. For those who believe that segregation must be ended, but that it can only be ended by consent, and never by force, there is nothing weak in the civil rights plank.

There was no ambivalence in Stevenson on the issue. He saw it clearly for what it was, and understood fully that the position he took left him trapped between intransigents. To him, this simply demonstrated the futility of any coercive course that would further polarize those who had to be brought together if there was to be orderly progress for the black minority. But when the adrenaline is flowing, the way of the moderate is hard—hence the testiness some mistook for vacillation. At an early full-dress strategy session, a relaxed evening at Bill Blair's family mansion when George Ball, Ben Cohen, Jane Dick, Jack Fischer, and Arthur Schlesinger joined the nuclear staff, Stevenson said, "You know, what I'd really like to do is attack the administration from A to Z—go down the line, call them on every point. I'm tired of this statesmanlike stuff." Bill Wirtz replied, "You might like to do it, but you would hate to have done it." The occasion never arose.

16

"We Can Straighten Up Our Backs..."

At Mobile Bay, where he polished off the remnants of the Confederate fleet, Adm. David Farragut, USN, provided one of history's most memorable quotations when he ordered his helmsman: "Damn the torpedoes! Full speed ahead!" Ninety years later, a hundred and fifty miles to the north, a middle-aged black woman acted in similar spirit when she refused to yield her seat on a Montgomery bus to a white passenger. And Rosa Parks also uttered a statement destined to echo down the years: "I was just plain tired, and my feet hurt."

In his *Dictionary of Quotations,* Bergen Evans noted that the admiral's command might have been recorded among famous last words had not the Confederate torpedoes proved to be defective. In the end the same thing was true of the antiquated segregation ordinances of the city that proudly called itself the "Cradle of the Confederacy." But this would be demonstrated only in the denouement of the drama that unfolded over the year following Mrs. Parks's arrest at Christmastime, 1955.

The remarkable young man who stage-managed the ensuing confrontation between Montgomery's white and black communities found that Rosa Parks was perfectly cast for her heroine's role. A comely, impeccably respectable, hard-working seamstress for a leading department store, her innate dignity and strength were captured by the lens of the TV camera, which Martin Luther King, Jr. soon came to recognize as the indispensable focus of his protest movement. Mrs. Parks was so impressively in character, indeed, that King found himself called upon to refute the suspicion of out-of-town reporters who, like many local white leaders, assumed that she must have been a plant by the NAACP.

In *Stride Toward Freedom,* his account of the Montgomery bus boycott, King insisted that Mrs. Parks's act was "an individual expression of a timeless longing for human dignity and freedom. She was not 'planted' there by the NAACP or any other organization; she was planted there by her personal sense of dignity and self-respect. She was anchored to that seat by the accumulated indignities of days gone by and the boundless aspirations of generations yet unborn. . . ." But if there was no conspiracy in Montgomery, Rosa Parks's act of defiance was something more than the spontaneous reaction of a simple black woman whose feet hurt. Her seamstress job may have seemed menial by white standards, but as a skilled, salaried employee of the fashionable Montgomery Fair she was firmly established in the black middle class. She had served as secretary of the state chapter of the NAACP, and had visited Myles Horton's radical Highlander Folk School in Tennessee, then one of the rare integrated centers in the region. The man who went bond for her was E. D. Nixon, a Pullman porter strongly influenced by his union's outspoken leader, A. Philip Randolph, a connection that inspired him to take the lead in calling for a bus boycott. And, once the boycott took hold, Bayard Rustin of the Fellowship of Reconciliation came down from New York to provide sophisticated counsel and organizing skills.

King himself was astonished when black resentment erupted so spectacularly in the old city where seventy thousand white citizens fondly believed they enjoyed a good relationship with fifty thousand blacks—one that for many years had not been marred by any publicized acts of racial violence or even a public exchange of unpleasantries. The young pastor had settled in at Montgomery only a few months before, called to fill the pulpit at the Dexter Avenue Baptist Church. There he presided over a red brick, stained glass citadel of black respectability which, since Reconstruction days, had occupied a place of dignity diagonally across the square from the state capitol where Jefferson Davis was sworn in as president of the Confederate States of America.

Newly returned to the South from graduate studies in Boston, King gravitated naturally to the local NAACP chapter, and the fledgling Alabama Council on Human Relations of the

Southern Regional Council, the only interracial organization in town. It was a disillusioning experience. "I found the Negro community the victim of a threefold malady—factionalism among the leaders, indifference in the educated group, and passivity in the uneducated," he wrote. "All of these conditions had almost persuaded me that no lasting social reform could ever be achieved in Montgomery."

King was one of forty leading black citizens who responded to E. D. Nixon's summons to a meeting on Friday, the day after Rosa Parks's arrest. They agreed to call a mass boycott of the city buses on Monday, December 5. Leaflets would be distributed throughout the black community on Saturday, and on Sunday ministers in the leading churches would urge support. With no more preparation than that, King had grave doubts that the movement could succeed. But on Monday morning his wife Coretta rushed back from a front window with the glad tidings that the first bus passing their house at 6:00 A.M. was empty. Those traversing the black neighborhoods would stay that way for another year.

Late Monday afternoon the ad hoc steering committee converted itself into the Montgomery Improvement Association and elected King, one of its youngest members, president. He went home to prepare for his first appearance in what was to become a historic role. A mass meeting had been called for 8:00 P.M., and, as he was to do many times in the years ahead, he withdrew to a quiet place to examine his conscience, asking himself the question that would haunt him throughout his short life: "How could I make a speech that would be militant enough to keep my people aroused to positive action and yet moderate enough to keep this fervor within controllable and Christian bounds?"

His answer was to expand upon Rosa Parks's homely description of her reaction when the bus driver demanded her seat: ". . . there comes a time when people get tired. We are here this evening to say to those who have mistreated us so long that we are tired—tired of being segregated and humiliated, tired of being kicked about by the brutal feet of oppression." The lilting cadences of his resonant baritone, soon to become familiar around the globe, brought forth the traditional harmonic response from the thousands who jammed the church and overflowed into the streets around it. He offered the old promise of salvation, touching all the chords of folk memory, but now there was a difference. He was, the black journalist, Louis Lomax, wrote, "the first Negro minister I ever heard who [could] reduce the Negro problem to a spiritual matter and yet inspire the people to seek a solution on this side of Jordan, not in life beyond death."

He used the gospel freely in that first message of exhortation and restraint, and he was conscious, certainly that he was addressing not only the sea of black faces before him but the mass of whites beyond, who would receive his words second-hand, stripped of the magic of communion. To these he offered reassurance in a fashion that would also remind them of their ancient guilt: ". . . in our protest there will be no cross burnings. No white person will be taken from his home by a hooded Negro mob and brutally murdered. There will be no threats and intimidation. We will be guided by the highest principles of law and order."

MANY of the black leaders thought the boycott should be limited to one day, doubting their ability to long hold in line the 17,500 blacks who rode the buses twice a day to and from work. The city fathers of Montgomery were convinced that this would be the case, and initially greeted the protest with something close to amused tolerance. If that contemptuous but comparatively benign mood had held, the movement might well have died aborning. When King led his negotiating committee to City Hall on December 8, the demands presented were so moderate they could have been granted without doing any violence to the basic concept of Jim Crow. The MIA did not demand an end to segregation, only that blacks be seated from the back of the bus on a first-come, first-served basis, and that whites, who would seat from the front not be given an absolute priority on seats when there was an overlap. They also asked for a guarantee of courteous treatment, and that black bus drivers be hired for predominantly black routes.

One of the three city commissioners indicated willingness to meet the demands, and another was leaning in that direction when Jack Crenshaw, attorney for the privately owned bus company, intervened with the argument that such concessions couldn't be granted without an amendment to existing segregation laws. This was a dubious proposition since the conditions demanded by the MIA were already in effect in Mobile, where the same bus company held the franchise. Asked to stay behind for private discussion after departure of the press, King heard Crenshaw candidly state the real objection: "If we granted the Negroes these demands they would go about boasting of a victory they had won over the white people; and this we will not stand for." The young pastor was shocked; he had come to City Hall believing the justice of his cause so evident, and the relief sought so mild, reasonable white men were bound to see the light.

In retrospect, Crenshaw's response seems a peculiarly obtuse manifestation of arrogance since the Chicago-owned bus company had no inherent commitment to Jim Crow, as such, and did have a considerable interest in maintaining the goodwill of the blacks who made up 75 percent of its passenger load—a pattern that had emerged across the South as the automobile freed the affluent of dependence upon public transportation. But, whatever else may be said of Crenshaw's insistence on holding the line, it cannot be written off as irrational. In the context of that time it would appear that the shrewd white lawyer sensed the real implications of Rosa Parks's defiance before King did.

All this was taking place in the prolonged moment of suspense that followed the Supreme Court's school desegration orders. In the winter of 1955–56 there was no movement toward compliance in Alabama, but any qualified lawyer who studied *Brown I* and *Brown II* had to conclude that the statutory basis for Jim Crow had been undermined. And any politician had to be aware that pressure for last-ditch resistance was building on the white side. If the boycott failed, its leaders would be discredited and the black community presumably would relapse into its usual apathy. On the other hand, concessions which eased but did not eliminate the demeaning injustices of Jim Crow might buy a little time, but would bring to light grievances far more compelling than the seating arrangement of city buses.

KING always believed that his presence in Montgomery at this moment in history was providential. If so, included in the divine purpose was the education necessary to prepare a political innocent for the great tasks that lay ahead. When the boycott was over and victory was his King cited the lessons he had learned: "I came to see that no one gives up his privileges without strong resistance; I saw further that the underlying purpose of segregation was to oppress and exploit the segregated, not simply to keep them apart." The fact that it required so searing an experience to remove the scales from the eyes of a sensitive, intelligent twenty-six-year-old black who had grown up in Georgia explains a great deal about King and the movement he led.

"As far back as I could remember, I had resented segregation," he wrote, and yet, as a boy growing up in the solidly middle-class "golden ghetto" of Atlanta, he had rarely been touched by it. His father, a powerful preacher and community leader, pastored a congregation of four thousand at Ebenezer Baptist; his mother's father had filled the same pulpit. "Daddy King," as he later was called to distinguish him from his famous son, refused to ride the Atlanta streetcars and buses by way of protesting Jim Crow—but didn't really need to since he always had an automobile at his disposal. So young Martin grew up surrounded by respectable black peers, and would not be exposed to intimate contact with whites until he reached maturity. At black Morehouse College he demonstrated uncommon scholastic ability; when he journeyed forth from Atlanta to Crozer Theological Seminary in Pennsylvania, and on to Boston University for his Ph.D., he enjoyed the special dispensation reserved for educated blacks with a religious vocation and he moved into the closest approximation of integrated society the nation then afforded.

He met his wife, equally sensitive and intelligent, in Boston, where she was doing graduate work at the New England Conservatory, coming there after graduation from Antioch College in the Quaker stronghold of Yellow Springs, Ohio. Coretta Scott's childhood in Marion, Alabama, had not been quite so sheltered. But she came from a family that had farmed its own land since Reconstruction, and her father was a solid man of property who could afford to send his daughters to a private high school founded by the abolitionists, and on to college. In a memoir written after the martyrdom of her husband, Corretta fondly recalled their courtship and formal wedding, setting down details that could have come from the diary of any white Alabama bride of the period. The black poet, Maya Angelou, tells of a white woman who responded to the intelligence that the poet's grandmother had owned the only black general store in Stamps, Arkansas, by exclaiming, "Why, you were a debutante!" Not quite, but Miss Angelou noted that proper black girls in small Southern towns were imbued with the same Victorian values as their white counterparts.

Coretta wanted to stay in the North, and Martin had promising opportunities to do so after his graduation from B.U. But he thought he had a duty to his people to return to the South, and Coretta came to share his sense of mission. Her description of the poor blacks in Montgomery as she first saw them from her new perspective might have been set down by one of the abolitionist ladies who made the round trip in reverse: "When they spoke to a white person, their backbones seemed to crumple, they seemed to diminish." That would never happen to Coretta Scott King, nor to her husband, who made the head-high march the major instrument of his movement. "We can straighten up our backs and walk erect now," he told the humblest of his followers. "We are walking to freedom in dignity."

WHEN King suddenly came into the ken of white Montgomery and, as the boycott held, of the nation at large, he began to be described as symbolizing the New Negro, a self-confident replacement for the docile Sambo of old. A *New York Times* reporter checking out the thesis recorded the response of a black mail carrier: "It's not a New Negro—it's just us old Negroes, the same old folks. It's not a New Negro—it's the new times. Only we know it, that's all, and the white folks here haven't caught on to it yet."

There was also a new visibility. Before World War II troubles like those in Montgomery were reported in brief dispatches sent by telegraph to major newspapers where, unless they involved major acts of violence, they were considered of marginal interest. Now the coaxial cable carried instant motion pictures to television news directors with an insatiable appetite for action involving confrontation and suspense. Montgomery provided a historic backdrop for a simplified morality play, and the casting was perfect.

The white antagonists provided the counterpoint high drama requires. On December 18 when King went to City Hall for a negotiating session, he found the secretary of the Montgomery Citizens Council in attendance, and thereafter the screw began to turn. First there was harassment by the police, and then, at the end of January, while the pastor was away speaking at a rally, a stick of dynamite was exploded on the front porch of his parsonage—injuring no one and doing little damage, except to the nerves of the white policemen and reporters who found themselves surrounded by a threatening black mob when they arrived at the scene. Here was the perfect setting for King's message of nonviolence, delivered as he stood on his splintered doorstep, urging his restive neighbors, "If you have weapons, take them home; if you do not have them please do not seek to get them. . . .

"We must love our white brothers, no matter what they do to us," he continued. "We must make them know we love them. Jesus still cries out in words that echo across the centuries: 'Love your enemies; bless them that curse you; pray for them that spitefully use you.' This is what we must live by. We must meet hate with love. Remember, if I am stopped this movement will not stop, because God is with the movement. Go home with this glowing faith and this radiant assurance."

Messages of support, often accompanied by donations of cash, came flooding in from all parts of the nation. The impromptu car pool which had been organized to transport the black faithful was augmented by the purchase of fifteen new station wagons, each registered in the name of a black church. The means were at hand for an indefinite confrontation, and the attention of the media helped maintain morale. The reporters searched for color among the bit players in the drama, and found an abundance in the ordinary black's ingrained capacity for irony, honed by the long tradition of slyly putting down "old massa."

There was the worker who lived more than fifteen miles from his job and arranged to be driven there each morning, but always was dropped just over the hill, where he slung his coat over his shoulder and trudged wearily into his boss's sight. "Ain't you gettin' tired, John?" The Man would inquire. "Ain't it gettin' to be a mighty long way?" And John would sigh, and say, "It sure is, Mr. Charlie, it surely is. But we never did rightly know from the Bible just how far it was that Christ walked from Bethlehem to Jerusalem, did we?" There were white matrons who drove their own cars into the black neighborhoods to make sure their maids got to work on time. It was one of these inadvertent chauffeurs who observed to her help that the bus strike was just terrible. "Yes, ma'am, it sure is," came the reply, "and I just told my young'uns that this kind of thing is white folks' business and we just stay off the buses till they get this whole thing settled." And a quote certain to loosen the pursestrings of a sentimental Yankee was the affirmation of an old woman, later excerpted as the title of a book written in praise of the movement: "It used to be my soul was tired and my feets rested; now my feets tired but my soul is rested."

The publicity worked the other way, too. In the summer of 1956 Sen. Sam Englehardt of the Alabama Citizens Councils told Ted Poston, a black reporter for the *New York Post:* "The bus boycott made us. Before the niggers stopped riding the buses, we had only eight hundred members. Now we have thirteen thousand to fourteen thousand in Montgomery alone." Among them were all three members of the Montgomery City Commission.

WHILE King and his supporters were being harassed by state legal action, Robert Carter of the NAACP was counterattacking in federal court, where he won a two-to-one ruling holding that Montgomery's bus segregation statutes were unconstitutional on their face. On November 13 word came that the United States Supreme Court had affirmed the finding. This meant that the state cases against the MIA were moot—and, more than that, it removed constitutional sanction from Jim Crow on all forms of public transportation, in Montgomery and everywhere else.

Eight thousand blacks turned out to celebrate the famous victory and renew their pledge to stay off the buses until the Supreme Court order reached Montgomery and was actually put into effect. That night forty carloads of hooded Ku Klux Klansmen rode through black neighborhoods. In earlier days streets would have emptied and houses gone dark in the face of the implied threat; this time blacks stood on the sidewalks and lighted porches and, King wrote, "behaved as though they were watching a circus parade." On December 20, a little over a year after Rosa Parks refused to yield her seat, the Supreme Court order was served on the parties. At 6:00 A.M. the next morning a bus arrived at the stop outside the once-bombed parsonage and King stepped aboard with two of his black colleagues and a white minister, paid his fare, and sat down on the front seat.

"I believe you are Reverend King, aren't you?" the driver said. "We are glad to have you aboard this morning."

The happy ending of the crusade was not to be quite that neat. The legal harassment and economic pressure tactics of the Citizens Council had been of no avail, and now, in the pattern that would recur over and over in other Southern cities, unreconstructed Klansmen returned to the old ways. Buses traveling on ill-lit streets were fired on with such regularity the City Commission ordered suspension of all runs after 5:00 P.M. In early January a wave of bombings struck four black churches and the homes of the Rev. Ralph Abernathy, King's closest associate, and a Lutheran minister, the MIA's most conspicuous white supporter.

This proved to be the movement's coda, finally pushing the white establishment beyond the line of toleration, bringing forth a resounding front-page editorial by my old friend Grover Hall of the *Advertiser* under the heading, "Is it safe to live in Montgomery?" Clearly it wasn't, and leading white ministers and businessmen came forward to agree with Hall that the issue was no longer segregation versus integration, but law and order. Seven white men were charged with the bombing, five were indicted by a grand jury, and the prosecutor made an all-out effort to convict them—failing, as many others were to do, only because the prosecution came to dead end with a white jury that simply refused to render a guilty verdict. "Justice had once more miscarried," King wrote. "But the diehards had made their last stand. The disturbances ceased abruptly. Desegregation on the buses proceeded smoothly."

THE high drama in Montgomery touched off protest movements in half a dozen other Southern cities, and excited interest in all of them. King's example inspired a new militancy among the younger black ministers who were beginning to take over the leading pulpits from older, more accommodating men. On the practical side, MIA pinpointed an area where blacks had inescapable economic leverage; there wasn't a transit company in the region that could make a profit, or even long survive, without their continued patronage. So it was that when he went to Atlanta in early January to meet with sixty black leaders from twenty-two communities across the South, the organization King founded was first called the "Southern Leadership Conference on Transportation and Nonviolent Integration."

By this time he had formulated the doctrine he would espouse for the rest of his life. He had been attracted to the idea of passive resistance as a moral imperative when he read Thoreau's *Essay on Civil Disobedience* during his undergraduate years. At Crozer Seminary he had been exposed to the theories of nonviolence advocated by Mahatma Gandhi, and he had pursued this line of thought with his philosophy professors at Boston University. But it was only after activism had been thrust upon him that he began to see a practical lesson for American blacks in Gandhi's famous Salt March, which marked the beginning of the end of British colonial rule in India.

In the beginning King was moved only by the challenge of applying, under duress, the teachings of Christ. "It was the Sermon on the Mount, rather than the doctrine of passive resistance, that initially inspired the Negroes of Montgomery to dignified social action," he wrote. But, reflecting on the teachings of Gandhi, he began to perceive that the commitment to nonviolence did not have to be passive: "Non-violent resistance had emerged as the technique of the movement, while love stood as the regulating ideal. . . . Christ furnished the spirit and motivation while Gandhi furnished the method."

King's new organization was announced at a press conference at which the founders affirmed their conviction that "non-violence transforms weakness into strength and breeds courage in the face of danger," and offering the pledge: "Not one hair of one head of one white person shall be harmed." An incredulous *New York Times* reporter asked King, "Do you really mean that, even if the others start the violence?" The newly anointed leader replied, "Individuals had better speak for themselves on that. But I mean it." The reporter queried the sixty men present one by one, and each nodded assent.

When it reconvened on February 14 in New Orleans, the group had grown to ninety-seven members from thirty-five communities in ten states, had broadened its protest to include all forms of segregation, and decided to give its first priority to a voter registration drive. The essentially religious character was reaffirmed, however, in the change of title to Southern Christian Leadership Conference. A telegram was dispatched over King's signature urging President Eisenhower to convene a White House Conference on Civil Rights comparable to those he had sponsored on education and juvenile deliquency. The message included a touch of nonviolent pressure: "If some effective remedial steps are not taken we shall be compelled to initiate a mighty Prayer Pilgrimage to Washington." There was no response and the pilgrimage was scheduled for May 17, 1957, the third anniversary of *Brown.*

King had now received his secular anointment, a cover story in *Time,* and the old line black leaders threw their resources behind the SCLC's first march on Washington. When the great day came they were all there on the steps of the Lincoln Memorial—A. Philip Randolph, Roy Wilkins, Adam Clayton Powell, Mordecai Johnson, surrounded by celebrities from show business and sports: Ruby Dee, Harry Belafonte, Sidney Poitier, Sammy Davis, Jr., Jackie Robinson. The *Washington Post* estimated that twenty-five thousand people, mostly black, had assembled on the Mall when Mahalia Jackson's powerful voice rolled out, "I've Been 'Buked, I've Been Scorned." The climax came in King's peroration, which was more a supplication than a demand:

Give us the ballot . . . and we will transform the salient misdeeds of bloodthirsty mobs into abiding good deeds of orderly citizens. . . .

Give us the ballot . . . and we will fill the legislative halls with men of goodwill. . . .

Give us the ballot . . . [now the crowd was chanting the opening phrase with him] . . . and we will place judges on the benches of the South who will do justice and love mercy. . . .

Give us the ballot . . . and we will quietly and nonviolently, without

rancor and bitterness, implement the Supreme Court's decision of
May 17, 1954.

This was Martin Luther King's first coming, and he presented only a truncated version of the dream of redemption he
would hold out in his second, nine years later, when he
attracted ten times the multitude, kept the network cameras on
the celebration from beginning to end, and touched the conscience of the nation with his moving vision of the great day
"when all of God's children, black men and white, Jews and
Gentiles, Protestants and Catholics, will be able to join hands
and sing in the words of that old Negro spiritual: 'Free at last!
Free at last! Thank God Almighty, we are free at last!'"

But, if the white community was not yet listening to the
young Georgia preacher in 1957, the black community was
electrified by his message. In the *Amsterdam News* James Hicks
cited King as "the number one leader of sixteen million
Negroes in the United States. . . . At this point in his career the
people will follow him anywhere." The Prayer Pilgrimage
marked the shift of the center of the civil rights movement
from North to South, and the black cause gained a moral depth
and breadth of appeal it had not had before. But, as King
recognized, in the critical days ahead it would have to be a force
sufficient unto itself. In *Stride Toward Freedom* he cited another
of the hard lessons he had learned in Montgomery: "As a result
of the Citizens Councils' activities most white moderates in the
South no longer feel free to discuss in public the issues involved
in desegregation for fear of social ostracism and economic
reprisals. What channels of communication had once existed
between whites and Negroes have thus been largely closed."

It wasn't much better in the North. The pilgrimage did not
succeed in opening the door of the White House; the best the
administration would offer in response to Adam Clayton
Powell's importuning was a conference for King and Abernathy
with Vice-President Nixon and the cabinet's lonely liberal,
Labor Secretary James P. Mitchell. King found the vice-
president polite, cool, and noncommittal, and the secretary
unwilling to go beyond a recitation of existing programs
presumed to benefit blacks.

". . . the forces of good will failed to come through," King wrote. "The office of the President was appallingly silent, though just an occasional word from this powerful source, counseling the nation on the moral aspects of integration and the need for complying with the law, might have saved the South from its present confusion and terror." Before the year was out, the confusion and terror came to a head on my own turf, in Arkansas, where President Eisenhower was forced to make his first affirmative gesture of support for the Supreme Court by calling out the United States Army to put a stop to the calculated defiance of Orval Eugene Faubus.

17

⁓

Showdown at Little Rock

A few days before the opening of the 1957 school term Benjamin Fine, education editor of the *New York Times,* turned up at my office at the *Arkansas Gazette* in the course of checking out the plan under which a handful of blacks were scheduled to be admitted to Little Rock's two-thousand-student Central High School. This orderly transition, Fine thought, might provide a model for thousands of other districts just now beginning to face up to the reality of the three-year-old mandate of the Supreme Court.

I thought so too. Those on the newspaper who covered day-to-day developments anticipated nothing more in the way of resistance than passing verbal fireworks. Comparing notes with Ben Fine I was impressed again with the elaborate preparation that had followed the school board's initial announcement, just five days after *Brown I,* that it would comply with the Supreme Court mandate as soon as the requirements for implementation were spelled out. When *Brown II* came down a year later, Virgil Blossom, the district's energetic superintendent, had a blueprint ready.

The "Blossom Plan" was projected to go into effect upon completion of two new high schools, one a modern, fully equipped plant to replace the antiquated black Horace Mann school in the central city, the other to accommodate the spreading white suburbs on the western fringe. Pupils would be assigned to grades ten through twelve on the basis of residence, but all black schools would continue as presently organized and staffed, and those of either race who objected to their assignment would be free to transfer. As desegregation proceeded downward grade by grade over a period of six years it was assumed that most minority students would stay where they were, as was the case with the great majority of those assigned to Central; all but 9 of the 516 eligible blacks had elected, or had been persuaded, to remain at Horace Mann after counseling sessions with black and white administrators.

Limited and gradual though it was, the Blossom Plan had met the test of deliberate speed when the NAACP challenged it in federal court. The superintendent, an earnest former football coach and natural-born Rotarian, said he thought desegregation premature but considered it his duty to meet the requirements of the law. He peddled his formula in hundreds of speeches before civic clubs, parent-teacher associations, and church groups, and defended it before black audiences as the maximum that could be sold to the white community. I had some reservations, particularly as to the top-down formulation, but I did not question Blossom's good faith, nor that of the solid citizens who made up the school board. Both the *Gazette* and its afternoon competitor, the *Arkansas Democrat*, endorsed the plan. So did the City Council, the Chamber of Commerce, and the Ministerial Alliance. There was no reason to doubt that it had solid support in the white community, and grudging acceptance among blacks.

But the spirit of compliance manifest in Little Rock did not hold throughout the state. In the plantation belt of eastern Arkansas most of the local politicians spoke out in the same vein as their compatriots on the other side of the Mississippi, and some openly lined up with the Citizens Councils. The ingrained populist resentment against meddling Yankee outsiders spread up the river valleys and into the hills, where blacks were few. It was only in the urban centers that moderation prevailed. In Little Rock, respectable citizens who may have had covert sympathy for the aims of the Citizens Council were unwilling to rally around the standard waved by its hyperactive spokesman, Amis Guthridge, a maverick lawyer who had no standing with his fellow members of the bar.

When I came back to Arkansas in the summer of 1956 after ten months with the Stevenson campaign, the resistance movement was still largely rhetorical and seemed to be contained. The governor, Orval Faubus, was rated liberal by Arkansas standards and had kept his national credentials in order by joining the state's labor leaders in support of Averell Harriman for the Democratic presidential nomination. Faubus greeted *Brown II* with as moderate a statement as any made by a major Southern officeholder: "It appears that the Court left some degree of decision in these matters to the federal district courts. I believe this will guarantee against any sudden dislocation. . . . Our reliance now must be upon the good will that exists between the two races—the good will that has long made Arkansas a model for the other Southern states in all matters affecting the relationship between the races."

In that summer's Democratic primary Faubus was challenged by James D. Johnson, a South Arkansas politician who was by all odds the most aggressive and effective of the diehard segregationists. The governor shrugged off Johnson's charge that his passivity was about to subject white Arkansans to the horrors of wholesale race-mixing, and won a second two-year term by a wide margin. I was never close to Faubus, as evidenced by my inability to persuade him to back Adlai Stevenson, but I had known him since 1948 when he came down from the mountains of Madison County to join Sid McMath in the statehouse. On the record it seemed reasonable to assume that the governor's public reaction to the Supreme Court decision represented his private conviction, and that he would stand by it.

In hindsight I can see signs that should have provided due warning that Faubus would abandon his moderate stance as public opinion hardened in the South between the spring of 1956 and the fall of 1957. If he had never been a race-baiter, he had based his political career on the parochial resentments of backcountry voters, and his willingness to cut deals with the kind of county political bosses who flourished in the plantation country. As a surprise last-minute entry in the governor's race against McMath's successor, Francis Cherry, a lackluster conservative up for what was ordinarily an automatic second two-year term, Faubus unveiled his ingratiating hillbilly persona in the course of an old-fashioned Jeff Davis-style campaign against a stuffy, thin-skinned opponent peculiarly susceptible to it.

As a nominal supporter of Cherry I did not take Faubus's bid seriously until he confounded the odds-makers by holding the incumbent below a majority and forcing him into a runoff. This was the depth of the McCarthy era, and when Cherry's handlers were panicked by the upset they decided to counter with Communism-by-association, dredging up a charge that Faubus, as a teen-ager, had attended long-defunct Commonwealth College, a left-wing self-help school established in the Ozarks during the depression years. The Commonwealth College story was old, thin stuff at best, and the fact that Faubus might have been a student there was hardly surprising since his father, old Sam Faubus, was well known in the hills as a proudly unreconstructed Eugene V. Debs socialist, one of those self-educated radicals who kept the militant populist faith alive in the little towns of the backcountry South.

When the Cherry people brought around copy for an advertisement setting forth the Commonwealth College "expose" I told them the *Gazette* would not accept it, and that if it were published elsewhere we would denounce the smear in the strongest possible terms. The material appeared in a campaign circular and I let fly with both barrels in a front-page editorial. Whatever else he might be, I wrote, Faubus certainly was not a Communist, and the injection of such a patently spurious issue into the campaign only served to discredit Francis Cherry.

Now Faubus, in his turn, panicked and issued what amounted to a flat denial that he had ever set foot on the Commonwealth campus—this in the face of documentary evidence in our own files that he had at least been present long enough to be identified in a school publication. Edwin Dunaway, a former prosecuting attorney and state supreme court justice who shared my outrage at the smear, asked me to meet privately with him and Faubus. I found the candidate in a funk, convinced that he was done for. The truth, he said, was that he did attend Commonwealth, but left after a few weeks because he objected to some of the more extreme notions advocated there, such as free love. I suggested that he had better make that explanation public and that he should do so at once in order to minimize the effect of the false denial. Dunaway, already on the phone raising money for a television broadcast, had reserved time by personally guaranteeing the cost. I agreed to try to put together a coherent statement of Faubus's version of his brief career at Commonwealth, and some choice remarks on the character of those who had attempted to use it against him.

Faubus gave the *Gazette*'s editorial, Dunaway's air time, and my speech draft credit for staving off a defeat in his maiden race that might have nipped his gubernatorial career in the bud, and he continued to acknowledge his debt when I encountered him in the years after we became prime adversaries. Faubus, a sly man with a political needle, thus reminded Judge Dunaway and me that we shared a burden of responsibility with Sid McMath, who once said, "I brought Orval down out of the hills, and every night I pray for forgiveness."

By the spring of 1957 the groundwork for massive resistance, up to and including abandonment of the public school system, had been laid in statutes enacted by eight Southern legislatures. Those who needed a high-sounding rationale followed the lead of the Richmond editor, James Jackson Kilpatrick, who reached back to the Kentucky-Virginia interposition resolutions of 1798 to provide a historical gloss for another try at nullification: "This right rests in the incontrovertible theory that ours is a union of sovereign states, that the Federal government exists only by reason of a solemn compact among the states. . . ." Those who spoke as candidly as the hyperbolic Kilpatrick echoed his sentiments, as quoted in *Time*: "The Negro is fundamentally and perhaps unalterably inferior; he is also immoral, indolent, inept, incapable of learning, and uninterested in full racial equality. The segregationist South has no guilt about keeping the Negro in his proper place—that is to say, in separate schools." To that end the legislators shouted through packages of bills the like of which had not been seen since the days of the Know-Nothings.

Orval Faubus did not appear to encourage the tide of sentiment that swept the Arkansas general assembly part-way into this company, but neither did he demur when he was presented with measures declaring the right of interposition, creating in its name a State Sovereignty Commission. The package was, I wrote in the *Gazette*, more an expression of pique than a practical program of resistance, since all the operational provisions were patently unconstitutional. Faubus seemed to share that view when, in July, the rambunctious legislature having gone home, he rejected a demand by the Citizens Councils that he interpose his police powers to halt the coming desegregation of Central High. "Everyone knows no state's laws supersede a federal law," he said.

But now the militant segregationists began to acquire

heavyweight backing from out of state. In Mississippi, Senator Eastland complained, "In Arkansas, where the governor will not take action, racial integration has already started. . . . If the Southern states are picked off one by one under the damnable doctrine of gradualism I don't know if we can hold or not." Local Citizens Council rallies, which had rarely attracted more than a few score of the faithful, began featuring out-of-state firebrands who openly encouraged violence. A barrage of letters, telegrams, and telephone calls from all parts of the South was concentrated on the governor's office in an orchestrated campaign that climaxed on August 22 with a flying visit from Gov. Marvin Griffin of Georgia, a colorful mountebank who had teamed up with the president of the Citizens Councils of America, Roy Harris of Augusta, to set the pace for the resistance movement.

Griffin and Harris told a Citizens Council rally that any red-blooded Southern governor would employ all means necessary to block the desegregation of a single white school. Roy Harris spelled out what that meant while Griffin nodded agreement; in Georgia, when the time came, the governor would turn out the State Highway Patrol, the National Guard, and every able-bodied man who could be enlisted to turn back blacks at the schoolhouse door. Faubus did not attend the rally, but he put up Griffin and Harris in guest quarters at the Governor's Mansion, and joined them next morning for breakfast. Brooks Hays, the Little Rock congressman who served as an honest broker in the ill-fated effort to negotiate with the Eisenhower administration, cited the Georgians' visitation as the turning point: "The pressure was mounting on [Faubus] to follow a course similar to the one advocated by Griffin. His political future might well be at stake."

Virgil Blossom visited Faubus several times to plead for a public pledge to use the powers of his office to maintain order. He found the governor increasingly withdrawn and evasive. One week before school opening, at a private meeting with the full school board, Faubus surprised all those present by urging that the district initiate further delaying action in state court, where he could guarantee that an appropriate order would be issued. "Under no circumstances will the board enter into collusion with a state agency to counteract the federal court order," replied the board's counsel, A. F. House, senior partner in the state's leading law firm. "Well," Faubus replied, "I will still get a court suit. A suit will be filed, and the judge will order you to delay."

The secretary of the council's auxiliary, the Mothers League of Central High, duly turned up in chancery court seeking an injunction on the ground that her children would be endangered if admission of blacks engendered mob action. Chief Marvin Potts of the Little Rock police testified that his men had found no evidence of any planned violence, and Blossom said this was also true of the other police intelligence sources available to them, including the FBI. Faubus took the stand to testify vaguely that he had been told that white and black students had been found in possession of revolvers, and intimated that he had other evidence of impending trouble he was not at liberty to divulge. The foreordained injunction was promptly issued, and the groundwork for interposition had been laid. The Citizens Council strategy, I wrote in next morning's *Gazette*, had paid off: "The governor abjectly surrendered when it was no longer possible to continue straddling the issue."

On Friday, just four days away from school opening, Little Rock's school officials were back in federal court. Judge Ronald J. Davies, who had access to a voluminous FBI report that found no evidence of impending mob violence, declared the chancery court injunction void in the absence of any testimony to support it, ordered the school board to proceed with desegregation on schedule, and enjoined any further interference by "all persons, in any manner, directly or indirectly."

There followed a weekend of frantic maneuvering. Winthrop Rockefeller, Faubus's appointee as chairman of the Arkansas Industrial Development Commission, came down from his mountaintop ranch to plead with the governor not to interfere with the admission of the black children. Sid McMath and his law partner, Henry Woods, were busy trying to line up moderate politicians who might offset some of the pressure on Faubus from eastern Arkansas and the state capitals of the Deep South. Edwin Dunaway, informal leader of the distraught liberals, was keeping a line open to the black community—where tension had been rising since the evening of Governor Griffin's visit, when a rock crashed through a picture window at the home of Daisy Bates, the state president of the NAACP. The attached note was to the point: "Stone this time. Dynamite next time."

Faubus's increasingly inflammatory public statements now constituted a virtual invitation for segregationist extremists to fulfill his prophecy of mob action. Without the guarantee of backup support from the state police and the National Guard the dispirited Little Rock police were in poor shape to handle a riot of any magnitude. As the result of a recent election changing the form of municipal government, Mayor Woodrow Mann and the city councilmen were scheduled to leave office in a few weeks, and these lame ducks were hardly disposed toward forthright action. The police chief was an avowed segregationist who said he would do his duty, and probably would, but there were reports that the fire chief had refused support with the pressure hoses essential to mob control.

Monday was Labor Day, and downtown was virtually deserted when Hugh Patterson and I met with J. N. Heiskell to review the situation. The publisher had been making the round of his sources in the business community, and his findings confirmed what I had heard from the politicians. Now that Faubus was openly allied with the segregationists, the community's leaders, without any effective exception, were heading for the storm cellars. If the *Gazette* held to its position it was virtually certain that we would stand alone, exposed to the full force of the economic pressures the Citizens Councils could muster with the backing of the state government. Those of us on the news and editorial side were ready to man the battlements, but I didn't think I had the right to make that decision since it was the owners, represented by Heiskell and Patterson, who would suffer the heaviest penalty. Mr. J. N. turned his chair to look out across the quiet streets and said, "I'm an old man, and I've lived too long to let people like that take over my city." Patterson's testy response was, "It's a silly question. I don't see why the hell you even thought you had to raise it."

On Monday night, without prior notice to any concerned party, Faubus ordered the Arkansas National Guard to take over the building and grounds of Central High because of "evidence of disorder and threats of disorder." Tuesday morning the black children stayed home, but that afternoon Judge Davies called the governor's hand, stating his assumption that the state troops had been called out to uphold the law, and again ordering the desegregation plan into effect. Next morning my front-page editorial was a prophecy and a warning:

. . . the issue is no longer segregation vs. integration. The question has now become the supremacy of the government of the United States in all matters of law. And clearly the federal government cannot let this issue remain unresolved no matter what the cost to this community.

. . . If Mr. Faubus in fact has no intention of defying federal authority now is the time for him to call a halt to the resistance which is preventing the carrying out of a duly entered court order. And certainly he should do so before his own actions become the cause of the violence he professes to fear.

Since he often told me he always read the *Gazette*'s editorials, I assume Orval Faubus read that one when he arose, as usual, shortly after dawn on Wednesday, September 4. If so, he was not impressed. At 9:00 A.M. the nine black children reported to Central High and were turned away by armed guardsmen while members of the Citizens Council stood across the street and cheered.

THERE are literally volumes of speculation on how and why Orval Faubus arrived at that fateful decision, and then refused to back down during the seventeen days of low- and high-level negotiation with Washington that followed. He never really denied the element of political expediency. When Winthrop Rockefeller pleaded with him not to block the Blossom Plan Faubus told him, "I'm sorry, but I'm already committed. I'm going to run for a third term, and if I don't do this Jim Johnson and Bruce Bennett (the segregationist state attorney general) will tear me to shreds." He was correct, I think, in figuring that such a race would require segregationist credentials. But there were less drastic means of obtaining them—as some of his contemporaries in the Upper South demonstrated by denouncing the Supreme Court decision in the resounding language of the Southern Manifesto and pledging to continue the battle on every legal front, which had the effect of transferring the burden of enforcement to the federals. It seems probable that in the beginning Faubus had something like this in mind. But once he seized the high school he found he had passed the point of no return. If he yielded to the federals, or even seemed to, he would have to forget his plan to stand for reelection—and this was a peculiarly difficult decision for a man who quite literally had no option that would maintain any approximation of the prestige and standing he now enjoyed.

Faubus had had no consistent career until he belatedly made one for himself in state politics. He was the owner and editor of the weekly newspaper at Huntsville, the seat of remote Madison County, but its earnings were so nominal he made out by also serving as postmaster. From the time he was big enough to shoulder an axe he worked alongside his father in the hickory woods, intermittently attending the one-room school from which he graduated at eighteen. In the summers he and his wife joined the migrant fruit and berry pickers who followed the harvest from Louisiana to Michigan, and one year he worked in the logging camps of the Pacific Northwest.

There was nothing in this background to make him a racist. His father once said that Orval had never seen a black man until he was full grown and went off to Missouri to pick strawberries. Moreover, in the formative years he was exposed to the tutelage of old Sam, a fiercely egalitarian radical who held that social justice required that all working people, white and black, stand shoulder to shoulder against the privileged classes. When Orval betrayed the old man's teachings and thereby became a prime object of media attention, Sam Faubus refrained from denouncing his flesh and blood to the reporters who sought him out in his little house up on Greasy Creek. But, throughout his son's long career in the statehouse, he regularly wrote sharply critical letters that appeared in the *Gazette*'s "From the People" column over the signature Jimmy Higgins. He identified himself only after I had moved to California, where I received a letter in his shaky handwriting saying he now felt free to tell me that he was Jimmy Higgins, and wanted to commend me in his own name for my stand against his erring son.

Even as a little boy, Sam Faubus once pointed out, Orval could never stand to be looked down upon. As an unexpected tenant of the Governor's Mansion he had ample reason to feel that the Little Rock establishment resented his populist assault on Francis Cherry, and tended to write him off as a rude demagogue. He suspected that the liberal Democrats, who should have been his political allies, didn't take him seriously. He saw, correctly, that when the Blossom Plan worked through to its conclusion the affluent whites in the suburbs would be largely exempt from integrated schools while the working-class whites in the downtown section would have to send their children to class with blacks. His most durable antagonist, Daisy Bates of the NAACP, believed that it was this personal resentment that pushed him into the arms of the segregationists. "I could see what was happening to Orval after he got in office," she once told me. "The liberals thought he was a political accident and wouldn't be there long, and they had little to do with him. When he put those troops around Central High it was the people in Pulaski Heights he was really trying to get at. I told Edwin Dunaway: You all may deserve Orval Faubus, but, by God, I don't!"

ROBERT SHERRILL, reviewing Faubus's unprecedented fourteen years in the governor's office, noted that his tenure was characterized throughout by a kind of galvanic groping: "There is in Faubus's makeup a weakness that, in momemts of pressure, makes him act seldom from logic, often from fear, and even more often from whatever the last stress happens to be before action is demanded of him," he wrote in *Gothic Politics in the Deep South.* That seems a fair characterization of the course that led him to the seizure of Central High, and left him with no plan of action when he found himself in the inevitable confrontation with President Eisenhower—who seemed to have no more idea what to do next than Faubus did. "Attorney General Herbert Brownell, Jr., was without any immediate strategy or policy to pursue," Lyle Wilson of United Press reported from Washington.

Into this power vacuum moved the Southern-born publisher of the *Washington Post,* Philip Graham, a potent behind-the-scenes political operator whose grand design to promote Lyndon Johnson into the presidency was being badly skewed by mounting racial tension in the South. In *The Powers That Be* David Halberstam cited the showdown at Central High as the occasion that appeared to push Graham around the bend into the nervous breakdown that led finally to his suicide:

His activities became frenzied. He became a self-appointed manager of the Little Rock crisis. He was on the phone day and night to everyone: the White House; presidential advisors Sherman Adams and Maxwell Rabb; Nixon; Bill Rogers; Harry Ashmore, the Little Rock editor; Brooks Hays, the Little Rock congressman; black leaders Thurgood Marshall and Roy Wilkins. Trying to think of anyone Ike might listen to. Calling on his White House reporter, Eddie Folliard, to pass on notes to Ike. Calling Ike's friends to get him to move. Trying to move Faubus a little, wondering what might affect Faubus, thinking of Truman. Truman was a good Baptist and a traditionalist, maybe Truman would call Faubus. But who would call Truman? Brooks Hays, that's who. Hays was a national lay Baptist leader and so Graham called Hays to call Truman to call Faubus. Anything. There was a touch of desperation to it all. . . .

Hays made the call to Truman, and another to Sherman Adams, Eisenhower's chief of staff, suggesting that the president invite Faubus to Washington to talk things over. From this point on he became the link between the two parties, and there could hardly have been a weaker one. Thoroughly honorable, highly intelligent, richly humorous, and devoutly Christian, Hays was, despite his fourteen years in Congress, still something of a political innocent—entirely too trusting to deal effectively with the devious Faubus and the hot-eyed men who were now breathing on his neck. In *A Southern Moderate Speaks,* a detailed account of his fruitless service as go-between, Hays wrote that he never had any doubt that the federal government would, and should sustain the Court order. His one great concern, he told Sherman Adams, was that the governor, "not be driven into the arms of the few extremists in the Southern governor's group." His old friend Sherman, he wrote, was rather sympathetic on this score, which could only mean that innocence was not confined to the Little Rock end of the line.

It took Hays three days to persuade Faubus to meet the White House's condition that he request the meeting, and include in his telegram an affirmation of his "desire to comply with the order that has been issued by the District Court in this case. . . ." By this time Eisenhower was operating out of his vacation headquarters on the golf course of the Newport Country Club in Rhode Island. On the eve of their departure for the summer retreat of America's biggest rich, Hays wrote in his diary: "It seems to me that time, not substance, presents the difficulty. The governor is not opposed to the School Board decision being carried out, he simply thinks that a delay is essential to the maintenance of peace." That, in essence, was the proposition Faubus presented at Newport, and Eisenhower seemed to have some sympathy for it. But, inevitably, Attorney General Herbert Brownell, Jr., shot it down by observing that the matter, after all, was not in the hands of the executive, but in the courts, which had already allowed the Little Rock School Board three and a half years to work out a plan to admit nine black children under an order that granted another six years to complete the opening of the grades. On its face, the Blossom Plan was the minimum any court could conceivably approve without abandoning the Supreme Court mandate altogether.

Formal statements from both parties emerged from the meeting beside the verdant fairway. The key passages in the governor's, cleared in advance by Adams and Brownell, were clear enough:

I have never expressed any personal opinion regarding the Supreme Court decision of 1954 which ordered integration. That is not relevant. That decision is the law of the land and must be obeyed. . . .

The people of Little Rock are law abiding, and I know that they expect to obey valid court orders. In this they shall have my support. In so doing it is my responsibility to protect the people from violence in any form. . . .

In his companion statement the president expressed confidence that the governor intended "to respect the decisions of the United States District Court and to give his full cooperation in carrying out his responsibilities in respect to these decisions."

The Newport Compact lasted just six days. In Judge Davies's courtroom, at a session called to hear argument on the injunction procedure brought by federal attorneys, Faubus's lawyers declined to introduce, or listen to, any testimony, walking out after declaring, "The position of the respondent, Governor Faubus . . . must be firm, unequivocal and unalterable. The governor of the state of Arkansas cannot and will not concede that the United States in this court or anywhere else can question his discretion and judgment as chief executive of a sovereign state when he acts in the performance of his constitutional duties." School officials, Mayor Mann, and Police Chief Potts again testified that they had no evidence of plans for concerted mob violence, and the same finding was included in a voluminous FBI report turned over to the judge by the government attorneys. The commander of the National Guard testified that his orders from the governor were to place off limits to blacks all schools previously operated exclusively for whites. Judge Davies reached the inescapable conclusion that the state troops were being used to bar desegregation of Central High in direct defiance of his previous order. That night Faubus responded by ordering the troops removed, and departed for the Southern Governors Conference at Sea Island, Georgia, where he would receive the warm embrace and hearty congratulations of his host, Marvin Griffin. He had not budged from the position he occupied before Brooks Hays arrived on the scene with a hope and a prayer.

On Monday morning, September 23, a semblance of the mob Faubus had been predicting finally materialized at Central High. A thousand whites of assorted age and sex assembled there, along with upwards of a hundred newsmen, who in the seething confusion were never able to determine how many were activists and how many curious bystanders. The fire chief had carried out his threat to refuse the use of his trucks and pressure hoses, and the police had to spread themselves in a thin line around school grounds covering six city blocks. Throughout the morning groups of howling, cursing demonstrators repeatedly charged the barricades. With the approach of noon, when classes were due to break, the situation would be complicated by an outpouring of students and the tough cop in charge, Assistant Chief Eugene Smith, concluded it would be impossible to cover all possible entrances to the school building. He recommended withdrawal of the blacks, and not long after they had been safely taken out a back entrance I talked with him by radio relay. "How do you feel, Gene?" I inquired. "My feet hurt," he replied. I remarked that this seemed an odd affliction for a man who had spent the morning standing firm. "Hell," he said, "I've walked a hundred miles today. I told my men that if any sonofabitch even thought about falling out I'd shoot him in the back of the head, and I had to be in position to deliver."

On that and the following day my office at the *Gazette* took on the atmosphere of one of the combat command posts I had manned in my days in the infantry. Most of the out-of-town correspondents were working out of our city room, an arrangement we welcomed since our own staff was spread thin and this gave us access to their reports. In the midst of the constant coming and going I was receiving telephone calls from all points on the compass, including a number from the frenetic Phil Graham in Washington. One of these, in the course of which he transferred me to Deputy Attorney General William Rogers, was referred to in news reports and gave rise to the durable myth that I was responsible for the dispatch of federal troops to Little Rock.

Rogers asked for my appraisal of the situation. I told him I thought the city police had done all that could be expected of them, that I had great respect for Gene Smith and accepted his judgment that the situation was beyond his control in the absence of backup state forces, which obviously were not going to be available. There was certainly a high risk of further trouble; Smith had told me that the most aggressive members of the mob were from out of town, some from out of state, and this had been borne out by our reporters' check of license plates of automobiles parked near the school. Now we were receiving reports that white goon squads were roaming through black neighborhoods. Sensational radio and TV accounts had raised tension to flash point, and anyone who was out to cause trouble would find plenty of opportunity. I thought the situation likely to grow worse if there were not an unmistakable show of force. I have no idea whether this information influenced Rogers; in any case my report included nothing that was not published next morning in the *Gazette,* and the same information was already available to him from other news sources—and from the scores of FBI agents who had been sent in to augment the resident force.

Another call came from J. William Fulbright, who had not

been heard from since Faubus called out the Guard three weeks before. My long-standing friendship with the senator had survived his signing the Southern Manifesto, but it had been a good many months since he had consulted me on a political matter. Now he asked if there was anything he could do that might ease the situation. For the moment, I replied, the problem was clearly one of protecting life and property, and that would seem to give him an opportunity to call Faubus at Sea Island and urge that he make state police and National Guard troops available to back up the local authorities—and that if he, like everybody else who tried, failed to get a satisfactory answer he should announce that fact. Well, he said, he was leaving for England in a few hours for a series of lectures at Oxford, and he thought it would be best to avoid a statement of any kind until his return. Some weeks later, when federal troops had restored calm to the beleaguered city, Fulbright's assistant, John Erickson, called to report that the senator had completed his tour at Oxford and would soon be heading home. He had asked Erickson to see if I had any suggestions. Tell him, I said, that he might as well enroll for the second semester.

A DETACHMENT of the 101st Airborne Infantry was flown to Little Rock from Fort Campbell, Kentucky, after Mayor Mann sent a telegram stating that the situation had passed beyond control by local authorities and that he could obtain no assurance of support from the governor. With the arrival of the disciplined troopers the Battle of Little Rock came to an abrupt halt. In terms of actual casualties it hadn't been much of a fight. Two black newsmen and a black passerby had been beaten; three white reporters and two photographers had been manhandled before being rescued by police; and Gene Smith had had the pleasure of felling a visitor from Benton with his billyclub. There were twenty-five arrests at the school site, and a few others had been brought in for creating disturbances elsewhere.

However, the psychic damage was heavy. The television and still cameras had sought out the naked face of hatred, and certainly it had been in evidence. The pushing and hauling of a few hundred frenzied men and women was magnified in the consciousness of the world to the point where Little Rock became the symbol of brutal, dead-end, resistance to the minimum requirements of racial justice. The impression still lives that the city was the scene of sustained race rioting so widespread the United States Army had to be called in to put it down. The fact is that no one, black or white, then or later, was injured seriously enough to require hospitalization. The only role for the army was to provide unmistakable evidence that, after all his vacillation, President Eisenhower was finally prepared to see that the orders of the federal courts were carried out.

This was the real significance of Little Rock; Faubus had forced a reluctant president into an irrevocable commitment to use his powers to protect and guarantee the declared rights of black citizens wherever they might be denied. Those who soon would rally by the thousands to march with Martin Luther King and the new generation of militant young leaders were no longer at the mercy of local authorities, the mobs they so often encouraged, and the state courts that were usually rigged against them. And everywhere outside the shrinking redoubt where the Citizens Councils held sway, public opinion was beginning to form behind the black cause. Orval Faubus was a hero to the mob; the nine courageous black children he failed to keep out of Central High were heroes to the world.

18

State of Siege

*F*or two years after Orval Faubus's seizure of Central High School the city of Little Rock served the national media as a microcosm of the South. By adopting the Citizens Councils' massive resistance strategy the governor jerked Arkansas out of its natural orbit in the Upper South, where moderate leaders managed to keep the reflexive states' rights challenge to federal authority within constitutional bounds; overnight he became presumptive spokesman for the bitter-enders who held sway in South Carolina, Georgia, Alabama, Mississippi, and Louisiana. To maintain this posture it was necessary for Faubus to keep Arkansas' urban population under what amounted to a state of siege. But the latent opposition was always there, and any correspondent who had the wit to plumb beneath the chaotic surface events could see the outline of the emerging political force that ultimately would bring Arkansas—and the rest of the South—into conformity with the Supreme Court's desegregation mandates.

So it was possible, and convenient, for the media to chart the course of the fever racking the region at the point where it seemed to have the highest temperature reading. In time this would shift the focus to Mississippi and Alabama, but for now Little Rock provided continuation of the morality play Martin Luther King had stage-managed in Montgomery. Television's oversimplified treatment reversed the usual symbolism; in the first act good, personified by black, had prevailed over evil, personified by white. In the second act evil was again triumphant. And the man who dominated the stage in Little Rock soon demonstrated that he was willing to try anything to keep the plot moving.

As the action ebbed and flowed over a period of months

the nation's leading journalists vied for the assignment. The
New York Times provided a measure of the progression; the very
first arrival from out of town, Ben Fine, was sent down on the
assumption that he would produce an inside-page think piece;
he was soon joined by John Popham, the newspaper's resident
expert on Southern politics; finally the lead went to Homer
Bigart, a veteran war correspondent. At one point *Time* and
Life, drawing upon bureaus in Chicago, Atlanta, and Dallas,
had twenty-two staffers on the ground. Present-day gray emi-
nences of television, then energetic young legmen, were there:
John Chancellor, Harry Reasoner, Howard K. Smith, Mike
Wallace, Sander Vanocur. Little Rock, Reasoner wrote in his
memoir, *Before the Colors Fade*, was the place "where television came to influence, if not to maturity. As in the case of
the Vietnam War a decade later . . . you could not hide from
it."

When the microphones clustered and the red lights of the
TV cameras began to glow, Faubus became a caricature of his
usual, canny self—but a highly effective one as he discovered
that sophisticated outlanders of the press corps, no less than
red-necked voters at the branch-heads, could be diverted by
sheer preposterosity. He set the tone when a hard-nosed
interrogator pointed out that his lawyers' defiant withdrawal
from Judge Davies's hearing on the use of the National Guard
contradicted his statement at Newport that he accepted *Brown*
as the law of the land. He had agreed to that language, he said,
because the president's men insisted upon it. "Just because I
said it," he added, "doesn't make it so." It was hard to think of a
follow-up question.

Remarkably, these convolutions also continued to bemuse
the White House. Since the federal troops were confined to the
area immediately around Central High, and their mission was
limited to guaranteeing peaceful entry for the black children,
President Eisenhower could hardly take seriously Faubus's
protest that Arkansas had been reduced to the status of an
occupied territory. He first used that characterization in a
network broadcast in which he recalled that his National Guard
unit had been one of those sent to the relief of the 101st
Airborne at Bastogne: "Today we find the members of that
famed division, which I helped to rescue, in Little Rock,

Arkansas, bludgeoning innocent bystanders . . . and with the warm, red blood of patriotic American citizens staining the cold, unsheathed knives. . . ." The only warm, red blood ever spilled on the 101st's picket line came from the chin of a lone demonstrator foolish enough to grab the rifle of a paratrooper, who responded with the butt as the manual of arms quite reasonably prescribes. I would have thought that this kind of gratuitous insult to an ornament of General Eisenhower's wartime command would have ended any possibility of his treating further with a man who had already double-crossed him once. Nevertheless, the president agreed to another negotiating session—this one initiated by the Southern Governors Conference. LeRoy Collins of Florida served as chairman of a delegation made up of three other moderates, Luther Hodges of North Carolina, Frank Clement of Tennessee, and Theodore McKeldin of Maryland. Marvin Griffin also was appointed by Collins, but for reasons that soon became apparent he did not show up for the meeting at the White House just six days after the black students entered Central High under federal protection.

Faubus, through the governors, assured the president that he was now prepared to use the National Guard, which had been federalized and removed from his command, to uphold the law. The White House announced that "upon a declaration on the part of the governor of Arkansas that he will not obstruct the orders of the federal courts and . . . will maintain law and order, the president will direct the secretary of defense to return command of the National Guard to the governor. Thereupon, as soon as practicable, all federal troops will be withdrawn." This compact didn't last out the day.

At Little Rock Faubus issued a statement approved in Washington, but added two words of his own; the key passage as he revised it qualified his original assurance to provide that "the orders of the federal courts will not be obstructed *by me.*" The White House indignantly rejected this as obviously abrogating the agreement, and Governor McKeldin declared that Faubus "now stands alone as the only man of prominence in all America who wants the troops of the federal government kept in Little Rock. By his ignominious double-crossing of the sincere and serious governors . . . he has elected to pile infamy on the heap of disgrace which he had inflicted on the great state of Arkansas . . ."

Back before the cameras, Faubus was asked why he reneged on this second statement with the White House. "Now, just a minute," he replied. "By adding the words 'by me' you mean they wrote their statement and then wrote mine? I write my statements from this end of the line. They can write theirs from that end." But hadn't he agreed to the language as presented by the four governors on his behalf? "That is true. The negotiations were on the basis of those two points and I agreed to those two points." Wasn't this, then, a case of reneging? His reply was one of the resounding non sequiturs the reporters were soon referring to as "Faubus Specials": "They want me to take troops and put bayonets in the backs of students of my state and bludgeon and bayonet my people."

Now all the stops were out. Taking his lead, and much of his text, from the most incendiary Citizens Council literature, Faubus did not allow his own past experience to inhibit his use of the Red smear. Two years before, his segregationist primary opponent, Jim Johnson, had regularly linked the governor and the *Gazette* as "tools of the NAACP," which in turn was identified as a Communist front. Faubus, having earned absolution through interposition, expanded the conspiracy to include all those who supported the Little Rock School Board. The Communist goal, he proclaimed, was to breach the pattern of segregation in the South so as to undermine that ultimate bastion of the Free World; to that end the Supreme Court, President Eisenhower, the Department of Defense and even J. Edgar Hoover had been drawn into a scheme to single out the sovereign state of Arkansas as a demonstration project in race-mixing.

No Arkansan this side of paranoia could take this sort of thing at face value. Beyond the fringe of true believers the propaganda barrage was seen for what it was—a broadside vicious enough to silence those who urged compliance with a court ruling most whites found objectionable even when they were persuaded they had no choice but to accept it. Normally responsible conservatives, who had always considered Faubus a demagogue, tended to write off his excesses as a necessary means to the end of maintaining segregated schools. This was a resurrection of what used to be called the "Longstreet dalliance" after the Confederate general whose standing order was: "Just hold on a little longer, boys, help is on the way." It would take a while for the realization to sink in that Faubus's extreme course not only precluded effective political reinforcement, but also destroyed the fall-back positions legal strategists had prepared as an extended line of retreat that would maintain the substance of segregation while yielding on the periphery.

With legal delaying action no longer possible, and the presence of the federal troops precluding any further effort to physically bar black students from Central, the segregationists turned to a guerrilla campaign intended to force their withdrawal. The immediate object was to panic the parents of white students and destroy their confidence in the ability of the school administration to maintain an orderly educational process, or even to safeguard their children. Concurrently, there was a campaign of harassment within the school by a few dozen white students acting with the encouragement of parents allied with the Citizens Council or its auxiliary, the Mothers League. The air was filled with rumors of bomb threats, skirmishing in the halls and classrooms, and improper conduct by members of the 101st, the latter reaching a low point when Faubus released a wholly groundless charge that troopers had been caught peeking into the dressing room at the girls' gym. Since all this was orchestrated from the governor's office, the media could not ignore it. None of these reports ever proved to have real substance, but truth was always chasing the lie, and when it caught up another lie was off and running.

The other primary institutional target was the *Arkansas Gazette*. With enthusiastic backing from the governor, the Citizens Councils called upon Arkansans to cancel their subscriptions. Thousands responded, and perhaps as many more were denied access to the paper through disruption of the circulation operation as young carrier boys were threatened and roving bullyboys—on some occasions including uniformed members of the state police—dumped bundles of papers from delivery points and street sales racks. The *Gazette* became the sole voice of opposition as the *Democrat* quickly abandoned the school board. This was to be expected, since the amiable publisher, K. August Engel, had begun his journalistic career as a bookkeeper, and had never been known to take a position on any issue that threatened his balance sheet. Now, by simply retreating to neutrality on the editorial page, and opening the news columns to the uncritical display of whatever sensational charges and countercharges Faubus and the council leaders chose to offer, the second-place *Democrat* was handed an opportunity to grow fat on the *Gazette*'s blood. When the next figures of the Audit Bureau of Circulation became available, *Time* magazine recorded the result:

Backed by Governor Faubus, the White Citizens Councils tried hard to bring the *Gazette* to heel with a boycott. Last week Publisher Patterson acknowledged that the boycott had reduced daily circulation 10.6 percent to 88,068 and Sunday circulation 9.7 percent to 97,449 for the six months period ending in March. Over the same period the *Arkansas Democrat*, which carefully avoided taking a stand on Faubus' defiance of federal authorities, gained more than 6,000 readers for both its daily and Sunday editions, now trails the *Gazette* on weekdays by 2,800 and leads it on Sunday by 3,000.

It is awkward to treat an institution as a conspirator, so Faubus and the council publicists worked hard at personalizing the *Gazette*'s perfidy. J. N. Heiskell, too venerated a figure to serve as a convincing villain, was cast as an aged dupe betrayed by a subversive outlander planted in Arkansas years before to pave the way for the ultimate coup of the race-mixers. The Judas role, of course, was mine, and so I was listed along with Virgil Blossom, Daisy Bates, Sid McMath, Woodrow Mann, and the members of the school board as a prime target for individual harassment. We were all subject to a constant public assault on our patriotism, integrity, and morals in statements by Faubus and the council leaders, and by newspaper ads and circulars sponsored by the segregationist organizations. The latter were free of even the minimum restraints of taste or libel, and the efforts at satire were usually based on what Robert Sherrill has termed "scrotum sociology." A fair sample was the fictitious social item to the effect that Mrs. Bates had given birth to twins, sired by me, and had named one Satchmo and the other Ashmo.

There was also an orchestrated campaign of intimidation

by threat of physical violence. By mail and telephone I was subjected to a barrage of anonymous warnings that assassins were stalking me and my family. The incessant calls on my home telephone obviously were a by-product of the organized bucket-shop operation used to tie up the newspaper's switchboard and block incoming classified advertisements. Much of this was on the level of the phony bomb threats at Central High, designed to spread panic or, failing that, to disrupt necessary routine. But, as the perpetrators intended, no one could be sure whether all these threats were in fact empty. Free-lance segregationists with an uncertain grip on reality had been unleashed across the South, and the widely circulated charges by Faubus and the council publicists set up tempting targets.

I was advised to pack a gun, as many an embattled Southern editor had done before me—and some, like Hodding Carter over in the Delta, were still doing. I had a few pistols around the house, brought home from Germany as souvenirs of the war, and in combat I had strapped a .45 automatic to my hip each morning as a part of the uniform of the day. But a handgun seemed to me useless in this situation; if any of my anonymous callers ever tried to carry out his threat it would be by ambush, or with a planted stick of dynamite. As to the others, I decided the best way to call their bluff and discourage their effort was simply to follow my normal routine.

It required a measure of physical courage for those of us on target to defy this kind of intimidation, but our very prominence afforded some measure of protection; those on the other side who were still rational would figure that an attack on one so conspicuous would pass beyond the toleration of the police and courts and, if not, would certainly bring in the federals. But this applied only with a large discount, if at all, to Daisy Bates, the feisty head of the NAACP who became the inspiration and guardian of the black children who came to fame as the Little Rock Nine. She had no assurance of even routine police protection in the black neighborhood where she lived, and the reach of the federal troops did not go beyond the escort to and from school provided for the students. Not only was she exposed to night-riders, but whenever the occasion warranted—and sometimes when it didn't—it was her practice to walk into the most hostile gathering and confront her white antagonists. Once, in the days when she was jousting with the school board over the tokenism of the Blossom Plan, she came to the *Gazette* to berate me for not joining her in the attack. I observed that one part of the problem was that in negotiating with her the board found itself in the position of the church fathers who dealt with Joan of Arc. She seemed to find this flattering, as, in a sense, it was. There were times when the desegregation effort turned on her raw courage; I doubt that the black students could have withstood the pressures of that disoriented school year without her undaunted presence.

THE number of Arkansans subjected to threats of violence was quite small, and in the end none of us suffered any physical harm. But thousands of others were faced with perhaps an even more taxing test of moral stamina. Public advocates— lawyers, politicians, newspaper editors, and the like—are con- ditioned to controversy by temperament and experience. Those in more sheltered callings, and certainly schoolteachers and administrators would be included here, usually have no occasion to acquire a thickened skin. For such as these to suddenly find themselves objects of opprobrium and scorn is likely to be an unnerving experience. Yet at Central High the key members of the staff held firm and carried along their faint-hearted colleagues in a fashion that kept the school functioning in relatively good order, and in doing so they rallied the support of the great majority of the two thousand white students and their parents.

The Little Rock Nine deservedly became heroic symbols of their people's struggle to attain their newly guaranteed rights. But there was little publicity for the minority of white students who actively supported them, or for the majority who calmly accepted the new dispensation, wanted to get on with their education, and refused to be stampeded. Principal Jess Mat- thews, and the vice-principals, J. O. Powell and the redoubtable Elizabeth Huckaby, emerge in her published journal, *Crisis at Central High,* not as social crusaders, but as dedicated profes- sional educators determined to carry out their responsibilities under conditions none of them had ever dreamed they would have to face.

The degree of personal involvement in the crisis varied,

but no one avoided it entirely. At the *Gazette* I watched with pride as pressure converted young staff members into seasoned veterans. Reporters, and particularly photographers, whose cameras made them marked men, encountered real hazard on some assignments, and unpleasantness on most. At public meetings dominated by segregationists the governor adopted Jeff Davis's old trick of pointing out a *Gazette* reporter to the audience and then piously urging his inflamed supporters not to do him any harm since he was only a helpless vassal of "Old Ashmore." But the newsmen had a platform from which they could be heard in reply, the support of colleagues of like mind, and the sense that they were on the right side.

It was harder on those in other departments of the newspaper. James Williamson and Leon Reed, the advertising and circulation directors, were functioning as damage control officers, and in the beginning they were steadily losing ground. They and their men were salesmen, used to going out with a smile and a shoeshine to push their product, assuming that they would at least get a respectful hearing. Now they discovered that some of their best customers were reluctant to be seen in public with them. But, if they were less in the public eye, under Hugh Patterson's aggressive leadership the business-side people were soon on the offensive.

When the Citizens Council attempted to extend the boycott to advertisers, sending out letters threatening to blacklist any who continued to take space in the *Gazette*, Patterson ordered the text of the broadside published on the front page. He figured, correctly, that the Jewish owners of the leading department stores, who set the pace for lesser advertisers, would be particularly sensitive to the implications of this effort to employ bigotry as an economic weapon. There was no significant shift of lineage to the *Democrat*, but the combination of lost income and heavy additional expense involved in fighting the circulation boycott opened a fiscal vein; by the time the *Gazette* restored its lead over the *Democrat* the owners had lost more than a million dollars in earnings, and the newspaper had been driven closer to the brink than Patterson, for tactical reasons, was willing to admit.

THE kind of deep, social cleavage that divided Little Rock has been unique to Southern cities in recent times, and it still arouses curiosity among those who viewed its symptoms from afar. Those of us who were most conspicuously tagged as symbols often found ourselves being praised and blamed for the wrong reasons. In one of his TV retrospectives, Bill Moyers probed the effect of local resistance to desegregation on the personal life of Frank M. Johnson, Jr., the federal judge who, from his bench in Montgomery, handed down many of the most critical court rulings, beginning with the order that gave Martin Luther King victory in the bus boycott. On that occasion Johnson was junior member of a three-judge panel, and he told Moyers he, as a Republican appointee from the hills of northwest Alabama, suffered far less opprobrium than did his colleague, Judge Richard Reeves, considered one of Montgomery's own, who was publicly denounced as having forfeited his right to be buried in Confederate soil. Johnson recalled that he opened the judicial conference by announcing that he had no doubt bus segregation was unconstitutional. Judge Reeves agreed, and the whole business didn't take more than five to ten minutes. Moyers shook his head. "History," he said, "seems to require more drama than this."

Judge Johnson conceded that over the years there had been a few melodramatic moments as he proceeded to hand down decisions that desegregated parks, mental institutions, and prisons; abolished the poll tax; ordered redistricting on the basis of one man-one vote, and provided protection for Martin Luther King's march on Selma. A cross had been burned on his lawn, and his mother's house had been dynamited on the mistaken assumption that he lived there. How then, Moyers, wanted to know, did he find the courage to go it alone? Why, he wasn't alone, the judge explained; he no doubt incurred the dislike of a good many people, but then he and his wife also had a good many friends. But wasn't he ostracized there in the Cradle of the Confederacy? Well, Johnson said, it's sort of hard to ostracize someone who does his own ostracizing. The fact was he and Mrs. Johnson had always attended large social and ceremonial gatherings only out of a sense of duty, and they were both relieved when the invitations fell off. A man who had rather be out fishing than attending a formal reception can turn a situation like that to his advantage.

Judge Johnson's description applies generally to the situation as it affected me and my family during the troubles in Little

Rock. By natural process of prior selection most of our close friends shared the views expressed in the *Gazette,* and those whose opinion shaded off to the right or left maintained our company because they enjoyed arguing with us. As in Judge Johnson's case, the invitations we didn't get were those we had just as soon not have had. There was some tension, of course. After a while a general weariness set in, and hostesses would announce at dinner that discussion of "the issue" was banned for the duration of the meal in the interest of digestion. Usually the imposed truce lasted no more than two or three minutes before purpling faces were again thrust across the napery. As they had been in the Civil War, families were divided; my notoriety caused some embarrassment for my brother back in South Carolina, a staunch supporter of Jimmy Byrnes, but he never disavowed me—explaining that family pride also would have prevented him from disowning an idiot child. In general, life went on pretty much as before at the social level, and at that of casual contact. As Hodding Carter once observed, Southerners will generally treat you politely until they make up their minds to kill you.

As Faubus moved, or was pushed by his segregationist supporters, into an ever more extreme position, he further lost respectability. And when, in March, he formally announced for a third term, he raised alarming practical considerations for many members of the business establishment. Regulatory commissions were removed from outright statehouse boodling by long-term staggered appointments, but their independence was based on the assumption that no governor would serve more than two terms. If Faubus gained a third he would be able to appoint a majority on the Public Service, Banking, and Insurance commissions—and to undo the reforms that had made the Highway Department independent in the wake of scandals in which he had been a leading figure. Although the odds were long that he could ride the segregation issue to reelection, two respectable candidates entered the primary against him—Chancery Judge Lee Ward of Paragould in northeast Arkansas, and Chris Finkbeiner, a wealthy Little Rock meatpacker. Even more significant, the old Dixiecrat, Ben Laney, and the dethroned white knight, Francis Cherry, joined

Sid McMath in open opposition—testifying from their own experience in the governor's office that machine rule was a certainty if Faubus gained control of these prime sources of patronage.

Faubus, of course, did win, and by a wide margin. But now he faced another dead-end situation. The Citizens Council guerrilla campaign had failed to force withdrawal of the black students from Central High, but it had finally worn down the school board. In May, the board went back to federal court to seek suspension of the desegregation schedule on the ground that the school administration was powerless to prevent internal disruption in the face of the continued opposition of the state government, and the absence of effective support from Washington. The case was back where it had started, in the district court presided over by Judge Harry J. Lemley, and the delay was granted. In August, however, the Eighth Circuit Court of Appeals reversed Judge Lemley, agreeing with Thurgood Marshall's contention that suspension of the Blossom Plan would be a signal to segregationist leaders throughout the South that they could halt the legal process by simply encouraging violent opposition.

The six-to-one opinion of the appellate court was unequivocal: "We say that the time has not come in these United States when an order of a federal court must be whittled away, watered down or shamefully withdrawn in the face of violent and unlawful acts of individual citizens. . . ." Asked for reaction, President Eisenhower said his feelings were exactly the same as when he ordered in the troops. So, said Orval Faubus, were his. A month later all nine justices of the Supreme Court signed a decree affirming the circuit court ruling, and interposition was formally interred.

Now Faubus played the last card in the Citizens Council deck. In anticipation of the Supreme Court ruling he had called a special session of the legislature to rubber-stamp bills empowering him to close desegregated public schools and transfer their assets and tax income to private academies. All Little Rock high schools were closed by his order on September 15, and two days later he directed the school board to lease its buildings to a newly incorporated Little Rock Private School

Corporation. The board complied, but before the day was out the circuit court of appeals enjoined transfer of the property. The Supreme Court followed with another unanimous ruling holding that "evasive schemes for segregation" cannot be used to nullify Court orders. Nothing was left but to find rented quarters for a genuinely private school supported by tuition and donations. The closing of the three public high schools left 3,261 white students and 1,069 blacks cut off from any accredited institution unless they chose to leave the city—as hundreds of the more affluent did.

The actual manifestation of massive resistance began to bring the city's leaders out of the storm cellars into which they had retreated when it was merely threatened. "The most dangerous form of pride is neither arrogance nor humility," James Agee once wrote, "but its mild, common denominator form, complacency." It was this that had kept the solid citizenry from recognizing that they were doing something more than dashing the hopes of the black minority when they abandoned the School Board. The closing of the schools dented the establishment's complacency, and in November it was shattered. Brooks Hays, still staunchly defending Faubus as a good Christian who may have had some bad advice from Marvin Griffin, ran well ahead of the segregationist mouthpiece, Amis Guthridge, in his Democratic primary race for renomination, and assumed that, as always, he would have no serious opposition in the general election. But Dr. Dale Alford, a physician who had become suffused with political ambition during service as the only pro-Faubus member of the Little Rock School Board, suddenly entered the race as a write-in independent. An aide in the governor's office with extensive experience as a hatchetman took leave to manage Alford's campaign, designing for the good doctor a one-plank platform: moderation, even the watered-down version espoused by Hays, was "treason to the South." Alford's majority was only 1,200 out of 60,000 votes cast, and the scent of skullduggery hung over the election, but an effort to get a reversal in the state courts, and finally in Congress, failed. Faubus had reminded any who still had doubts that he would treat a local politician just as cavalierly as he would the president of the United States.

School closing also activated a leading citizen who had

never been touched by the pervasive myopia. Adolphine Fletcher Terry, qualified by ancestry and affluence as Little Rock's premier grand dame, lived in a white-columned antebellum mansion near the center of the old city, convenient to the extensive business property she inherited from her banker father. She had been in the forefront of every progressive movement since she came home after graduation from Vassar in 1902 to march with the suffragettes. Now she arrived at my office at the *Gazette* to announce the formation of the Women's Emergency Committee to Open Our Schools (WEC). "It is evident," she said, "that the men are incapable of doing anything. I have sent for the young ladies." And down from the Heights they came, concerned mothers of school-age children and older matrons looking for an outlet for their general sense of outrage. They organized under Mrs. Terry's designated field commander, Vivion Brewer, Smith '21, and immediately found plenty to do.

In November, the school board members declared the situation hopeless, bought up Virgil Blossom's contract, and resigned. This forced a special election, and the lines formed behind a Citizens Council slate and one made up of anti-Faubus business and professional men backed by the WEC. The result was a draw, with three elected from each side, which left the board deadlocked into the spring. When the segregationist members began pressing for a purge of "disloyal" school employees, the list being headed by the ablest administrators and teachers in the system, the anti-Faubus members forced the maneuver into the open, precipitating a recall contest.

The ladies of the WEC now were joined by a new ad hoc group of civic leaders called STOP (Stop This Outrageous Purge). The segregationists countered with CROSS (Committee to Retain Our Segregated Schools). As battle was joined under these resounding acronyms Grainger Williams, the strong-minded new president of the Chamber of Commerce, brought in his troops to join the PTA and assorted educational organizations marching under the banner of STOP.

When Faubus saw the tide turning he went on television in a paid broadcast, drawing class lines as he urged "honest, hard-working" citizens in the downtown precincts to rally against the "Cadillac brigade" descending upon the polls from the high ground of the western suburbs. Will Mitchell, the corporation lawyer who headed STOP, countered in a rebuttal broadcast: "Governor, let us alone. Let us restore our community to the rule of reason." The election was a clean sweep; the three pro-Faubus board members were recalled, and the three anti-Faubus members were retained. The schools would be open in the fall, and the slow process of desegregation would be resumed.

THE defeat of the segregationists at Little Rock resulted from a political fusion reminiscent of the one forged by the Redeemers—a coalition of the country club set and the black community. Not all the white voters could be assigned such exalted status, of course, but that's where the leadership came from. This working relationship held for the next ten years, and grew in effectiveness until, reinforced by its emergence in the lesser cities of the state, the salt-and-pepper combination overwhelmed the rural populists, bringing to the governor's office as Faubus's successor a multimillionaire Republican socialite, Winthrop Rockefeller—the only Arkansas mountaineer, I once observed, who owned his own mountain. And, as the number of black voters increased steadily throughout the region, the coalition with affluent whites would be replicated in the Deep South, finally bringing to an end the decade of demogoguery and confrontatin still to come.

A minority of the whites—Adolphine Terry and the battle-scarred liberals who had fought at her side in earlier campaigns, and a growing number of younger people—saw the cause as one of advancing justice for the blacks, and, now that the respectability barrier had been breached, these became more open and effective in opposing segregation in all its aspects. But for most it was an exercise in pragmatism. The governor's excesses had driven them to accept the lesser of two evils—and they were secure enough to recognize that there would be no drastic change in the pattern of social relationships, certainly not at the level where their own domination was, if anything, reinforced.

But it did put the black and white leadership in touch with each other in a fashion that had not existed before. Brooks Hays, for example, had been accepted as an expert when he reported to a pussy-footing committee of former Chamber of Commerce presidents that he had heard encouraging words on voluntary withdrawal of the Little Rock Nine from a few elderly preachers and discredited political fixers; no one present had any inkling that these so-called leaders had long since been written off as Toms by the black rank and file. "I was determined not to make any contacts with the NAACP officials, either national or local," Hays wrote. "I disagreed with their tactics and, in the Little Rock situation, I could not even discuss the question with them without appearing to approve projection of the national organization into Little Rock's difficulties." This was the obverse of his failure to recognize that by the time he arrived on the scene Faubus had already thrown in with the Citizens Councils; the NAACP was irrevocably projected into the local situation, and anyone who refused to consult with Daisy Bates and her associates could have no sense of the deep conviction that moved the mass of blacks. As their counterpart said in Montgomery, these were not necessarily "New Negroes," but even the most timorous had begun to believe that a new day was dawning.

Despite all the harsh language, an indispensable reservoir of goodwill survived at the interpersonal level. Most blacks made a distinction between real, adrenaline fired segregationists, and what they called "mouth segs," those who out of habit upheld the forms of white supremacy but bore no generalized animosity toward blacks and frequently displayed marked sympathy and kindness at the level of individual contact. This perception was particularly sharp among those who dealt with whites in their most unguarded moments, notably domestic servants and the attendants at the city's private clubs and better restaurants. Louis Martin, a White House aide in the Kennedy, Johnson, and Carter administrations, once said that no black could stay in politics as long as he had without becoming a cynic. This was also true of the bartenders and waiters at the Little Rock Club, who may have had a more intimate view of the inner working of the political process than Martin did.

That downtown watering hole for the establishment was the source of many of the splendid ironies that sustained my confidence that Orval Faubus's cut-rate rerun of Fort Sumter would have no lasting effect other than to prolong his tenure in the statehouse, and that this would prove to be irrelevant to the evolution of the new patterns of desegregation certain to come. The bar at the club was something of a communications center for leading politicians, and unless I had business elsewhere I ordinarily lunched there.

After the siege began, there were usually a dozen or so correspondents around the *Gazette* office at lunchtime, many of them friends from my campaign days with Adlai Stevenson, and I regularly wound up at the club with several guests. There was no provision for payment by a nonmember, so their food and drink necessarily went on my tab—the sort that is signed upon arrival, leaving it up to the waiter to add appropriate charges as the meal proceeds. This represented a quantum jump in my ordinary scale of entertaining, but after several months it suddenly dawned on me that the monthly bill was no higher than usual.

This called for a private consultation with Herbert Douglas, the rotund black man who presided over the bar. "Herbert," I said, "I think I know what you and the others are doing, but we can't let the club absorb the cost of all the booze and food I'm laying out for these visiting firemen." He took a swipe with his bar rag and leaned closer. "It ain't costing the club nothing." How could that be? Now there was a broad gold-flecked grin. "Oh, we just lay it off on the segs." The intelligence that the board bill for out-of-town journalists the governor considered his natural enemies was being paid by his supporters was bound to get around in so intimate a setting, and it might have seemed to the uninitiated that this would be due cause for an outraged confrontation with the House Committee. But I never heard of a complaint, and my guess is that the segs who learned of it either thought it funny, or inevitable. After all, for some years Herbert Douglas had been a leading light of the Urban League, and when he disappeared from behind the bar each summer it was explained that the club always gave him leave to attend the national convention, usually in the company of one of his best customers, Judge Dunaway.

Not all the true believers were so benign. On Saturdays, when downtown offices were closed and the club was nearly empty, I often shared a table with Major General Edwin A.

Walker, who had recently been assigned to the Arkansas-Oklahoma Army Reserve District. A tall, handsome bachelor, Ted Walker had had a distinguished career as an artillery-man in Korea, and came to Little Rock from a division command in Hawaii. When the contingent from the 101st was sent to Little Rock, and the National Guard federalized, command automatically passed to Walker as senior officer in the area, and his comportment in those difficult circumstances was a model of aloof correctness. Since he avoided personal comment on the situation at Central High, issuing such statements as were unavoidable through a public affairs colonel sent down from the Pentagon, we talked of other things when I ran into him at the club. The other things soon began to raise my hair.

The general began to pass on to me *Common Sense* and other extreme right wing tracts devoted to the Communist conspiracy presumed to be controlling the government of the United States. I might have dismissed this as a manifestation of the hardened political arteries common in the military, but Walker also began confiding his personal problems. His steady upward march through the ranks of the regular army had been abruptly terminated by his assignment to the post at Little Rock, a sinecure normally reserved for colonels or brigadiers marking time until retirement. In Walker's mind, an unidentified "they" was responsible for this outrage—the same "they" who had begun to plot against him as far back as his cadet days at West Point. Now "they" had heaped upon him the final indignity by placing him in a position where duty required him to further the Communist scheme to undermine segregation in the South.

I used the occasion of a visit to Washington to warn a Pentagon general I knew that a public relations time-bomb was ticking away in the Little Rock command post. The brass knew all about it, it turned out, and that was why the public affairs colonel always did the talking when there was no way to avoid exposing the general to the press. The lid blew off in 1961, in Germany, where Walker had been assigned command of a division in the NATO forces. After a service newspaper revealed that he was using John Birch Society literature in indoctrination courses for his troops, he was relieved, and to still the ensuing flap in Washington, allowed to resign. In

September 1962, Walker turned up at Oxford, where federal marshals stood off a mob trying to bar James Meredith's admission to the University of Mississippi. This time he was on the other side, in the forefront of the attacking skirmish line as twenty-nine of the defending marshals suffered gunshot wounds before federal troops arrived to restore order.

After his enforced retirement, the general went back to live with his mother in Dallas, and became a sort of wandering segregationist minstrel, campaigning for George Wallace, coming back to Little Rock as an honored guest of the Citizens Council, which dispatched Amis Guthridge to meet him at the airport. Confused and inconclusive evidence linked shots allegedly fired at his house in Dallas to the assassination of President Kennedy. He last turned up in the news in 1976, when he was arrested in a public restroom on morals charges.

These are footnotes to an episode that itself has become a footnote to the history of the vast change in the pattern of race relations the nation has experienced in the quarter century since *Brown*. But they are, I think, essential to understanding the spectacular surface events that dominate most accounts of the period. They reinforced my own conviction that the South was not entering upon what the more excitable chroniclers began referring to as the Second Reconstruction, but was finally disposing of the remnants of the First.

19

❧

Northern Exposure

*I*n December 1959, I received a long letter from Ralph McGill embodying his usual mixture of irony, gossip, and profound insight into the changing political landscape of the South. "I am sure you have noticed that Reverend Martin Luther King is moving to Atlanta and assuming a pulpit here," he wrote. "I view this, I am sure, in much the same manner as that of citizens of medieval walled cities who heard that the great plague was coming. I have the highest esteem for the Reverend, but he could not have come at a worse time."

The Georgia legislature would be in high gear by February 1, King's scheduled arrival date, and McGill foresaw a showdown on Marvin Griffin's pledge to use his police powers to close any public school that admitted blacks. A federal district judge had warned Atlanta school officials that application of the state's pupil placement plan to close one school would result in the closing of all schools. "This," McGill wrote, "has them snarling and snapping."

Actually, by the end of 1959, the precedents invoked by Orval Faubus's defiance in Little Rock had invalidated massive resistance statutes everywhere. The snarling and snapping would be over the carcass of a dead horse. In Virginia, the cradle of interposition, Gov. James Lindsay Almond had staged a rerun of Appomattox, informing his legislature that the time had come to deal with "fact, not fiction; a condition and not abstract theory; reality, not surmise and wishful thinking." The governor went on to lay before the lawmakers the report of a commission he had appointed to study the future of Virginia's public schools. It was summarized by the long-suffering *Rich-*

mond Times-Dispatch in an editorial aimed at its interpositionist stablemate, the *News Leader*:

It squarely faces the cold fact that no state legislative assembly can enact any law effectively against overwhelming federal force, or arm any governor with power to undo what the federal judiciary has done. It points out, contrary to the advice of some who should know better, that the police power cannot be exercised by any agency of a state to reverse or negate a federal decree; that a state cannot interpose its authority or power between the federal government and the object of a federal law or decree. . . . If those Virginians who express bitter opposition to integration of any sort whatever are prepared for the ultimate abolition of all public schools, it would clear the air if they should say so. There is no other way to stop all mixing in the public schools.

In Prince Edward County local officials accepted the challenge and the public schools were closed from 1959 until 1964, leaving the education of both whites and blacks to private academies without tax support. But elsewhere across the South school districts undertook at least token compliance when they were faced with a court order. In the Deep South the last line of resistance, manned by the Citizens Councils with occasional support from Klan-style night-riders, was to be a campaign of intimidation aimed at keeping blacks from applying to the federal courts in the first place.

Martin Luther King's presence in Atlanta, and the establishment there of the expanding headquarters of the Southern Christian Leadership Conference, would, as McGill foresaw, provide a new locus for the civil rights storm center. King, as field commander and symbol, would take on increasing importance in other aspects of the movement, but he was never to be directly involved on the school front. This remained the province of the NAACP, which continued to place primary reliance on litigation. In the beginning, the old-line leaders tended to look askance at the young preacher and his doctrine of nonviolent protest. "All that walking for nothing!" Thurgood Marshall said when the federal court banned integration on Montgomery buses. "They could just as well have waited while the bus case went up through the courts, without all the work and worry of the boycott." With the law now firmly on the side of black plaintiffs in the school cases, it hardly made sense to meet mass white pressure tactics with counterpressure from black demonstrators. SCLC accepted the division of labor, and aimed its initial effort at opening voting rolls to blacks.

IT was a time of transition in the rights movement, and in my own professional career. When the Little Rock schools reopened under the Blossom Plan in the fall of 1959 I felt free to accept a long-standing invitation to join Robert Maynard Hutchins at the Fund for the Republic, on whose board of directors I had served since 1955. The *Gazette*, I thought, would restore its economic health much more readily without me. The newspaper and I had been awarded Pulitzer Prizes for the stand against Faubus, and the local establishment had turned out at a dinner in our honor. But I had the feeling that in that company my status as a vindicated prophet would continue to occasion considerable discomfiture.

I was already in Santa Barbara at the Fund's new Center for the Study of Democratic Institutions when McGill wrote at Christmastime to complain that my departure had left him naked and alone: "All the White Citizens Councils now are repeating in their publications that in Little Rock the mayor who advocated desegregation is gone, the school principal and the editor are gone, and they are urging the same treatment for me." But if I was now removed from the Southern front of the civil rights movement, I had hardly abandoned my concern with the central issue that had again become a determinant in the nation's domestic politics. Indeed, I had chosen Hutchins's offer from among a number of possibilities because it afforded an opportunity to view the shifting patterns of race relations in broader perspective. My agreement was to devote half my time to setting up a mass media project at the Center, leaving me free to accept other assignments, including one from the *New York Herald Tribune* for a series on the condition of blacks outside the South. Thus I would spend most of the first spring of my emancipation, not in the salubrious environs of the Center's elegant quarters in an old estate overlooking the Pacific, but in Harlem.

The projected *Herald Tribune* series was the central topic of McGill's long letter. There were few journalists in the country in 1960 who could have matched the prescience of the rumpled old editor gazing out from the eye of the emotional hurricane still gathering force in the South. McGill was concerned that I not allow my new Yankee associates to lead me into the simplified view that racism alone was the root of the spreading misery and rising tensions in the slums of the nation's great cities. In the wake of the continuing migration prompted by the mechanization of agriculture, he wrote, "we are developing a dangerous segment of population of youthful age who won't be able to find employment. I think this is something new in our society. To be sure race enters into it and aggravates it. The Puerto Ricans, the Italians, the Jews and the Negroes all have their clashes in New York and Chicago, but it grows largely out of idleness, frustration and economic lacks. These unemployed and uneducated thousands can, at best, hold fringe jobs. If they get married they can't support a wife; so they drift into petty crime and then into major crime."

If this seems a commonplace diagnosis some twenty years later, it had little currency in the public consciousness when I went to New York in early 1960. The assignment grew out of the appointment of a new editor at the ailing *Herald Tribune,* Robert M. White II, summoned from his family's newspaper in Mexico, Missouri, deep in the section called "Little Dixie." Coming from that background, White was surprised to discover that none of New York's dailies paid more than cursory attention to the city's black community, now sharing the northern end of Manhattan with Puerto Ricans and spreading across both rivers into once-distinctive white ethnic neighborhoods in the other New York boroughs and the New Jersey river towns. My assignment from Bob White was open-ended, to take whatever time was required for a dispassionate look at the colored 20 percent of the city's population. The final product was a series of articles syndicated to twenty-five major newspapers across the country and published as a book by W. W. Norton under the title *The Other Side of Jordan.*

HARLEM in the twenties and thirties had been the fashionable last stop for a night on the town in New York. The Cotton Club and the Savoy were in their glory as fountainheads of jazz. There were dozens of glittering supper clubs where the prohibition law and closing ordinances could be bent for a price, and black hustlers were available to steer white customers to whatever private debauchery they might fancy. It was a place where Satchmo blew his golden horn, and high-yellow girls strutted under blue spotlights, and old Bojangles tapped out his loose-limbed rhythms on the hardwood staircase. The leading black intellectuals maintained a branch of bohemia there, and Carl Van Vechten could, without violating the prevailing standards of literary propriety, identify the exotic enclave as "Nigger Heaven."

In the years after World War II all that changed. The gradual lowering of the color bar permitted the jazz musicians to move downtown, to Birdland, Eddie Condon's, and the Embers, and their black aficionados could follow them to a ringside table even if they couldn't rent an apartment in the neighborhood. The performing arts opened to blacks, and writers and intellectuals found their way into the mainstream. As the upper class moved out of Harlem the new underclass of unskilled migrants from the South moved in, sharing the ghetto with Puerto Ricans and West Indians flooding in from the Caribbean. There was no longer any attraction for whites uptown, except for the shopkeepers who continued to operate most business and service establishments, and the landlords who could turn a profit from decaying apartment buildings as density increased and services diminished. On quiet side streets there still was some decent housing for middle-class blacks who could afford it, and touches of fading elegance on Sugar Hill, but the usual residential block was one of those once described by Thomas Sancton as "a hundred Delta cabins, plus tuberculosis."

But Harlem was not yet a place where a white skin was an invitation to attack. After spending six weeks there, I wrote: "There are, of course, dark turnings into which a man wearing an air of prosperity and a little gone in liquor would proceed only at his peril—but if he were rolled an objective investigation would probably reveal that it was done without particular malice, and without regard to race, creed or color. In the brightly lighted commercial areas, where the ordinary humdrum business of life goes on, a man with a white skin has no difficulty making innocent passage. If he is looking for trouble he can probably find it, and wind up carved like a Thanksgiving turkey. But if he minds his own business he will be treated with courtesy and respect—the special, almost painful politeness that any close-knit community reserves for the identifiable stranger in town."

The black migrants had left a heavy Southern imprint—restaurants bearing crudely hand-lettered signs advertising chitlins and greens, pogies and whities; store-front preachers shouting salvation while lumpy old women writhed in religious ecstasy; swarms of pink-heeled barefoot children making the same shrill, obliviously happy sounds I had heard in every black neighborhood I ever knew. It was, therefore, no surprise that when I came to discuss contemporary affairs with this constituency's political leaders I found that only their pigmentation distinguished them from those I had been dealing with all my life.

For good reason, J. Raymond Jones, Harlem's Democratic district leader, was nicknamed "The Fox." His rise in politics began under Mayor William O'Dwyer, who had talked of making him the first black leader of Tammany Hall. Jones was not interested, he told me, for reasons of simple arithmetic; there was no way to parlay the black votes he could deliver into a combination that would insure continuity in citywide leadership; the clout was not yet there to take over from the Irish, the Jews, or the Italians. "You will note," he said, "that Bill O'Dwyer is not around any more, and I still am." Jones's latest coup had been to bring together as the United Harlem Leadership Team the two most effective black elected officials, Congressman Adam Clayton Powell and Borough President Hulan Jack, who had long been at odds. This involved bringing Powell back into the Democratic fold after his bolt in 1956 to support President Eisenhower. In the process Jones had scuttled a coalition with the Puerto Rican leadership, and precipitated an open break with Carmine De Sapio, the Tammany leader.

This, in Jones's view, represented a simple application of algebraic principle: "Put Jack's and Powell's groups together and we swing 20 percent of the votes in Manhattan. Swing those votes right and we ought to wind up with 20 percent of the jobs. If we do that we don't need the Puerto Ricans—and anyway the break with them makes Carmine nervous, and that's good for us." This kind of politicking required a solid, readily identifiable bloc vote, and, in theory at least, maintaining it ran counter to the integrationist ideal espoused by traditional black leaders.

Politics to The Fox was a game of power, and it couldn't be played without counters: "Sure the white liberal leaders in the past have done a lot of things that needed doing. But why did they support antidiscrimination laws and public housing and all the rest? Because the Negro vote has been growing steadily and they couldn't ignore it. I say it has grown big enough so that Negroes can take over their own show. We're not leaving our old friends, we're just tending to our own business." He was particularly scornful of the effort to have public agencies drop racial identification in their record-keeping. "A lot of our people listen too much to sociologists. Silliest damn thing I ever heard of. How am I going to bargain for Negroes if I can't prove where they are?"

Jones worked behind the scenes, leaving the limelight to a man whose natural equipment for political campaigning was as impressive as that of any officeholder I have ever known; at the top of his form there were few better orators than the handsome Reverend Adam Clayton Powell, and his most florid effusions reflected the genuine erudition of a graduate of Colgate and Columbia. Upon the base of the eleven thousand members of Harlem's Abyssinian Baptist Church he inherited from his father, who served as pastor before him, Powell had created a solid personal following that made him one of four blacks in Congress—and had kept him there for eight terms despite recurring scandals growing out of a life-style that hardly seemed appropriate for a Baptist preacher, or within the means of a moderately paid public servant. He flaunted his taste for Upmann cigars and Napoleon brandy, maintained an expensive suite at a midtown hotel and a beach house in Puerto Rico, and made frequent trips to European watering spots, traveling with an entourage like a heavyweight champion's—door-openers, coat-holders, check-grabbers, telephone-answerers, and several remarkably pretty girls.

I went to the weathered charcoal-gray stone pile that is the Abyssinian Church one Sunday afternoon to hear the Reverend Powell preach. In the austere auditorium, facing a primly starched congregation that filled every pew, he stood before a strangely wrought brass cross presented to the church by the Lion of Judah, Haile Selassie. Powell had lately added the appeal of African identity to his message to black audiences, and this day he was riding it hard: "I came back from the Bandung Conference in 1955—five years ago—and I went to the White House and I told Mr. Eisenhower the shape of the future. 'Mr. President,' I said, 'I have been there, and I have seen, and I have heard. And I say to you, Mr. President, this is the truth America must recognize if we are to survive: The timetable of freedom is no longer in the white man's hands!'" This produced a muted, rising sigh from the faithful, and evidently helped inspire them to forgive their pastor's well-publicized trespasses, including the income tax evasion for which he was currently under indictment.

After the service I met Powell in the pastor's study behind the nave. He greeted me, feet on carved desk, cigar in one hand, brandy snifter in the other, his pastoral robe with its doctoral chevrons thrown open to display a monogrammed silk shirt. The discourse that followed, I learned from reporters who covered him regularly, was the standard blend of candor and cynicism he used with white interviewers. He cheerfully conceded that he had sabotaged a number of housing, education, and social measures of prime interest to blacks by appending sometimes practically meaningless antidiscrimination clauses. "Sure, I'm a maverick," he said. "I'm an irritant. Just keep on turning the screw, turning the screw. Drip, drip, drip makes a hole in the marble." But he insisted that the technique provided leverage to produce votes from the most conservative whites. "When one of those hard-core Dixiecrats gets in trouble with his constituents down home he comes around and asks me to attack him in public. I'm usually willing to oblige, quid pro quo."

As Powell no doubt intended, it was impossible to tell how much of this could be taken at face value. One of his standard gambits was the off-the-record revelation that he was in fact a white man passing as a black. It was commonly known that his mother was a white German immigrant, and, according to Powell, his slave grandmother was an Indian whose black husband had been cuckolded by his white master. "But if you print that," he said, "I'll sue for libel." In a television interview

Mike Wallace had said, "I hear you have quite a bit of white blood," and Powell had replied, "Yes, probably more than you, Mike." This was, I thought, another example of his uninhibited self-indulgence, a way of amusing himself with the kind of gallows humor I had noted among the more intelligent of his white Southern counterparts.

But there could be no doubt that Powell had a sure sense of the shifting black mood, and stood ready to exploit it. This put him at odds with contemporary black leaders, whom he regularly denounced by name when they reacted to his excesses by branding him a racist demagogue. A few weeks after our interview, in an address before the Cliosophic Society at Princeton, Powell sounded the antiestablishment tocsin that would soon be reverberating on campuses across the land:

The thrust of the Negro mass has impaled accidentally the Northern "liberal." The thrust of the Negro today is sweeping away from underneath him the foundations on which he has stood so long—that of being the Great White Father or the Great White Mother of the Negro people. Desperately, with contrived organizations and committees, plus certain captive Negroes—and that is a refined phrase for Uncle Tom—the Northern "liberal" is trying to hold on.

ADAM CLAYTON POWELL's formula for political longevity, like Orval Faubus's, used real and fancied racial grievances to invoke a defiant separatist spirit, and employed militant rhetoric as a substitute for a coherent plan of political action. At the operating level Ray Jones translated the bloc vote produced by this appeal into jobs and constituent services, trading off with the leaders of the other ethnic blocs that had long dominated municipal government in New York. But if The Fox worked within the system, Powell, like Faubus, employed a rhetoric that tended to push the more agitated of his followers beyond the live-and-let-live boundary of practical politics. In Harlem the failure to absorb the growing underclass into a productive work force created grievances beyond the reach of the usual City Hall trade-offs. At the same time, the end of European colonialism and the rise of independent new nations in Africa aroused a new spirit of racial chauvinism. James Booker, the *Amsterdam News* columnist the *Herald Tribune* retained as my indispensable guide and counselor, relayed the sardonic judgment of the streetwise: "If you got Lumumba and Mboto, who needs Amos and Andy?"

The pro-African sentiment aroused in the twenties by the Black Star movement led by Marcus Garvey was enjoying a revival at all levels. The emotional response to the clash between Israel and the Arab nations added a sharp edge to the endemic anti-Semitism rooted in the grievances of Harlemites against Jewish shopkeepers and landlords. James R. Lawson, a public relations man with clients among the new African nations, even pitched a low inside curve at the venerated Ralph Bunche, whose Nobel Prize recognized his peace-keeping efforts in the Middle East, invoking a chorus of boos by introducing him at an African Freedom Day rally as "the George Washington of Israel."

I spent some time at the United Nations discussing the rising tide of pro-African feeling with Bunche and, through his good offices, with representatives of some of the new African nations. Like most black intellectuals, Bunche welcomed identification with the African past as a boost to his people's pride and self-identify, so badly eroded by the years of slavery and second-class citizenship. But he deplored the absurdity of some of the claims being made in the name of purportedly suppressed black history, and he was particularly alarmed by the naked hatred of whites being preached by those who called themselves Black Muslims. The growing movement was generally regarded as grotesque by the African and Middle Eastern diplomats I talked with, but there was no one to say so officially, for, like a born-again Christian, a man could embrace the faith simply by declaring it. Anyone who accepted Allah as the one God, faced toward Mecca to pray, and observed the dietary proscriptions of the Koran, as the Black Muslims professed to do, met the minimum test for membership.

THE black Nation of Islam came into being in Detroit in 1931 under the leadership of Elijah Poole, son of a Georgia Baptist preacher. The theology of the man who thereafter called himself Elijah Muhammad was at variance with that of orthodox Muslims in important respects, notably in its account of Mr. Yacub, who was said to have been exiled from Mecca and, "embittered toward Allah now, decided, as revenge, to create upon the earth a devil race—a bleached-out white race of people. . . . It was written that after Yacub's bleached white race had ruled the world for six thousand years—down to our time—the black original race would give birth to one whose wisdom, knowledge and power would be infinite." This, according to Elijah, was a mysterious stranger who revealed to him that he was "the One to whom the Jews referred to as the Messiah, the Christians as the Christ, and the Muslims as the Mahdi." Before he disappeared without a trace the stranger designated Elijah Supreme Minister and assigned him the task of organizing temples in the big city ghettoes to serve as the basis for self-sufficient black communities. In Chicago, where he settled, the Black Muslims operated their own school, grocery stores, restaurants, garment manufacturing plants, and a rudimentary department store.

Those who converted joined a closed black society with a rigidly puritanical code of conduct. They were required to accept the Muslim proscription against pork and alcohol, but this was only the beginning: Messenger Elijah extended the list to include narcotics, tobacco, fornication, lying, stealing, dancing, gambling, cosmetics, domestic quarreling, movies, and sports. A daily bath was mandatory, and the faithful were enjoined to indulge in no more sleep than health required, and to avoid long vacations. These divine laws were enforced by the Fruit of Islam, a select corps of disciplined young men trained in judo and karate, who served as bodyguards for the Messenger and his ministers and brought suspected sinners before the Temple for trial. The penalty for the more serious offenses was excommunication from, as the Messenger put it, "the only group that really cares about you."

It followed that these stringent requirements placed a low ceiling on recruitment; in 1959 there were only seven temples, none with a membership of more than a few thousand. Since its antiwhite preachments were largely confined to meetings where only blacks were allowed past the guarded doors, and the members were enjoined against overt insubordination to civil authority, the sect was generally welcomed by local officials impressed by the orderly, hard-working character of the membership. The Black Muslim movement might have remained in obscurity had not Elijah chosen as the minister of Temple

Number Seven in New York a remarkable young man named Malcolm Little. He also was the son of a Baptist minister, but, unlike the soft-spoken Elijah, before his conversion he had prided himself on a reputation as the "baddest nigger" in Harlem.

Malcolm X—the converted thus replaced a surname presumably inherited from a slave-owning white—saw the light while serving time in a Massachusetts prison. Upon his release his converted brother arranged his apprenticeship for the Muslim ministry. Visitations to the Messenger in Chicago resulted in recognition of mutual need—that of Malcolm for a personal savior, of Elijah Muhammad for a charismatic front man who could extend the Muslim appeal beyond the few who so far had answered the call.

Assigned to Harlem, Malcolm began his mission by "fishing," as he called it, at store-front churches. The strict moral code kept the catch small; he identified the early converts as "usually Southern migrant people, usually older, who would go anywhere to hear what they called 'good preaching.'" When I came to know him I had no doubt Malcolm could provide that, although I never had the privilege of hearing it, failing in my efforts to persuade him to lift the color bar and let me attend one of his services at Temple Number Seven. And I could understand how his blend of mysticism and passion, coupled with a blanket indictment of the white world, would appeal to blacks hopelessly trapped at the bottom of society.

In those days the Messenger would not receive a white journalist, but Jimmy Booker managed to arrange an interview with Malcolm. I was, like most of those who faced him in the years to come, impressed by the young minister's obvious intelligence and steel-edged drive. Well over six feet, whip thin, with a bronze complexion and close-cropped rust-colored hair, he had been called "Detroit Red" in his earlier incarnation as a numbers runner, dope peddler, pimp, and second-story man. He practiced these trades in New York until a bookmaker came after him with a gun; to avoid a shootout he decamped for Boston, where a burglary conviction earned him seven years in prison and the leisure to educate himself for his new mission of liberating blacks from the white man's yoke.

In the five years before his politics of rage caught up with him, Malcolm X was to become a ranking American celebrity, a media star whose shock value guaranteed him prime time on television and space in newspapers and magazines. But when I first sat across the table from him in a Harlem restaurant he was still relatively unknown. His devotion to black separatism, he said, was a heritage that predated his conversion to Islam; in the small towns of Michigan where he grew up, his father had preached the gospel according to Marcus Garvey as well as that of the Baptist church, and, despite an official verdict of accidental death, Malcolm was convinced that he had been murdered by white men as a result. "Garvey was right as far as he went, but he was wrong in urging blacks to go back to Africa to achieve freedom from white oppression," he said. "We're going to build our own society here in the United States. We're going to have our own all-black state."

His scorn for white liberals and fellow-traveling blacks in the civil rights movement made Adam Clayton Powell's strictures sound like an accolade. Anyone who expected blacks to improve their lot in a white dominated society was "integration-mad," and if he wore a black skin he was a "house nigger" for the whites. Any black intellectual who challenged Muslim doctrine was written off as "Uncle Thomas, Ph.D." In our several hours of conversation he was always on the offensive; any topic I tried to introduce was bent to fit his litany—the white man was the devil, his God was false, his professed commitment to justice a part of the "tricknology" he used to delude blacks. And he had his own version of scrotum sociology, an apparent obsession with the white man's sexual exploitation of black women, which he equated with rape, and the white woman's alleged lust for black men, which he considered understandable. I could not doubt his sincerity when he punctuated this diatribe with a reiterated, "I *believe* in anger."

Malcolm was then pressing the Messenger to ease his ban against communicating the Nation of Islam's message through the mass media, and the beginning of his leap to national prominence came when he persuaded Elijah to cooperate in the production of a Mike Wallace TV documentary, "The Hate That Hate Produced." In his *Autobiography* Malcolm described the network program as ". . . a kaleidoscope of shocker images . . . Mr. Muhammad, me, others speaking . . . strong-looking, set-faced black men, our Fruit of Islam . . . every phrase was edited to increase the shock mood. As the producers intended, I think, people just sat about limp when the program went off."

Exposure on the visual medium demonstrated that Malcolm's personal appeal extended far beyond poor, ignorant, disturbed members of his race. No black, including those who most vehemently denounced the Nation of Islam as destructive and demagogic, was untouched by it. In the five years before the break with Elijah Muhammad that led to his assassination, Malcolm became a powerful, if negative, force in the black community. His rise paralleled that of another looming media star, Martin Luther King, Jr., whose nonviolent doctrine of Christian love was the antithesis of Malcolm's bitter preachment.

IN an introduction to *The Autobiography of Malcolm X,* M. S. Handler, a white *New York Times* reporter, wrote that his wife described her first meeting with Malcolm by saying it was like having tea with a black panther:

The description startled me. The black panther is an aristocrat in the animal kingdom. He is beautiful. He is dangerous. As a man, Malcolm X had the physical bearing and the inner self-confidence of a born aristocrat. And he was potentially dangerous. No man in our time aroused fear and hatred in the white man as did Malcolm, because in him the white man sensed an implacable foe who could not be had for any price—a man unreservedly committed to the cause of liberating the black man in American society rather than integrating the black man into that society.

The physical description was apt enough, and I suppose that after he became a regular on the television talk show and college lecture circuit the menacing persona he perfected did spread a good deal of fear along with the anger he ignited. But no sophisticated white could take seriously the bizarre theology Malcolm preached, or accept as a realistic goal the separatist state he proposed. This was also true of sophisticated blacks, those in the middle class Malcolm excoriated. Whitney Young of the Urban League attributed the preoccupation of the white media with the Black Muslims to "a kind of guilt feeling, saying, 'Beat me, Daddy, I feel guilty.' "

The posthumously published *Autobiography* was actually

written by Alex Haley, the talented author of *Roots,* and it is a remarkable document—or rather two documents. The major portion is a first-person account of Malcolm's brief life, as extracted by Haley in interviews over a period of two years, rendered faithful to the subject's view of himself by an agreement that "nothing can be in this book's manuscript that I didn't say, and nothing can be left out that I want in it." But Haley protected his professional reputation by stipulating that he could include an epilogue of his own without clearance by Malcolm. In a critical but sympathetic essay he underscored the inevitablity of the break between Elijah and his disciple, finding it rooted in Malcolm's growth, not only in celebrity but in sophistication, rather than in the ostensible causes cited by each—on Malcolm's side his discovery that the Messenger was a fornicator who had sired illegitimate children by at least two of his young secretaries, and on Elijah's, the tactical blunder committed by Malcolm when he affronted a shocked and grieving nation by contemptuously dismissing the assassination of President Kennedy as a matter of chickens coming home to roost.

Haley's epilogue tends to support the belief that Malcolm reversed his antiwhite stand in the months after he parted with Elijah and made his own pilgrimage to Mecca. When he called a press conference to announce his new Organization of Afro-American Unity he described it as a nonreligious, nonsectarian movement to unite blacks for a constructive program to secure human rights. "My trip to Mecca has opened my eyes," he said. "I no longer subscribe to racism. I have adjusted my thinking to the point where I believe that whites are human beings—as long as this is borne out by their humane attitude toward Negroes."

Unsuccessful efforts were made to bring the new Malcolm together with Martin Luther King, but the Christian minister always declined and the two never met. Malcolm did go to Selma on the eve of the famous march, when King and others had been jailed, and an alarmed Andrew Young insisted that Coretta King address a rally on her husband's behalf because he feared the ex-Muslim might push the throng over the line into violence. After the meeting Malcolm told Mrs. King he was leaving town, but gave her a message for her husband: "I want Dr. King to know that I didn't come to Selma to make his job difficult. I really did come thinking I could make it easier. If the white people realize what the alternative is, perhaps they will be willing to hear Dr. King."

But Malcolm had been double-talking violence in this fashion all along, and he continued to offer asides that tended to make the skeptical, including me, doubt that he was entitled to the martyrdom some have conferred upon him. The purpose of his new organization, he said, was to convert the black population to active self-defense against white supremacists. "Whether you use bullets or ballots, you've got to aim well," he said. "Don't strike at the puppet, strike at the puppeteer." Would he now accept white members? His reply was one of those zingers he used with great success to titillate reporters: "If John Brown were active, maybe him." And when he announced that he had information that his former associates had ordered his execution, he added: "There is no group in the United States better able to carry out this threat than the Black Muslims. I know, because I taught them myself."

If he now professed to hate whites only on a selective basis, it was clear that he was still as far from King's commitment to nonviolence as he had ever been. In that regard there was increasing ambivalence among black intellectuals as they responded to the rising tide of black consciousness. Kenneth Clark thought the condemnation of whites by the Muslims aroused an inescapable emotional response from blacks because "they are not inventing, nor for that matter are they even exaggerating or distorting the basic facts." That, he thought, posed a problem for King: "There is also an unrealistic, if not pathological basis in King's doctrine. . . . It would seem, then, that any demand that the victims of oppression be required to love those who oppress them places an additional and probably intolerable burden on these victims."

In the course of the long hot summer of 1964, when random arson flared in cities across the north, the *New York Times* reported a meeting of black intellectuals who agreed that Martin Luther King could appeal to middle- and upper-class blacks, but that Malcolm X alone could secure the allegiance of those at the bottom, and concluded: "Malcolm X is going to play a formidable role, because the racial struggle has now shifted to the Urban North. . . . If Dr. King is convinced that he has sacrificed ten years of brilliant leadership he will be forced to revise his concepts. There is only one direction in which he can move and that is in the direction of Malcolm X." It was an illusion shared by many white radicals, who were delighted with Malcolm's broadside attack against middle-class America, and thought they could see in it the long-awaited stirring of revolution among the black *lumpenproletariat*. But when a *New York Times* poll asked blacks who among their leaders was doing the best job on their behalf, almost three-fourths named King, one-fifth Roy Wilkins of the NAACP, with only 6 percent citing Malcolm X.

The one ability of Malcolm that no one disputed was his prowess as a publicist, measured by his capacity to attract attention to himself. Playing on the media's Pavlovian response to the sensational, he regularly manipulated even those most devoutly opposed to him and his works. The *Saturday Evening Post* snapped up publication rights to the *Autobiography*, and introduced it with what amounted to an apology to its readers: "If Malcolm X were not a Negro, his autobiography would be little more than a journal of abnormal psychology, the story of a burglar, dope pusher, addict and jailbird—with a family history of insanity—who acquires messianic delusions and sets forth to preach an upside-down religion of 'brotherly hatred.' "

Yet Malcolm's account of his youth seems remarkably free of overt discrimination. He tells of a kind of Huck Finn boyhood in rural Michigan, hunting and fishing with the white kids, joining them in turning over a neighbor's privy on Halloween, attending a high school where his white classmates elected him senior class president—and, he says, some tried to introduce him to sex with their sisters or girl friends. He writes of being befriended by a number of whites when he got in trouble with the law, and the poverty that afflicted the Littles seems no different in kind or degree from that suffered by many white families in those depression years. He made no effort to portray himself as Robin Hood; most of the victims in his outlaw days were black, and most of the beneficiaries white—the Mafia operators who skimmed the profits from the dope and numbers he peddled, and the lesbian madam for whom he pimped. The real impact of discrimination on Malcolm was spiritual—the sense that even whites who befriended him looked upon him as a kind of mascot, something less than a man, and it was this, not his identification with the poor, that gave his rage resonance with blacks of all classes.

His cavalier disregard for the consequences of his actions carried over into his second incarnation and, I suspect, into the third. In Boston he organized a burglary gang he said included a married upper-class white woman who had been his mistress for years, her young sister, and two black males. To put them in awe of him he played a game of Russian roulette, thrice spinning the cylinder of a revolver containing one bullet, snapping it against his temple. "Never cross a man not afraid to die!" he instructed his hysterical accomplices, and added proudly, "I never had one moment's trouble with any of them after that." In his epilogue, Alex Haley tells how, after the book was in final draft, Malcolm told him he had palmed the bullet and the Russian roulette game had been a fake. Haley started to change the passage, but Malcolm stopped him: "No, leave it that way. Too many people would be so quick to say that's what I'm doing today, bluffing."

I never saw Malcolm after his break with the Black Muslims, but I am certain that my verdict would have paralleled that rendered by Robert Penn Warren, who interviewed him when he established the Organization of Afro-American Unity. "He trusts to his magnetism—and his luck," Warren concluded in *Who Speaks for the Negro.* "He may end at the barricades, or in Congress. Or he may even end on the board of a bank." Malcolm ended, riddled with bullets, on the stage of Harlem's Audubon Ballroom, slaughtered, as he had prophesied, by black men presumed to have been dispatched by his former brethren. Shortly thereafter an explosion and fire destroyed Temple Number Seven, and the Nation of Islam, as founded by Elijah Poole and propagated by Malcolm Little, had run its course as a national institution.

THE obituary comment after Malcolm's demise on February 21, 1965, was mixed. In a eulogy at the funeral the actor-playwright, Ossie Davis, said: "Malcolm was our manhood! This was his meaning to his people. And in honoring him we honor the best in ourselves . . . our own black, shining prince—who didn't hesitate to die, because he loved us so." Few dissented from the view that the fallen Muslim had contributed to a necessary elevation of black self-esteem. But many questioned whether there wasn't a less destructive path to the same end, for there was no escaping the corrosive basic ingredient in the gospel according to Malcolm. "The Black Muslim movement evinces aspects of the psychology of redemption which we know well from Christianity, the Communist Party and psychoanalysis," Warren wrote. "And it openly offers, in addition, a powerful attraction not officially advertised by those other communions: hate."

Malcolm's implacable black adversary, Roy Wilkins of the NAACP, accorded him a kind of immortality: "Master spellbinder that he was, Malcolm X in death cast a spell more far-flung and more disturbing than any he cast in life." The spell would survive primarily among black intellectuals, and among the young of both races who sought to incorporate the race issue in the inchoate protest movement that broke out on the nation's college campuses and, briefly, spread to the streets.

The principal tender of the flame was the gifted, best-selling black author, James Baldwin. At the heart of his tormented, sex-oriented fiction, and his sulphurous polemical writing, was the conviction Baldwin shared with Malcolm—that the race issue that plagued America had its beginning in the rape of Africa by European whites, and could never be cured by those who are stained with the guilt of slavery. Thus, whatever befalls a black man is the fault of the white majority. In London, when he received word of Malcolm's death, he pointed at a white reporter: "You did it. . . ."

Baldwin had risen from his beginnings as a boy evangelist in Harlem not only to be accepted but honored by the larger American society, helped all along the way by the white establishment, which conferred upon him the Saxon Memorial Trust Award, Guggenheim and Partisan Review fellowships, a Ford Foundation grant, and, finally, enough returns from royalties to permit him to live among the wealthy expatriates in the South of France. This did nothing to temper his view. "My countrymen impressed me, simply, as being, on the whole, the emptiest and most unattractive people in the world," his protagonist, the bisexual Leo Proudhammer, says in *Tell Me How Long the Train's Been Gone*. Baldwin rejected the integrationist goals of the civil rights movement. But he was far too perceptive to regard separatism as a practical alternative. His eloquence served to enshrine Malcolm X's politics of rage, while demonstrating its futility. Leo Proudhammer put it this way: "There was no reason not to kill—I mean no moral reason. But there were too many—too many; they were everywhere one turned, the bland, white, happy, stupid faces."

20

Breakthrough in Congress

By the end of the 1950s civil rights had become something more than a side issue in national politics, primarily useful to Republicans as a means of arousing Southern Democrats and thereby embarrassing their liberal Northern brethren. Philip Graham, the energetic publisher of the *Washington Post,* concluded that the time had come to turn this equation around in a fashion that would advance his budding career as a kingmaker. To that end he persuaded Lyndon Johnson that he could become a serious contender for the presidency if he were willing to emerge as the first Southern politician in modern times to champion the cause of the black minority. It turned out to be a historic sales effort.

As the tireless, arm-twisting Senate Democratic majority leader Johnson had gained recognition among Washington insiders as a formidable political power. But his public image, as he was to complain throughout his career, was distorted by his Confederate antecedents and his earthy, flamboyant style. "Southern political personalities, like sweet corn, travel badly," A. J. Liebling wrote in *The Earl of Louisiana.* "They lose flavor with every hundred yards away from the patch. By the time they reach New York they are like golden bantam that has been trucked up from Texas—stale and unprofitable."

In those days Johnson was a study in frustration, his boundless ambition thwarted, as he saw it, by the liberals who dominated the Democratic Party and contemptuously wrote him off as a parochial wheeler-dealer. He identified me with Adlai Stevenson, whose inner circle he thought infested by his detractors, and when I ran into him in Washington it was only a matter of time before he impaled me with his clublike forefinger and demanded: "Why doesn't Arthur Schlesinger like me?"

In *The Powers That Be* David Halberstam suggested that "it was not so much the accent that put the liberals off, it was the smell of oil and gas that tainted Johnson's public image." To Phil Graham, the talented upward-striver who moved in as the tall Texan's mentor, neither aspect of the problem seemed too serious. "Graham saw Johnson as a political extension of himself," Halberstam wrote, "liberal, pragmatic, partially populist, from a semideprived Southern background. A man who knew the real world and who . . . had an overall sense of moral purpose." On his own behalf the young publisher had parlayed these assets into a secure position among the leaders of the liberal establishment. He was confident he could sell Lyndon Johnson to the party's leaders as the ablest of the surviving New Dealers, one who had entered politics as a protégé of Franklin Roosevelt and had kept the faith despite necessary services to his Texas oil and gas constituency.

I found myself in general agreement with Graham's grand design when he sketched it to me one night at dinner in early 1957. The rising tension in the South over desegregation, and the increasing unrest in the black ghettoes of the North, were very much on his mind. He had tried, he said, to push the Eisenhower administration into an active role of support for the Supreme Court's *Brown* ruling, but had found it impossible to shake the president's devotion to the status quo. What the situation called for was a healer, one who could bridge the widening gap between liberals and conservatives as FDR had done in the crises brought on by depression and war. The race issue, he thought, was producing a dangerous polarization, and only a Southerner who was willing, and equipped, to "go national" could deal effectively with it. Johnson, he had decided, was the man, and the device for launching him into his new orbit was at hand—a civil rights bill sent up by Republican political strategists in anticipation that, as usual, the raucous opposition of the Southern bloc would defeat the measure and provide campaign ammunition for the coming congressional elections.

In the light of later legislation the Civil Rights Act of 1957, the first to be passed by Congress in eighty-two years, was mild even in its original form, which included as Part III a provision that would have empowered the attorney general to seek injunctions on his own motion against any who sought to deprive others of their civil rights—thus giving the Justice Department an affirmative role in furthering school desegregation. Before Section III came up for final action, however, President Eisenhower pulled the rug from under its Republican sponsors, remarking at a crucial press conference, "I personally believe if you try to go too far too fast in laws in this delicate field that has involved the emotions of so many Americans, you are making a mistake."

Lyndon Johnson moved in. When Senator Russell of Georgia branded Part III "a cunning device to integrate the races" the majority leader proposed a substitute that would eliminate the offending section. Harris Wofford, a young Washington lawyer who was on the Hill lobbying on behalf of the civil rights forces, described Johnson in action as he began to pull the two sides together: "He did talk at least two different lines—one when his arms were around Sen. Hubert Humphrey, with whom he discussed the maximum they could get, and the other when he was hand-in-arm with Sen. Richard Russell, saying there had to be some kind of 'nigra' bill."

While Johnson was working over his colleagues, Phil Graham, with the same driving energy and bulldozing technique, was bringing around key civil rights leaders, whose first instinct was to reject Johnson's version as an unacceptable compromise that would only serve to take the steam out of their movement. The tide turned when Graham dragooned reluctant endorsements from Roy Wilkins of the NAACP and a white liberal bellwether, Joseph Rauh of Americans for Democratic Action.

On August 29, after a fourteen-hour filibuster by Strom Thurmond, the Civil Rights Act of 1957 passed the Senate by a vote of sixty to fifteen. As a tour de force for Lyndon Johnson it had few parallels in the modern history of Congress. "The miracle of '57," the Washington columnists, Rowland Evans and Robert Novak, dubbed it. A battle-scarred veteran of Capitol Hill deadfalls, former Secretary of State Dean Acheson, cited the measure as "among the greatest achievements since the war, and, in the field of civil rights, the greatest since the Thirteenth Amendment." Johnson, as Graham had assured him he would, managed to go national without losing his

Southern base. "The party that seemed about torn in two by the controversy achieved greater unity than it had had in two decades," Richard Rovere wrote in *The New Yorker*.

And there was, as it turned out, a good deal more to the compromise bill than met the jaundiced eye. It created, finally, the Civil Rights Commission that had been on the congressional agenda since Harry Truman proposed it back in 1948. This was an independent, bipartisan body, and while its functions were investigatory and advisory, it did have the power of subpoena. When the more militant black leaders denounced the commission as a charade, Roy Wilkins replied, "If you're digging a ditch with a teaspoon and a man comes along and offers you a spade, there is something wrong with your head if you don't take it because he didn't offer you a bulldozer."

THE Civil Rights Act provided that the commission should be made up of six members, with no more than three chosen from one political party. President Eisenhower's appointments were characteristic—on the Democratic side two segregationist former governors, John Battle of Virginia and Doyle Carlton of Florida, and the moderate Dean Robert Storey of Southern Methodist University Law School; as Republican appointees Eisenhower named as chairman Pres. John Hannah of Michigan State University and, as the only black member, the conservative assistant secretary of labor, J. Ernest Wilkins. As had been the case with the Supreme Court when he appointed Earl Warren, the president unintentionally provided the catalyst that would move the commission off dead center. What was presumed to be a nonpolitical appointment went to Fr. Theodore Hesburgh, president of Notre Dame University, who then had no track record in public service.

By June the new agency was in business with an initial appropriation of $750,000. Harris Wofford was a key figure on the nuclear staff, summoned by Hesburgh from a leading law firm after he read a memorandum in which Wofford contended that the commission's most vital role might be to restore communication between the races. The biracial advisory committee to be established in each state, Wofford wrote, could provide the means through which the Southern white "might realize that there is a new Negro in his midst, not sent from the

North, not primarily stirred up by outside agitators, but by the Constitution and the Christian Church. And the Negro might see that there are other, wiser Southern voices than the jeers and catcalls of racist mobs and the ranting or slipperiness of political demagogues."

The thirty-two-year-old lawyer was uniquely qualified for the role Father Hesburgh literally thrust upon him. Although he had grown up in solid, middle-class Republican respectability in Scarsdale, New York, his roots were deep in the South, where he spent his first six years. His great grandfather, Col. Jefferson Llewellyn Wofford of Lexington, Mississippi, led the Confederate infantry in the last battle of the Civil War at Blakeley, Alabama. Not far from there, at Craig Field outside Selma, Wofford, as an eighteen-year-old World War II air force volunteer, had his first exposure to the realities of race relations in the Deep South.

After the war he spent some time in India, where he was attracted to the Gandhian philosophy of nonviolence. He concluded a 1952 law school thesis on patterns of segregation in the South with the observation that what the region needed was "a Negro with a touch of Gandhi in him"; the Montgomery bus strike convinced him that one such had arisen and he became an early confidant of Martin Luther King. Wofford's thesis was written while he studied civil rights law at Howard University, the first white to matriculate there since suffragettes attended classes in the days when they were barred from all other schools by their gender. In *Of Kennedys and Kings,* a memoir which recounts his experiences as chief civil rights adviser to the New Frontier, he told of the reaction of his family to his decision to enroll at Howard:

My parents were terribly upset, fearing for my career. It was a shock to my grandmother in Tennessee, but as an active churchwoman she braced herself and sent me an Episcopal prayer against race prejudice. For my other grandmother from Little Rock, it was the end of the world. Ironically, she was the one who started my interest in India and Gandhi and first encouraged me to break out of the family's Republican fold. She was a devoted Democrat who adored both Franklin and Eleanor Roosevelt. She also was an inveterate traveler who took me around the world for six months when I was twelve. But to stop me from enrolling in a predominantly Negro university she pleaded, "You can go there to teach them, to help them, but you can't go and be a student with them." When her arguments failed, she literally collapsed and my father and I had to carry her upstairs while she shouted, "If God made them equal, I hate God! I hate God! I hate God!"

Wofford provided an initial link between the commission and the black civil rights leadership—and found that Eisenhower's choice of commissioners had produced universal skepticism. The commission was empowered to investigate complaints that the right to vote was being denied by reason of race, but for the first eight months of its existence not a single complaint was filed. It could be assumed that this resulted from a combination of inertia and fear of retaliation among blacks in those rural Southern precincts where the abuses were most flagrant—but it also meant that the black leaders were making no effort to even test the new agency. "You are willing to lead people to jail," Wofford told King. "Why can't you get them to file an affidavit?" The answer was that the black leaders doubted that the commission had the power, or the will, to protect those who would be singled out if they agreed to testify before a public hearing.

The first complaint, from Gadsen County, Florida, was wholly spontaneous. But when the response was an immediate field investigation by trained, thoroughgoing agents who inspired confidence in the federal presence, word began to get around, and soon SCLC was helping spread it. By the end of the year complaints had been received from twenty-nine counties in eight states; fifteen of these were among the hundred where 1956 black voter registration averaged less than 6 percent even though blacks constituted a majority of the population.

By 1959, when the commission was in full swing, blacks were voting more or less freely in the Southern cities, and it was only in the rural backwaters of the Deep South that the traditional combination of fraud and strong-arm tactics was still used to keep them away from the polling place. At the state level the political leadership tacitly accepted an expanding black electorate as a fact of life and had begun to deal with its spokesmen. However, in the states where the Citizens Councils rode high overt support for breaching the white primary was still considered hazardous to the political health of those who privately welcomed the change.

When urban blacks became a political force in Louisiana, a true believer named Willie Rainach got himself named chairman of a joint legislative committee and set out to reduce their registration from 130,000 to 13,000. But when Rainach pressured state officials to refuse to divulge voting records to the agents of the Civil Rights Commission, Gov. Earl Long met privately with its representative, Berl Bernhard, and told him: "You're here to help the niggers vote, and I am for you because they're my niggers and I want their votes. . . . Now, we're never going to talk about my helping you, but I'm gonna get my state registrar to give you the records you need, and after you talk to him, you remember, you never saw me."

There was no such sub rosa assistance available in Alabama. The commission's first real showdown came there when the attorney general, John Patterson, who was also governor-elect, blocked the effort to obtain voting records for Lowndes County, where no blacks were registered although they made up 82 percent of the population. The commission voted unanimously to hold a hearing in Montgomery, and issued sixty-six subpoenas for witnesses. Circuit Judge George C. Wallace, who would succeed Patterson as governor after vowing that no candidate would ever "out-nigger" him, told the press: "I will jail any Civil Rights Commission agent who attempts to get the records."

This adamance hardened the resolve of the three Southern commissioners, who were able to preface their public statements at Montgomery by citing their Alabama kin and Confederate ancestors. None of the white people present, said Governor Battle, "believe more strongly than I do in the segregation of the races as the right and proper way of life in the South." But voting was a constitutional right, and those records must be provided. The record of the hearing was turned over to the Department of Justice, the government filed suit, and Judge Frank Johnson overrode the interposition of Judge Wallace and issued the appropriate order.

In addition to voting, the commission had selected two other areas for study: discrimination in housing, and in education. The Southern members readily approved a full-scale effort in the first, since the most appalling examples were to be found in the ghettoes of non-Southern cities. The starting point was the 1958 report by the independent Commission on Race and Housing established and financed by the Fund for the Republic. As a director I had been asked by Robert Hutchins to review the voluminous material summarized in the published report, *Where Shall We Live?*, and found it a sober, compelling documentation of the failure of more than a decade of federal slum clearance and public housing programs. Although billions had been spent, the inner cities continued as enclaves where unscrupulous landlords, with the concurrence of private lending institutions and local public officials, reaped unconscionable profits from minority tenants trapped by de facto segregation.

The Civil Rights Commission's hearings in major cities confirmed these findings, pointing up two levels of discrimination—that against middle-class blacks financially able to afford decent housing in neighborhoods that barred them because of race, and that against the poor, who were not immediately concerned with the "white noose" of surrounding suburbs that now characterized every major metropolitan area. These slum-dwellers were among the nearly 70 percent of nonwhite families whose income level gave them no choice but to live in overcrowded apartments officially classified as substandard because of dilapidation or lack of plumbing. The Civil Rights Commission confirmed the prior finding that a joint public-private effort, heavily involving the federal government, was urgently needed.

Predictably, the commission found its effective unanimity threatened when it turned to the matter of school desegregation. This was still considered a uniquely Southern problem, and any probing into the sensitive area was bound to have immediate political repercussions. To placate the Southern members public activity was confined to a single hearing, and this was limited to representatives of schools already in transition, a requirement that eliminated the necessity of dealing with the Deep South's massive resistance. School officials from the border states, plus Arkansas, North Carolina, Tennessee, and Texas, gathered at Nashville to compare notes. The consensus was that where the proportion of blacks to whites was low—the 30 percent "tipping point" formula was beginning to enter educational jargon—desegregation could be achieved on a step-by-step basis without impairment of educational quality. Indeed, some of the educators thought that the pressures created by *Brown* might be used to make badly needed general improvements. Honest acceptance of the proposition that the only reason to delay admission of black students to white schools was not their color, but their deficient educational background, might convert the drive for equalization from a device to stall integration to an orderly means of achieving a genuinely open system.

As it approached the end of its initial two-year term, the extent to which the commission had succeeded in its healing mission was put to the test among its own members, who were now required to submit a summary report to the president. From the beginning, Father Hesburgh had argued the case against segregation in terms of natural law: "Civil rights are important corollaries of the great proposition, at the heart of Western civilization, that every human person is *res sacra*, a 'sacred reality,' and as such is entitled to the opportunity of fulfilling those great human potentials with which God has endowed man." In addition to steady moral purpose, the priest also brought to communion with his Southern colleagues a taste for fishing and bourbon whiskey. Employing both when the commission met at his order's retreat at Land O' Lakes, Wisconsin, Hesburgh and Chairman Hannah managed to get approval for major elements of the final report to the president, with only one partial dissent. "I'm a tiger on voting," Battle told Hesburgh, but he couldn't go along on school desegregation. "Don't give me any theological stuff. I know what the Bible says, I try to be a Christian, but I'm an old dog. My wife tells me you're right, but it kills me and I just can't do it."

The commission made no specific recommendation on the school issue but did emphasize "fundamental premises" affirming that the choice was between ending compulsory segregation and abandoning public education. It urged an executive order to define the constitutional objective of equal opportunity in housing and to direct all federal agencies to shape their policies to that end. The only call for direct action was the recommendation for appointment of temporary federal registrars to qualify blacks to vote when the Civil Rights Commission found evidence of arbitrary denial by local officials. This assumed that the life of the commission would be extended.

When the members came to the White House to present their report, President Eisenhower listened politely, and expressed amazement that three Northerners and three Southerners could agree on any aspect of civil rights. "It's because we're all fishermen," Father Hesburgh explained. But the president was a golfer. The only recommendation he passed on to Congress was extension of the commission's tenure for another two years, which was approved in the Civil Rights Act of 1959. Dwight Eisenhower left office as he entered, declining to give civil rights a place on his personal agenda. When the big four of black leadership—King, Wilkins, Randolph, and Lester Granger of the Urban League—came again to the White House with a nine-point proposal for executive action, the president gave his answer in a murmured aside to King as he walked him to the door. "Reverend, there are so many problems . . . Lebanon, Algeria . . ."

THE incumbent was required to vacate the White House at the end of 1960 under the two-term constitutional amendment. The Republican heir apparent, Vice-President Richard M. Nixon, was not, as he conceded, overly endowed with charisma, and this guaranteed a wide-open race among the Democrats. Adlai Stevenson, the party's titular head, made it clear that he had no intention of entering the spring primary marathon. Anticipating that the other contenders would kill each other off, some of Stevenson's undaunted admirers, including Eleanor Roosevelt, began setting the stage for another draft, but the putative candidate offered no encouragement and told me privately he thought it had no chance of succeeding.

The most spectacular primary bandwagon was mounted by Sen. John Fitzgerald Kennedy of Massachusetts. Pierre Salinger, who was to become White House press secretary, called me in California to ask me to come aboard, but as long as there was a possibility of a Stevenson candidacy I didn't want to appear to be defecting. Moreover, I had become fond of Kennedy's leading primary opponent, Hubert Humphrey, and I was also attracted to the idea that Lyndon Johnson, on the strength of his virtuoso performance on civil rights, might fill the role of healer prescribed for him by Phil Graham. So I sat out the primary season, which narrowed the leading contenders to Kennedy and Johnson and left the final decision to old-fashioned horse trading at the Democratic National Convention in Los Angeles.

Bob White asked me to cover the convention for the *Herald Tribune,* and I was happy to accept since it provided an opportunity for a reunion with two of my favorite colleagues, Ralph McGill and William Calhoun Baggs, editor of the *Miami News.* When we pooled our findings among the delegations where we had personal contacts, we concluded that the Stevenson draft movement was going nowhere. There was no other galvanizing force in the convention capable of producing a coalition sufficient to stop Kennedy, although Lyndon Johnson was still giving it a good try.

On the second day, I filed a prediction that the ticket would be Kennedy-Johnson, and when my friend William S. White, the Washington columnist, heard I had done so he urged me to kill it. My sources were all wrong, he insisted; as a professional Texan and long-time confidant of the majority leader he *knew* there was no way on God's green earth for anyone to persuade Johnson to take second place on anybody's ticket—and certainly not on that of a Yankee upstart.

The fact was that I had no inside sources. Most delegate-counters by this time had concluded that Kennedy had locked up a majority, but when they started checking out the vice-presidential choice they ran into a spate of rumors and speculation. Robert Kennedy and most of the Ivy League liberals were horrified at the notion of their champion running with Johnson, and many of the Texan's intimates shared White's belief that pride would prevent his accepting the vice-presidency. But I was convinced that in the end two masterful politicians—as these certainly were—would yield to the pragmatic requirements of the elective process.

Kennedy, with the handicap of his Catholic religion to overcome, had to have a Southern running mate, and the Texan was the only one of consequence who had purged himself on civil rights. Johnson, in his turn, had reached the top of the ladder in Congress, and, from a number of private conversations with him in recent years, I was convinced that he cherished the national role he had begun to play and was anxious to be rid of the encumbrance of his Texas constituency. The place on the Kennedy ticket was the only opportunity that promised lateral, if not upward, movement within his political life expectancy.

So, in this backhanded way, the civil rights issue became a dominant factor in the nomination of an American president, and, according to the reckoning of most observers, the black vote it engendered probably provided the narrow margin by which Jack Kennedy defeated Richard Nixon in the general election. But by that time I was removed from the political scene.

In the course of the Los Angeles convention I met with William Benton, owner of *Encyclopaedia Britannica,* to discuss appointment as editor-in-chief of that venerable publication. Hutchins, the long-time chairman of *Britannica*'s Board of Editors, had recommended me, and Benton concurred. There would be pro forma interviews with the publishing company's operating executives in Chicago and London, but, as in all matters of consequence, the autocratic Benton's word was final. It was agreed—or at least I thought it was—that I would maintain my base in Santa Barbara in order to work with Hutchins, the board of editors, and a select group of advisors in developing the format for the first totally revised edition of the massive, twenty-four-volume encyclopaedia in more than fifty years—this to be published in 1968 to mark the two hundredth anniversary of *Britannica*'s birth in Edinburgh. Lord Geoffrey Crowther, the vice-chairman, welcomed me aboard with a sardonic query: "Has it ever occurred to you that you will be editing a book you won't live long enough to read?"

21

❦

Action on the
New Frontier

With the formidable *Britannica* assignment to occupy me, the 1960 presidential campaign became
the first in many years in which I had no personal involvement.
I thought well of Jack Kennedy, although our contacts had
been casual, and from his standpoint may have been negative,
since about all he was likely to remember was that at the 1956
convention I had been the messenger who brought him the
news that Stevenson had turned down his bid for a place on
the ticket. Many of my companions from the 1952 and 1956
campaigns joined the Kennedy entourage, and Benton, a
former Democratic senator from Connecticut, was an active
supporter.

There were frequent reports from the front. A colleague
at the Center for the Study of Democratic Institutions, John
Cogley, was an advisor on the tricky religious issue and traveled
with Kennedy to Houston for his confrontation with the Baptist
ministers. Harris Wofford, head of the campaign's civil rights
section, came to visit his mentor, the philosopher Scott Buchanan, a senior fellow at the Center, and dropped around to
compare notes. It was Wofford who initiated the famous
telephone call from Jack Kennedy to Coretta King that is
generally credited with solidifying the black support that put
the Democrats over the top in states with decisive electoral
votes.

It was hardly a surprise that King had wound up behind
bars in Atlanta on October 19 after leading a protest sit-in at
Rich's department store. It was now his practice to refuse bail
on such occasions, insisting on being locked up by way of
dramatizing his personal protest against what he considered
unjust laws. "I'll stay in jail a year, or ten years, if it takes that

319

long to desegregate Rich's," he told the waiting press. But the incident caused a considerable flap in the Kennedy camp, where Wofford had an understanding that the SCLC leader, while not openly endorsing the Democratic nominee, would be "neutral against Nixon," and to that end would postpone until after the election the kind of racial confrontations that would disturb Kennedy's lukewarm Southern supporters.

Mayor William Hartsfield worked out an agreement with the black leaders to postpone their protest for thirty days while he negotiated a desegregation agreement with Atlanta merchants, and King and the fifty blacks who had gone to jail with him were released. But in neighboring De Kalb County, a Ku Klux Klan stronghold, a local judge ordered King jailed on the ground that his Atlanta arrest constituted violation of the parole he had been granted after conviction on a minor traffic charge some months before. King was then spirited away to a state prison under sentence of six months at hard labor—a move that understandably frightened Coretta King, who telephoned Wofford. Kennedy was persuaded to place a call to Mrs. King, who promptly announced to the press that she was confident that the Democratic contender would do what he could to obtain her husband's release, and added, "I have heard nothing from the vice-president or anyone on his staff."

Bobby Kennedy did some discreet telephoning of his own to the De Kalb County judge, and King was returned in a blaze of media attention to a moving welcome at Ebenezer Baptist Church. His staunch Baptist father announced from the pulpit that he was withdrawing his public endorsement of Nixon: "I had expected to vote against Senator Kennedy because of his religion. But now he can be my president, Catholic or whatever he is. . . ." Jack Kennedy was reported to have greeted this conversion by expressing surprise that Martin Luther King, Jr., could have been sired by a bigot. "But, then," he added, reflecting on the life and times of Old Joe Kennedy, "we all have fathers."

This was the Kennedy brothers' first exercise in the kind of crisis management that would characterize their relationship with black activists during the thousand days of the New Frontier. It was also a harbinger of the growing cleavage between militants and moderates in the civil rights movement

—the internal contest for leadership that would plague King until he joined the young president in the hall of martyrs. He had tried to keep his agreement to hold down racial confrontations until after the election, but his hand had been forced by aggressive young blacks enlisted in a new organization SCLC inspired and helped found—the Student Nonviolent Coordinating Committee (SNCC).

"SNICK," as its youthful adherents called it, had its genesis in the spontaneous action of four students at North Carolina Agricultural and Technical College. After reading King's *Stride Toward Freedom*, Joseph McNeil, eighteen, began needling three fellow freshmen, Ezell Blair, Jr., Franklin McCain, and David Richmond, suggesting that the four organize their own antisegregation boycott right there in Greensboro.

On Monday afternoon, February 1, 1960, the four young men went to Woolworth's variety store, made a few purchases, and then sat down at the lunch counter and ordered coffee. When the waitress informed them that Woolworth's didn't serve colored people, Blair replied that they had in fact just been served at other counters. The first response of the management, and the police who came to patrol the aisle behind them, was to simply ignore the polite, neatly dressed young men who had suddenly abandoned the role Harry Golden identified as that of "the vertical Negro," who was welcome to spend his money as long as he stayed on his feet. The Greensboro Four sat at the counter, unserved but unmolested, until the store closed at 5:30 P.M.

The next day twenty students joined the protest, taking virtually every seat at the counter, and stayed until closing time; by the third day enough had volunteered to permit organizing the "sit-in" in shifts. The A & T basketball team played the role of Johnny Appleseed, leaving behind lunch-counter sit-ins in the five cities where it played during the next few weeks. By instinct, the Greensboro Four had touched the same sensitive nerve that had rallied blacks to support the Montgomery bus boycott.

To most whites, segregation in places of public accommodation seemed to impose no more than minor inconvenience upon the blacks who were barred from their presence—and at its inception this form of Jim Crow had not directly touched the mass of blacks who could not afford access to most of the establishments where it was practiced. But the black middle class, to which the students belonged, was growing, and like its white counterpart regarded the automobile as a mark of status. For these, Jim Crow made travel a nightmare. "Nothing," John A. Williams wrote in *The King God Didn't Save*, "is quite as humiliating, so murderously angering, as to know that because you are black you may have to walk half a mile farther than whites just to urinate; that because you are black you have to receive your food through a window in the back of a restaurant or sit in a garbage-littered yard to eat."

I was in Harlem when the sit-ins began to spread across the South, and I heard the moving firsthand reaction of an aging crusader who was battling Jim Crow long before the young protestants were born. One quiet Saturday afternoon I sat in the shabby offices of the Brotherhood of Sleeping Car Porters discussing with A. Philip Randolph the new Negro American Labor Council he had formed to battle racial discrimination within the ranks of the AFL-CIO. Of necessity, his own union had come into being segregated—its thirty-five thousand members accounting for almost half the total number of blacks in the AFL as late as the 1930s—but now its founder had concluded that such exclusivity was no longer tolerable.

The basic philosophy of the trade union movement, Randolph contended, called for an end to discrimination, not just economic discrimination but all forms of demeaning treatment. That was why he had openly challenged the AFL–CIO hierarchy from the floor of its last convention, outraging Pres. George Meany to the point that the old plumber shouted at the old porter, "Who the hell appointed you the guardian of all the Negro union members in America?" That would have seemed to be challenge enough for a man entering his seventies, but Randolph had just made another commitment. Gazing down on the teeming streets of Harlem, the old man told of being literally taken off a train in North Carolina by a delegation of black college students who found out his travel schedule and came aboard unannounced at an operating stop.

"They scared the life out of the porter, and he tried to keep them out," he said. "I think he even told them I wasn't on the train, but they knew better, and they just pushed him backward into my compartment. He kept saying, 'For the Lord's sake, Boss, don't go with these people. They're wild!'

"But they told me they had a car waiting, and they needed me on their campus, and would take me on to Charlotte to meet my appointments. So I went with them, and when we got there the whole auditorium was full of students and they had been waiting for hours. The president and some of the faculty came in to greet me, and they looked pretty nervous, and I guess I couldn't blame them. That whole place was full of electricity. You could feel it.

"I got up to talk to them, and when I looked out over those young faces there wasn't but one thing I could say. I told them I would do what I could to help. That's what I'm doing now— trying to help the best way I know how."

As the movement spread from campus to campus, the NAACP and the New Congress of Racial Equality (CORE) sent field representatives to work with the college students, and in April SCLC financed a conference of sit-in leaders at Shaw University in Raleigh. Martin Luther King was there, and came away disturbed that many of the youngsters seemed to look upon nonviolence only as a tactic, and grew restive when he tried to discuss the underlying philosophy.

"There is another element in our struggle that makes our resistance and nonviolence truly meaningful," King told them. "That element is reconciliation. Our ultimate end must be the creation of the beloved community. The tactics of nonviolence without the spirit of nonviolence may become a new kind of violence." But a Virginia delegate responded, "I don't dig all this." The issues to him were money, jobs, and scholarships for poor blacks.

A fifteen-member planning group met in Atlanta in May and paid tribute to King by including "nonviolent" in the title chosen for the organization they formed. The statement of purpose proclaimed: "We affirm the philosophical or religious ideal of nonviolence as the foundation of our purpose, the presupposition of our faith and the manner of our action. . . ." But the Student Nonviolent Coordinating Committee spurned the role of youth affiliate to SCLC and asserted the independence that was to be its hallmark.

A meeting in October to perfect a permanent organization stressed a minimum of structure and a maximum of spontaneity. SNCC was intended to be, and for the most part was, an exercise in participational democracy. Robert Moses, who became a dominant influence, once proposed that all offices and committees be abolished, and that those present simply walk out the door and "go where the spirit say go and do what the spirit say do."

By September 1961, the Southern Regional Council reported, over a hundred cities in the Southern and border states had been the site of demonstrations, sit-ins, picketing, marches, or mass meetings. At least seventy thousand people, some of them white, had been involved in protesting segregated lunch counters, restrooms, and recreational facilities; thirty-six hundred, mostly students, had been arrested.

That spring CORE had modified its supporting role for SNCC's student activists, launching on its own motion the first of the Freedom Rides that would bring interracial teams down from the North to protest Jim Crow. In February the veteran organizer, James Farmer, left his post as program director of NAACP to become head of the activist pacifist organization. He targeted bus terminals, now covered by a Supreme Court ruling which extended the segregation ban the Interstate Commerce Commission (ICC) originally limited to interstate vehicles. "Our purpose," Farmer said, "is to provoke the Southern authorities into arresting us and thereby prod the Justice Department into enforcing the law of the land."

The ultimate object of this maneuver was John F. Kennedy and his brother Robert, the new United States attorney general. Farmer was not moved by the great wave of affection for the Kennedys among rank-and-file blacks that followed their intervention on behalf of Martin Luther King. At the popular level this was sustained by the excitement of the transition from the staid Eisenhower administration to the glamorous New Frontier. There were gestures toward the black constituency in the cool presidential style—as when JFK noticed that there were no blacks in the Coast Guard contingent at his inaugural and ordered a racial inventory of that and all other federal services. And there were some notable, if largely symbolic, black appointments below the cabinet level: Andrew Hatcher to the White House staff as associate press secretary, Robert Weaver as director of the Housing and Home Finance Agency, Carl Rowan as ambassador to Finland, Thurgood Marshall to the Circuit Court of Appeals. In the early months the Kennedy performance was dazzling to white and black alike; Norman Mailer, joining a chorus of intellectual hurrahs, predicted that Kennedy's regime "would be an existential event; he would touch depths in American life that were uncharted. . . ."

But, like Farmer, most of the other leaders of the civil rights movement entertained doubts that any of this would touch the well-charted depths where the mass of poor blacks were huddled. They understood that the obligation Kennedy owed black voters was offset by the debts he had incurred among reactionary Democratic leaders who held the line for him in Southern states also essential to his victory. To Clarence Mitchell, the NAACP's veteran Washington lobbyist, the New Frontier looked "suspiciously like a dude ranch with Sen. James O. Eastland as general manager." If it didn't look quite that way from an inside perspective, the liberals who had found places in the White House also had their reservations.

To Arthur Schlesinger, Kennedy displayed a "terrible ambivalence about civil rights. While he did not doubt the depths of injustice or the need for remedy, he had read the arithmetic of the new Congress and concluded that there was no chance of passing a civil rights bill." Even more inhibiting, the president feared that a protracted filibuster would produce drastic reaction among increasingly restive blacks that would "place a perhaps intolerable strain on the already fragile social fabric."

In May Robert Kennedy addressed the University of Georgia Law School, pledging to pursue amicable, voluntary solutions to problems of racial discrimination wherever possible. But he warned that "if the orders of the [federal courts] are circumvented, the Department of Justice will act. We will not stand by and be aloof. We will move." Ralph McGill praised the speech in the *Constitution,* which was not surprising since Kennedy had privately consulted him on what to say. "Never before, in all its travail of by-gone years," McGill wrote, "has the South heard so honest a speech from any Cabinet member." And Georgia-born Louis Martin, who also had been consulted on the advance draft, sent a warm message: "Congratulations are pouring in from brothers everywhere, here and abroad. If you keep up this way, one of these days I might be able to go back home."

But by this time James Farmer had assembled a band of thirteen Freedom Riders in Washington, and had begun training them in the nonviolent tactics they would use on their highly publicized trip south. In Virginia and North Carolina the White Only signs came down in the terminals the day before the Riders arrived. But in South Carolina, predictably, the signs were still up, and at Rock Hill white toughs attacked John Lewis—the future chairman of SNCC—when he tried to enter a restroom. There, and elsewhere on the way to Atlanta, local police acted to protect the Riders against mob action. But now the trajectory would take them across the Deep South to New Orleans, and the mounting publicity served to alert the Ku Klux Klan. A mob was waiting at Anniston when the first of the two buses bearing Freedom Riders crossed into Alabama. Turned back by police at the terminal, the Klansmen followed the bus out to the highway, where they halted it, set it afire, and manhandled the fleeing passengers. A flying squadron of blacks led by the Reverend Fred Shuttlesworth of SCLC picked up the Riders and took them on to Birmingham by automobile.

The second bus avoided the mob at Anniston, but when it arrived at the Trailways station in Birmingham the Klan had turned out scores of its members to greet the Riders with pipes, chains, and baseball bats. A detailed battle plan for this operation had been forwarded to Washington by the FBI, whose paid informant within the Klan reported that Police Commissioner Bull Connor had agreed to give the bullyboys twenty minutes before he sent in his police, saying that he wanted the Freedom Riders beaten "until it looks like a bulldog got ahold of them."

The Klansmen carried out their mission in exemplary fashion, leaving the Riders so bloodied an eyewitness said he couldn't see their faces. Bull Connor explained to reporters, many of whom had been alerted the day before, that he didn't have any police on hand at his headquarters a few blocks away because it was Mother's Day and he had let them all go home.

Gov. John Patterson, a presumed Democratic loyalist who had been an early Kennedy supporter, responded to the president's public call for the restoration of law and order by declaring: "The people of Alabama are so aroused I cannot guarantee protection for this bunch of rabble-rousers." John Siegenthaler, a Tennessee journalist who served as public affairs assistant to Bobby Kennedy and was equipped with a presumably helpful Southern accent, was dispatched to Birmingham and managed to get the battered Riders to the airport and aboard a plane to New Orleans.

The bizarre events in Alabama had become an international media event, and an acute embarrassment to President Kennedy on the eve of departure for a summit conference with Nikita Khrushchev. "Tell them to call it off!" he ordered Harris Wofford. "Stop them!" In the absence of James Farmer, who had been called back to Washington by the death of his father, Bobby Kennedy almost managed to carry out these instructions, getting agreement from CORE to suspend the rides during a cooling-off period. But up in Nashville, young John Lewis, having returned there after his tour of duty in the Carolinas, decided that suspension of the Freedom Rides would be an intolerable surrender to the segregationists. Against the advice of SCLC leaders, he recruited sit-in veterans from the local campuses and used SNCC funds to buy them tickets on a bus headed for Birmingham.

There Lewis and his party encountered one of the few examples of fairly humane treatment to be found in the extensive civil rights record of Bull Connor. Taken into "protective custody" by the police upon arrival, they were held overnight in the city jail. After dark the following day, they were loaded into police cars, driven a hundred and fifty miles north to the Tennessee border, and left there on the side of the highway. Lewis was in the car with Bull Connor, and recalled that they laughed and joked all the way. But this uptown version of the classic ride out of town on a rail didn't work. Lewis got to a telephone, arranged to have a car sent down from Nashville, and with seven of his followers headed straight back to the Greyhound bus terminal in Birmingham, where they bought tickets for Montgomery.

Now the cooling off, if there was to be any, would have to

be done on the other side. Bobby Kennedy got on the telephone, where he was to spend many hours cajoling and threatening state and local officials. He made a deal, or thought he did, with Governor Patterson, who agreed to provide an escort of state police to take the bus containing the Freedom Riders to Montgomery, and on to the Mississippi state line as it headed for Jackson. Fred Shuttlesworth, the outspoken Birmingham SCLC leader, chortled, "Man, what's this state coming to! An armed escort to take a bunch of niggers to a bus station so they can break these silly old laws"—a chortle that may have had something to do with the governor's refusal to extend state police protection into the local jurisdiction at Montgomery, where the waiting mob was even more vicious than those at Anniston and Birmingham. Siegenthaler himself was among the victims, kicked unconscious and left lying in his own blood for nearly half an hour after he tried to rescue a girl who was being clubbed.

Now the federals were forced to take police action on their own. Bobby Kennedy sent in his deputy, Byron White, and four hundred riot-trained United States marshals—the special force that had been brought into being after the use of army troops at Little Rock had seemed to invoke memories of the Civil War. I had never taken much stock in this notion, since it seemed to me Little Rock actually demonstrated that the dress of an armed man didn't make any real difference; what was required to end mob violence with minimum casualties was a show of unmistakably superior force, and the protests would be heard no matter whether the federals wore civilian clothes or combat fatigues. My view was borne out at Montgomery, and a year and a half later at Oxford in the case of James Meredith's admission to the University of Mississippi. The marshals performed valiantly on both battlefields, but the mob action was not quelled until, at Montgomery, Governor Patterson finally turned out the National Guard, and, at Oxford, federal troops arrived.

The crisis at Montgomery came when King arrived to address a mass meeting. The marshals managed to get him from the airport to Ralph Abernathy's First Baptist Church, and to protect him and his audience of fifteen hundred against the mob that surrounded the building until the National Guard arrived hours later. From the pulpit King proclaimed: "We hear the familiar cry that morals cannot be legislated. This may be true, but behavior can be regulated. The law may not be able to make a man love me, but it can keep him from lynching me." When he expressed these sentiments over the telephone during the long, terror-filled night, complaining that the attorney general was not doing enough, Bobby Kennedy's respect for the cloth lapsed. "Now, Reverend," he said, "you know just as well as I do that if it hadn't been for those United States marshals you would be as dead as Kelsey's nuts right now."

Kennedy went to work trying to secure safe passage for the Freedom Riders after they crossed into Mississippi. He made a deal with Senator Eastland; there would be no violence, Eastland guaranteed, but the Freedom Riders would be arrested as soon as they tried to sit in at the Jackson bus station. Kennedy thought this fair enough; his primary interest was in protecting the Riders against further physical harm; the arrests would dramatize the issue, and bail could be arranged. But when he publicly called for suspension of the Freedom Rides to permit a cooling-off period, James Farmer replied, "We've been cooling off for a hundred years. If we get any cooler we'll be in a deep freeze." And King shocked the attorney general by rejecting the proposal for bail, saying the Riders were honor bound to accept and serve their sentences.

"It's a matter of conscience and morality," King explained in another of the interminable telephone conversations. "They must use their lives and their bodies to right a wrong." This, the attorney general replied, was nonsense; this kind of pressure tactic was not going to have any effect on him, or on his brother. When King observed wryly that maybe it would if Freedom Riders began to come down by the hundreds of thousands, Kennedy construed it as a threat. King was sorry about that. "I'm deeply appreciative of what the administration is doing. I see a ray of hope, but I am different from my father. I feel the need of being free now!"

In the wake of this telephonic impasse King told his associates, "You know, they don't understand the social revolution going on in the world, and therefore they don't understand what we're doing." Kennedy in his turn relayed his frustration to Wofford: "This is too much! I wonder whether they have the best interest of their country at heart. Do you know that one of them is against the atom bomb—yes, he even picketed against it in jail!"

The president, facing delicate negotiations with allies and with the Russians on the impending European tour, refused to make any personal, public intervention in the matter. His reading of public opinion reinforced his decision to keep the presidential profile low while Bobby Kennedy and his aides managed the crisis; a June Gallup poll showed 63 percent disapproval of the Freedom Rides in principle, but 70 percent approval of the use of federal marshals to protect the Riders against mob action—with a reading of 50 percent in the South. A *New York Times* editorial supporting the call for a cooling-off period reflected the prevailing liberal view: "Nonviolence that deliberately provokes violence is a logical contradiction."

FOR better or worse, the strategy that would prevail through the remainder of the Kennedy administration was set. Victor Navasky summarized it in *Kennedy Justice*: "The trick was to encourage the inevitable integration, but never at the cost of disturbing the social equilibrium." A growing body of critics charged that the president's concern with holding together a congressional majority in support of his cold war programs, including the space race, caused him to sacrifice controversial— which by definition meant effective—civil rights measures, and unduly limit executive intervention. The glamor of the New Frontier no longer provided a diversionary shield against charges of expediency, equated by some with moral weakness. But, aside from the predilections of the president and the coterie of pragmatists David Halberstam scornfully labeled "The Best and the Brightest," the dramatic events precipitated by the Freedom Rides demonstrated that the federal system imposed severe limitations on direct action by Washington in response to a black-white confrontation. And, I think, these justified Bobby Kennedy's efforts to defuse by negotiation, even though his misjudgment of recalcitrant white Southern politicians sometimes produced counterproductive and even ludicrous results.

It was the unhappy lot of Burke Marshall, civil rights chief in the Justice Department, to explain to importunate seekers of federal action that, "we do not have a national police force, and *cannot* provide protection in a physical sense for everyone who is disliked because of the exercise of his civil rights. . . . There is no substitute under the federal system for the failure of local law enforcement responsibility. There is simply a vacuum, which can be filled only rarely, with extraordinary difficulty, at monumental expense, and in a totally unsatisfactory fashion."

Supreme Court decisions had greatly broadened the range of civil rights entitled to federal protection, but it could be invoked only on clear showing of denial or default by local authorities, and in most cases this meant after the fact. Burke Marshall complained that this was not understood, and he was probably right so far as the general public was concerned. But the black leaders understood it very well and, indeed, made it the basis of their strategy. "Our philosophy is simple," James Farmer said. "We put on pressure and they react."

In the case of the Freedom Riders the first reaction was violence against nonviolent demonstrators, or jail sentences for violations of state laws the federal courts were bound to hold unconstitutional; the next was intervention by the federal government, which could not stand by while its authority was challenged by mob rule; the third was action by appropriate federal agencies to remove the original cause of the demonstrations. In the wake of the riots in Alabama and the mass arrests in Mississippi, the attorney general petitioned the ICC to strengthen regulations requiring the end of segregation in interstate terminals, and the Justice Department began systematic enforcement in railway stations and airports as well as bus terminals.

By the end of 1962 CORE declared that its objective had been achieved. A Freedom Highway campaign followed, concentrated on national motel chains such as Howard Johnson and Holiday Inn, usually carrying the day with the mere threat of a boycott. For the first time in history, Farmer said, a Negro could drive along the nation's highways secure in the knowledge that when he became tired and hungry he could find a place where he would be welcome to stop and rest.

Nonviolence was still the watchword of the national black leadership, but there was no longer anything passive about it—and, except in the case of King, not much talk of loving the white enemy.

22

∾

The Uses of Duplicity

*T*he Fund for the Republic was created by the Ford Foundation, handed $15 million, and sent forth to do what it could to advance the cause of civil liberties and civil rights. It became functional in 1954, with the appointment of the parent foundation's displaced chief executives, Paul Hoffman and Robert M. Hutchins, as chairman and president. Recognizing that the new philanthropy was entering upon an area of mounting controversy, Hoffman and Hutchins tried to insure its respectability by assembling a board made up of members drawn from the top drawer of the American establishment. This protective coloration, however, did little to allay the fear and suspicion that has always attended the effort to apply in practice the principles enunciated in the Bill of Rights; the postwar Red scare that prompted the creation of the Fund guaranteed it a stormy reception. "A group of the most responsible, respectable, and successful business and professional men in the country have banded together in a Herculean effort to roll back the creeping tide of what is known as McCarthyism," Eric Sevareid told his CBS audience. Sen. Joseph McCarthy, Congressman Carrol Reece, and the other congressional anti-Communist crusaders could not be expected to take this challenge lying down, and their fuglemen in the media joined in a systematic attack upon the integrity and patriotism of all those associated with the Fund.

When I joined the board in November 1954, the Fund had come under heavy fire on its civil rights as well as its civil liberties flank—the issues of free speech and desegregation having been joined in the fevered right wing propaganda campaign touched off by the cold war. The Fund was still in the grant-making business, and there was an urgent need for its philanthropy in the South, where local financial support for interracial organizations had dried up. Many of the conventional foundations were intimidated by charges of subversion hurled even at the social agencies of mainline religious denominations. The Southern Regional Council was in desperate condition when the Fund came to the rescue with the largest single grant it was to make, providing funds to expand the Atlanta headquarters and hire professional staff for affiliates in states where effective communication between the races had literally broken down. Grants also went to the National Council of Churches, the Catholic Interracial Council, and the American Friends Service Committee. The Commission on Race and Housing was established and funded.

As the 1950s drew to a close the anti-Communist fever abated, and there was measurable progress on the race front. Joe McCarthy had demonstrated that there is a limit beyond which a demagogue is bound to self-destruct, and the return of the Democrats to power had made liberalism respectable—if not exactly dominant—in Washington. Hutchins felt free to end the Fund's philanthropy and use the remaining $5 million of Ford money to launch a study of the underlying causes of the national condition one of his consultants, the Princeton historian Eric Goldman, described as "a vast impatience, a turbulent bitterness, a rancor akin to revolt . . . a strange rebelliousness quite without parallel in the history of the United States." Hutchins, as usual, was ahead of his time when he established the Center at Santa Barbara with the mission of identifying and defining the basic issues that would make Goldman's description even more pertinent in the decade to come.

In the South the cult of massive resistance was losing ground in all the states except Alabama and Mississippi, and the indigenous black protest movement had become a factor that had to be dealt with, not only by politicians, but by businessmen vulnerable to boycott. In an introduction to a new edition of *The Negro in America*, an edited one-volume version of *American Dilemma*, Myrdal's principal collaborator, Arnold Rose, wrote:

Neither those who insisted that changes would occur extremely slowly (or not at all), nor those who held that rapid change would occur if—and only if—Negroes joined white workers in class warfare, have received corroboration by the actual course of events since 1944. The facts are that social change in the area of race relations in the United States has been rapid within the framework of our democratic, modified-capitalist system.

Rose was addressing himself to race relations in the nation as a whole, and he cited evidence of a significant shift of majority attitudes—in the South toward acceptance of social change, in the North toward apprehension, now that the race problem could no longer be treated as an aberration peculiar to another region. In 1964, when the federal government began to recognize the necessity for broader programs to eradicate the effects of discrimination, Adam Clayton Powell offered an astute appraisal of the divergent forces within the movement.

In the South, it's the middle-class and upper-class Negroes, the preacher, the teacher, the student, and they're fighting for the golf course and the swimming pool and the restaurant and the hotel and the right to vote. But when you leave the South, where only one-third of the Negroes now live, you have a revolution of the masses. Not the classes. And that revolution is interested in schools, housing, jobs. And the Civil Rights Bill will not help them at all.

But Powell added a warning that many intellectuals of both races chose to ignore as they responded emotionally to the increasing volume and abrasiveness of radical rhetoric: "The day the Negro changes from nonviolence to violence, he is finished, and the Black Revolution has to start all over again at some future date."

That was the lesson Martin Luther King was trying to teach, but increasingly he was being challenged on his home grounds.

Voting rights were not really at issue any longer; none but the most extreme Southern demagogues still attempted to defend their denial. The Civil Rights Bill of 1960 was not only shepherded but introduced by Lyndon Johnson, and he included in it as Part III the extension of enforcement powers he had excised from the Republican version in 1957. It was in this politically defensible area that the Kennedy administration concentrated its primary civil rights effort. Many of the national black leaders were disappointed, and some were bitter. Roy Wilkins, on behalf of the Civil Rights Leadership Conference, urged the president to promulgate a code governing the whole of the executive branch, arguing that he had the power, without congressional sanction, to end the "massive involvement of the federal government in programs and activities that make it a silent, but nonetheless full partner in the perpetuation of discriminatory practices." Harris Wofford, now in the White House, urged Kennedy to issue the executive order to end discrimination in housing he had promised during the campaign. The president demurred, and the attorney general concurred.

The black leaders had no real choice but to go along, but the regional cleavage was emphasized when Martin Luther King stood virtually alone in public endorsement of the strategy. Voting rights had been a primary objective of SCLC since its founding, and he used his influence to persuade the rambunctious young people in SNCC to concentrate on a registration drive. Now, in late 1961, King gave comfort to the White House with a policy statement: "The central front . . . we feel is that of suffrage. If we in the South can win the right to vote it will place in our hands more than an abstract right. It will give us the concrete tool with which we ourselves can correct injustice."

But outside the South the administration's emphasis on voting rights was regarded as a betrayal. In retrospect, Burke Marshall said of the Kennedys' strained relations with the black activists: "It was as if they were asking Negro leaders to divert their energies, and those of their organizations, into channels that would require as little change and movement as possible." The feeling was shared by some of the more restive members of SNCC, who seized upon a term coming into high fashion in the radical vocabulary to charge that King had been "co-opted" by the Kennedys.

That suspicion, unworthy as it proved to be, was reinforced when the administration actively encouraged private foundations to finance a major Voter Registration Project. Steven Currier of the Taconic Foundation obtained pro forma endorsements from CORE, SNCC, and the NAACP as well as SCLC, but it was King's organization that was most closely identified with the major project, underwritten by $339,000 from Taconic, $225,000 from the Field Foundation, and $219,000 from the Edgar Stern Foundation. The seminal undertaking, a residential training school for field workers, was established in Georgia under the direction of two young ministers who were to become key associates of King, Andrew Young and Wyatt Tee Walker.

Andy Young, the best known of King's spiritual heirs, had what he recalls as a sheltered childhood in New Orleans. His father, a prosperous dentist, sent him to a private school, to Howard, and on to Hartford Theological Seminary. Ordained in the United Church of Christ, he pastored for a while in the Alabama black belt, feeling a "need to be around plain, wise, black folk. I thought, then, poor people who knew suffering and love and God could save the world." But by the time SCLC came into being Young had headed back north, serving from 1957 until 1961 as one of three black executives in the National Council of Churches. He brought considerable sophistication to his new assignment at the Dorchester Center, fifty miles south of Savannah, where the Voter Education Project was established in the old academy built by missionaries in Reconstruction days. There, young volunteers, most of them recruited by SNCC, were given do-it-yourself civics courses and sent forth to run similar training centers in their home towns. By February 1962, fifty-two such schools were in operation in Georgia, Alabama, Mississippi, Virginia, and South Carolina.

Both Young and Walker gravitated to King's personal staff, and Young in particular found himself caught in the crossfire between SNCC and the parent organization. The young field workers were rarely content to confine their activities to training and organizing blacks to register and vote; their impulse was to move on all fronts, and most of them yielded to it. Moreover, they were impatient with King's tactic of choosing limited targets of opportunity in the Southern cities where clearly defined goals could be achieved; the SNCC workers, now being reinforced by volunteers coming down from the North, wanted to confront segregation head-on in areas where it was most malignant. "We tried to warn Snick," Andy Young has recalled. "We were all Southerners and we knew the depth of depravity of Southern racism. We knew better than to try to take on Mississippi." But Snick already had a cadre of field workers there, left over from the Freedom Rides. After their arrest at Jackson their militancy was honed by sentences served at the notorious Parchman Prison Farm and the tutelage of white radicals attracted by what was rapidly becoming the most widely publicized arena of social protest. At McComb, where they attempted to organize one hundred and fifty high school students for a protest march, the SNCC stalwarts were cheered on by the field representative of the newly hatched Students for a Democratic Society. His name was Tom Hayden.

THE tension between SNCC and SCLC first came into the open at Albany, then a town of fifty-six thousand and the fourth-largest in Georgia. The population was 40 percent black, and included a substantial middle class bolstered by the faculty and students of the black college located there. It was, in fact, a reasonably civilized community, at least by comparison with the black belt counties that surrounded it in Georgia and across the line in Alabama. But two Parchman veterans who established SNCC headquarters there in late 1961, twenty-two-year-old Charles Sherrod and eighteen-year-old Cordell Reagan, found a ready response to their militance in the NAACP Youth Council chapter on the Albany State college campus.

Stimulated by agitation among the youngsters, the leading black elders were swept up in what was called the "Albany Movement." This touched off protest demonstrations, which the police treated with restraint, arresting some demonstrators but promptly releasing them on bail without physical abuse. What was needed, SNCC headquarters advised, was national publicity, so a biracial group of eight Freedom Riders was dispatched from Atlanta to stage a sit-in at the railway station.

The arrest of the Riders produced a protest march by four hundred students, who were herded into an alley and methodically booked. Now the elders decided to send for Martin Luther King, and, over the objection of SNCC leaders, he came to Albany accompanied by Ralph Abernathy and Ruby Hurley, southeastern regional director for the NAACP. A thousand people turned out at Shiloh Baptist Church to hear King exhort: "Keep moving! Don't get weary! We will wear them down with our capacity to suffer." But when King led two hundred and fifty followers to City Hall for a prayer vigil, he encountered a different kind of policeman from any he had dealt with before.

Police Chief Laurie Pritchett greeted the marchers politely, asked for their parade permit, and booked them all when it turned out they didn't have one. In the weeks that followed, the arrest total rose to 737, and some 400 of these followed King's injunction and remained in jail. The chief accomplished his mass roundups with grave professional courtesy. Coretta King described the procedure:

He tried to be decent, and, as a person, he displayed kindness. He would allow the protesters to demonstrate up to a point. Then he would say, "Now we're going to break this up. If you don't disperse you'll be arrested." Our people were given fair warning. Often they would refuse to disperse, and would drop on their knees and pray. Chief Pritchett would bow his head with them while they prayed. Then, of course, he would arrest them, and the people would go to jail singing.

The protests dragged on into the fall of 1962; before the Albany Movement finally petered out, 5 percent of the black population had served some time in jail. That, in retrospect, was perhaps the most significant thing about it, for it demonstrated that King, despite his own erratic performance, still commanded the loyalty of middle-class blacks. Few of the tangible goals of desegregation were obtained, primarily because honest divisions on tactics among black leaders were compounded by jealousy. Among the younger blacks the commitment to nonviolence did not hold; on at least two occasions rocks and bottles were hurled without provocation at police who were actually protecting protest marchers. Andy Young, his voice breaking, confronted three husky black youngsters: "You're too yellow to march! But you stand over here and throw things and give us a bad name. Those folks who marched could hold their heads up high. Not y'all."

This time the whites involved in the serial media events came out ahead. "We met 'nonviolence' with 'nonviolence,' and we are indeed proud of the result," Chief Pritchett said. It was, a segregationist City Hall politician explained, simply a matter of killing them with kindness. "Albany was successful only if the goal was to go to jail," Ruby Hurley of the NAACP concluded. King and Abernathy were behind bars three times between December 1961 and August 1962.

On one of those occasions, in July, the ambivalence of King's relationship with the Kennedy administration produced a tragicomic denouement. A Democratic gubernatorial primary was in progress, and the president's leading supporters were backing the moderate Carl Sanders against the super-segregationist Marvin Griffin. Demonstrations against King's arrest, now freighted with the possibility of violence, were the last thing the Democratic leaders wanted. Among other telephone calls made by Burke Marshall was one to Coretta King assuring her that everything possible was being done to insure her husband's release. Next morning an unidentified, well-dressed black man made bail for King and Abernathy and, contrary to their past policy, both accepted. "I've been thrown out of lots of places in my day," Abernathy said, "but never before have I been thrown out of jail."

From the beginning King was under pressure from Washington to close out the Albany Movement on whatever terms he could get. Bobby Kennedy, keeping lines open to both sides, sent a telegram to Chief Pritchett congratulating him on keeping the peace. Coretta King wrote that her husband was deeply offended by the gesture, seeing it, correctly I think, as an indication of failure to understand the complexities of SCLC's leadership role. More serious was King's growing conviction that the FBI, whose agents swarmed into Albany, was not only failing to provide effective protection for embattled black demonstrators, but was doing so deliberately. He instructed his followers not to report civil rights violations to the agency, charging that it would be futile, and might even be counterproductive, since most of the FBI men were Southerners. This caused the eruption from the hypersensitive J. Edgar Hoover that presaged one of the most infamous abuses of police power the nation has ever known. The Reverend King, Hoover asserted, was "the most notorious liar in the country," and from that time on the apostle of nonviolence was at the top of his personal enemy's list.

The collapse of the Albany Movement was seen as a personal failure for King, although he came to it late and never really controlled the actions of the protest groups. The usually sympathetic national media generally agreed with the verdict of the *New York Herald Tribune,* which called it "one of the most

stunning defeats in his career"—and King understood very
well that the image he projected to the nation was central to his
ability to deal effectively with politicians in Washington and the
white power structure in the South. At the same time, any loss
of national prestige accentuated his difficulties with black
followers growing increasingly impatient with his insistence on
nonviolence and reconciliation. By the time Albany relapsed
into its normal, segregated state, SNCC workers were openly
and contemptuously referring to him as "De Lawd."

But Albany was a learning tree. "There wasn't any real
strategy," Andy Young said. "We didn't know then how to
mobilize the masses. We learned in Albany. We put together the
team of SCLC staff people there that later won the victories."
The payoff would come the next year in Birmingham, where
King and his men joined battle on terrain, and against an
adversary, of their own choosing.

KING had no part in the next great civil rights eruption to
focus the media's attention. That came in Mississippi—now
seen in retrospect as the most recalcitrant of the states committed to massive resistance. There were no industrial centers to
provide a countervailing force to politicians beholden to the
dominant agricultural interests, which ranged from vast, mechanized corporate enterprises to patch farms where whites and
blacks contributed to the statistical reckoning that established
Mississippi as the poorest and least literate state in the union.
The planter class, which had once provided a civilized, if
reactionary, leavening for the political process, had largely
disappeared in the course of the transformation of the agrarian
economy. And there was no newspaper of wide circulation, no
Atlanta Constitution or *Arkansas Gazette* or Nashville *Tennessean,*
to raise a standard around which moderates might rally;
among the dailies the only voice of reason was that of Hodding
Carter's *Delta Democrat-Times* and it did not reach beyond
Greenville, a city of forty thousand on the western boundary.

For all these reasons, Mississippi was considered first in
another category: the proclivity for physical violence to turn
back the new demands being made by—or, in the most
spectacular cases, on behalf of—the black population. That
rank was confirmed by Claude Sitton, who succeeded John

Popham as the *New York Times* regional correspondent and ranged the South during the troubled years from 1958 to 1964. "Mississippi was bad," he recalled after he had settled into a more sedentary assignment as national affairs editor of the *Times*. "I always felt that Alabama was sort of mean, but Mississippi could be deadly. They'd kill you over there. And they did. . . ."

Yet, remarkably, Mississippi remained an island of calm in the years when massive resistance was bringing on federal incursions on both flanks. The principal reason was James Plemon Coleman, described by Robert Sherrill as "the last of the aristocratic governors; not truly aristocratic, of course, but such as is so designated in Mississippi, where the landed gentry claims a bloodline that disappears kindly into the groundmists four or five generations ago, an aristocracy of certitude that nothing will ever change. Coleman was the last response to that certitude, come just as it was unraveling and tearing along the edges into strange new fears and uncertainties."

Coleman managed to win election over five rabidly segregationist opponents in 1955, the year after the Supreme Court handed down *Brown*. He did so by correctly identifying the real issue as one of preserving order in the state. "What we need is peace and quiet," he insisted on the stump, when all about him were crying havoc. An able constitutional lawyer, he believed litigation could delay any but token desegregation of the schools for at least a generation—and he publicly denounced Orval Faubus when the Arkansan destroyed the legal line of retreat in his clumsy confrontation with the federal courts. In his inaugural address Jim Coleman promised, "Mississippi will be a state of law and not of violence. . . ." For four years he kept that pledge, explaining privately: "I believe in preserving segregation, but I don't believe in making war. In the first place, I am a loyal American, and in the second place, you can't win."

Peace departed from Mississippi in 1960 when the pragmatic Coleman left the governor's office. Sherrill was caustic in characterizing Coleman's successor: "Of Ross Barnett . . . the kindest and most accurate thing that can be said is that he is bone dumb." It could also be said that he, like Orval Faubus, was prone to failure of nerve when the heat was on. It was the combination of these characteristics that produced travesty at the University of Mississippi when a native son with a black skin presented himself for enrollment in September 1962.

JAMES MEREDITH was a stubborn loner, a self-starter who needed no mass movement to set him on the single-minded course that took him to Oxford. He had risen to staff sergeant in the air force during nine years of service, and was attending the black state college at Jackson when he decided to finish his education at Ole Miss. Inspired by President Kennedy's inaugural address, he wrote on the same evening for an application form and returned it with an accompanying note: "I am an American-Mississippi-Negro citizen. With all of the occurring events regarding changes in our educational system taking place in our country in this new age, I feel certain that this application does not come as a surprise to you. I certainly hope that this matter will be handled in a manner that will be complimentary to the University and the State of Mississippi."

When his application was rejected, Meredith turned to Medgar Evers, the state director of the NAACP, and in June 1961 suit was filed on his behalf. The Mississippi members of the federal bench were the most unreconstructed in the South; Meredith was turned down twice in district court, then won in the Fifth Circuit Court of Appeals—only to have the Fifth Circuit's reversal reversed by one of its own members, Judge Ben Cameron. When his brethren vacated his stay order, Cameron issued another, repeating the procedure three more times before this unprecedented roundelay was terminated by Supreme Court Justice Hugo Black, who ordered the University to admit Meredith at once.

The Kennedys were determined not to repeat President Eisenhower's mistake in ignoring Orval Faubus's defiance of the courts until he had no recourse but to call out the 101st Airborne. Bobby Kennedy promptly got on the telephone to begin wheeling and dealing with Barnett. When the governor continued to stall, the attorney general strengthened his bargaining position with a court order citing him for contempt, obtained after Barnett conveniently appointed himself the university's acting registrar and personally refused to enroll Meredith. This, of course, was a media event, featuring the governor standing in the schoolhouse door—in this case that of the lovely old red brick Lyceum that housed university administrative offices. He adorned the occasion with one of the non sequiturs enshrined in the memory of reporters who covered him. As the would-be student, the only black within half a mile, approached in a sea of white United States marshals, the governor politely inquired, "Which of you is James Meredith?" Satisfied that he had the right man, he read an executive decree barring him from the campus "now and forevermore." The federal men withdrew and the circuit court of appeals promptly cited Barnett, giving him a week to purge himself of contempt on penalty of jail and a running fine of $10,000 a day.

Barnett was ready to capitulate, or seemed to be, when Bobby Kennedy entered into another of his protracted telephone negotiations. The governor pledged that there would be no violence when Meredith came on campus, and promised that his state police would be on hand to preserve order. But he wanted a show of federal force to demonstrate to his constituents that he was standing firm to the bitter end. He would step aside, he said, once the federal marshals confronted him with drawn pistols. Kennedy protested, "I think it is silly going through this. . . . To me it is dangerous, and I think it has gone beyond the stage of politics."

To meet the attorney general's objection to the possibility of a misfire the governor proposed that all guns on both sides be unloaded. So a scenario was worked out that called for Barnett to arrive at the campus gate flanked by unarmed state troopers. They would be met there by Chief U.S. Marshal James P. McShane and thirty of his men. McShane would draw an unloaded pistol, the troopers would step aside, and Meredith would pass through. Barnett objected that one pistol wasn't enough; he wanted all thirty unloaded federal sidearms drawn to show the people of Mississippi that he had acted only to prevent bloodshed. Kennedy proposed that instead of drawing the marshals just slap their holsters. The governor and the troopers actually got into position at the campus gate to act out this preposterous melodrama, but the sight of the threatening mob outside unnerved Barnett, and he messaged Washington to turn back the thirteen-car convoy bringing Meredith into Oxford.

Now Jack Kennedy prepared to use his trump card, presidential prestige. On Saturday he reserved network television time to explain to the American people the impasse at Ole Miss, and sent word to Barnett that he was going to recite the full record of the futile effort to effect a settlement. Barnett called back to offer still another deal—to arrange to have Meredith enrolled secretly in Jackson while he and the lieutenant governor decoyed the mob by taking their stand at Oxford. The president agreed, and at the end of the conversation turned in wonder to his aides: "Do you know what that fellow said? He said, 'I want to thank you for your help on the poultry program.'"

Now the comedy was over and the tragedy began. Barnett reneged on the Jackson arrangement, but agreed that his state police would stand by to support the marshals on Sunday evening while Meredith was taken onto the campus by a back way. President Kennedy issued a proclamation federalizing the Mississippi National Guard and ordered a regular army detachment to stand by at Memphis. Now he made his postponed television broadcast, unaware that Ross Barnett had already double-crossed him by ordering withdrawal of the state police in the face of a growing mob on the campus. The president appealed to the tradition of chivalry at Ole Miss: "The honor of your university and state are in balance. I am certain that the great majority of the students will uphold that honor." But students were now only a small minority among the self-appointed vigilantes who surrounded the embattled marshals at the Lyceum, where Deputy Attorney General Nicholas Katzenbach established his command post.

The members of the mob had flocked to the campus from the backwaters of Mississippi and beyond. Earlier in the week my erstwhile luncheon companion, Edwin A. Walker, major general, USA, retired, had been on radio with a call for action that invoked memories not only of Little Rock, but of Shiloh: "It is time to move. We have talked, listened, and been pushed around far too much by the anti-Christ Supreme Court. Rise to stand beside Governor Barnett. . . . Now is the time to be heard. Ten thousand strong from every state in the union. The battle cry of the republic: Barnett, yes, Castro, no. Bring your flags, your tents, and your skillets. . . . The last time in such a situation I was on the wrong side. . . . This time I am out of uniform and I am on the right side and I will be there."

Meredith, under protection of twenty-four marshals, was safely hidden away in a dormitory at the other end of the campus as darkness fell and the mob around the Lyceum grew in size and fury. The state police disappeared, and the battle-cry sounded loud and clear: "Kill the nigger loving bastards!" Rocks and bottles pelted the federal men, and by eight o'clock they had to resort to tear gas to turn back their attackers. Then came Molotov cocktails, iron bars, bricks, jagged projectiles from shattered concrete benches—and, finally, rifle fire. At ten o'clock Katzenbach told Washington the troops would have to be called in, and the president issued the order. The first unit to arrive was Troop E, 108th Armored Cavalry, Mississippi National Guard, under the command of a nephew of Oxford's most illustrious citizen, William Faulkner, whose fiction includ-ed no more savage a scene than the one enacted that Sunday evening just down the street from the old family homestead.

The casualty list provided a measure of the extent of the battle. Nearly a third of the marshals, 166, were wounded, 28 by snipers' bullets. Forty soldiers of Troop E were hit by missiles or shotgun blasts, including Captain Faulkner, who suffered two broken bones. There were two deaths, one a white citizen of Oxford who may have been an innocent onlooker, and the other a correspondent for *Agence France Presse*, Paul Guilhard. Claude Sitton said of the bearded Frenchman's death: "He was shot in the back of the head. He was taken right off the campus . . . made to kneel behind a tree and was shot in the back of the head . . . pure out-and-out execution." Although not a single shot was fired by the federal forces, Ross Barnett greeted the evidence with still another non sequitur. Blame for the riot, he said, belonged to "inexperienced, nervous, trigger-happy" marshals.

The addresses of the two hundred participants arrested by military police before the mob was dispersed attested the efficacy of General Walker's rallying cry; only twenty-four Ole Miss students were listed along with those from Georgia, Louisiana, Tennessee, and Texas who joined Mississippians drawn from the state's redneck precincts. I recall being struck at the time by the fact that there were no Arkansans among those hauled in by the MPs. I suppose the veterans of Little Rock had either seen the light, or learned how and when to depart.

WHEN it was all over at Oxford, and James Meredith was attending classes on the subdued campus, the Mississippi state senate passed a resolution declaring its "complete, entire and utter contempt for the Kennedy Administration and its puppet courts." But this display of pique only provided evidence that the dead-end politicians had nothing else to say. The controlling reality was that the Kennedys had demonstrated in practice the course the attorney general had promised to follow in his University of Georgia speech; the administration would play along with Southern officials trying to save face with segregationist constituents, but it would not tolerate violence and could not be intimidated by the threat of it.

The only serious criticism came on tactical grounds. Some black civil rights leaders were disappointed that the president had confined himself to an appeal for law and order in his television address on the night of the riot, and did not bear down on the moral issue. I was myself surprised that Bobby Kennedy would treat seriously with a tower of Jell-O like Ross Barnett for as long as he did, and would allow himself to be a party to the ludicrous scenario for a phony confrontation at the campus gate. He had not yet learned that any Southern leader who had thrown in with the hard-line segregationists could no longer be depended upon to play the political game according to the usual rules.

The national media generally saw the result as a victory for Kennedy. Hugh Sidey, *Time*'s White House correspondent, characterized it as an "overwhelming setback for Southern racism." In his intimate biography of JFK, Sidey reported that neither Kennedy ever agonized over the possibility that they might have to use troops; that had been settled before the negotiations began. Barnett's outlandish maneuvering could not be said to have purged him of contempt, but the Kennedys chose not to pursue the matter. Burke Marshall was told not to file the affidavit that would have activated the contempt citation, and in 1965 the case was formally dismissed as moot. In dissent, Judge Minor Wisdom of the Fifth Circuit wrote: "What cannot be overestimated . . . is the importance of federal courts standing fast in protecting federally guaranteed rights of individuals. To avoid further violence and bloodshed all state officials, including the Governor, must know that they cannot with impunity flout federal law."

In fact that lesson had been learned, at the state house level at least. Resistance would continue for a while, but those in high office would be careful to keep a safe distance from the bullyboys who employed the last resort of violence. After Oxford, elected defenders of the Southern Way found it prudent to acknowledge their obligation to maintain law and order, and were always found ostentatiously looking the other way when it broke down.

23

〜

Parting of the Ways

*T*he civil rights movement reached flood stage in the mid-1960s. In the five years following Martin Luther King's Project "C"—for "confrontation"—at Birmingham in the spring of 1963 an estimated 1,117,600 Americans participated in 369 civil rights demonstrations; 15,379 were arrested, 389 were injured, and 23 were killed. What had begun as an all-black protest against institutionalized discrimination in the South spread across the whole of the nation, and whites, particularly the young, flocked to the cause.

Birmingham provided the ideal stage for the drama that precipitated the burgeoning. The national audience had no difficulty in sorting out the cast of characters made more than life size by the selective eye of the television camera. The officials who governed the city, which had grown to near 350,000 in 1960 with a 40 percent black population, entertained no reservations as to segregation on moral or any other ground. A raw product of the industrializing New South, Birmingham was born late in the last century with the exploitation of iron and coal deposits in the surrounding north Alabama hills, and was generally devoid of the civility that characterized older Southern cities.

Local politics was dominated by the men who ran the Alabama outpost of United States Steel, and the related heavy industries attracted by its product. Down in Montgomery they were known as the Big Mules and they pulled their weight in state politics too. In return for their bounty they received tax breaks and cooperation in containing the influence of labor unions—the surefire way of achieving the latter being to exploit the race prejudice of the rednecks who made up much of the work force in the mines and mills. In 1960 I described the smoky, brawling city as Gary, Indiana, with a Citizens Council. Harrison Salisbury, the veteran *New York Times* correspondent, was more specific: "Birmingham's whites and blacks share a community of fear."

After the Reverend Fred Shuttlesworth formed the Alabama Christian Movement for Civil Rights in 1956, the bombing of black leaders' homes became so frequent the area where most of them lived was christened Dynamite Hill. The active presence of the Klan was attested by fifty cross-burnings and numerous threats against local synagogues. Night-riders castrated a black man and whipped a black preacher with chains. In a *Times* series that documented these atrocities, and suggested that many more went unrecorded, Salisbury wrote: ". . . every inch of middle-ground has been fragmented by the emotional dynamite of racism, reinforced by the whip, the razor, the gun, the bomb, the torch, the club, the knife, the mob, the police, and many branches of the state's apparatus."

Project "C" was launched at the behest of Shuttlesworth, who had affiliated his organization with SCLC. The immediate objective, desegregation of commercial establishments and public facilities, was limited and clear-cut; areas of high resistance, such as the schools, were not involved. King, recognizing the need for a dramatic victory to improve the declining fortunes of SCLC, saw Birmingham as a prime target of opportunity: "With a strong base in the Shuttlesworth-led forces in the Negro community, the vulnerability of Birmingham at the cash register would provide the leverage to gain a breakthrough in the toughest city in the South." The prime tactical consideration was cited by Wyatt Tee Walker, one of the key SCLC field commanders: "We've got to have a crisis to bargain with. To take a moderate stand, hoping to get help from the whites, doesn't work. They nail you to the cross."

King was being steadily pushed toward greater militancy by his associates, by increasingly vocal black critics outside the South, and by events. After the debacle at Albany, civil rights lost priority in Washington. "The issue no longer commanded the conscience of the nation," King wrote in *The Nation* after a January 1963 meeting with the Kennedys at the White House, where he was told the administration would not push for major civil rights legislation at the coming session of Congress.

The administration sought to demonstrate to Negroes that it has concern for them, while at the same time it has striven to avoid inflaming the opposition. . . . If tokenism were our goal this administration has adroitly moved us toward its accomplishment. But tokenism can now be seen not only as a useless goal, but as a genuine menace. It is a palliative which relieves emotional distress, but it leaves the disease and its ravages unaffected. It tends to demobilize and relax the militant spirit which alone drives us forward to real change.

AFTER Albany it was commonly charged that King had proved to be a poor organizer—overly reliant upon charisma to rally a spontaneous following, and upon divine guidance to point the way to appropriate action. The black journalist, Louis Lomax, saw those who came to leadership from the pulpits of black Southern churches as tending to confuse God's will with their own personal desires and ambitions. "Men such as Martin are natural-born revolutionaries," Lomax wrote in his 1962 book, *The Negro Revolt*. "They have what it takes to get people out in the streets yelling and dying for a cause. But when the revolution is over, the republic would be better off if someone else took over the executive leadership."

I suspect my friend Lomax would have tempered that judgment had not his own death intervened before King scored his greatest triumphs. Although King may have been devoid of some of the attributes of the conventional executive, it is difficult to make such an appraisal since the tumultuous activities that marked his brief career as a leader were anything but conventional. It is evident that he did command the personal loyalty of the talented, strong-minded, temperamental, often jealous young ministers who surrounded him, and he used this to maintain an effective degree of cooperation among them. At Birmingham he proved to be a master of planning and tactics.

One lesson learned at Albany was that the old radical device of bringing pressure by flooding the jails with prisoners required careful preparation and timing. Another was that every demonstration had to have a core of trained, disciplined participants to serve as highly visible role models for those who turned up in response to the excitement of the moment. And, finally, King and his men now fully understood the possibilities of television; the cameras were at once a measure of protection against the extremes of physical violence since they were irrefutable eyewitnesses, and the means by which he could project images that would force the reluctant politicians in Washington to step up the federal intervention that was his ultimate objective.

There is no doubt that a compelling factor in King's decision to move on Birmingham in April 1963 was the presence there of the ideal adversary for his purposes— Theophilus Eugene Connor, commissioner of public safety. When a contested mayor's election promised to install a moderate in city hall and end Bull Connor's career as chief law enforcement officer, King rejected the counsel of those who urged that he delay the demonstrations. The last thing he wanted was another encounter with a police chief who would follow Laurie Pritchett's example and defuse the black crusade with civility. He was counting on Bull Connor's police dogs and firehoses, and his own inevitable sojourn in the Birmingham jail, to restore the movement's command of the nation's conscience.

They did just that. Beginning with lunch-counter sit-ins on April 3, demonstrations of various size and character continued for a month. As planned, the jails were flooded with blacks. In the beginning the police acted with restraint; the dogs were on display, but they were kept on leash, and King's field commanders had to rely on numbers to impress the covering media. Wyatt Tee Walker made the happy discovery that white reporters could not distinguish between black demonstrators and black bystanders. "All they know is Negroes, and most of the spectacular pictures printed in *Life* and in television clips had the commentary 'Negro demonstrators' when they weren't that at all," he said. Marches were delayed, sometimes for an hour or two, until a crowd had gathered. On one occasion fifteen hundred curious citizens trailed Walker's little band of twenty-two trained demonstrators. "They followed us down the street, and when the UPI took pictures they said: fifteen hundred demonstrators—twenty-two arrested. Well, that was all we had."

On April 10 an Alabama state court issued an injunction against further demonstrations by the SCLC, and King elected to defy it in person. On Good Friday he led fifty hymn-singing blacks from Zion Hill Church to City Hall, reaching the downtown sector before Birmingham's finest ended the march by escorting them to jail. Perhaps as a demonstration of his new militancy, perhaps simply in anticipation of a long stay, King doffed his usual sober preacher's garb and appeared in blue workshirt and denim trousers. While in jail he wrote his famous open letter to eight Birmingham clergymen who had characterized him as an "outside agitator" and deplored the demonstrations as extremist. The Apostles, he noted, were also outside agitators, and Jesus was considered "an extremist for love." He echoed Thoreau and Gandhi in his assertion of a moral obligation to disobey unjust laws—saying that this certainly applied to those directed against a minority that had no part in their making. And, as always, he closed on a redemptive note: "One day the South will know that when these disinherited children of God sat down at lunch counters they were in reality standing up for what is best in the American dream and for the most sacred values of our Judeo-Christian heritage."

Martin Luther King behind bars could not be ignored by the White House, and once again there was a call from the president to Mrs. King to assure her that he was keeping an eye on the situation. In the meantime Andy Young, who was always kept out of jail to maintain contact with the white establishment, was negotiating behind the scenes with the moderate, but still powerless mayor-elect, Albert Boutwell, and the downtown store owners. There was some progress, but no agreement, and Young recalled this as the low point of the campaign. What was needed was a direct confrontation with Bull Connor's forces, and Young proposed a "children's crusade." King approved, and the SCLC headquarters staff fanned out through the black schools to urge children to come to the Sixteenth Street Baptist Church for the showing of SCLC films; while there they were instructed in the techniques of nonviolent protest. In short order they mobilized six thousand children of all ages, and on May 2 began sending them out from the church staging center in successive waves.

The police arrested the crusaders in wholesale lots, sending them off in school buses when they ran out of patrol cars; by nightfall 959 children and 10 adults had been jailed. But on that and succeeding days thousands more made their way downtown by various routes, trooping through the stores singing "Ain't gonna let nobody turn me 'round" and "On my way to Freedom Land." Young, who went with them, found that the children's display of courage and discipline was having a profound impact on the store owners.

And now King's men finally got the confrontation they sought. The dogs were unleashed and the fire hoses came into play as black adults by the thousands came swarming into the downtown streets. The SCLC field commanders began spending most of their time trying to cool the restive crowds. Burke Marshall arrived from Washington, and the telephone lines began humming—with cabinet officers like C. Douglas Dillon of Treasury and Robert McNamara of Defense importuning big business associates to pressure their counterparts in Alabama. They got results from such as Roger Blough, chairman of the board of U.S. Steel, who instructed the Big Mules to see that order was restored. Gov. George Wallace assembled more than five hundred members of his state highway patrol on the outskirts of the city, and federal troops were on alert at nearby bases.

Marshall managed to avoid direct federal intervention by persuading King to accept a truce, during which negotiations with the store owners would continue. When the local politicians resisted King's demand for amnesty for all the jailed blacks, Bobby Kennedy enlisted four national unions to send $40,000 each to secure the bail bonds that released 790 demonstrators. On May 10 the store owners signed an agreement to desegregate all facilities, and pledged to begin hiring blacks in clerical and sales positions. "The city of Birmingham has reached an accord with its conscience," King said, terming the agreement "the most significant victory for justice we've ever seen in the Deep South."

In the established pattern, official capitulation to black demands was followed by unofficial resort to violence. The Klan staged a rally just outside the city, and that night dynamite demolished the front half of the home of Martin Luther King's brother, the Birmingham pastor, A. D. King. A half hour later another package of dynamite exploded at the A. G. Gaston Motel, named after its owner, the city's wealthiest black, who made its facilities available as headquarters for the SCLC principals and much of the out-of-town press. The response was a miniature race riot that lasted most of the night. Black mobs rampaged through a nine-block area, producing spectacular TV footage, but the casualty figures were low; there were no serious injuries and the *Birmingham News* estimated property damage at only $41,775.

Two weeks later the Alabama Supreme Court affirmed Mayor Boutwell's right to take office, and Bull Connor's tenure as police commissioner came to an end. The Big Mules had decided that their city would pay the price of limited desegregation to maintain the peace, and there was only one further headline-making atrocity, one so wanton not even the most dedicated segregationist could publicly condone it—the September bombing of the Sixteenth Street Baptist Church during Sunday School, which killed four teen-age girls and injured twenty others.

AFTER Birmingham capitulated the state government of Alabama also began to accept the inevitable—although George Wallace would never admit that he had in fact gone back on his inaugural pledge: "Segregation today, segregation tomorrow, segregation forever!" When the University of Alabama opened its summer session on June 11, the little governor was on hand, as he had promised, to stand in the schoolhouse door to bar the entry of two black students. He tried for a full rerun of Ross Barnett's Mississippi scenario, but the Kennedys offered only a short version. This time Nick Katzenbach arrived accompanied by the commanding general of Alabama's federalized National Guard. Wallace was given a podium and allowed to make a brief speech to the television cameras, but he had agreed in advance that he would step aside on his fellow Alabamian's order.

The farce at the schoolhouse door was followed on the nation's TV screens by a speech by President Kennedy, who finally parted company with his more cautious advisors and zeroed in on the moral issue. Citing the statistics that measured the great disparity between the condition of the black minority and that of the white majority, he asked, "Who among us would be content with the counsels of patience and delay?"

The fires of frustration and discord are burning in every city, north and south. Where legal remedies are not at hand, redress is sought in the streets in demonstrations, parades and protests, which create tensions and threaten violence—and threaten lives. . . . We face, therefore, a moral crisis as a country and a people. It cannot be met by repressive police action. It cannot be left to increased demonstrations in the streets. It cannot be quieted by token moves or talks. It is time to act in the Congress, in your state and local legislative body, and, above all, in all our daily lives.

That speech committed Kennedy to the kind of legislative program he had told King in January he believed Congress would not accept. Birmingham had made the difference. The police dogs and fire hoses arrayed against big-eyed, pigtailed little girls on the six o'clock network news had touched the nation's conscience. The president, with his usual irony, told the civil rights leaders at a White House meeting in late June, "I don't think you should be totally harsh on Bull Connor. He has done as much for civil rights as anybody since Abraham Lincoln." To the shock engendered by the naked display of brutality, King had added the positive force of his eloquent espousal of the Christian doctrine of love. He was ready now to preach his greatest sermon, with the whole of the nation as his congregation.

T HE March on Washington on August 28 was in a very real sense the culmination of Project "C." It was arranged by the black leadership to support the administration's broadened legislative package, and all the major civil rights organizations were involved, with Bayard Rustin serving as principal organizer. But, inevitably, it became King's showcase. At first the great in-gathering was opposed by the Kennedys, but the president soon recognized that there was a limit to his ability to dissuade the black leaders and he joined them. In July he endorsed the project at a press conference, saying that it wasn't really a protest march but a peaceful assembly seeking redress of grievances in the great American tradition.

There was jockeying among the black leaders behind the scenes, and some public condemnation by black radicals, but in the end King's spirit of reconciliation prevailed. Young John Lewis, assigned to speak on behalf of SNCC, arrived with a fiery oration proclaiming: ". . . we will take matters into our own hands and create a source of power outside of any national structure. . . . We will march through the South, through the heart of Dixie, the way Sherman did. We shall pursue our own 'scorched earth' policy and burn Jim Crow to the ground—nonviolently." He reluctantly agreed to reduce his Sherman-esque threat to a promise to "march with the spirit of love and the spirit of dignity we have shown here today."

A considerable majority of white Americans saw some part of the March on Washington on television, and most, I am convinced, were deeply moved by King's "I have a dream" peroration. Not even a diehard segregationist could fail to be impressed by the great throng that spread across the mall before the Lincoln Memorial—at least 250,000 people, 70 to 80 percent of them black, comporting themselves through the long day with great dignity. For most in the television audience it was their first exposure to what Arthur I. Waskow identified as a new phenomenon in *From Race Riot to Sit-In*, citing the response of a girl marcher when asked who she thought was likely to participate in this mass phase of the civil rights movement: "Anybody who's black—and glad."

"Millions of Negro Americans have throughout our history been black and sad," Waskow wrote. "The Negro rioters of 1919 were black and bitter; many civil rights workers for many decades have tried to act like angry whites. But only in the 1960s did large numbers of Negroes embrace their blackness and channel their ancient anger into joyful protest." The *Brown* decision had kindled new hope, and now the gains made in the South by blacks acting on their own motion, limited though they were, had added a surge of pride, raising the black consciousness so long repressed under the calculated humiliation of legalized segregation.

I was the only Southerner in a group that watched the March on television in California. When King had finished sketching his vision of the beloved community, there was not a single wisecrack to be heard from those often brittle sophisticates, and I doubt that there was a dry eye among them. Yet I think that I, like all Southerners, was touched in a different way—in my case not so much by King's implied promise of absolution for guilt inherited from slave-owning forebearers, as by pride that this man, so uniquely one of the South's own, had become, for the moment at least, the nation's chaplain. There were still racists in the South, I knew, who would react to the spectacle with fear, and the twin passion, hatred. But no white Southerner would ever again dismiss Martin Luther King and his cause with contempt; he was certified as a force to be reckoned with.

Much has been written about the importance of King as a role model for his people. His was a role that came out of ingrained values of the old America—that near-archaic society that survived longest in the South. King understood that Southerners were, for the most part, still praying people, despite all the aberrations of their leaders a people who thought of themselves not only as God-fearing but as law-abiding. With his doctrine of reconciliation he had provided blacks the means to appeal to values deep in the Southern consciousness, bypassing the defensiveness aroused by what Southerners perceived as external threats to their way of life.

"THE march on Washington was in many ways the high point of 'gladness' in the civil rights movement of the 1960s," Waskow wrote, "and the high point of the coalition between the various elements in the country, white and black, that support-ed the demand for racial equality." King had come now to the paradox that shaped the remainder of his career; as his influence with the white leadership grew, and with it his ability to put through reformist changes in the system, so did his opposition from the radical Left. In part, this resulted from a regional division of interest; dismantling the structures of institutional segregation represented real gains for Southern blacks, but it had only symbolic meaning for those in the non-Southern ghettoes, whose problems were largely econom-ic, and were worsening. Increasingly, the difference was reflect-ed in ideological, or perhaps more accurately, temperamental cleavage within the civil rights movement. Most of the leaders still stood, philosophically at least, with King, who insisted that there was no practical alternative to working within the system. But in the black ghettoes, as in the third world, there were rising expectations that enhanced ancient frustrations, and there was a growing response to the professed revolutionaries who wanted to bring the system down.

The black cause had a magnetic attraction for whites who

saw the capitalist, middle-class American society as hopelessly corrupt, but the fragmented Marxist movement, with its elaborate theoretical superstructures had little to do with the surge of black-oriented radicalism. Those who gave it voice were for the most part highly individualistic intellectuals who were unlikely to march in any mass movement, but who had begun to make a cult of alienation. King and the mainline black leaders were perforce integrationists, while their black adversaries were uncompromisingly antiwhite; they usually did not go all the way with the Black Muslim's separatism, but proclaimed a kind of spiritual segregation. James Baldwin and the talented dramatist, Lorraine Hansberry, posed the issue with a famous question: "Who wants to integrate with a burning house?"

Baldwin's *The Fire Next Time* was excerpted in *The New Yorker* in the spring of 1963, and its passionate eloquence sent thrills through the white intellectual establishment. One result was a meeting in New York in late May where Bobby Kennedy was confronted by a group assembled by Baldwin, including a young Freedom Rider who for some three hours led an unrelenting rhetorical assault on the attorney general. "They don't know anything," the shaken Kennedy said. "They don't know what the laws are—they don't know what the facts are—they don't know what we've been doing or what we're trying to do. You couldn't talk to them as you could to Roy Wilkins or Martin Luther King. . . . It was all emotion, hysteria. They stood up and orated. They cursed. Some of them wept and walked out of the room."

Black moderates at the session—among them Harry Belafonte, who would remain a dedicated supporter of Martin Luther King—allowed the onslaught to go on with no effort to defend Kennedy. Kenneth Clark explained their silence by arguing that the speakers were simply "trying to say that this was an emergency for our country, as Americans." The theory, or at least the contention, was that this purpose could not be served by the intelligence available to the Kennedys, not even that provided by such a perceptive black observer as Louis Martin, who had just warned the attorney general that "the accelerating tempo of Negro restiveness and the rivalry of some leaders for top billing coupled with the resistance of segregationists may soon create the most critical state of race relations since the Civil War." The Baldwin thesis was that the message would be received by whites only after their sensibilities had been sufficiently lacerated.

THERE could be no doubt that a new racial showdown was coming, and *Look* asked me to appraise the situation in an article published in mid-July. I used Baldwin's one-sided confrontation with Bobby Kennedy as a point of departure, comparing his adamance with that offered, in reverse, by George Wallace. These polar positions, I contended, were a measure of the gap between the rhetoric and the reality of this phase in the evolving pattern of race relations:

Governor Wallace can cause trouble, but he cannot prevail. The feudal system he seeks to maintain has been falling apart under its own weight for more than a generation. . . . Those whose power is recognized in the title Big Mules are still balky, but they have decided to get back to making money.

Mr. Baldwin can lend momentum to the drive for Negro rights, but he can produce neither the millennium nor the holocaust. His tortured eloquence flutters the intellectuals, and his revolutionary words thrill the alienated of all complexions. But the mass of American Negroes do not reject the existing social order, seeking only to share fully in its bourgeois blessings.

Actual violence, I wrote, was an unthinkable weapon for a minority outnumbered ten to one by whites, who controlled the means of forcible subjection. Yet the complacency of the white majority, and the lack of conviction among the political leadership, made the threat of spontaneous violence the blacks' most valuable tool, enhanced by the fact that it had been fashioned by their declared enemies. I cited John Bartlow Martin's 1957 report on a tour of the region, *The Deep South Says Never:* "He had reported what he had heard, and most of those with whom he talked believed what they told him—that the white folks would rise up en masse if a colored man set foot across the existing boundaries of segregation." Yet when the test came the resistance quickly collapsed, for the actuality of mob violence proved to be intolerable to urban Southern whites. After nearly a decade of angry words and wild promises, the great confrontation had produced no more corpses than those handled by a metropolitan police morgue on a hot Saturday night. So it was that Martin Luther King was bound to his course of nonviolence, not only by his vows of conscience, but by the most elementary tactical considerations:

So long as violence is directed against Negro demonstrators, elemental standards of justice and Federal guns are automatically on their side. Let Negroes initiate the attack, or even reply in kind, and the balance will shift—and without this essential support Negroes again will be a helpless minority in an aroused white community.

Martin Luther King not only subscribes to, but has given real meaning to, the battle cry of the movement: No white man has a right to ask a Negro to wait any longer for equality. But, as a practicing Christian, Dr. King also has to recognize that every white man has a right to insist that the quest for equality not be marked by a trail of blood.

It is on this critical point that Dr. King has had to part company with a good many of those who have lately swung aboard the freedom train. He speaks for justice. They cry out for vengeance.

Although I would not realize it until some years later, my delineation of the gap between the rhetoric and the reality of the struggle was demonstrated by the striking photograph spread across two pages of *Look* to illustrate the article. "Negroes join hands to keep from being knocked down by water from the fire hoses used in Birmingham," the caption said. But Wyatt Tee Walker, who was there when the picture was made, recalled: "So they gathered in the park, and the firemen set up their hoses at two corners. And the mood was like a Roman holiday—it was festive. . . . They'd been saying, 'Turn the water hose on, turn the water hose on!' Then somebody threw a brick and they started turning them on. So they just danced and played in the spray. This famous picture of them holding hands, it was just a frolic, they'd get up and run back and it would slide them along the pavement. . . ."

I do not intend to suggest that there was any lack of real danger, and real heroism, in Birmingham. But it is an essential fact that, while they still tried to observe the forms of journalism, the TV crews were bound to treat the demonstrations as theatrical events. This made it possible for King and his men to provide high, symbolic drama at low actual risk; if it had not been so I doubt that he would have allowed Andy Young to send forth little children to defy Bull Connor's forces. I think he sensed that, while the firemen might use enough pressure to slam so inviting a target as Fred Shuttlesworth against a wall, they were not going to employ such force against children. He wrote of watching another encounter when the firemen simply defied Bull Connor's shouted order: "Turn on the hoses, dammit!", finding in the spectacle reaffirmation of his faith in the possibility of reconciliation. And that, of course, was a tactical as well as a moral consideration; there could be no victory for his cause unless it brought racial peace. He thanked me for the *Look* article and said he agreed with my conclusion: "The central problem facing all parties at this stage of the civil rights movement is to bring the mass of Americans of both races to accept the kind of accommodation that will achieve harmony as well as justice."

BRIEFLY, the success of the March on Washington tended to paper over the differences among the black leaders, but as the Kennedy civil rights package began its slow progress through the congressional obstacle course, the lobbying effort was left to the old Leadership Conference while those who favored street agitation began to go their separate way. "Almost every week a new civil rights organization with a new philosophy is born in the metropolitan area and another man or woman is acclaimed a civil rights leader," the *New York Times* reported. Inevitably, rhetorical violence, amplified by television's insatiable taste for the sensational, produced the real thing. In the July heat, four days of rioting erupted in Harlem over an alleged case of police brutality and spread to Bedford-Stuyvesant. James Farmer and Bayard Rustin took to the streets trying to cool tempers, but one of their new rivals, Jesse Gray, called for "a hundred revolutionaries ready to die." The casualty list: one dead, forty-eight policemen and ninety-two civilians injured.

Mayor Robert F. Wagner summoned Martin Luther King for advice, and after conferring at City Hall the two made a tour of Harlem, where King was spattered with thrown eggs. From his pulpit, with what must have been conscious irony as well as his customary political expediency, Adam Clayton Powell complained of meddling: "No leader outside Harlem should come into this town and tell us what to do." In late July, King joined Wilkins and Randolph in a call for "a broad curtailment, if not total moratorium, of all mass meetings, mass picketing and mass demonstrations until after election day." There was reason for their concern; the term "white backlash" had entered the national political vocabulary with the foray across the Mason-Dixon line by another meddling outsider, George Wallace, who had entered the Democratic presidential primaries and garnered 34 percent of the vote in Wisconsin, 30 percent in Indiana, and 43 percent in Maryland.

James Farmer of CORE and John Lewis of SNCC were not impressed and refused to take the pledge. They were leading spirits in the Freedom Summer project, launched in the fall of 1963 as a joint effort by a number of civil rights organizations to recruit and train Northern college students to join field workers in a massive voter registration project in Mississippi. By midsummer, 1964, these young people were involved in political action on the national front, and demonstrations were essential to their effort to embarrass, if they could not convert, the elders of the Democratic Party.

Freedom Summer injected Northern radicals, white and black, into the Southern movement in a fashion that challenged King's leadership on his home ground. A vibrant young man dubbed the "Magnificent Barbarian." was beginning to gain influence in SNCC at the expense of the Southern student founders. Stokely Carmichael first crossed the Mason-Dixon line when he came down from Howard on CORE's Freedom Ride, and his introduction to the Southern Way included a term in Parchman Prison Farm. Born in Trinidad, reared in Harlem, he was one of the exceptional students assigned to the Bronx High School of Science. "Stokely—bright, quick and wild—read Karl Marx, met white liberals," Carl Gardner wrote in a vignette included in his biography of Andrew Young. "Dated white girls, became a showpiece in Park Avenue salons and the bohemian haunts of Greenwich Village, like a piece of African sculpture on an elegant plaster mantel, the Nubian prince. Wondered if niggers weren't passe." He would, before he passed on to the Black Panthers in the seventies, precipitate a face-to-face showdown with King on the issue of Black Power.

24

～

Dawn of the New Left

*I*n the 1960s what had begun as an issue of civil
liberties was finally transformed into one of civil
rights—now conceived to entail the obligation of the federal
government not only to protect the black minority against
oppression by the white majority, but to provide relief from the
economic disabilities imposed by a century of second-class
citizenship. Many leaders were involved as the black cause
developed into a mass movement, but four were ultimately
responsible for the transition: John and Robert Kennedy,
Martin Luther King, Jr., and Lyndon Johnson.

These men played out their roles on a brightly lit stage,
and their performance has been publicly appraised by their
political associates, by journalists and scholars, and by assorted
intimates. All four left behind more or less autobiographical
works, and the voluminous material that can be loosely called
biographical has continued to pour forth, ranging from ador-
ing to scurrilous. There is an inescapable *Rashomon* effect, as in
the famous Japanese movie where the same event drastically
changes shape when it is seen through the eyes of each of
several participants. And this is enhanced by the fact that three
of the four were martyred at the height of their powers, while
the one who escaped an assassin's bullet always thought he was
misunderstood, traduced, and finally driven from office by
ungrateful partisans who should have been devoted supporters.

I had some personal contact with all four during the
crucial years, but could never have been counted in the
entourage of any. It is my belief, reinforced by the record now
available, that I shared with Jack Kennedy, King, and Johnson
a common perception of the emerging pattern of race rela-

tions. I do not think this could have been said of my views and those of Bobby Kennedy.

The Kennedy brothers are usually treated as jointly deserving credit, or blame, for key developments on the civil rights front; in the beginning they operated from the same power base, one as president, the other as attorney general, and were seen as reigning figures in the closest approximation of a political dynasty the American republic has known. But it is generally agreed that there was a significant temperamental difference between the two, and one does not have to indulge in amateur psychiatry to assume that the tragic death of the older Kennedy had a profound effect on the younger. But, long before he suffered that trauma, it was evident that Bobby's response to men and events was personalized in a way that contrasted with Jack's usual cool detachment.

I think it is fair to say that the matter of race was an abstraction to both Kennedys when they first faced the necessity of dealing with it. Sons of Irish Catholic arrivistes, inheritors of enough wealth to guarantee personal independence, they were inspired and often goaded by a father whose driving ambition had taken him as far as the Court of St. James, and who would accept no limit on the careers of his progeny. Superimposed upon this essentially European consciousness was an uppercrust New England education with its abolitionist overtones. The Kennedys would, in the way of their Harvard classmates, treat the injustice of the Negro's lot as a given, and ascribe it primarily to the stubborn perversities of white Southerners.

When Harris Wofford joined Jack Kennedy's 1960 campaign as civil rights advisor, he brought Martin Luther King to see the candidate. The talk went well, but when it was over King said he thought Kennedy lacked a "depthed understanding" of civil rights—what a less formal man would have called a "gut feeling." I think that remained true of the president to the end. In 1965 when Robert Penn Warren recorded interviews with black leaders, most, if somewhat less bluntly, echoed the judgment of James Forman of SNCC, who said he was nauseated by the deification on the civil rights issue that followed the assassination. "The president did intellectualize the issue," he said, "but it was a cold intellectual issue and political issue with him. He moved only when there was pressure and he had to move."

Bobby Kennedy's approach to civil rights seems to have been a progression—from a personal disinterest expressed in the view that those who worked in the cause were soft-headed bleeding hearts, to a pragmatic acceptance of the black vote as essential to his brother's presidential election, to an almost mystic identification with all the poor and dispossessed. At their first meeting in 1957, when Bobby served as chief counsel to the Senate committee investigating labor racketeering, Wofford found that he fully lived up to the reputation he had already acquired in Washington as "an arrogant, narrow, rude young man." Kennedy devoted most of their brief conversation to a moralistic diatribe on the evils of communism that would have done credit to Joe McCarthy—a reflection of the cold warrior attitude that also would be tempered only after his brother's death. As to his racial views, it is not insignificant that in those days he had no difficulty in maintaining a close working and personal relationship with his committee chairman, John Mc-Clellan of Arkansas, one of the Southern primitives.

As attorney general he was the chief wheeler-dealer with Southern politicians on racial matters, and in this role he engaged in a sustained feud with the Civil Rights Commission. "You're second-guessers," he told the commissioners at an early meeting on voting rights. "I am the one who has to get the job done." He dismissed the contention that the commission had a statutory duty to investigate violations. "I can do it, and will do it, my way, and you're making things more difficult," he said, and began to treat the commission as a runaway grand jury. Berl Bernhard, the director, was often at loggerheads with the attorney general; after he made his sub rosa deal with Earl Long to obtain voting registration records in Louisiana he was ordered at the last minute to cancel a scheduled hearing in New Orleans.

"Do you know what you're doing?" Kennedy demanded in a 1:00 A.M. phone call. "If you continue with your hearing and make race a big issue, Delesseps Morrison will lose the primary election for mayor and you will have destroyed one of the truly moderate politicians in the South. I want it called off—now." When Bernhard asked what reason he could give the press for

cancelling the hearing the peremptory response included an
echo of Uncle Earl Long's admonition: "If you're not smart
enough to give a good reason I don't know why my brother
nominated you. And remember, you never talked to me." The
commission chairman, Father Hesburgh, wrote Wofford that he
was deeply disappointed by "the Administration's stance on
civil rights progress versus practical politics."

By the end of the decade revisionist were turning out
bestsellers charging that the panache of Camelot, followed by
the emotional reaction to the martyrdom of the two Kennedys
and King, had served to conceal the limitations and, some
thought, the essential cynicism, of their collaboration. They
were all, in varying degree, pragmatists. And as the 1970s
approached, pragmatism went out of intellectual fashion. The
demands of their calling in the new age of television put them
in a position where even their most idealistic efforts were in
another sense self-serving. For King, particularly, this meant
that in order to exercise leadership he had to accept and even
encourage the kind of aggrandizement that incites the hostility
of those who feel themselves eclipsed; he could, and did,
donate to the cause the cash that came with his 1965 Nobel
Peace Prize, but the personal prestige it brought him necessarily was his stock in trade. He was a moral leader, and I know of
no instance in which it could fairly be said that he violated his
conscience, but his mission required him to play a political role,
which necessarily entailed compromise.

"In Negro life there is a unique and unnatural dichotomy
between community leaders who have the respect of the masses
and professional political leaders who are held in polite disdain," King wrote in his last published work, the 1967 *Where Do
We Go From Here: Chaos or Community?* "Those who lead civil
rights groups, churches, unions and other social organizations
are actually hybrids; although they bargain for political programs, they generally operate outside partisan politics." For
King this involved a kind of political jujitsu—backing his moral
appeal to the white community with the actuality or the threat
of disruptive demonstrations that would pressure white leaders
into concessions. He was constantly confronted with the problem of how far he could go before his strategy became
counterproductive; according to both his moral compass and

his tactical judgment that point came when his followers were about to lapse, or be goaded, into violence; then he settled for what he could get, which was often less than he had demanded.

Most idealists, I have found, respond with a kind of rage when someone reminds them of the old cliché that politics is the art of the possible. But it remains an elemental truth, even though it is often used to justify inaction or compromise with principle. In a representative government, elected officials cannot ignore public opinion if they are to survive in office, and in the 1960s some states and many congressional districts still had controlling majorities not yet conditioned to accept the kind of social change the civil rights movement required. This meant that in Congress there was an irreducible minimum of opposition to legislation that would advance school desegregation, ban discrimination in public facilities, secure black voting rights, and guarantee equal employment opportunity. It did not follow, however, that all Southern members of the two houses were equally opposed to all these measures. Nor did it mean that some previously reflexive opponents could not be brought around if the political risk could be shown to be diminishing.

The recognized master of this congressional calculus was now a member of the administration. When the civil rights leaders met with Jack Kennedy in the White House to urge him to follow up on the momentum created by the March on Washington, the president, after reminding them that his approval rating in public opinion polls had already dropped from 60 percent to 47 percent, turned the floor over to his vice-president. Lyndon Johnson, pointing out that cloture would have to be overridden by a two-thirds majority, ticked off the numbers: "We have about 50 votes in the Senate, and about 22 against us. What counts are the 26 or so votes that remain. To get those votes we have to be careful not to do anything which would give those who are privately opposed a public excuse to appear as martyrs."

The most striking thing about the Kennedys' handling of civil rights was that they made so little use of Johnson's finely honed political instinct and formidable manipulative skills. His own congressional voting record could be read as a chart of the practical limits of civil rights support for those with a Confederate constituency. He voted with the Southern bloc on racial

matters during his ten years in the House, and in his successful
race for the Senate in 1948, the year of the Dixiecrat rebellion,
he termed Harry Truman's civil rights program "a farce and a
sham" and gave lip service to the classic states' rights position.
But he never indulged in nigger-baiting, in or out of Congress,
and, within the limits of Texas's segregated society, he insisted
that blacks get their fair share under any program he had
anything to do with. By the time he pulled off the "miracle of
'57," pushing through his compromise version of the Republican civil rights bill, he had convinced the mainline black leaders
that his heart was with them, even if his down-home style
continued to put off black as well as white intellectuals.

When Wofford tried to line up Roy Wilkins for Kennedy in
the 1960 run for the presidential nomination, the NAACP
leader told him, "If you ask me who, of all the men in political
life, I would trust to do the most about civil rights as president,
it would be Lyndon Johnson." A similar ex post facto judgment
was rendered by the first black cabinet appointee, Robert C.
Weaver, who served under both Kennedy and Johnson: "I
think Kennedy had an intellectual commitment for civil rights
and a broad view of social legislation. Johnson had a gut
commitment for changing the entire social fabric of this
country. . . . I don't think we would ever have got the civil
rights legislation we did without Johnson. I don't think Kennedy could have done it."

No one who had seen the big Texan in action as majority
leader could have doubted his capacity to deal with the kind of
recalcitrant politicians Bobby Kennedy was encountering in
Southern statehouses. Yet it was not until June 1963, when
Kennedy's civil rights bill was stranded in committee and
apparently going nowhere, that Johnson was asked for advice
on breaking through the Southern bottleneck. The request was
almost off-hand, a telephone call from Ted Sorensen. But it
elicited a reply from the pent-up Texan that ran to twenty-
seven pages when transcribed, and contained some of the best
advice Jack Kennedy never took. It was Johnson's thesis that
the way to influence the Southerners in Congress was to rally
support in their own region:

I wouldn't have him go down there and meet Wallace and get in a
tussle with him. I'd pick my own time and my own place. The hell with

confronting those people. But I think he ought to talk frankly and freely, rather understandingly and maybe fatherly. He should stick to the moral issue and he should do it without equivocation.

I know these risks are great and it might cost us the South, but these sorts of states may be lost anyway. The difference is: if your president just enforces court decrees, the South will feel it has yielded to the force. But if he goes down there and looks them in the face, these Southerners at least respect his courage. They feel that they are on the losing side of an issue of conscience.

Merle Miller, in his invaluable oral biography, *Lyndon,* includes a description by Harry McPherson, a Johnson aide, of the vice-president practicing what he preached. Sitting in the presiding officer's chair in the Senate, Johnson fell into conversation with the dignified John Stennis of Mississippi, and asked how he stood on the public accommodations section of the bill. Stennis said he thought his people never would stand for it, and he couldn't support it. McPherson continued:

Johnson said, "Well you know, John, the other day a sad thing happened. Helen Williams and her husband, Gene, who have been working for us for many years, drove my official car from Washington down to Texas, the Cadillac limousine of the vice-president of the United States. They drove through your state, and when they got hungry, they stopped at grocery stores on the edge of town in the colored areas and bought Vienna sausage and beans and ate them with a plastic spoon. And when they had to go to the bathroom, they would stop, pull off on a side road, and Helen Williams, an employee of the vice-president of the United States, would squat in the road to pee. And you know, John, that's just bad. That's wrong. And there ought to be something to change that. And it seems to me that if the people of Mississippi don't change it voluntarily, that it's going to be necessary to change it by law."

"Well, Lyndon, I'm sure there are nice places where . . ."

Then the vice-president just said, "un-huh, un-huh," and sort of looked away vacantly and said, "Well, thank you, John." And Stennis left. Johnson turned around to me and winked. It represented . . . the first time I had ever really had the feeling that the comprehension of the simple indignity of discrimination was deep in Johnson.

There was a mutually respectful, if something less than intimate, relationship between the president and vice-president. The difference between them on civil rights was almost entirely one of priority, and this, I suppose, can reasonably be translated into a question of commitment. But I think Jack Kennedy has been unfairly criticized in that regard by many of the revisionists; he, after all, had the final responsibility for the whole of the presidential agenda, and it is gratuitous to second-guess his reluctance to jeopardize the shaky coalition that supported his foreign and domestic policy by forcing a showdown on civil rights in the Senate. Hindsight doesn't alter the reality he faced—that the odds were long against Congress passing the civil rights package without the kind of debilitating amendments that would have been unacceptable to the civil rights leadership. I recall having lunch with James Reston of the *New York Times* in Washington a few days before the president departed on his star-crossed journey to Texas. It was that veteran observer's judgment that the whole of Kennedy's domestic program was hopelessly stalemated in Congress, so much so it raised serious doubt that he could win a second term in the coming election.

It is possible that the odds on civil rights legislation might have been changed had Johnson been given a primary role. But there was no chance of that in the face of the implacable hostility of Bobby Kennedy, which began with his frustration over the president's selection of his running mate, and was enhanced by an inherent conflict of personality. His feeling of resentment and contempt was shared by the "Irish Mafia," the inner circle of Kennedy loyalists, and by some of the White House intellectuals, who scorned the vice-president's earthy personal style. And, of course, the hypersensitive Texan responded in kind. I asked Elizabeth Carpenter, who viewed developments from the perspective of the vice-president's office, what part Johnson played in devising civil rights strategy. "None," she replied. "There not only wasn't any real consultation, there wasn't even any communication. Days would pass without so much as a telephone call from the White House. And Lyndon figured, correctly I think, that if he volunteered any advice it would guarantee Bobby's opposition to whatever he proposed."

ON November 22, 1963, rifle shots fired from a window of the Texas Book Depository in Dallas portended the end of the impasse on civil rights. When Lyndon Johnson set out to make his inherited presidency a memorial to Jack Kennedy, it was more than a sentimental gesture, although sentimentality was a powerful strain in Johnson's complex character. It also represented a masterful politician's recognition that the martyrdom of his gallant young predecessor would, temporarily at least, unite the American people and provide, in the deceased president's name, a leverage on Congress he had never known in life.

Four days after the state funeral Johnson began summoning the black leaders to the White House, one by one. James Farmer remembered sitting in the Oval Office for almost two hours, following the thread of conversation through the incessant phone calls that always characterized Lyndon Johnson at work. Many of these came from the Hill, and had to do with the stalled civil rights legislation: "He said he was running into great difficulty, but he's got to get the bill through, he's got to get it through. . . . " Whitney Young recalled his first reaction when the press called him for comment on the succession: "I said I had always felt that if I ever turned on the radio and heard the president of the United States speaking with a deep Southern accent that I would panic. But I did not feel that way at all. I felt by that time that Lyndon Johnson would do exactly what he did."

Before he made his first presidential appearance at a joint session of Congress, Johnson met with the top men of the Kennedy administration and some of his old friends to talk about what he ought to say to smooth the transition. He was advised, as Kennedy so often had been, that it would be best to let the civil rights bill lie fallow until after election, that the presidency had only a limited amount of political capital to spend and that it should not be squandered on a measure that would never get through. Abe Fortas recalled that Johnson's reply was, "Well, what the hell's the presidency for?" When he stood before Congress he said:

No memorial oration or eulogy could more eloquently honor President Kennedy's memory than the earliest possible passage of the civil rights bill for which he fought so long. We have talked long enough in this country about equal rights. We have talked for one hundred years or more. It is time now to write the next chapter—and to write it in the books of law.

I urge you again, as I did in 1957 and again in 1960, to enact a civil rights law so that we can move forward to eliminate from this nation every trace of discrimination and oppression that is based upon race or color. There could be no greater strength to this nation both at home and abroad.

The House began work on the administration's civil rights bill on January 31; it passed, 290 to 130, on February 10. With Johnson's blessing, the original version had been strengthened in its enforcement provisions and expanded to include FEPC. The real test would come in the Senate, where minority delaying tactics could be overriden only by invoking cloture, and that required a two-thirds majority. If it came to that, racist opposition would be bolstered by libertarians who thought curtailing debate for any reason was a violation of sacred principle. But when moderate senators approached their old horse-trading friend to urge that he sacrifice the public accommodations and FEPC sections in order to insure enactment of the other titles, they found that those big ears had gone deaf.

Johnson enlisted Hubert Humphrey to carry the bill in the Senate. Humphrey recalled that he was simultaneously flattered and taunted: "He called me up on the telephone, and he said, 'You have this great opportunity, Hubert, but you liberals will never deliver. You don't know the rules of the Senate, and your liberal friends will be off making speeches when they ought to be present. . . . No, your bomb-throwing friends will be out making speeches to the already-converted—for a fee. And, Hubert, I'm not sure that you yourself . . .'" The only possible response to that was, "Damn you, I'll show you!" The president's final admonition to his floor manager was that he must line up the Republican minority leader, Everett Dirksen: "You've got to let him have a piece of the action. He's got to look good all the time. . . . Don't you let those bomb-throwers, now, talk you out of seeing Dirksen. You get in there to see Dirksen! You drink with Dirksen! You talk to Dirksen!" And, finally, perhaps the hardest task of all for the loquacious Minnesotan: "You listen to Dirksen!"

The ultimate recognition of the president's determination came from the leader of the opposition, Richard Russell. The Georgian said on the floor of the Senate, "I have no doubt that the president intends to throw the full weight of his powerful office and the full force of his personality—both of which are considerable—to secure the passage of this program. . . ." And privately Russell said to Johnson's aide, Bill Moyers: "You tell Lyndon that I've been expecting the rod for a long time, and I'm sorry that it's from his hand the rod must be wielded, but I'd rather it be his hand than anybody else's I know. Tell him to cry a little when he uses it." And he may have.

When the time came to invoke cloture Humphrey and the bomb-throwers produced 71 votes, 4 more than needed. One was cast by Clare Engel of California—dying of a brain tumor and unable to speak, he was brought onto the floor in a wheelchair and recorded his aye by pointing to his eyes. After cloture 115 amendments were offered, and all were voted down. On July 2, by a vote of 73 to 27, the measure passed the Senate. That night Lyndon Johnson signed it into law and went on television with a speech designed to ease the burden of the old friends who had fought him and lost. His Southern accent added reassurance to his reminder that the states had not been stripped of all their rights: ". . . the act relies first on voluntary compliance, then on the efforts of local communities and states to secure the rights of citizens. It provides for the national authority to step in only when others cannot or will not do the job. . . ."

Capitulation came from Dick Russell in a form Lyndon Johnson, and every other Southerner, could understand. The venerable senator went home to enjoin Georgians to obey the law "as long as it is there." If this still seemed to hold out some hope for ultimate reprieve, the most influential of the unreconstructed members of Congress was now telling his fellow citizens what they did not choose to believe when the word came from the Supreme Court—that the requirement that black citizens be allowed to fully exercise their civil rights was the law of the land.

LYNDON JOHNSON had rammed through by far the most sweeping civil rights measure in the nation's history. The mainline black leaders were in sight of the goals they had long ago set for themselves, and the public opinion polls showed a marked tempering of resistant white attitudes. Desegregation, if not integration, had gained acceptance across the center of the political spectrum, and racism, in any overt form, was rapidly losing respectability.

Militant opposition was now largely confined to Mississippi and Alabama, and to such isolated redoubts as Leander Perez's political satrapy in Plaquemines Parish south of New Orleans. And in Alabama the tide was clearly turning. While George Wallace was out picking up dissident Democratic votes in Northern presidential primaries, he was being derided at home for his erratic and futile bluffing in the case of desegregating Alabama schools. The conservative *Alabama Journal,* the capital's afternoon daily, termed his maneuvers "mock warfare in which the administration has volunteered itself, and the state on the losing side." The governor's fire-and-fall-back tactics, the *Journal* said, had earned him "the Southeastern Conference title for the most desegregation in the shortest time."

That left Mississippi. In July 1964 the Southern Regional Council summed up race relations in the Magnolia State: "Here every datum of economics and every fact and twist of history have conspired to keep white people deeply and ofttimes harshly resistant to change, and its Negro people ill-equipped for it." Such was the target chosen by a coalition of national civil rights organizations for the Freedom Summer project. The stated objective was voter registration, and there was good reason for the choice. In November 1963 Wiley Branton, director of the Voter Education Project, reported that only 3,871 blacks had been added to the voting rolls in Mississippi after two years of effort, and announced that funds budgeted for the state would be diverted to areas where real progress was being recorded.

Field workers for SNCC, however, were unwilling to pull out. They had put together a cadre of native leaders under the banner of COFO—Council of Federated Organizations—which had the support of NAACP, CORE, and SLC. Aaron Henry, a Clarksville dentist and state NAACP president, was then nominal head of COFO, but its moving spirit was SNCC's charismatic Robert Parris Moses, Harlem born and Harvard educated. After failing in its effort to crash the Democratic primary polling places with unregistered blacks, COFO staged a statewide mock election, with Henry as candidate for governor. Ninety thousand blacks voted, nearly a quarter of those eligible, and more than three times the number actually on the rolls. This was the genesis of the Mississippi Freedom Democratic Party, and it marked the emergence of an energetic white New Yorker, Allard Lowenstein, as a perennial burr under the saddle of the national Democratic leadership.

IN the spring the National Council of Churches set up a training center at Western College for Women in Oxford, Ohio, and some seven hundred student volunteers flocked in from Swarthmore, Cornell, Yale, Harvard, Mount Holyoke, Bryn Mawr, Smith, Colorado, Stanford, the University of California, and other less prestigious institutions. The minimum requirements were that they be eighteen years of age, able to pay their own way, and willing to live with black families in the field. This invasion force was backed by a hundred paid SNCC field workers, another forty from CORE, a hundred clergymen, and a corps of volunteer lawyers from the NAACP Legal Defense Fund and several liberal lawyers' organizations.

The first contingent of Freedom Summer volunteers arrived in Mississippi in June, to be greated by the burning of six black churches; another twenty-one would go up in flames before the summer was out, the Klan having struck upon this form of sacrilege to augment the traditional cross-burning. Night-riders roamed the state virtually without restraint. President Kennedy's speech on civil rights signaling victory in Birmingham had been greeted in Mississippi by the sniper assassination of Medgar Evers, field secretary for the NAACP, and the white man indicted for his murder had been set free by a white jury; from January to August 1964, thirty blacks were victims in cases where the evidence, such as it was, indicated that their murderers were white.

On June 21 an atrocity in Neshoba County proved that the planners of Freedom Summer had been correct in their assumption that lethal violence against white youths could not be covered up, as was usually the case when local authorities dealt with offenses against uppity blacks. Michael Schwerner, a New York social worker on CORE's staff, and Andrew Goodman, a Queens College student, were arrested for speeding, along with

James Chaney, a black CORE field worker. They were not seen again until six weeks later when their mangled bodies were dug out from under an earthen dam on a farm six miles south of the county seat, Philadelphia.

Lyndon Johnson sent the federals into Neshoba County in force after the three young men disappeared. The number of FBI agents assigned to Mississippi was increased tenfold, and J. Edgar Hoover himself appeared, along with a cowed Gov. Paul Johnson, at the opening of a new, vastly expanded headquarters in Jackson. Hoover publicly paid his respects to local law enforcement authorities; the FBI's investigations, he said, were being hampered by "water moccasins, rattlesnakes, and rednecked sheriffs, and they all are in the same category as far as I am concerned." He was specific in the case of Neshoba, where his men, with the assistance of a paid informer and search parties provided by the United States Navy, finally located the bodies of the martyred civil rights workers. In that area, he said, "law enforcement is practically nil, and many sheriffs and their deputies participate in crime."

AGAINST this background, Freedom Summer was projected to the Democratic National Convention, assembled in Atlantic City for the anointment of Lyndon Johnson and his running mate, Hubert Humphrey. The Mississippi Freedom Democratic Party sent a delegation to challenge the seating of the regular Democrats. The MFDP didn't have a legal leg to stand on, but it had a powerful moral argument—and, when it came down to it, the old issue of party loyalty, since there was good reason to believe the Democratic organization was prepared to deliver the state's electoral vote to Barry Goldwater, the Republican nominee. The president, perforce, stood with the leadership in upholding the party rules while trying to avoid the embarrassment of a legalistic rejection of MFDP. The problem for the party elders was compounded by the fact that the regular Mississippi Democrats were lead by Gov. Paul Johnson, whose idea of a knee-slapping campaign joke was to identify NAACP as standing for "niggers, apes, alligators, coons, and possums." "Are we going to seat a delegation sent by a man like that?" thundered Joe Rauh, who had taken charge of the legal representation for MFDP.

Lyndon Johnson sent in his first team to work out a deal. The mainline black leaders, King, Wilkins, Farmer, and Aaron Henry, chairman of the contesting delegation, endorsed the result. It provided that the regular Mississippi Democrats would have to take an oath to support the party ticket, which would certainly vacate some seats; two MFDP delegates would be given full voting, which meant speaking, rights, while the others would be seated as honored guests; in the future no delegation would be admitted from a state where the party process denied any citizen the ballot. But SNCC and CORE militants led by Stokely Carmichael rebelled, and staged a sit-in on the convention floor. "When the convention resumed deliberations three turbulent hours later," Thomas R. Brooks wrote, in *Walls Come Tumbling Down*, "the sympathy won by the upright stance of MDFP . . . had been all but wiped away by the intransigence of a handful of militants."

THE black vote, growing in size as migration continued to overpopulate the big city ghettoes while the franchise opened across the South, went virtually unanimously for Lyndon Johnson. His identification with the black cause cost him the handful of electoral votes he lost—those of Alabama, Georgia, Louisiana, Mississippi, and South Carolina, the only states Barry Goldwater carried in addition to his native Arizona. But the Texan's overwhelming 61 percent of the popular vote left the Deep South isolated and politically disarmed; Johnson had achieved a level of popular support no president had known since the Oval Office was occupied by the man he idolized and emulated, Franklin Roosevelt.

In the honeymoon year after he achieved the presidency in his own right, Johnson put through a domestic program that in many ways surpassed that produced in the first hundred days of the New Deal. Poor Americans in general, and blacks in particular, were the primary beneficiaries of his soaring vision of a Great Society. He created the Department of Housing and Urban Development, charged it with literally rebuilding American cities, and appointed a black cabinet officer to head the effort; he launched programs that gave the federal government responsibility for supporting public education from kindergarten through college; in deference to Lady Bird, who called it "beautification," he included a major environmental package; he overrode the resistance of the American Medical Association to expand social security to cover basic health services, including hospitalization; and he anticipated the feminist uprising by including women in his affirmative action programs.

Willard Wirtz, his secretary of labor, said, "When you think of what happened in 1965, you turn around two centuries. Just take civil rights and women, to mention two—he turned the whole country around." Hugh Sidey recalled how he did it: "During 1965 in particular . . . Johnson would zero in on a congressman or a senator and get what he wanted. . . . I would be amazed at some of the devices he would use. He would lie, beg, cheat, steal a little, threaten, intimidate. But he never lost sight of that ultimate goal, his idea of the Great Society."

WHEN what amounted to the last stand of the hard-core white militants in the South came at Selma, Alabama, Johnson was ready to show Bobby Kennedy how redneck resistance ought to be handled. The issue was voting rights, and the initial adversary was Sheriff Jim Clark, an obtuse advocate of Bull Connor's strategy of head-knocking intimidation. Clark employed a mounted posse of deputized bullyboys to turn back a protest march through the heart of the black belt that stretches from Selma to Montgomery. Network television cameras had the scene in sharp focus when the mounted men fired tear gas grenades and rode their horses into marchers confined by banked approaches to the Edmund Pettus Bridge across the broad Alabama River. Seventeen blacks were wounded seriously enough to require hospitalization, among them the leader, John Lewis of SNCC, whose skull was fractured.

Martin Luther King arrived, and so did the president's personal emissary, LeRoy Collins, former governor of Florida and now head of the new Federal Community Relations Service. On March 9 George Wallace's state troopers joined Sheriff Clark's men to bar the way when King arrived at the bridge at the head of fifteen hundred marchers, including a number of whites come down from the North to lend moral support. King turned back, as he had promised Collins he would do if he could not proceed without invoking violence. That night three white Unitarian ministers were assaulted on a Selma street, and one of them, the Reverend James J. Reeb of Boston, died a few hours later. All around the country there was a rising chorus of demands for federal intervention, and when the president seemed to demur, civil rights pickets appeared outside the White House for the first time during the Johnson tenure.

On March 13 George Wallace was summoned to Washington to meet with Johnson in the Oval Office. The president, as he usually did, cleaned up his published account of the confrontation, noting in his memoir, "I kept my eyes directly on the governor's face the entire time. I saw a nervous, aggressive man; a rough, shrewd politician who had managed to touch the deepest pride as well as prejudice among his people." The president appealed to that pride to prod Wallace into agreeing to use his state force to protect the marchers as they walked the fifty-three miles to the capital. Happily, Nick Katzenbach was present and has provided an unexpurgated report of the encounter:

He [Wallace] was . . . trying to tell the President that it was his responsibility to turn off the demonstrations. President Johnson's response was, "You know, George, you can turn those off in a minute." He said, "Why don'tcha just desegregate all your schools?" He said, "You and I go out there in front of those television cameras right now, and you announce you've decided to desegregate every school in Alabama." Wallace said, "Oh, Mr. President, I can't do that, you know. The schools have got school boards; they're locally run. I haven't got the political power to do that." Johnson said, *"Don't you shit me, George Wallace."*

On March 17 Judge Frank Johnson in federal court at Montgomery upheld the right of the Selma marchers to proceed in peace, and enjoined Governor Wallace to prevent any interference, official or otherwise. Pleading that he did not have forces at his command adequate for the job, Wallace sent a telegram asking the president to "provide sufficient federal authority." The president pointed out that the governor had ten thousand Alabama National Guardsmen at his disposal. But, Wallace replied, the state couldn't afford to pay the cost of mobilizing the guard. With the trap snapped shut, the president agreed to help the governor carry out his admitted responsibilities by federalizing the guard and picking up the tab. So, with helicopters overhead and military vehicles full of white Alabamians fore, aft, and on the flanks, Martin Luther King set off to Montgomery with thirty-two hundred marchers. By the time the procession reached the square before the capitol in Montgomery the ranks had grown to twenty-five thousand, and King proclaimed, "We are on the move now—no wave of racism can stop us."

Johnson used the emotional force generated at Selma to launch a new 1965 voting rights act drawn to his specifications by Katzenbach, who was told, "I want you to write the god-damnedest toughest voting rights act you can devise." The president went up to the Hill to present the measure in person to a joint session, and there had rarely been a more dramatic moment in the House chamber than the one he contrived for the members, and the national television audience, as he slowly emphasized his peroration in his Texas twang:

What happened in Selma is part of the larger movement which reaches into every section and state of America. It is the effort of American Negroes to secure for themselves the full blessing of American life. Their cause must be our cause, too. Because it is not just Negroes, but really it is all of us who must overcome the crippling legacy of bigotry and injustice.

And we shall overcome.

WHEN Johnson went again to the Hill in January 1966 to present the State of the Union message, he said, "This nation is mighty enough, its society is healthy enough, its people are strong enough to pursue our goals in the rest of the world while still building a Great Society here at home." A Harris poll published on January 9 seemed to bear him out. The president's approval rating stood at 67 percent, and that of the 1965 Congress at 71 percent, in contrast to the 35 percent recorded two years before under Kennedy. The specifics of the Great Society achieved overwhelming endorsement: medical care for the aged approved by 82 percent, aid to education by 90 percent, the voting rights bill by 92 percent.

But when he spoke of the nation's goals in the rest of the world the president was committing himself to continue the "dirty little war" in Indochina that was the end product of the anti-Communist containment policy pursued by Democratic and Republican presidents for more than twenty years. As he examined his options, it was temperamentally impossible for Johnson to accept a decision to, as he put it, cut and run. Soon he would find that to avoid abandoning the Vietnam campaign he would have to expand it—and so began the escalation that splintered the formidable political coalition he had put together by his own main strength.

The first cracks appeared among those ostensibly committed to the civil rights crusade. The increasing cost of the distant, unpopular war, in terms of lives, inconvenience, and money, soon turned the restive young and many of their supportive elders against American involvement in Indochina. One who saw it coming was Virginia Foster Durr, sister-in-law of Hugo Black, whose friendship with Lyndon and Lady Bird went back to the days when, in the flush of their own youthful idealism, they came north to find a place among the Young Turks of the New Deal. Now they would face "the horror of the dichotomy in his presidency—all the people who were for him on the civil rights issue were against him, mostly, on the war issue."

And, of course, both issues were so emotionally charged there was no possibility of orderly debate when the two seemed to merge. Soon there was a plaintive ring to the invocation of Isaiah 1:18, the Bible verse Johnson had used with considerable success all his political life: "Come now, and let us reason together, saith the Lord." Reason was in short supply on the streets and college campuses where what was called the "New Left" took shape, and, as the pressures mounted, in the White House as well.

Freedom Summer was a portent. There was a touching idealism and a large measure of gallantry to be seen among the white students who came down to the hazardous backcountry of Mississippi, and a display of extraordinary courage and stamina among the blacks who made them welcome. It is a moving experience to read the account of those days rendered in their own words by leaders and followers in *My Soul Is Rested*, the admirable oral history compiled by Howell Raines. If their immediately measurable accomplishments were few, there can be no doubt that the young people's presence contributed to the ultimate success of black Mississippians in building their own freedom movement. But the weakness of the self-styled New Left could be seen at its inception—the transient commitment of so many who responded to the challenge and excitement but faded away in the face of the drudgery of systematically organizing people whose values were so foreign to their own; the confusion of self-indulgence with self-sacrifice; above all, the refusal to face the realities of rural Mississippi in the belief that an elevated consciousness could simply rise above the individual limitations imposed by poverty and ignorance upon even the most stalwart blacks.

It is not surprising that as the years passed the nostalgia of many of the aging veterans of Freedom Summer came to be colored by disillusionment. Many had approached improvement of the lot of the submerged black population not as a cause in itself, but as a means of venting their rage at the whole of American society. David Halberstam, who reported on the Ohio training camp for the *New York Times,* found that a number of the students were "so alienated that they might just as well, psychologically, have been Communists—because they hated their own country so much, and distrusted its every word and action. They had moved into the civil rights thing because it was the most tangible way to express their discontent." Such as these could not abide the thirty-sixth president of the United States. Charles de Gaulle once said that John F. Kennedy was a mask on the face of America, while Lyndon Johnson *was* America.

25

〜

Comes the Revolution

The Center for the Study of Democratic Institutions was situated in one of the elegant mansions built in the hills around Santa Barbara early in the century as a retreat for the big rich. The location, and the purpose proclaimed for the institution by its patrician founder, Robert M. Hutchins, invited description as an ivory tower or, in current jargon, a "think tank." It is a measure of the confusion of the sixties and seventies that the Center also was regarded by some as a hotbed of insurrection.

Hutchins, who had spent his life practicing boardsmanship in the upper reaches of the American establishment, held that the only way to sell a new idea was to make it sound old. So he had no objection when supporters of the Center compared it to the academy of ancient Athens, or the mountaintop monasteries where intellectuals repaired during the Dark Ages to continue their speculation on the nature of man. He was a traditionalist who believed the heritage from the incubators of Western civilization mandated constant challenge to the conventional wisdom. In 1956, explaining why he had decided to terminate a notable academic career to assume an activist's role in the fight to preserve civil liberties, he wrote:

A lifetime of experience and reflection has supplied me with reasons for defending the faith in which I was brought up . . . faith in the independent mind. Its educational consequences were belief in free inquiry and discussion. Its political consequences were belief in democracy, but only in a democracy in which the minority, even a minority of one, could continue to differ and be heard. Those who desire to conform, but are prohibited or hindered from doing so by intolerance and prejudice, must be aided; the non-conformist conscience must not be stifled. Hence my interest in the Fund for the Republic.

Blacks, of course, were most conspicuous among those who were denied the right of conformity, and with it the protections, opportunities, and amenities available to the white majority. But at the beginning of the 1960s the federal government accepted and began to act upon the obligation to guarantee the civil rights of the minority. The immediate issues growing out of the effort to obtain justice for blacks were holdovers from the old America, and there was reason to believe they were being ameliorated by the passing of time and the changing of generations. Hutchins concluded that new, and deeper dislocations now beset the contemporary culture.

The basic issues of the midcentury, in his view, arose from the unprecedented rate of technological change, and these were hardly touched upon by the outmoded ideology that dominated what passed for political debate. "No existing theory of politics, economics, society, or international relations can explain or account for the facts of contemporary life," Hutchins wrote. "Our situation has changed too fast for our ideas, and so our ideas have degenerated into slogans. . . . Most of us retain individualistic, liberal ideas, but we live in a bureaucratic culture. It remains to be seen whether our ideals can be made applicable to our culture, or whether we can make our culture conform to our ideals."

The Center was designed to test that proposition by subjecting the institutions that had evolved under the American Constitution to reexamination by the best minds Hutchins could find. Distinguished consultants were signed on, among them A. A. Berle, Clark Kerr, I. I. Rabi, Reinhold Niebuhr, John Courtney Murray, Robert Gordis, Eugene Burdick, Eric Goldman, Rexford G. Tugwell, George Shuster, Harrison Brown, Henry R. Luce, Scott Buchanan, Stringfellow Barr, and William O. Douglas. All of these were to spend some time at Santa Barbara engaged in what Hutchins visualized as a continuing dialogue intended "to define and clarify the basic issues of our time, and widen the circles of discussion about them." They would be followed over the next twenty years by some two thousand participants in Center conferences, symposia, and convocations—ranging from a dozen persons around the table in the old mansion on Eucalyptus Hill to great public occasions in major cities in this country and abroad. Some of these, certainly, were among the best minds of the time, a good many were well-known academics or prominent public figures, and all were at least open to the notion that understanding the parlous condition of twentieth-century man required hard, original thought.

It soon became apparent that there were no purely domestic concerns at this level of examination. Despite the presumed separation of powers, our democratic institutions were demonstrably interdependent and could no longer function, as the founding fathers had hoped they might, in effective isolation from the world beyond the seas. It might be thought that at this elevation the peculiarly American phenomenon of the civil rights movement would have little bearing on broader questions of global concern, but the race issue, as always, proved to be inescapable. The unjust treatment of the black minority represented not only a failure of the nation's ideals and religious precepts, but provided a litmus test of the built-in inadequacy of institutions presumed to guarantee equality of opportunity, if not of person.

Conservative defenders of the American faith—and, popular suspicion notwithstanding, they were well represented at the Center—held that the bumping and grinding of countervailing forces, while it produced some friction, also smoothed the way for individual advancement on the basis of merit and served as a guarantee of an open, if not classless, society. But no concept of meritocracy could be said to have embraced the black population under the federal system as originally conceived, and this was a primary reason for the increasing concentration of power in Washington under judicial edict. Now, just as the legal barriers to black advancement began to fall, it was beginning to be evident that cybernation, the engineering advance that made possible automation of manufacturing, processing, and record-keeping, was rapidly eliminating the kind of jobs that had always provided the marginally skilled entry into the mainstream.

The Center's continuing dialogue, as Hutchins conceived it, was open-ended, intended to expose a given issue to all relevant points of view. It was a clarifying rather than a problem-solving enterprise; the object was not to tell the citizenry or their leaders what to think, but to alert them to what they ought to be thinking about. And so, if it was to rise above the conventional wisdom, the dialogue must include those with radical ideas. This meant a regular procession of men and women actively involved in, or at least sympathetic to, the ferment on the college campuses that drew its initial motive power from the civil rights movement—and would, as it progressed to a stage of self-professed revolution, take on what its participants perceived, from a considerable distance, to be the uninhibited life-style of ghetto blacks.

BOB HUTCHINS had an instinctive sympathy for the youth movement. He liked to think of himself as a utopian, and he clung to the Rousseauian notion that the young, like the noble savage, started out in life free of the corruption a materialistic society imposed upon their elders. In what his long-time intellectual companion, Mortimer Adler, considered the best speech he ever made, Hutchins told the 1935 graduating class at the University of Chicago:

I am not worried about your economic future, I am worried about your morals. . . . Believe me, you are closer to the truth now than you ever will be again. Do not let "practical" men tell you that you should surrender your ideals because they are impractical. Do not be reconciled to dishonesty, indecency, and brutality because gentleman-ly ways have been discovered of being dishonest, indecent, and brutal. . . . Courage, temperance, liberality, honor, justice, wisdom, reason, and understanding, these are still the virtues.

But when what came to be called simply "The Movement" emerged on the campuses a quarter century later, most of Hutchins's prescribed virtues were conspicuously missing. From the beginning, the fledgling radicals were militantly antiintellectual; rationality, they proclaimed, had submerged mankind in a materialist quagmire by supressing the liberating sensory aspects of human nature.

One strain of the Movement went back to the Beats of the 1950s who protested the conformity of their "silent generation" of college students by dropping out of society. Theirs was a hedonistic cult of alienation that celebrated self-gratification as a form of protest, and subscribed to no formula for reforming society. Three writers who attracted considerable attention in the mass media gave the Beats their public image: Jack Kerouac, Allen Ginsberg, and William Burroughs. Two of these, Ginsberg and Burroughs, were ostentatiously homosexual, and one form of their protest was to insist that sexual practices should be totally uninhibited. They achieved their popular reputations by describing these as explicitly as possible.

Ginsberg, who settled in the San Francisco Bay Area, saw himself as a messiah as well as a poet, and it was at Berkeley that the counterculture he epitomized first took root among students. Bright, restless children of the middle class were assembled at the University of California, and the Beats' appeal to naturally rebellious adolescents lay in part in its contrast with the concept of truth as beauty that still held sway in academe. "It was no coincidence that the truth of the Beats was normally ugly, undisciplined, cruel," Milton Viorst wrote in his chronicle of the sixties, *Fire in the Streets*. "The Beats' concept was truth as protest—and so the concept passed into the consciousness of a generation which seemed convinced that the defining characteristic of America was hypocrisy. The generation took delight in being personally unkempt, using vulgar language, living in filthy pads. This was truthful. This was authentic. . . ."

The Beats were principally an aberration of the white middle class, and had little appeal for blacks. Still, blacks were prime symbols of what was regarded as the failure of liberalism, and so they had a fascination for the counterculture. The connection was made by Norman Mailer, an existentialist rebel who shared the Beats' corrosive disdain for middle-class values and their obsession with sexuality. In a prescient 1957 essay, "The White Negro," Mailer endowed the counterculture segment of the Movement with the designation "Hippie," derived from the term "hipster" he applied to a new character on the bohemian scene. This was "the philosophical psychopath," a white rebel who adopted the life-style of the ghetto black, living immoderately for the moment, smoking marijuana, speaking street jargon, seeking not love but a good orgasm.

The author's treatment had the effect of converting the derogatory stereotype of Sambo into a role model for the rebellious young. In the dregs of a corrupt society, Mailer wrote, paranoia becomes a necessity, and so the black "kept for his survival the art of the primitive, he lived in the enormous present, he subsisted for his Saturday night kicks, relinquishing the pleasure of the mind for the more obligatory pleasures of the body, and in his music he gave voice to the character and quality of his existence, to his rage, and the infinite variations of joy, lust, languor, growl, cramp, pinch, scream and despair of his orgasm."

In The Movement the sensory strain of the counterculture managed to blend, more or less, with a rational, often puritanical radicalism that had its roots deep in the American past. It would have been hard to find more sharply contrasting personalities than those of two men generally recognized as among the founding fathers, Ginsberg and A. J. Muste. As director of the Fellowship of Reconciliation, an outgrowth of the draft-resister movement of the First World War, Muste was committed to Christian pacifism. His brand of Gandhian nonviolent protest attracted two young blacks who were to become leading figures in the civil rights movement, James Farmer and Bayard Rustin. There was linkage here, too, with traditional American socialism—the Eugene V. Debs-Norman Thomas variety that attempted to translate Marx's authoritarian doctrine into social democracy.

When my colleague at the Center, Paul Jacobs, published *The New Radicals*, he dedicated it to Muste. His co-author, Saul Landau, made his dedication to C. Wright Mills, the Columbia University sociologist who coined the term "New Left." Mills, who found Western society in the strangling grip of a power elite, thought Marx was out of date because the working class proletariat had failed to prove a revolutionary agency of change; he pinned his hope that society might be uprooted and turned upside down on the young: "Who is it that is thinking and acting in radical ways? All over the world . . . the answer is the same: it is the young intelligentsia."

THE Movement was never to attain philosophical coherence, nor effective organization. The first was impossible for partially educated free spirits who expected their further development to result not from disciplined intellectual inquiry but from the liberated libido. The prospect of the second was doomed by the commitment to what was called "participatory democracy"—the refusal to delegate authority even to members of the peer group in the belief that true freedom required that each individual must do his own thing. In their sympathetic appraisal, Jacobs and Landau wrote that "to be in The Movement is to search for a psychic community, in which one's own identity can be defined, social and personal relationships based on love can be established and can grow, unfettered by the cramping pressures and life-styles so characteristic of America today." A psychic community, by definition, could hardly be expected to undertake a program of concerted action, yet for a time there were those who hoped, and others who feared, that this elitist handful was the cutting edge of revolution.

Leaders did emerge, largely by force of personality, superior energy, and the exercise of the kind of self-discipline The Movement rejected in principle. The most influential of these was Tom Hayden, a brilliant, hard-working student at the University of Michigan. He was a big man on campus at Ann Arbor, having become editor of the *Michigan Daily* in his senior year. In the process, he had been politicized through association with the student offshoot of the old League for Industrial Democracy whose Socialist founders included such intellectual notables as Jack London and Upton Sinclair. In the spring of 1960, the League sponsored a conference on civil rights at Ann Arbor, and two of its black staff members, Farmer and Rustin, were there to report on the sit-ins in the South. When it was over, SLID had changed its name to Students for a Democratic Society.

That summer Hayden spent his vacation in California, and stopped off at Berkeley, where the student movement had precipitated a police bust by sitting in at a San Francisco hearing of the House Committee on Un-American Activities. He arrived in his role as journalist, still, as he said, half in the establishment, still the ambitious young reporter who expected to become a famous correspondent. Fifteen years later he recalled the visit as a seminal experience: "What Berkeley did was define my politics, and turn me on to the idea of student power. I got very exhilarated by that, and within a year I had plunged deeply into SDS." Being turned on was essential to the Hippie creed, and for these it was sufficient unto itself. To Tom Hayden, power meant action—power, that is, in a form that turned out to be the antithesis of the gospel of universal love proclaimed by the flower children.

Idealism, as a by-product of innocence, comes easily to the young. For many, disillusionment begins with discovery of the limitations imposed by the human condition and the imperfection of the institutions mankind has fashioned in the long journey outward from the cave. Hayden and his peers added the conviction that they were the first to face up to this reality, and this led to the conclusion that their elders had consciously betrayed them. ". . . if the problems were there all these years, why did *we* have to discover them?" he demanded. "Where was liberalism at?"

The idea that liberalism was the true enemy of The Movement prevailed when SDS held its first national convention in June 1962. Twelve campus chapters, with a total of eight hundred members, sent delegates to a United Auto Workers camp at Port Huron, north of Detroit. They were joined by representatives of SNCC, the Young Democrats, the campus branch of ADA, the Student Peace Union, the NAACP, the Young People's Socialist League, and CORE—fifty-nine participants, all told, forty-three of whom had the power to vote and exercised it by electing Hayden president, and issuing the manifesto he had largely fashioned, "The Port Huron Statement."

"We are the people of this generation, bred in at least modest circumstances, housed now in universities, looking uncomfortably to the world we inherit," the statement began. This was, I suppose, intended as expiation, for surely the gathering at Port Huron must have recognized how far removed it was from most of the people of its generation—including, particularly, the blacks. They had never known privation, and, indeed, could experience it only by a deliberate act of abnegation. "The ambition to escape from poverty is no spur to action in their lives," Jacobs and Landau noted. And Hayden, even then more tactician than ideologue, divined that their upward-striving parents would continue to support their downward-striving offspring even if they disapproved. Viorst attempted to identify the characteristics that distinguished those who made a genuine commitment to The Movement from those who were transiently attracted by its flamboyant defiance of middle-class conventions:

It never consisted of more than a minority at any university, but its members were consistently the brightest and most energetic on campus. Jews were disproportionately represented, and so were the "red diaper" children of old-time radicals. But if there was a typical activist among the huge diversity within The Movement, it was the offspring of a family of professionals, usually well-to-do, with liberal political convictions. Unlike the young black in civil rights the white student had no identifiable self-interest in promoting his cause. For better and worse his concerns were less practical than moral, his goals not reformist but often millenarian.

The rhetoric of the twenty-five thousand-word Port Huron Statement was both plaintive and militant, but the programmatic sections contained little that wasn't already on the liberal reformist agenda: universal controlled disarmament, supervised military disengagement in Vietnam, enlarged foreign aid for the third world, realignment of the political parties, restructuring corporations to increase their social responsibility, increased job opportunities for blacks in the public sector, a sweeping antipoverty program. After SDS had passed into history and Hayden had decided to work within the system, he still resented the suggestion that this could hardly be construed as a radical manifesto. He told Viorst:

. . . our notions of Marxism were in many ways fucked up. We had no experience, no intellectual background. But everybody there knew what we were doing. We had certain deviations from what we considered to be Marxism because we preferred ourselves to be *New Left*. But we were conscious of what we were driving at, which was a revolutionary change in the American structure.

Michael Harrington, a sometime colleague at the Center, was at Port Huron as an observer for the League for Industrial Democracy, a pillar of the Old Left that, through its student division, had financed the organizing effort. However the manifesto might be parsed as to Marxist theory, SDS violated a basic precept of SLID when it refused to ban Communists from participation in the Movement. This, Harrington complained, was a return to "united frontism" and was intolerable to those who still bore scars from battles with the Communist party USA as it followed the twisting party line dictated from Moscow. The parting with the Old Left was foreordained in any case, for SDS, like the other elements of The Movement, was embarked on what soon was recognized as a generational rebellion. "You can't trust anyone over thirty," became the slogan of the college generation—or at least of the most articulate segment on the most exalted campuses.

THE rebellion first impinged upon the consciousness of the general public in 1964 when a spontaneous Free Speech Movement produced a series of highly telegenic media events on the University of California campus. The Hippie counter-culture was already flowering at Berkeley, as well as in the Haight-Ashbury district of San Francisco across the bay, but the straight world tended to forgive its untidy vulgarity because of its professed sweetness and light. On campus youthful idealism was still being channeled within the system; Jack Kennedy was a generational hero, and the Berkeley campus provided the highest percentage of volunteers from any university when the Peace Corps was launched. Others went down to Mississippi for Freedom Summer, and one of these, Mario Savio, emerged as the leader of student protest after a bungling administrator sought to shut down the traditional "Hyde Park" area at Sather Gate where student activists of all persuasions made their speeches and signed up followers. Two days after the ban went into effect, Savio was in his usual place behind a table on the plaza soliciting funds for Friends of SNCC when he, along with four others, was arrested by campus police. Protest erupted in the name of free speech.

Clark Kerr, who headed the vast, multicampus California system, sensed that the surface issue was a symptom of frustration among students lost in a maze of computerized bureaucracy. One of the badges of the Free Speech Movement was an IBM card with the legend, "I am a UC Student: Do Not Fold, Bend or Mutiliate." In the 1963 Godkin lectures at Harvard, Kerr coined the term "multiversity" for these monuments to explosive postwar growth, and noted that their students faced genuine problems in establishing their identity as members of the cloistered academic community presumably still located somewhere among the high-rise buildings and parking lots.

"The undergraduate students are coming to look upon themselves as a 'class,'" he warned. "Some may even feel like a *lumpenproletariat.*"

That, of course, is precisely what did happen at Berkeley. Specific issues of university administration, with which the officers, the faculty, and the regents had the power to deal, gave way to social causes beyond their control—most of these derived from the civil rights movement, which also provided techniques of sit-in and demonstration often directed at off-campus business enterprises. Repercussions in the political community were inevitable. Ronald Reagan, who had marked his transition from movie actor to practicing politician by nominating Barry Goldwater at the 1964 Republican convention, campaigned for governor with a promise to end the "sit-ins, the teach-ins, the walk-outs, and organize a throw-out." At the first meeting of the university's board of regents after his inauguration, ex officio member Reagan saw to it that Clark Kerr was fired.

Kerr was only one in a lengthening procession of ranking university officials who found themselves caught between a rebellious student faction and an alarmed political establishment. Although it had no students, and its permanent "faculty" never amounted to more than twenty or so residential fellows, the ferment on the campuses deeply affected deliberations at the Center for the Study of Democratic Institutions. Before the decade was over it would be simultaneously condemned by student revolutionaries as a citadel of the intellectual enemy, and by Everett Dirksen as the incubator of the New Left.

Taking his cue from the *Chicago Tribune*, the Republican minority leader charged that the Center had sponsored a 1965 Santa Barbara gathering that featured such firebrands as Stokely Carmichael, and espoused nothing less than guerrilla warfare. "They mean business and they went out there to get money from the Ford Foundation to carry out this nefarious business," Dirksen said. Aside from the fact that Hutchins's Center—which he described as a "wholly disinherited" subsidiary—was the last place anyone would go to seek Ford Foundation money, the 1965 "New Politics" meeting that so aroused the *Tribune* and the senator was not sponsored by the Center, although a few of those associated with it attended out of conviction or curiosity. The *Tribune* lumped these together with some notables who certainly had not been present— among them Martin Luther King, and Gens. Vo Nguyen Giap of North Vietnam and Lin Piao of Red China—and declared: "This is criminal syndicalism. . . . Everybody who has a stake in this country had better take this conspiracy seriously before the greatest civilization the world has ever known is leveled. The Justice Department should stop fiddling and go after those who are working toward the friction point of revolution and all their 'angels,' not excepting the Santa Barbara clique and rich patrons, with more money than brains, who enjoy conniving at their own destruction."

THE Movement attracted some of the Center fellows and repelled others, but no one who was seriously engaged in studying democratic institutions could ignore it. From the beginning, it seemed to me, the tenuous connection between the civil rights movement and the SDS's loose grouping of white middle-class students could not possibly survive, since all the self-professed black revolutionaries I knew were militantly antiwhite. This issue produced the ultimately fatal policy split in SNCC. Those who wanted to insulate the young activists against any degree of control by their elders, including Martin Luther King, prevailed. Those who wanted SNCC to remain wholly Southern, denying active membership to Northerners, black or white, lost out. When Northern black militants began to assume key leadership roles, they reopened the question of white participation. Stokely Carmichael opposed the Freedom Summer project because it included white students, and when the decision went against him declared that he would work only with blacks. Carmichael never really tempered that position, and in 1967, when he published *Black Power: The Politics of Liberation in America*, he wrote off the Movement in contemptuous terms:

. . . many young, middle-class white Americans, like some sort of Pepsi generation, have wanted to "come alive" through the black community and black groups. They have wanted to be where the action is. . . . They have sought refuge among blacks from a sterile meaningless, irrelevant life in middle-class America. They have been unable to deal with the stifling, racist, parochial, split-level mentality of their parents, teachers, preachers and friends. Many have come seeing "no difference in color," they have come "color blind." But at this time, and in this land, color *is* a factor and we should not overlook or deny this. The black organizations do not need this kind of idealism, which borders on paternalism.

This kind of rhetoric had a profound appeal for some of my brethren at the Center. W. H. Ferry, who had joined the Fund for the Republic as a vice-president in its early days, had a passionate commitment to the underdog that kept him in a permanent state of simmering moral indignation. This led him to the conclusion that the American upperdog was beyond redemption, and by 1968 he was insisting in *Center Magazine* that white Americans would never accept any effective degree of integration, and that an increasingly segregated society was therefore inevitable:

My proposition, in short, smashes the liberal dream. It eliminates the democratic optimistic claim that we are finding our way to a harmonious blending of the races. It changes the words of the marching song to "We Shall *Not* Overcome," for what was eventually to be overcome was hostility and non-fraternity between black and white. My proposition dynamites the foundations of the NAACP, the Urban League and similar organizations. It asserts that blacktown USA and whitetown USA, for all practical purposes and with unimportant exceptions, will remain separate social communities for as long as one can see ahead. I am not sure, but it may also mean that blacktown will become a separate political community.

At that extremity Ping Ferry had moved into the philosophical company of James Baldwin and Malcolm X, and his proposition seemed to me more an exercise in morbid pessimism than a call for revolution. At the other, optimistic, extreme, were devotees of the flower-strewn Hippie counterculture. They shared the faith of Charles Reich, whose *Greening of America* introduced the concept of consciousness-raising to fashionable circles when it was excerpted at length in *The New Yorker*. To Reich, a law professor at Yale who had participated in Center deliberations, the millennium was at hand. "There is a revolution coming," he wrote. "It will not require violence to succeed. . . . It promises a higher reason, a more human community, and a new and liberated individual. . . . This is the religion of the new generation."

OVER the years the Center's dialogue ranged across all the positions between these two poles. The moral aspect of the race issue had due emphasis. At one point the resident fellows included two Episcopal bishops. The semi-unfrocked James A. Pike had earned a deserved reputation as a preacher of the social gospel, and Edward Crowther had been exiled from his Capetown diocese for his opposition to the Union of South Africa's apartheid policy and practice. The social scientists who charted changes in the black community were regularly heard from, and the senior among them, Gunnar Myrdal, was in residence for a year. Harvey Wheeler, a political scientist fascinated by the scientific avant garde, pursued such esoteric enterprises as B. F. Skinner's experiments with operant conditioning of pigeons, which the Harvard psychologist thought could be used to rid humans of their aggressive instincts—a final solution for the race problem, no doubt, but one that required psychological manipulation to move the whole of society away from the traditional concepts of Western civilization, as Skinner conceded when he titled his expository work *Beyond Freedom and Dignity*.

Two holdovers from the staff of the Fund for the Republic, Paul Jacobs based in Berkeley and Joseph Lyford in New York, were engaged full time in field investigations of ghetto conditions. Jacobs fancied himself a revolutionary but it always seemed to me that he was disqualified by his antic sense of humor, sybaritic tastes, and inability to commit himself to any organized enterprise. He was conditioned by the left wing intellectualism of his alma mater, CCNY, but when he signed on with the Marxist crusade he gravitated to the Trotskyist remnant. As a labor organizer on the west coast he was at odds with the most radical of American unionists, Harry Bridges. He once took me to lunch in Jerusalem at what he said was the only decent restaurant in town; it was run by an Arab. Jacobs was often accused of anti-Semitism by his fellow Jews, and seemed to bear them out by his highly publicized fascination with the Palestine Liberation Organization. His reports from the black ghettoes were uniformly alarmist, and he obviously derived great pleasure from using them to frighten staid white audiences. His 1967 *Prelude to Riot* was actually a postlude, a kind of celebration of the conflagration in Watts and the long hot summers that followed. Its conclusion was a characteristic anecdote, in which he recounted a conversation with a depressed black friend:

"What's bugging you," I asked.
"I had a nightmare last night," he said. "You know, the last time in Watts I was out in the streets trying to cool it. Well, in my nightmare it happened again, but this time I wasn't cooling it, this time I was up on a roof with a rifle, sniping. And down below in the street, there was a white guy and I shot him. I killed him. And you know who he was? He was you. I killed you."
His nightmare is becoming our reality.

Jacobs subtitled *Prelude* "A View of Urban America From the Bottom." But, like his other works, it struck me as an impressionist sketch by a romantic excursionist who never really got in touch with any of the ordinary people living and suffering in the ghettoes. His perspective was in sharp contrast to that of Joe Lyford, whose *Airtight Cage* was a fine-grained documentation of the social pathology he found in a 120-block area of Manhattan's west side where he maintained his own residence. Watching the flight of white neighbors before the influx of blacks and Puerto Ricans, he enlisted the Center's support for what turned out to be a three-year study that detailed the previous failure of the holdover urban renewal schemes and the dubious beginnings of the new social programs launched in the early days of the Great Society.

Lyford's denunciation of the political leadership was no less scathing than Jacobs's. He found that the shortcomings of the ostensibly enlightened social experiments undertaken from the New Deal through the New Frontier resulted from the "good German" mentality of the white majority, which looked the other way while municipal functionaries used federal funds to sweep the dregs of the larger society into enclaves where the helpless poor were huddled. As long as the misery in the ghettoes remained out of sight, the affluent taxpayer was willing to pay the cost of welfare programs devised by theoreticians who had no idea of the real conditions of daily life among people who were, in the main, already socially incapacitated. It was here that Lyford parted company with the romantic radicals. He found that his ghetto neighbors were no more capable of launching, or sustaining, the revolution The Movement proclaimed than they were of pulling themselves up by their own bootstraps, as the social Darwinians prescribed.

Conditioned by my own experience, I was never able to make the leap of faith The Movement required. At the Center I was struck by the failure Lyford emphasized— the inability, or at least the unwillingness, of most intellectuals to address the reality of the black condition. In his *Center Magazine* "Farewell to Integration" article, Ferry wrote, "It is doubtless clear that there is next to nothing here about blacktown's reactions to my proposition. This is because I do not know what they are. I mistrust polls of black opinion. Until recently it has made no difference what blacks think." Lyford, who checked countless interviews of his own against opinion data, thought it made all the difference in the world. "When in rare instances an opinion research firm assigns Negroes to interview their neighbors in a Watts or a Harlem," Lyford wrote, "the results contrast sharply with the picture conveyed by those who insist that the black community is in steady sympathy with the black practitioners of violence, or by those who see the rioters as symbols against racial injustice."

In those days police brutality was a prime issue among New York's liberal Reform Democrats, but Lyford found that the presumed victims in the ghettoes actually wanted more and tougher cops on their streets to protect them against the wanton violence of black neighbors and the depredations of white criminals who took refuge there. I summed up his conclusion in an introduction to *The Airtight Cage:*

If adversity has shaken the poor's grip upon reality, affluence seems to have done the same for the rest of the community. Lyford diagnoses the prevailing American disease as a form of auto-anesthesia, a self-induced ability to ignore the sights, sounds and fetid smells of the human scrap heap every city seems to require—or at least to be unable to alleviate, even now when we have more wealth than we can count and have run out of the traditional economic excuses for poverty.

THE Movement ran its course in less than a decade. Its demise would have come sooner, I believe, had its motive power continued to derive from the inchoate rage of affluent young whites linked precariously to the small band of black militants. The mainline black leadership was appalled by it, seeing in its inflammatory rhetoric an incitement to the outbreaks of urban arson they considered ultimately destructive of their cause. Roy Wilkins may have been reflecting his own middle-class bias, but the evidence has borne out his contention that the typical black, North no less than South, "is a very practical and pragmatic animal, and he had never lost sight of the elementary facts of survival, and he has never forgotten that he's a ten percent minority."

The split among the young black activists came along North-South lines, when Stokely Carmichael set up a registration project in Lowndes County, Alabama, and announced his intention to found a new, all-black party under the Black Panther symbol. "To me, the only good thing the vote could do was wreck the Democratic Party and spring off a revolution in America," he said. John Lewis, SNCC's chairman, who bore as many scars as any of the band of native sons who first defied the conventions of the Deep South, opposed the move as dead-end separatism, and Carmichael said, "After that, I wanted his blood." He got it at the SNCC convention in Nashville in May 1966, when Lewis resigned in protest against the evident abandonment of the principle of nonviolence.

Within eighteen months, SNCC's national headquarters in Atlanta was closed and the *Constitution* estimated that the scattered active members numbered no more than a hundred and fifty. Ralph McGill wrote an obituary for the movement in *Center Magazine:* "SNCC, like Carmichael, is a melancholy story. From its beginning in North Carolina, through the freedom rides, the freedom schools, and the long contests with segregation before the public accommodations law, SNCC was an inspiring organization. I do not think I have ever seen any more courageous, any sweeter or more dedicated lot of young people. They endured jails, abuses, brutalities. Some were killed. When Carmichael opted for an anti-white Black Power group he cut them off. . . ."

The term "Black Power" came into currency as a gesture of direct defiance of Martin Luther King when, a month after his elevation at Nashville, Carmichael joined King in the last joint effort of SCLC and SNCC. The two met in the Memphis hospital room of James Meredith. The loner who broke the color bar at Ole Miss characteristically had set forth on a solo protest march, heading south from Memphis into the Mississippi delta. Just across the state line an unemployed white drifter arose from the bushes to bring him down with three blasts of birdshot from a shotgun. King and Floyd McKissick, then national director of CORE, flew in to take up where the wounded Meredith left off, and were joined by SNCC's new chairman.

King's published version of the strategy session next day makes no mention of the presence of Roy Wilkins of the NAACP and Whitney Young of the Urban League. But Carmichael, in an interview with Milton Viorst, said they were present until he deliberately forced their withdrawal. "King's role was dangerous to us," he said. "We wanted to pull him to the left. We knew if we got rid of Young and Wilkins the march [was] ours." He described how it was done:

Wilkins came to the meeting and he already had a statement. He was going to make the march to support some legislation, some nonsense that Johnson had. And when he came up with that, everyone else was mad, because they didn't like him much anyway. So I started acting crazy, crusing real bad. I said, "You sellin' out the people and don't think we don't know it. We gonna getcha." And all the SNCC people in the meeting were yelling, "Right on!" We ought to shoot him on the spot." We wanted to let them know that it would be impossible to work with us. . . . Young and Wilkins fell completely into the trap and stormed out of there.

King, Carmichael, and McKissick, with a gaggle of followers from the three participating organizations and a full complement of reporters and television crews, set forth on foot from the spot on Highway 51 where Meredith's blood still stained the pavement. For more than two weeks they marched south, camping out on the roadside at night. On the first day King noted that when the marchers came to the stanza of "We Shall Overcome" which refers to whites and blacks together, the Snick voices faded out. He asked why and was told, "This is a new day, we don't sing those words any more. In fact the whole song should be discarded. Not 'We Shall Overcome' but 'We Shall Overrun.' "

The march was a highly successful media event, drawing

considerable crowds in the towns it passed through. At Greenwood, one of SNCC's district headquarters, the marchers were
greeted by a mass rally in a public park. Carmichael took the
platform to bring forth a roaring response from the crowd
when he made his first public call for Black Power. He knew he
would, he told Viorst, for he had sent advance men ahead to
sound out the temper of the local blacks and prepare them for
his coming. *In Where Do We Go From Here?* King described the
aftermath:

The phrase had been used before by Richard Wright and others but
never until that night had it been used as a slogan in the civil rights
movement. For people who had been crushed so long by white power
and who had been taught that black was degrading, it had a ready
appeal.

Immediately, however, I had reservations about its use. I had the
deep feeling that it was an unfortunate choice of words for a slogan.
Moreover, I saw it bringing about division within the ranks of
marchers. For a day or two there was fierce competition between those
wedded to the Black Power slogan and those wedded to Freedom
Now. Speakers on each side sought desperately to get the crowds to
chant their slogan the loudest.

A shaky modus vivendi was worked out, and King stayed
with the march, walking into Jackson on June 26 at the head of
a procession of fifteen thousand. He disassociated himself from
the Black Power slogan as best he could, issuing a statement
saying that "black supremacy would be equally as evil as white
supremacy." But the younger leader was offering the rhetorical
red meat the media craved, and the public relations coup he
had planned paid off: After Greenwood Carmichael was well
launched on the national talk show and lecture circuit with an
opening appearance on "Face the Nation."

The spiritual separation of King and Carmichael was
affirmed ten days out on the march at a Catholic parish house
in Yazoo City, where for five hours King pleaded with Carmichael and McKissick to recognize that Black Power carried
strong connotations of violence and would simply divert attention from the evils they were protesting in Mississippi. Carmichael, with McKissick's support, remained adamant, and finally
confessed, "Martin, I deliberately decided to raise this issue on
the march in order to give it a national forum, and force you to

take a stand for Black Power." King laughed and replied, "I have been used before—one more time won't hurt."

But it did hurt, as King made clear in a remarkable chapter in *Where Do We Go From Here?*, in which he offered a dispassionate, closely reasoned argument against compromising the nonviolent character of the movement he had launched. True to his concept of reconciliation, he declined to sign a statement condemning SNCC's antiwhite posture drawn up by A. Philip Randolph and endorsed by Wilkins, Young, Rustin, and others. He conceded the psychological importance of the Black Power battle cry as an assertion of manhood. But the erudite King knew the sources of his opponents' sloganeering better than they did, contrasting the new radical bible upon which they drew, Frantz Fanon's *The Wretched of the Earth*, with the Gandhian doctrines that were his own inspiration. "Beneath all the satisfaction of a gratifying slogan," he wrote, "Black Power is a nihilistic philosophy born out of the conviction that the Negro can't win. It is, at bottom, the view that American society is so hopelessly corrupt and enmeshed in evil that there is no possibility of salvation from within." He saw this as the ultimate contradiction of the Black Power movement:

It claims to be the most revolutionary wing of the social revolution taking place in the United States. Yet it rejects the one thing that keeps the flame of revolution burning: the everpresent flame of hope. When hope dies, a revolution degenerates into an undiscriminating catchall for evanescent and futile gestures.

Along with violence, separatism was also implicit in Black Power, and King saw that as another contradiction—a certain dead end for a black minority that had no possibility of achieving effective political and economic power in isolation from the white majority that controlled its sources. But King also had come to understand that, for the foreseeable future at least, blacks would have to use their racial identity to maintain a political bloc within the system—for their own individual protection, as well as to maintain pressure for change. Experience had taught him to appreciate the mordant thesis that runs through Walker Percy's fictional treatment of man's inhumanity to man:

Where there is a racially distinct minority whose well-being depends to a degree upon law and to a degree upon the good nature of the majority, the minority will be buggered precisely to the degree that the law allows—even when there is considerable good nature at hand. No man can hold out for long against another man's helplessness. Sooner or later one will be seduced and the other will be buggered.

Re-reading King's final testament more than a decade after it was written vindicates his reputation as a prophet. He wrote it during the time he lived with his family in a railroad flat in the Chicago ghetto, his residence there attesting his recognition that the American black's destiny now would be determined in the great cities. This was significantly different terrain from that upon which he had launched his civil rights crusade, and it demanded a change of tactics; the gains he had sought for his people in the South, and for the most part had realized, were precious in terms of human dignity but they had not in fact cost the white majority anything except pride. When he moved on, as he must, to deal with urban poverty he would have to demand something more tangible of whites than giving blacks a seat on a bus or at a lunch counter or in a public school classroom.

He had his share of frustration that year in Chicago, where he found himself negotiating with a wily Mayor Richard Daly, dodging among the entrenched factions in a city that operated by power brokerage. It was a far cry from dealing with the black-and-white moral simplicity of confrontation with the likes of Bull Connor. The effort to transplant SCLC across the Mason-Dixon line is usually written off as a failure—and it might well have turned out that way even if King had lived. Still, I find *Where Do We Go from Here?*, with its "Prospects and Programs" appendix, as clear-eyed an appraisal of race relations in the United States at the close of the sixties as anything compiled since with the benefit of hindsight.

But the case is moot. By the time the book came off the press no one in a position of authority was still listening to Martin Luther King when he spoke out on civil rights, and he was himself preaching on a different subject—the war in Vietnam. On April 4, 1967, he shrugged off the advice of the black political leadership and spoke his conscience from the pulpit of Riverside Church in New York. He had concluded that a man committed to nonviolence at home could no longer ignore violence abroad. "We are committing atrocities equal to any perpetrated by the Vietcong," he said. "The bombs in Vietnam explode at home—they destroy the dream and possibility for a decent America." He became co-chairman of Clergy and Laymen Concerned about Vietnam, and by that act broke with the most effective political supporter the civil rights movement had ever known, Lyndon B. Johnson.

26

The Long, Hot Summers

*T*he front-line leaders of the radical wing of the civil rights movement never had any use for the Center for the Study of Democratic Institutions, or for any other intellectual enterprise, but most of the theoreticians turned up on Eucalyptus Hill at one time or another during the 1960s. Few, if any, accepted nonviolence in the conciliatory Gandhian mode advocated by Martin Luther King, who condoned hatred for the oppressive system but required love for the oppressors. The young radicals insisted that middle-class America—*Amerika* as they began to spell it to provide a Nazi connotation—was corrupt beyond redemption and had no conscience to confront.

Yet, most still accepted nonviolence as a necessary tactic, recognizing that, at least until the masses were prepared to rise, The Movement faced overwhelming force which it could assume would be invoked to put down sustained disorder. The gentler souls believed, or wanted to believe, that a way could be found to mount a revolution within the system—that is, to somehow, without bloodshed, intimidate the controlling majority into yielding the advantages it enjoyed. The concept of nonviolent revolution had always seemed to me a contradiction in terms, and I found it difficult to believe that a central problem of political theory that had defied generations of philosophers would yield to thinkers who treated it as a brand new phenomenon.

The protest marches of Martin Luther King were often cited as examples of what came to be called "creative disorder," but this was a misreading of their essential strategy. King had prevailed because his methods contrasted with the use of force by his antagonists, and his objective had been to invoke federal intervention to restore law and order when local authorities refused to put down violence perpetrated by whites. In the big city ghettoes the situation was reversed. Here it was the rhetoric of the radical leaders that fed the flames, inciting rather than restraining insurrection. Disorder was certainly possible, but it was soon evident that keeping it this side of physical violence was not. Anyone who had lived through the Southern experience, where demagogues used white discontent to build an emotional surge of defiance, would have shared my surprise that anyone seriously thought it could be otherwise.

THE noncreative mass disorder that was to plague the nation for more than three years first flared on August 11, 1965 in a black neighborhood of Los Angeles called Watts. It came as a surprise, since blacks in California, where most had arrived since World War II, were probably better off than anywhere else in the country. The Urban League rated Los Angeles first among sixty-eight cities in terms of housing, employment, and available amenities; the overall unemployment rate among the city's half million blacks, at 7.9 percent, was less than double that of whites. But in Watts, the poorest of Los Angeles' nine black districts, 30 percent of adult males were jobless—and there, as it would be in the other hundred ghettoes put to the torch in the long hot summers to come, it was the younger of these who ran through the streets chanting a slogan adapted from a radio disc jockey: "Burn, baby, burn."

The Watts riot was touched off, as most of the others would be, by spontaneous reaction against routine police action—in this case the arrest of a drunken driver who was, or seemed to be, manhandled. Before order was restored six days later, a National Guard force of 14,000 had been brought in to impose a curfew over a forty-six-square-mile area. The casualty list stood at 34 killed, 898 wounded; arrests totaled 4,000; property losses were estimated at $45 million. This pattern, with only minor variations, was repeated in four cities in 1965, twenty-one in 1966, and seventy-five in 1967. It became so commonplace the Department of Justice established standards to distinguish a riot from a mere racial disturbance. In order to receive a riot rating the disorder had to last more than twelve hours, involve more than three hundred participants, and feature gunfire, looting, arson, and vandalism. The cities where these criteria were met were outside the South.

The mainline black leaders condemned the riots. They were "absolutely wrong, socially destable, and self-defeating," King said. Roy Wilkins added, "God help black Americans if this is their revolution, and these are their revolutionaries." But young radicals and black separatists praised the looters and arsonists as urban guerrillas and cheered them on, usually from the sidelines. The public and private agencies that investigated the rioting were unanimous in citing spontaneity and lack of leadership as its most conspicuous characteristics. It can be assumed that the FBI would have been delighted to link the radical leaders directly to the wanton destruction, but evidence of effective conspiracy was never forthcoming.

The common carrier of the seeds of destruction that spread from city to city was an organ of the establishment, television. Poor as the people of Watts undoubtedly were, nine out of ten of the houses there had TV sets, and they were turned on most of the broadcast day. Television served, first of all, to whet the resentment of the deprived by showing them, through beguiling commercials, a life-style among whites that contrasted sharply with their own. And it bore graphic tidings of racial disturbances elsewhere, accompanied by the most dramatic exhortations of black radicals. It is not hard to imagine the reaction of a frustrated ghetto youth when the charismatic H. Rap Brown of SNCC appeared on his TV screen to declare violence as American as cherry pie, and proclaim to a cheering audience of his peers, "The honky is your enemy. If you give me a gun I just might shoot Lady Bird." Theodore H. White charged that his electronic colleagues shared responsibility for Watts; television and radio coverage, he said, went "beyond reporting and become a factor in itself." And he posed a question that has remained pertinent and unanswered: "Can electronic reporting be curbed in the higher interest of domestic tranquility?"

King told a touching story about his futile visit to Watts, where he had gone with Bayard Rustin to see if he could help reduce the fever. In the midst of the havoc they stopped to talk with a twenty year old, who greeted them with an exultant, "We won!" Rustin responded, "How have you won? Homes have been destroyed, Negroes are lying dead in the streets, the stores from which you buy food and clothes are destroyed, and people are bringing you in relief." The happy rioter replied, "We won because we made the whole world pay attention to us. We made them come."

Gaining visibility, however, did not necessarily help their cause. An old friend, Doris Fleeson, the Washington columnist, was visiting in Santa Barbara when Watts blew, and we spent an afternoon watching the live broadcast from Los Angeles. Her husband, Dan Kimball, a tolerant, civilized Californian who had served as Secretary of the Navy under Harry Truman, was visibly shaken. Finally he erupted, "Goddamn them, that's my town they're burning down! They're animals—they ought to be shipped back to Africa!" I had not before heard that demand, colored by that depth of passion, outside the Deep South.

THE explosion of the Detroit ghetto in the third summer of rioting represented considerable escalation over the beginning in Watts. Street fighting continued from July 23 until July 30; thirty-seven blacks and three whites were killed and two thousand were wounded; arsonists touched off fifteen hundred fires; and looters contributed heavily to the $350 million in property losses. When the situation passed beyond control by city and state police and the National Guard, President Johnson answered Gov. George Romney's request for aid with five thousand airborne troopers. The rioting spilled outside black neighborhoods, prompting UAW president Walter Reuther to observe that Detroit had earned the distinction of being the first city with integrated looting.

On the fourth day, a posse of city police, state patrolmen, and National Guardsmen rushed into the annex of the Algiers Motel in search of snipers. They found no firearms on the premises, but they flushed out ten black men and two partially clad white women, and when they left an hour later two of the men were dead of gunshot wounds and all the others, including the women, had been badly beaten. The gifted writer, John Hersey, chose to focus on this encounter when his conscience moved him to abandon work in progress on a novel and turn his skills to reportage, probing the anatomy of what he considered "the most intransigent and fear-ridden issue in American life." He spent months in the charred Detroit ghetto interviewing the principals as the resulting murder case made its way through the courts.

The Algiers Motel Incident emphasized the point that Hersey thought was glossed over in the usual consideration of racism —the fact that sex, as exemplified by the white officers' reaction to the discovery of white women consorting with black men, played such a distorting role in the relationship between the races:

> . . . I believe it to be at the very core of racism. If real progress is to be made, it cannot be made simply by expenditures of funds, even in great sums, on "programs"; racism must be educated or coaxed or wrenched or stamped out of the centers of injustice and grievance— namely, out of police forces, courts, legislatures, unions, industry, schools, the civil service, and the bureaucracy of welfare.
>
> There are four main causes of racial violence: unequal justice, unequal employment opportunities, unequal housing, unequal education. . . . I believe [unequal justice] is the one that should be attacked first, because it is the cutting edge of irritation in the inner cities; because it is the prime cause of the deep anger of those without whom there would be no summer rebellions, the young black males; and because, to be practical about it, its remedy would not cost a cent. The remedy is in the minds of men. Unequal justice is experienced by the black population at two points: what happens with the cop in the street, and what happens with the prosecutor and lawyer and judge in court.

Most white Americans who had immediate responsibility for dealing with the cause and effect of the wave of riots were in general agreement with Hersey's analysis. The conventional wisdom in these circles embraced the proposition the author made when he wrote: "Perhaps the whole point of this book is that every white person in the country is in some degree guilty of the crimes committed at the Algiers." The National Advisory Commission on Civil Disorders appointed by President Johnson in 1967 agreed that the criminal justice system provided the flashpoint for rioting. Its report, signed by the chairman, former Illinois governor Otto Kerner, concluded: "Virtually every major episode of urban violence in the summer of 1967 was foreshadowed by an accumulation of grievances by ghetto residents against local authorities (often, but not always, the police)."

Johnson reacted to Watts with compassion and restraint.

". . . it is not enough simply to decry disorder," he said. "We must also strike at the unjust conditions from which disorder largely flows. . . . We must not let anger drown understanding. . . ." As the rioting spread he told Doris Kearns, a White House assistant, "As I see it, I have moved the Negro from D+ to C−. He's still nowhere. He knows it. And that's why he's out in the streets. Hell, I'd be there too. . . ." When he sent troops into Detroit, Johnson went to extraordinary lengths to see that they remained under civilian control, and to insure the use of only minimum force he ordered that their arms be unloaded and their bayonets sheathed.

Yet when the Kerner Commission report was issued Johnson greeted it with what, for him, amounted to silence. The commission, finding no evidence of conspiracy to account for the riots, attributed them to pervasive white racism, and concluded its report with the dire warning that the United States was "moving toward two societies, one white, one black— separate but unequal." Liberals who reflexively distrusted Johnson charged that he withheld endorsement because he feared the report would produce a white backlash in his coming campaign for reelection. John Hersey, his sensibilities rubbed raw by his close-up view of the aftermath of the Detroit riot, was outraged: ". . . the spectacle of this man running for cover from the conclusions of the commission which he created, and which he charged with the high task of seeking truth, was not only disgusting; it was positively inflammatory, for it denied the very thesis of the report. The Texan seemed to want to deny the charge of white racism."

Those around the president thought he backed away from the Kerner Commission for other reasons. Certainly he had never denied that the white community was responsible for the legitimate grievances that led blacks to riot, but he did not accept the conclusion that the two races were pulling apart into separate communities. He believed, and the evidence was with him, that the black and white middle classes in fact were coming together in a fashion that indicated a marked tempering of white racist attitudes. The afflictions of blacks in the underclass could properly be seen as the residue of the racist past, but the more compelling fact was that he had been able to persuade the representatives of white taxpayers to appropriate funds for programs aimed at alleviating them.

As to Hersey's denigration of mere "programs," he might have asked what other means were available to educate, coax, wrench, or stamp racism out of the centers of injustice and grievance. The Kerner report did not clash in any way with his own statements and actions, but the implications being read into it by his critics seemed to dismiss the efficacy of the Great Society programs in which he had invested so much of his political capital.

The War on Poverty had been launched in a blizzard of legislation, and Johnson was still sending measures to the Hill. There were general programs of health care and urban renewal that would reach into the ghettoes, and economic development undertakings intended to create new jobs—and a strengthened FEPC to see that blacks got their share. He had created a new agency aimed directly at the conditions Hersey cited: the Office of Economic Opportunity, established under the direction of the most idealistic member of the Kennedy clan, Sargent Shriver, whose brother-in-law had put him in charge of doing good works overseas as director of the Peace Corps. OEO programs included Job Opportunities in the Business Sector (JOBS) to provide placement for the hard-core unemployed; Head Start, which brought needed services to 1,300,000 preschool children in its first year; Volunteers in Service to America (VISTA), a domestic Peace Corps; a Neighborhood Youth Corps, providing 500,000 part-time jobs for teen-agers; Upward Bound, preparing disadvantaged youths for college through campus programs; a Community Action Program (CAP) coordinating local health, housing, and employment programs and offering free legal advice; and Foster Grandparents to work with homeless children.

Some of these programs were bound to falter, but in the season of riots, they were all more or less in place, and unprecedented sums of public money were being funneled through them to the ghetto communities. But the Kerner report implied that this was a mere trickle, and called for "adequate action" involving immediate expenditures totalling an additional $30 billion. That was the real stopper so far as the president was concerned.

The Vietnam war was now escalating month by month, and so was the cost of maintaining it. From the beginning, Johnson had played fast and loose with deficit financing in order to convince the voters that they could still have both guns and butter. As far back as 1965 he had justified his refusal to lay the actual cost of Vietnam on the line by telling those around him: "I don't know much about economics, but I do know the Congress. And I can get the Great Society through right now—this is a golden time. We've got a good Congress and I'm the right president, and I can do it. But if I talk about the cost of the war, the Great Society won't go through, and the tax bill won't go through. Old Wilbur Mills will sit down there and he'll thank me kindly and send me back my Great Society, and then he'll tell me that he'll be glad to spend whatever we need for the war."

ALTHOUGH there was a kind of half-baked Marxist element in the radical youth movement that produced talk about capitalist imperialism, there had been little concern with foreign policy in the beginning. Exaltation of the black cause by the militants, and celebration of personal liberation by the counterculturists, had been sufficient to attract the idealistic and the alienated who made up SDS. This began to change in the fall of 1964, when Lyndon Johnson used an incident in the Bay of Tonkin as an excuse to commit his administration to increased military involvement in Vietnam.

Escalation brought an end to automatic student deferment just as the monthly quota of draftees for military service was stepped up—tenfold in 1966 over the 1965 average of five thousand. Now the war came home to the campuses. The heightened prospect of military service gave the whole of the student generation, straights included, the kind of self-interest in antiestablishment protest that had been unique to blacks. When the Movement took up the antidraft cause, and began demonstrating to halt troop trains rather than to desegregate lunch counters, its tiny membership grew—and, more significantly, it acquired the tacit support of nonradical students and, in time, their concerned parents.

The spreading anti-Vietnam feeling hardly touched the black community. The *right* to military service on equal terms in an integrated armed service had been one of the first great achievements of the civil rights movement. Blacks were proud of the fact that they had earned their share of medals in the

Korean War, and they were now solidly emplaced as service careerists, particularly in the regular army where they were disproportionately represented among noncommissioned officers. A hitch in the service offered a better real income and better prospects for advancement than were available elsewhere for most poor blacks; if there was hardship and danger they were equally shared, and produced a kind of comradeship that tended to obliterate color lines. Asked if he encountered any discrimination in the corps, a black marine grinned and replied, "Oh no, not at all. They treat us all like niggers."

Within their own constituency there was no pressure on the mainline black leaders to join the anti-Vietnam protest. They were unmoved by the New Left party line, which identified Vietnamese Communists with the colored peoples of the third world and characterized American intervention in Southeast Asia as racist. But most of all they were concerned that identification with the anti-Vietnam protest would inevitably alienate the political support so recently gained and so essential to further black progress.

It could be assumed that a man of Martin Luther King's religious convictions would be opposed to the use of force in the conduct of foreign policy, but until 1965 he was not vocal about it. Linus Pauling, who won one of his two Nobel Prizes for his stand against the use of nuclear weapons, was in residence at the Center when award of the Nobel Peace Prize to King was announced. He felt, he told me, that he was bound to protest, since, however valuable King's services might be to his people, they had nothing to do with ending war. But, after the Selma march, King began to speak out, saying publicly, "It's worthless to talk about integrating, if there is no world to integrate in. The war in Vietnam must be stopped." Roy Wilkins, Whitney Young, Daddy King, and even Bayard Rustin, the veteran pacifist, urged him to stick to civil rights. And Lyndon Johnson, alarmed at this dissidence by the most influential of his black supporters, launched a characteristic campaign to keep King in the fold.

Vice-President Humphrey took King, Andrew Young, and the leaders of the NAACP, CORE, and the Urban League on a cruise down the Potomac aboard the presidential yacht. Humphrey was at his effusive best as he recalled the civil rights battles they had fought together and promised more triumphs in the future, but King and Floyd McKissick of CORE could not be moved. King continued to speak out, and in June 1966 his split with the administration was given public notice when the president convened a White House conference on civil rights; a subordinate member of SCLC was accorded vice-chairman status, while King was left off the program and invited to attend only as a guest.

It was hardly surprising that he was no longer welcome at the White House. King had taken a leading role in the Spring Mobilization, an umbrella organization that rallied a broad spectrum of church, pacifist, professional, Old Left, and New Left groups, including SDS—now trying to establish a united front with the nonradical student and faculty groups sponsoring antiwar "teach-ins" on leading campuses. When the Reverend James Bevel of SCLC, who served as organizer for a demonstration at United Nations Plaza in New York, was asked about the political implication of including radical contingents with mainline supporting groups, he replied, "We're going to get to the left of Karl Marx and left of Lenin. We're going to get way out there, up on that cross with Jesus." That was the tone of the address King delivered at United Nations Plaza to a throng estimated by the police at 150,000.

Bevel's explanation of the presence of the noisy radical fringe in the "Mobe," as they called it, aroused no sympathy in Washington. Carl Rowan, the black journalist who had served as director of the United States Information Service, was undoubtedly speaking the administration's sentiments when he charged in a newspaper column that King had created "doubt about the Negro's loyalty to his country." Rowan referred to allegations of subversive influence in SCLC being systematically leaked to journalists by J. Edgar Hoover and his men: "I report this not to endorse what King and many others will consider a 'guilt by association' smear, but because of the threat that these allegations represent to the civil rights movement."

Those who were arguing for unity among the black leaders were pleading for something that no longer existed. King told the cautious ones in SCLC: ". . . I could never again raise my voice against the violence of the oppressed in the ghettoes without having first spoken clearly to the greatest purveyor of

violence in the world—my own government." And he sent
Andy Young to represent him at a New York meeting in April
1967, called by Allard Lowenstein, the gadfly who touched off
the Mississippi Freedom Movement that plagued Lyndon Johnson at Atlantic City, and now was engaged in a concerted effort
to dump him in 1968. James Wechsler, editor of the *New York
Post*, and Norman Thomas joined Lowenstein in urging that
King head up a presidential ticket to dramatize the antiwar
protest, as Thomas had done so many times for the Socialist
cause. King declined, but left no doubt that he would like to see
Johnson replaced.

THE Center could no more avoid the divisive issues raised
by the anti-Vietnam movement than it could those pointed up
by the turbulence among supporters of civil rights. Robert
Hutchins was a gray eminence in the traditional antiwar
movement, a leading advocate of international organization to
curb the forces that had always propelled great powers into
armed conflict. At the Center the continuing project that
interested him most was that devoted to world order—indeed,
it was his view that purely domestic concerns had become
irrelevant, since American society, no matter how it might be
internally reformed, had no future in a world divided among
powers armed with the ultimate weapons of destruction.

Hutchins saw in the dramatic encyclical of Pope John
XXIII, *Pacem in Terris*, a possible breakthrough in the cold war.
The Vatican's overture aroused great interest in Moscow,
where it was viewed as a conciliatory gesture from the ideological citadel of Western anti-Communism. But normal diplo-
matic channels were still frozen by the postwar chill and there
was no follow-up in Washington or the other Western capitals.
Hutchins concluded that the only way to pursue the opening
would be through an East-West dialogue on a wholly unofficial
basis. To that end he proposed a great convocation in New York
that would bring together political, intellectual, and spiritual
leaders from both sides of the Iron Curtain to consider the
agenda Pope John set forth as "the requirements of peace." In
February 1965, the Center managed to convene what John K.
Jessup described in *Life* as "an extraordinary assemblage of the
world's shakers and movers."

Back full time at the Center as executive vice-president

after publication of the new edition of Britannica was post-poned and my assignment terminated, to the mutual pleasure of William Benton and me, I became principal organizer of the convocation, a role that would make me, in Hutchins's wry description, the Sol Hurok of the peace game. Aside from the substantive results we hoped would flow from this unprece-dented informal exchange among influential men and women on both sides of the great ideological divide, the convocation was conceived as a public relations exercise that might reopen a popular dialogue on the central issues. To round up the kind of celebrities who inspire widespread media coverage, I found myself again operating more or less full time in political circles in Washington and abroad.

Camelot was still in flower when planning for *Pacem in Terris* began. If my allegiance to Adlai Stevenson had limited my access to the inner circle of the Kennedy administration, I could rely on old journalistic comrades and influential Center associates to open doors for me. Chief among the latter was William O. Douglas, who had succeeded Elmo Roper as chair-man of the Center board, and who shared Hutchins's convic-tion that the future of civilization depended on establishing the rule of law in international relations. Justice Douglas had been brought to Washington by Joseph Kennedy, whom he succeed-ed as chairman of the Securities Exchange Commission, and he had been intimate with his sons since they were children.

Bill Douglas and I discussed with President Kennedy the possibility that he might use the *Pacem in Terris* convocation as a forum from which he could address the requirements of peace as defined by Pope John. He was attracted by the idea but had not finally committed himself before the assassination. Not long after Lyndon Johnson, another long-time intimate of Douglas, took over the Oval Office the two of us visited him there to urge that he open the convocation. He said it was too early for him to make a commitment, but he was not unduly discouraging. Douglas continued to importune the president, but as fall approached he found that Johnson "dodged, ducked, and evaded the proposition, changing the subject and finally shunting me off to the staff that was instructed to sabotage me politely."

By the time the two thousand *Pacem in Terris* delegates from twenty nations gathered in the great hall of the United Nations in February, the reason for the presidential U-turn was evident: Johnson had extended the air war across the border to North Vietnam and had initiated a massive buildup of American ground forces in the South. As the mounting conflict began to imperil the fragile great power detente prompted by the papal encyclical, we were urged by Ralph Bunche and others at the U.N., and by some of the foreign leaders who had participated in the first convocation, to convoke *Pacem in Terris II*. The Russians and the French were insistent that we try to bring in representatives of China, North and South Vietnam, and the other Southeast Asian nations. We assembled the second convocation in May 1967 in Geneva, and if we did not succeed in breaking through to the Chinese, sealed off as they were by American containment policy and their own cultural revolution, we did make contact with North Vietnam. In the course of these negotiations and their aftermath I went twice behind the enemy lines to Hanoi.

We collaborated with the State Department in all of this, or at least we tried to. My old friend Bill Baggs of the *Miami News*, now a Center board member, and I agreed to travel secretly when we were cleared for our first trip to Hanoi in January 1967. We brought back from a two-hour audience with Ho Chi Minh what we were convinced the North Vietnamese patriarch intended as a clear signal that he was prepared to discuss terms for the negotiated settlement President Johnson professed to seek. At the behest of the State Department we sent back an equally clear signal that the United States was willing to move the exchange to the level of official contact. But some weeks later we found that at the same time our message was going forward the president had sent through Moscow a hard-line response that effectively cancelled our effort. Baggs and I felt obligated to blow the whistle on this double-dealing.

Publication of our detailed account of "Duplicity in High Places" in *Center Magazine* produced headlines everywhere and brought down on my head the full wrath of the administration. An extensive statement issued by Assistant Secretary of State William Bundy didn't deny the facts of our case, but dismissed Baggs and me as petulant amateur diplomats. This gave me prominence among the critics of the war, whose number and stature were growing in the face of the president's evident determination to force a military settlement of the conflict.

I had thought from the beginning that we were fighting the wrong war in the wrong place for the wrong reasons, and after touring the countryside in North Vietnam under American aerial attack I was more than ever convinced that there was no way to force a surrender without the use of atomic weapons, at the risk of bringing in the Russians and the Chinese. But I also was convinced that the antiwar movement, in which the loyal majority was drowned out by the posturing of the radical fringe, had no prospect of pressuring Lyndon Johnson into accepting anything that could be construed as an American surrender. I could think of nothing more likely to harden Johnson's resolve than SDS pickets outside the White House chanting, "Hey, Hey, LBJ, how many kids did you kill today?" unless it was those who gladdened J. Edgar Hoover's heart by shouting "Ho Ho Ho Chi Minh, NLF Is gonna win" as they ran through the streets baiting policemen and trashing public facilities and private property.

I saw a good deal of Ralph Bunche in those days and was moved by his monumental sadness. The Nobel laureate could see his own life's work threatened by his government's policies, and he recognized that they were also cutting the ground from under the civil rights cause he had always championed with his quiet dignity. The other black Nobel laureate was no less sad when I talked at length with him in Geneva, where he came to address *Pacem in Terris II*. King was fully aware of the consequences of his stand against the war, but like the first Luther, he felt he could do no other. He was the only civil rights leader of the first rank in the various mobilizations, and there were few black faces to be seen among the peace marchers in any city, North or South. Aside from a few Marxist "third worlders," most of the black radicals scorned the peace demonstrations because of their domination by whites.

In 1966 President Johnson assured a group of black politicans that he was doing his best to put through another civil rights package strengthening federal authority to end discrimination in housing and in jury service, and to speed the end of segregation in the public schools. He broke out one of his favorite Texas aphorisms: "We haven't gone near as far as we're going to go in the next two years of my office, if the good Lord is willing and the creeks don't rise." But the creeks were already out of their banks. Johnson tried, but he couldn't hold wavering Democratic moderates, and Everett Dirksen came unhitched; the administration package died in the Senate ten votes short of cloture. In the 1967 State of the Union message civil rights drew only forty-five words, and these in passing as the president urged federal funds for a Safe Streets and Crime Control Act. "Our country's laws must be respected," he said. "Order must be maintained."

The war had become the overwhelming issue. If the radicals continued to make the most noise and provide the most sensational headlines and television film clips, a swelling tide of middle-class Americans were responding to demands for settlement of the conflict being voiced in the most respectable circles, including the pulpits of leading churches. Surburban matrons paraded sedately through quiet streets to hold candlelight vigils. Ken Galbraith, explaining his absence from these demonstrations, said, "My instinct is to express myself within the framework of the political process. I haven't marched; I don't carry signs. I have a certain asymmetric effect on parades." Hutchins, who was just short of Galbraith's six feet six, could have used the same excuse. I didn't have the altitude, but I was affected by a deterrent of my own—a growing aversion to the manner in which white middle-class parents were supporting the efforts of their sons to avoid military service, even to the extent of financing flight to Canada when local draft boards got tough on claims for educational deferment.

It was no longer possible to distinguish those motivated by opposition to the war on moral grounds from those who were simply avoiding a certainly unpleasant and possibly dangerous duty. "I've got these heavy questions now," a long-haired student at UC Santa Cruz confided to Art Seidenbaum, who published a collection of profiles of student activists in 1969. "I'm very far to the left, but I'm also a coward, a physical coward. I was arrested once, at the Humphrey demonstration, dressed as a saint, and I only got out of it because I was white and middle class and my parents cared enough." In an introduction to Seidenbaum's *Confrontation on Campus*, I wrote:

These, of course, are doubts that have always plagued the young. Most members of the preceding generation settled the question of personal cowardice in one of the traditional rites of manhood and sources of community: armed combat. This student generation, with at least the passive support of most of their elders, have rejected the initiation. They have condemned the tragic misadventure in Vietnam and their resistance has had a great deal to do with its ultimate winding down. But the distant war in some important ways may have wounded the well-to-do hedonists who stayed out of it even more grievously than it did the poor and black who have done most of the fighting.

There was no blinking the fact that the dead and wounded in Vietnam were for the most part blacks, Southern rednecks, and boys from ethnic neighborhoods—loyal Americans, that is, devoid of the affluence and influence that made draft evasion possible and even fashionable. The usual political division was blurred as the mounting cost of the conflict began to adversely affect businessmen not primarily engaged in providing military supplies; the most effective demand for an end to the war came from those normally on the Right, and the most effective support for its continuation until victory was achieved from those usually counted on the Left, as exemplified by perhaps the most vociferous proponent of Lyndon Johnson's hard line, Pres. George Meany of the AFL-CIO.

THROUGHOUT 1967 the indefatigable Allard Lowenstein beat the bushes trying to find a legitimate antiwar candidate to run against Lyndon Johnson in the Democratic primaries. To that end he toured the campuses, working to split the moderate student majority away from the radical SDS fringe. He enjoyed considerable success, and when he finally found a senior senator willing to make the run, his Conference of Concerned Democrats had available a ready-made, energetic, short-haired volunteer army ready to go doorbell-ringing in the primary states. The man he finally enlisted was Eugene McCarthy, the brilliant, iconoclastic Minnesotan who, from his seat on the Foreign Relations Committee, had become an outspoken critic of Vietnam policy. On November 30, McCarthy announced that he would enter selected primaries, including California's. I had seen a good deal of him in the years since we worked together in the Stevenson campaigns and I had no hesitation when he asked if I could support him.

I was then chairman of the advisory council of the California Democratic Party, a fairly high-powered group, most of whom shared my views on Vietnam. When I endorsed McCarthy, the White House sent word to Charles Warren, the California state chairman, to cut us loose from our party moorings, which he quite efficiently did. Another of my old friends, Blair Clark, former director of CBS News, became McCarthy's campaign manager, and I joined him for a swing with the candidate from Sacramento to San Francisco and down to San Diego. The turnout was impressive, although McCarthy, in conventional terms, wasn't.

The senator was the quintessential intellectual, equipped with a sharp wit and, when he bothered to use it, considerable charm. But the mechanics of the campaign bored him, and so did most of the people he was supposed to spend time wooing. However, the enthusiasm of his army of student supporters, who had sloughed off their counterculture trappings to "come clean for Gene," carried him to a surprise showing in the first primary on March 12 in New Hampshire where he won 42.2 percent of the vote and twenty out of twenty-four convention delegates.

This was not exactly a clear mandate to halt the war in Vietnam, but such a turnout for so lethargic a candidate represented a solid vote against Lyndon Johnson—so much so that Robert Kennedy, now U.S. senator from New York, announced as an antiwar candidate, and was promptly endorsed by Martin Luther King. Reaction to the Kennedy entry was mixed. McCarthy loyalists were outraged, but others in the anti-Vietnam vanguard professed to see evidence that the impetuous pragmatist had matured into a dedicated statesman.

I had spent a long day with this "new Bobby" a few months before in the course of a remarkable dialogue on the nuts-and-bolts of desegregation. The senator joined Robert Hutchins and me in New York for two extended sessions with Kenneth Clark, the black psychologist; Oscar Lewis, an anthropologist who specialized in the culture of poverty; and Neil V. Sullivan, who operated an extensive desegregation program as superintendent of schools in Berkeley. The transcripts of these sessions reveal Kennedy as a discerning critic of programs he had launched in full fervor in his earlier incarnation—notably Harlem Youth Opportunities Unlimited, which had been conceived as an exercise in federally financed participatory democracy.

Ken Clark, who had been a prime mover in HARYOU, now proclaimed the undertaking an expensive failure: "We transferred to the antipoverty program the inflationary manners of the educational establishment—salaries rather than services. If the day of reckoning comes when there is a tough, objective reexamination . . . a substantial number of these people will have to get back to reality." Kennedy agreed. "Twelve hundred people are in jobs at very inflated rates and they are not accomplishing anything," he said, and went on to a conclusion that would have echoes twelve years later in the presidential campaign of Ronald Reagan. "The schools can flunk students, but if we graded the schools we'd flunk them. . . . If we start examining what is happening to the money we would necessarily have to examine the school itself. A hell of a lot of money is involved. I'm willing to make a fuss if it will accomplish some good."

None of this came through when he took to the campaign trail and moved ahead of Gene McCarthy on a wave of passionate response from the young and disaffected. Harris Wofford, who traveled with him, thought that he "had come to see that the Enemy Within America was the enemy within him, and that he had done as well in taming the savageness in men and in himself as anyone I knew." An erstwhile critic who became a good friend, Anthony Lewis, agreed: "He changed— he grew—more than anyone I have known." But another veteran Washington commentator, William V. Shannon, found him guilty of romanticizing the youth movement at the expense of the substance of his campaign, presenting "such an astonishing perspective on public affairs it [was] hard to say on the basis of it whether Kennedy [was] seeking the presidency or the leadership of a new Children's Crusade."

BILL BAGGS, who was close to the Kennedys, and I were removed from the increasingly bitter competition between the embattled Irishmen by a message indicating that Hanoi would like to reestablish the contact disrupted when the Johnson administration openly attempted to sabotage *Pacem in Terris II* in Geneva. The State Department was interested, if hardly enthusiastic, and we again agreed that we would keep our

journey secret until we had returned and reported the results
—and, as a matter of importance to us, had a chance to
appraise the official reaction. In late March we made the long
swing through Southeast Asia and were in the North Vietnamese capital when, on March 31, Lyndon Johnson made his
surprise announcement that he was unilaterally curtailing the
aerial war, implying that he was prepared to meet Ho Chi
Minh's earlier terms for negotiation, and as a manifest of good
faith, was withdrawing as a candidate for reelection. We were
able to reassure the skeptical Vietnamese that to a man of
Johnson's ego this was an act of political immolation that must
be taken seriously and we brought out to the United States
embassy in Vientiane, Laos, the official *aide-mémoire* that opened
the way for the Paris peace talks.

On our last day in Hanoi our nominal host, Hoang Tung,
editor of the government newspaper, *Nham Dan*, came to the
villa where we were quartered to gently inform us that Martin
Luther King had been assassinated in Memphis, and that racial
violence was erupting across the country. Our reaction was set
down in the log of the journey that was the basis of the book
Mission to Hanoi that Baggs and I co-authored:

We were, in that dim dining room with its awkward French bourgeois
furnishing, literally on the other side of the globe from the scene of
the gentle King's death, and it felt as though we were on the far side
of the moon.

We had both known King well . . . and we could hear him again
at *Pacem in Terris* in Geneva, proclaiming in his measured, prophetic
tones, "I criticize America because I love her, and because I want to
see her stand as the moral example of the world." He had gone on to
indict his country for launching a war in Vietnam that has "exacerbat-
ed hatred between continents, and, worse still, between races." And at
Geneva he had concluded with words singularly fitting for this place
on this day:

". . . North Vietnam and/or the National Liberation Front . . .
may have understandable reasons to be suspicious, [but] life and
history give eloquent testimony to the fact that conflicts are never
resolved without trustful give-and-take on both sides."

We were asked to fly straight through to Washington, and
did so with only a brief stop to be brought up to date at the
embassy in Tokyo, where for the first time we learned the

details of the tragedy. It followed a march of striking Memphis sanitation workers in which young blacks defied King's instructions and converted the peaceful protest into a street brawl, shouting, "King is not our leader! We want Carmichael!" Andy Young reported he had never seen King so depressed and discouraged. But he rallied, and in a rousing, prophetic sermon the night before the white assassin's bullet brought him down, he told how the Lord had taken him to the mountaintop. "Like anybody else, I would like to live a long life," he told the faithful, in the familiar rhythmic cadence. "But I'm not concerned about that now. I just want to do God's will. And he's allowed me to go up to the mountain. And I've looked over and I've seen the Promised Land. I may not get there with you, but I want you to know tonight that we as a people will get to the Promised Land. . . ."

In a hundred cities and towns across the country King's murder was memorialized in the way that would have pained him most, with a wave of rioting that turned out thirty-four thousand National Guardsmen and twenty-one thousand federal troops to assist the police in restoring order, and cost the lives of forty-six persons, forty-two of them black. Worst hit of all was Washington. When Baggs and I landed at Dulles airport a State Department aide took us off the plane at the ramp to avoid the press. On a warm, bright afternoon we gazed through the haze of our fatigue upon a spectacle Americans had not seen since a detachment of Confederate cavalry rode across the Potomac to find that the besieged federal government had decamped and, fearing a trap, rode back across the river again. Now a curfew was being enforced to halt the arson and lotting perpetrated in the name of the apostle of nonviolence:

We rolled in awed silence down the broad avenues, past the White House, up 16th Street to our hotel in the heart of the downtown district. An occasional police car prowled past, or a military personnel carrier with armed troops, but nothing else moved. Down the whole length of 16th, from Lafayette Square to Scott Circle, past the grand hotels, the Soviet Embassy, the University Club, only one pedestrian was in sight, a single defiant Negro with no one to accost and, until a patrol car came by, no one to accost him.

Violence abroad, as Martin Luther King always said it would, had come home.

27

The Fires Die Down

*T*he fires of organized rebellion burned out with the advent of the seventies, leaving only a sullen glow in the black ghettoes. The Movement's last great television extravaganza was staged in Chicago at the 1968 Democratic National Convention, and achieved a record audience rating. In the first flush of near hysterical media reaction one of its principal perpetrators, Jerry Rubin, claimed a famous victory: "We wanted exactly what happened. . . . We wanted to create a situation in which the Chicago police and the Daley administration and the federal government and the United States would self-destruct." But the ultimate self-destruction was that of The Movement.

At Chicago the serious leaders of the anti–Vietnam War Mobilization were soon wholly eclipsed by Rubin and his clownish sidekick, Abbie Hoffman. These self-appointed gurus of the Youth International Party set the tone for the confrontation with Mayor Daley and his police. The Yippie faction professed to represent an amalgamation of the counterculture and the revolution, but it was in fact a public relations exercise based on a kind of running practical joke. "I was once in the New Left but I outgrew it," Hoffman explained. "I don't like the concept of a movement built on sacrifice, dedication, responsibility, anger, frustration and guilt. . . . You want to have more fun, you want to get laid more. . . ."

Remarkably, these antic hedonists were taken seriously on both the Left and Right. In *The Armies of the Night* Norman Mailer described Rubin as "the most militant, unpredictable, creative—therefore dangerous—hippie-oriented leader available on the New Left." Mayor Daley believed him when he announced that the Yippies were going to put LSD in the municipal water supply, and send thousands of naked youngsters running through downtown streets. And Rubin and Hoffman outraged his Irish puritan sensibilities with calculated needling—as when they published a list of demands that included such familiar items as the legalization of marijuana and also noted, "We believe that people should fuck all the time, anytime, whomever they want." When the Democratic delegates arrived, Daley had twelve thousand city police on twelve-hour shifts, with five thousand National Guardsmen and six thousand army troops standing by in reserve.

The Mobilization's leadership was fragmented when the middle-aged pacifist, David Dellinger, insisted on a policy of nonviolence. Tom Hayden and Rennie Davis more or less concurred, but the other SDS leaders refused to go along. The Black Panthers also boycotted the Mobe, and few blacks were to be seen at any time during subsequent encounters with the police. Fewer than two thousand people turned out for the opening Yippie Festival of Life; at least half were sightseers, and a goodly number were undercover police. But when the motley band moved downtown to Grant Park, across the street from convention headquarters at the Conrad Hilton Hotel, the magnifying lens of television was waiting.

"Rubin understood that a bottomless bank account could not buy the services that TV, if properly exploited, would furnish free," Milton Viorst wrote in *Fire in the Streets*. "Though it was often said that he was a media creation, and it was true, he himself directed the media in the creative process." Rubin, who entered The Movement as a graduate student at Berkeley, had worked on a Cincinnati newspaper during his undergraduate years, and there he had begun to sense the possibilities of media manipulation:

It was a conscious thing, and I guess it came from an intuitive understanding. You know, stopping troop trains, a little violence, students and police clashing on the railroad tracks. The media loved it.

They exaggerated the event on television, and then the papers exaggerated it some more. The people who read it or saw it exaggerated it even more when they talked about it to others. The process was like a riot, with thousands of people transmitting emotions from one to the other, and the emotions growing. They created myths, saying, "Wow, that's exciting!" Everybody wanted to do what we were doing in Berkeley, and from that the movement grew.

I was in Chicago for the convention, and in line of duty wound up in the middle of what was, with justice, called a police riot. I included my summary impression in a *Center Magazine* "Symposium on the Limits of Dissent":

If one takes Rubin seriously one might well share the alarms of Mayor Daley—who says he did what he did because he had information that assassins were abroad in his city, and that the very citadels of officialdom were threatened with assault and disruption. The consensus of the battle-scarred press, however, was that there were no organized strong-arm squads in the thin ranks of the Armies of the Night, and that the active *provocateurs* probably numbered no more than forty—and were armed against the Mace and the tear gas and nightsticks with nothing more lethal than stink bombs and an occasional extemporaneous brickbat.

Despite the lurid pictures on the nation's television screens the evidence is that both sides acted with remarkable restraint, except for one encounter outside the Hilton when the police commanders on the ground lost control, if in fact they tried to exercise it. I was there when their men charged into a crowd of young demonstrators swinging their billy clubs, and might well have wound up in a paddy wagon myself had I not been wearing press credentials. Not a single shot was fired on either side; fire hoses were never used; no one was killed or injured seriously enough to require hospitalization; the extent of the known casualties was 192 policemen treated for bruises and 425 demonstrators who received similar ministrations at the Mobilization's first aid stations.

But there was a harbinger of real tragedy to come. When I crossed over into Grant Park with Gene McCarthy on the last night of the demonstrations, after National Guard troops had replaced the blue-helmeted Chicago police, it suddenly struck me that the confrontation was now confined to one side of the generation gap:

The soldiers standing shoulder to shoulder with their rifles across their chests were of an age with those who writhed along their front scattering taunts and jeers and obscene invitations. These were boys from Skokie and Peoria and East St. Louis, largely bypassed by the affluence that underwrites a protest movement that has taken on the sound of revolution but so far has not achieved much more reality than the television dramas upon which all these young were suckled.

Here was the limit of dissent. The obtuseness of the Mayor and the brutality of his police were facts. But it was also a fact that no government could allow dissidents to disrupt its vital processes. There would always be a line somewhere manned by very young men in combat fatigues under orders to hold at any cost—and if they were pressed long enough and hard enough the time would come when the elevated gun barrels would come down and live rounds would slide home. This would be the ultimate tragedy, and the ultimate irony, for if reality ever overtakes the rhetoric the old and corrupt will be somewhere else when the young provide their own executioners. . . .

The gun barrels came down on May 4, 1970, on the campus of Kent State University. Seconds later four students were dead and nine wounded. Viorst wrote: ". . . the 1960s, as suddenly as they began at Greensboro, ended at Kent State. That is not to say that the counterculture vanished, or that radicalism died. . . . But, as an era when masses of people, most of them young, regularly took to the streets to challenge the practices of society, the 1960s ended with a thirteen-second fusillade in a small Ohio town. The decade ended because the civil rights movement, which was responsible for its conception, no longer contributed the seed to enrich it. . . ."

HAD Bobby Kennedy not been assassinated in Los Angeles after winning the California primary, his charisma might well have carried him all the way to the White House. It seems likely the debacle at Chicago, which so damaged the chances of the Democratic nominee, Hubert Humphrey, would have been avoided. Jerry Rubin wrote in *Do It!* that he had decided to call off the Yippie Festival of Life after Kennedy entered the race: "Some Yippies have hidden fancies of Robert Kennedy smoking pot in the White House." He changed his mind after Kennedy's death, providing a fair sample of his style with the explanation, "Sirhan Sirhan is a Yippie."

The presidential contest between Hubert Humphrey and Richard Nixon effectively disenfranchised those who were passionately committed to the antiwar cause and left The Movement without attraction for most of the young. In mid-1969 the hard core left in the SDS split between an openly Marxist faction that called itself "Progressive Labor" and what was to become an underground terrorist operation taking its name from a Bob Dylan song "Subterranean Homesick Blues," which says, "You Don't Need a Weatherman to Tell Which Way the Wind Blows." Progressive Labor took the Old Left line that the future lay with the working class, while the Third Worlders, who would provide the cadre for the Weathermen, were Maoists who exalted racial conflict as the core of the revolution. The P. L. leaders dismissed racism, and the rising demand for women's liberation, as divisive issues that would alienate workers; the Third Worlders wanted to make common cause with the violence-prone Black Panthers.

The showdown came at a raucous SDS convention in Chicago in June 1969. The Third Worlders, waving Chairman Mao's little red book, formed into a Weathermen caucus led by Bernardine Dohrn and Mark Rudd, who would soon go underground. The Black Panthers were on a parallel track. Stokeley Carmichael and James Forman quit in protest against collaboration with the "honky" SDS. Now centered in Oakland under the leadership of Bobby Seale and Huey P. Newton, the Panthers took on a paramilitary character, dressing in leather jackets and black berets and brandishing rifles at some of their protest rallies.

The Panthers' primary contribution to the radical cause was the generation of a series of purported martyrs as their leaders were systematically hauled off to jail. When Newton was convicted after a shoot-out with the Oakland police, the cry "Free Huey" echoed throughout what was left of The Movement. For a few years the black militants were the superstars at "radical chic" fund-raising affairs, and the symbol of insurrection in the eyes of right wing conservatives. *Newsweek* called them "the bad niggers of white America's nightmares," and in 1970 J. Edgar Hoover provided what they considered an accolade, terming them "the most dangerous and violence-prone of all extremist groups."

At their high point, the Panthers claimed a membership of three thousand to four thousand working out of forty storefront headquarters around the country. The party structure was thoroughly infiltrated by the FBI and local police "Red Squads," and the leaders and their prominent white supporters became prime targets of the Cointelpro operation Hoover ordered to discredit self-proclaimed revolutionaries through whatever dirty tricks his agents could devise—including tapes allegedly recording the sounds Martin Luther King made in bed with a woman, which the bureau tried to peddle to the media and, failing that, passed on to Mrs. King. This pressure, coupled with the internal tensions of such a frenetic movement, decimated the Panthers. By 1975 most of the headquarters were closed and the leaders scattered—Huey Newton in Cuba and Eldridge Cleaver in Paris were both avoiding criminal charges back home; Bobby Seale had resigned from the party under circumstances no one would discuss; Jonathan Jackson, Fred Hampton, and a score of others were dead.

Before the decade was out most of the black radical refugees had come home and gone straight. Bobby Seale ran for mayor of Oakland. In 1978 H. Rap Brown, who missed the Panther movement while serving a five-year prison sentence for armed robbery, was running a neighborhood grocery store in Atlanta. And Cleaver, author of the best-selling *Soul on Ice*, had become a born-again Christian and would ultimately wind up as a supporter of the Reverend Sun Myung Moon's Unification Church.

NOT all recanted. When he was heard from at all after he acquired an African wife and moved to Guinea, Stokeley Carmichael spoke as head of the All-African People's Revolutionary Party. Angela Davis was never to abandon the Marxist philosophy she absorbed as a graduate student under Herbert Marcuse; in the 1980 election she appeared on the Communist Party ticket as running mate for the perennial presidential candidate, Gus Hall. But now, back in the teaching profession at San Francisco State University, her public behavior was as conventional as that of the survivors of the Old Left who also enjoyed free passage in academia. About the only connection with her days of rage was the National Alliance Against Racism and Political Repression to which she still donated the $1,000 fees received when she went lecturing on other campuses. This depository was successor to the Angela Davis Defense Fund created in 1972 by a shower of offerings when the cry "Free Angela" reverberated around the radical-chic cocktail circuit when she faced trial in connection with a courtroom kidnapping and shoot-out in San Rafael that left the judge and three others dead in an abortive effort to force the release of the "Soledad Brothers" from a California prison.

This kind of derring-do had a far more profound effect outside the black community than it did within it. The nightmares of respectable black Americans were also haunted by "bad niggers"—and firsthand experience reminded them that victims of the Black Panthers were by no means all of the other race. In Los Angeles there was a spectacular shoot-out with Ron Karenga's Black Nationalists, and at Oakland an execution squad of the Symbionese Liberation Army gunned down a respected black school official in a parking lot. In the crime-ridden ghettoes it hardly seemed prudent to declare war on the entire criminal justice system and in effect challenge the police to a test of arms.

A survivor of the period when the extremist remnant of The Movement went underground and adopted outright terrorist tactics gave the black militants full credit as preceptors: "The Panthers set the tone for revolution in America at the end of the '60s," Susan Stern wrote in her memoir, *With the Weathermen*. "All the slogans, most of the gravitation toward Mao Tse-tung, the militaristic approach, all came from the Black Panthers. . . . They coined the fact for us that 'power comes from the barrel of a gun.' They gave white radicals a focus for their sprouting hatred—the pigs [police]."

Middle-class backlash against the excesses of black militants and their white running mates is usually listed as a prime factor in Richard Nixon's election to the presidency. Yet one of the most remarkable aspects of the period was the tolerance of rank-and-file citizens for the unbridled rhetorical assault upon their values and life-style, even when it was accompanied by threats to their lives and property. There was an automatic response in kind from the opposite extreme, and it is clear that by temperament Nixon belonged with the hard-line advocates of repression in the name of law and order. But it was not until well into his first term that he began to make a major issue of the manner in which the criminal justice system set free all manner of black and white dissidents. There was no great public outcry from the constituency Nixon claimed for himself —middle America—when the case against the Chicago Eight was dismissed on appeal. A jury found Angela Davis not guilty, and juries, judges, or appelate courts vindicated the heretical conduct of defendants enshrined in the annals of The Movement as the Harrisburg Seven, the Camden Seventeen, the Seattle Seven, the Kansas City Four, the Evanston Four, and the Gainesville Eight.

Nixon's posture in his 1968 run for the White House was that of a healer. He explained that he had taken the theme of his campaign from a sign held aloft by a thirteen-year-old schoolgirl at an Ohio rally: "Bring Us Together." This was, of course, at variance with his previous record as a bitterly divisive partisan, and his overwhelming lead in the opinion polls began to shrink when Hubert Humphrey belatedly went on the offensive. The narrow Republican victory over a divided Democratic Party could not be construed as a mandate of any kind so far as domestic policies were concerned. Nixon carried a comfortable majority in the electoral college, but he received only a minority of the popular vote: 43.4 percent against Humphrey's 42.7 percent. Another 13.5 percent and 45 electoral votes in the South went to the ultra-Right American Independent party ticket headed by George Wallace with Gen. Curtis LeMay as his running mate.

James Reston of the *New York Times* was to write of Nixon, "There is scarcely a noble principle in the American Constitution that he hasn't defended in theory or defied in practice." This was profoundly true of his record on racial matters, so much so, the only feasible method of appraising it was to follow the advice of his campaign manager, John Mitchell, who told a group of Southern black leaders: "Watch what we do, not what we say." What the president said in the opening months of his administration seemed to support the insistence of his media spokesmen that a "New Nixon" had emerged from the purgatory of his past defeats, but experienced Nixon-watchers found it prudent to reserve judgment until he began to translate the generalities of the campaign into specifics.

If Nixon had toned down his usual disdain for civil liberties in his run for the White House he had followed the standard conservative line in attacking the Great Society effort to extend civil rights for blacks to improve their prospects for economic advancement. "For the past five years," he charged, "we have been deluged by government programs for the unemployed, programs for cities, programs for the poor, and we have reaped from these programs an ugly harvest of frustration, violence, and failure across the land."

Yet the putative New Nixon seemed to be in evidence when the president appeared before the National Governors Conference to unveil a package of proposed changes in the welfare system, citing it as the cornerstone of a "New Federalism." The response among those who knew federalism best was near unanimous endorsement of the generalized reform program. The governors adopted a resolution by the leader of Republican liberals, Nelson Rockefeller of New York, urging Washington to take over the welfare responsibility lock, stock, and administration; support for states' rights had dwindled to the lone vote of Lester Maddox of Georgia, who presumably wanted welfare abolished altogether.

"There's irony in it, of course," said the New York City welfare commissioner, Mitchell I. Ginsberg. "Here, coming from a Republican, is something that amounts to a guaranteed annual income. We'll have to call it something else, naturally. Something to make it sound like the free enterprise system. . . . We'll have to move toward compulsory national health insurance, too, and Washington will have to dream up something to call that. But I don't give a damn what they're called as long as they get done."

He bespoke the sentiment of most of the liberals and mainline black leaders, who supported existing welfare programs in principle but had a good deal of criticism of them in practice—much of it stemming from the inequities and inefficiencies of administration divided among three levels of federal, state, and local government. By the time Lyndon Johnson left town there was fairly widespread disillusionment with his Great Society, which, in terms of the original grand design, remained financially undernourished. After the start-up phase, Sargent Shriver had expected his annual budget to increase to the range of $16 billion. "We ended up with 2 billion," he recalled, with Johnson explaining that "Bob McNamara had assured him they would spend 20 billion in Vietnam and the war would be done by December 1966. The idea was that we had to fight *this* war this year. Next year we'd get to the war on poverty. I think I knew then that 'next year' wasn't going to come."

But there were also failures that arose from the very

idealism of the OEO operation, which adopted the principle of "maximum feasible participation" by the poor in the management of community action programs. "It got out of hand," conceded Wilbur J. Cohen, Johnson's HEW secretary and loyal supporter. Kenneth Clark explained why:

The conflict between the newly stimulated, indigenous poor and entrenched political power brokers and controllers of political systems in local communities soon emerged as a major problem which had not been anticipated or prepared for. . . . Antipoverty programs became political pork-barrel-type programs and were taken over by sophisticated middle-class bureaucrats. In some cases upwardly mobile working-class individuals became either the products of or the puppets of the more sophisticated middle-class political controllers of these programs. Sometimes the upwardly mobile indigenous became sophisticated antipoverty hustlers.

The proposal to channel federal dollars directly to welfare recipients, eliminating much of the cumbersome and intrusive social service bureaucracy and the local power brokers, originated with a surprise White House staff appointee—Daniel Patrick Moynihan, a colorful Harvard sociologist who had served as assistant secretary of labor under Kennedy and Johnson. As the Nixon welfare program was translated into proposed legislation, it began to appear that the New Federalism package would pare the rolls and reduce the level of income for those who remained on them, and the suspicion grew that this was the president's real intention. Liberal and black support began to fall away, and Moynihan complained that his one-time compatriots were selling him and his program down the river. By the time the New Federalism disappeared from the White House legislative agenda, Moynihan was well launched on the course that would make him an ornament of what came to be called the "neo-conservative movement," and he was inspired to genuinely outrage the civil rights leadership with the suggestion that what the black ghettoes really needed was a period of benign neglect. Meanwhile, the president was systematically gutting Great Society programs by cutting back financial support and placing them in the charge of administrators fundamentally unsympathetic to their purpose.

Nixon's predecessor, relieving the tedium of retirement down on the ranch by regaling Doris Kearns with the remarkable soliloquies she recorded in *Lyndon Johnson and the American Dream*, expressed his own outrage at what was going on in Washington. He likened the Great Society to a beautiful daughter who was just beginning to get her natural growth. He could see her "getting thinner and thinner and uglier and uglier all the time; now her bones are beginning to stick out and her wrinkles are beginning to show. Soon she'll be so ugly that the American people will refuse to look at her; they'll stick her in a closet and hide her away and there she'll die." If that seems fanciful, and even a trifle paranoid, Nixon's actions bore him out. "There's a story in the paper every day about him slashing another one of my Great Society programs," the former president said, adding a characteristic Johnsonian touch: "I can just see him waking up in the morning, making that victory sign of his and deciding which program to kill."

Less jaundiced observers began to recognize the New Federalism as a device to sidestep the Supreme Court and reinstate the Old Federalism. The great battles of the Kennedy and Johnson years had been fought in Congress to obtain enforcement powers to insure federal intervention when local authorities refused to protect or advance the rights of blacks. President Nixon's signal to the Hill was full speed astern. By the beginning of his second term in the White House he had cemented a working relationship with the congressional segregationist bloc by acceding to their demand that he fire the civil rights enforcement chief at HEW. Leon Panetta's offense was carrying out his statutory duty to withhold federal funds from schools defying court-ordered desegregation. He departed the federal service with a valedictory statement that applied across the whole of the civil rights front:

Desegregated education has been upheld as legal principle, it has been pursued as public policy, with more success than many will admit, and it should not be undone where it is successful merely because of the rabid screams of those who make political hay out of racial antagonism . . . We need leadership to stand up and say the issue is obedience to law, the issue is a fair break for kids who have lost time and time again because of rank discrimination, the issue is the future of this nation's race relations. . . .

That kind of leadership was to be missing from the executive branch for another seven years, and Nixon was trying to remove it from the Supreme Court—as evidenced by the first two names he sent up for confirmation, those of Southerners presumably willing to reverse the trends of the Warren Court. In the meantime, the president worked on the Great Society Programs at the point where they were most vulnerable.

ALTHOUGH the term did not come into general usage until later, the necessity for "affirmative action" by the executive and legislative branches to advance desegregation was implicit in *Brown.* The Supreme Court mandated dismantling the de jure structure of segregated education in the South, but there was no requirement for action until black patrons initiated a lawsuit. And if local school officials continued to stall—as the great majority of them did—there would be no effective relief until a district judge took charge of the system and specified action to end the isolation of children in all-black schools. There was some movement toward voluntary compliance in districts where the proportion of blacks to whites was low, primarily in the Upper South and border states, but the great majority of black children continued to go to school, as they always had, among their own kind.

It was not until ten years later that Congress finally moved, at Lyndon Johnson's urging, to give the government a positive role in ending educational inequality as defined by the Court. The 1964 Civil Rights Act forbade the payment of federal aid to school districts that continued discriminatory practices and authorized the Justice Department to bring civil rights cases on its own motion. Vigorous enforcement by Johnson appointees in Justice and HEW, which administered the school funds, rapidly brought most Southern school districts into compliance. Within three years more than half the black children in the Southern states were attending predominantly white schools, and the process of desegregation was continuing with only minor resistance.

The primary means of accomplishing the redistribution of school population was busing. In the rural areas the adjustment was fairly simple, since a transportation network already served consolidated schools—often hauling black children past white schools in order to deposit them at segregated facilities much farther away from their homes. And busing was feasible, and relatively inexpensive, in most of the Southern cities, which were small enough so that children did not have to be carried inordinate distances in order to meet the standards of racial balance established by the courts. It was true, as some parents complained, that busing violated the traditional concept of the neighborhood school. But it was also true that there was no other practicable means of attaining the goal of desegregation in urban areas where racially separate schools were the product of patterns of residential segregation—the situation affecting most blacks living outside the South.

It is ironic that busing was certified as the sovereign remedy for school segregation not by the Warren Court but in a unanimous opinion signed by Richard Nixon's appointee, Chief Justice Warren Burger. The Burger Court held that within an existing school district proper racial balance required pupil transfer to eliminate de facto segregation—that is, assignment of black children to all-black schools not because of law but because of residence. This brought the prospect of court-ordered busing to the major cities of the North and West, where less than 30 percent of black children were enrolled in predominantly white schools. The result was noted in *Must We Bus?*, the Brookings Institution publication summarizing a decade of intensive research by Gary Orfield:

Shortly before the courts began to require citywide desegregation a new administration took office and brought the most sudden shift on civil rights policy in the century. President Nixon had in his campaign promised to restrain HEW's efforts in the South and to produce a more conservative Justice Department and Supreme Court. The conflict between the judicial requirements for busing and the President's active leadership of anti-busing forces produced a severe institutional crisis in HEW and Justice. Bureaucracies created to enforce civil rights laws found themselves with controversial responsibilities in a political climate that had suddenly changed.

Richard Nixon, the master of political duplicity, provided the rhetoric a substantial majority of non-Southern whites were soon using to denounce busing while still professing full sympathy for the goal of desegregation. The drive for equality in education, the president said in his 1972 message to Congress, had actually been set back, "a classic case of the remedy for one evil creating another evil." The public school had once been the nation's symbol of hope, but "in too many communities today it has become the symbol of helplessness, frustration, and outrage—of a wrenching of children away from their families, and from the schools their families may have moved to be near, and sending them arbitrarily to others far distant."

Given this clear signal from the president, *busing* became the code word conservatives in Congress used in their campaign to undercut the previous majority support for civil rights legislation. The 1968 fair housing act was the last positive step toward integration enacted on the Hill, and it was so watered down as to have little effect. In the next decade every session of Congress saw efforts to restrain school desegregation in the major cities of the North and West, where, with the exception of Boston, it had never been undertaken except on a limited, usually voluntary, basis. It was an era of double-talk in which most Americans continued to ignore the walled-in pockets of poverty in the inner cities that were causing accelerated deterioration of the American metropolis. Orfield wrote:

After a tumultuous decade of social and cultural change, a nation that had been torn by war, stunned by urban crisis, and shaken by assassinations was not prepared to recognize or cope with metropolitan apartheid. People denied that the problem existed, claimed that it was being solved, argued that blacks and Hispanics liked segregation anyway, or most often attacked the proposed solutions.

When the Los Angeles school district, the nation's second largest and one of the most thoroughly segregated, came under court order to initiate busing, I felt a distinct sense of déjà vu. Although couched in different terms, the objections to the only feasible means of achieving desegregation were those I had heard in Little Rock twenty years before, and they were being offered by laid-back Californians who prided themselves on having established the most open society known to man—and had seemed to prove it by electing as their governor a youthful alumnus of The Movement, Jerry Brown.

28

The Southern Strategy

The president who came to office professing an
ambition to pull the nation together sought reelection through a device deliberately designed to pull the electorate apart. What came to be called the "Southern Strategy" was
conceived in the course of the 1968 Republican campaign, but
was never unveiled because George Wallace preempted its basic
elements with his appeal to antiestablishment racists, who
typically were also hard-line advocates of total military victory
in Vietnam. Since Lyndon Johnson had made the Democrats
the "war party," and Hubert Humphrey could never extricate
himself from identification with the hawks, Nixon found it
expedient to pursue what seemed to be a soft, or at least a
muted line on both Vietnam and the so-called social question.
But as he prepared to enter the lists in 1972, he had at his side a
brash young strategist whose politics of polarization appealed
to Nixon's basic instincts.

Kevin Phillips first appeared on the national scene as the
occupant of a cubbyhole at John Mitchell's 1968 command post
on Park Avenue, across the street from Nixon headquarters.
Garry Wills encountered him there, and was impressed by his
candor. Phillips had become an expert on ethnic voting patterns in the Irish precincts of the Bronx, where he'd apprenticed in New York City politics. Now he was ready to extrapo-
late his findings into a national strategy. In *Nixon Agonistes* Wills
described how the engaging young lawyer elaborated on his
discovery of what he termed "the whole secret of politics—who
hates who."

In New York City, for instance, you make plans from certain rules of
exclusion—you can't get the Jews *and* the Catholics. The Liberal Party
was founded here for Jews opposing Catholics, and the Conservative
Party for Catholics fighting Jews. The same kind of basic decision has

to be made in national politics. The Civil War is over now; the parties don't have to compete for that little corner of the nation *we* live in. Who needs Manhattan when we can get the electoral votes of eleven Southern states? Put those together with the Farm Belt and the Rocky Mountains, and we don't need the big cities. We don't even want them. . . .

Nixon, Phillips figured, could write off the silk stocking Republicans—"those rich enough to stay in town and live in the safe areas, or to move only to the best suburbs, the red-hot types who go for Gene McCarthy; they have never felt the shove of fellow proles in the same block." Equally dispensable were the traditional Republican abolitionists, who were no longer of consequence even in their native habitat, New England. Phillips divined from his computer data that a new populism was emerging, one that came from the Right, not the Left as before. It would bring together the Catholic ethnics and the Protestant conservatives of the Sun Belt:

The clamor in the past has been from the urban or rural proletariat. But now "populism" is of the middle class, which feels exploited by the Establishment. Almost everyone in the productive segment of society considers himself middle-class now, and resents the exploitation of society's producers. This is not a movement *in favor of* laissez faire or any ideology; it is *opposed to* welfare and the Establishment.

Wills suggested that growth in black registration might throw off these calculations. "No, white Democrats will desert their party in droves the minute it becomes a black party," Phillips replied. "When white Southerners move, they move fast. Wallace is helping, too—in the long run. People will ease their way into the Republican Party by way of the American Independents." That, he pointed out, was the way Strom Thurmond had made the transition after his bolt to the Dixiecrats in 1948. "We'll get two-thirds to three-fourths of the Wallace vote in 1972," Phillips predicted.

It seemed to me quite likely that Wallace had become an active participant in the Southern Strategy when he declared himself a born-again Democrat and entered the 1972 presidential primaries. He conceded that he had no chance of winning the nomination against a field of no less than twelve fairly prominent contenders, and said he was out to rally a protest vote that would "send 'em a message." In Florida, where he confounded the pundits by coming in first, his appeal was the promise that a Wallace victory would insure that "President Nixon will do something to halt this busing in thirty days." It didn't take that long. Two days after the Florida primary the president proposed a moratorium on busing.

Kevin Phillips was probably correct in his assumption that Democrats who voted for Wallace in the primaries would cross over to vote for Nixon in the general election. But the Southern Strategy never had a real test in 1972, for another deranged gunman was stalking the presidential campaign trail, and at Laurel, Maryland, a bullet in his belly took the little Alabamian out of the race, and left him confined to a wheelchair for the rest of his life.

There was no real general election contest. In retrospect, it is evident that Nixon's handling of the Vietnam war, with its reckless incursion into Cambodia, only compounded the tragedy and added to the death toll, but by election time his so-called "Vietnamization" policy had reduced the American troop commitment and casualty rate, and Henry Kissinger announced from the Paris negotiating table that an honorable peace was in sight. Nixon was able to finesse the war issue and bill himself as the candidate of peace and detente, and his campaign appearances were so rigidly controlled by his media experts that his protestations were never effectively challenged.

The Democrats, fragmented by the debacle of four years before, yielded their nomination to the estimable George McGovern, of whom it would be said that he wanted to run for president in the worst way, and did. Nixon carried 60 percent of the popular vote and the electoral votes of forty-nine states—which would have been counted a landslide except for the fact that only 55 percent of the registered voters went to the polls, and the winner's personal mandate was left in question when the Democrats held onto their majority in the House of Representatives and actually increased it in the Senate.

IN THE time left to him before Watergate drove him from office, Nixon was distracted by such items as the forced resignation of his boodling vice-president, Spiro Agnew, so he did not quite finish off OEO and its community action programs. His staff was still working on the vestiges of the Great Society to the end, however, and on his fifth day in the Oval Office, Agnew's unelected successor, Gerald Ford, had on his desk an action memorandum from Ken Cole, Nixon's domestic affairs chief. From 1969 onward, the memo noted, Nixon had considered OEO "inappropriate" and had provided for its termination in the 1974–75 budget; this would be "consistent with philosophy that Community Action is more properly a state/local program and save the Federal Government over $300,000,000." Gerald Ford promptly put his initials in the box indicating approval.

No one had any reason to expect otherwise. The open, unassuming personal style of the amiable Ford had automatically altered the bunker mentality the White House acquired under the hag-ridden Nixon, but if Ford had any ideas about changing direction they were not revealed during his brief tenure as the most accidental of presidents. As House minority leader he had delivered 85 to 90 percent of his party's votes in opposition to the Great Society. He achieved the same percentage in support of the Nixon Administration—and cheerfully ran such shabby errands for the White House as the abortive attempt to impeach Justice Douglas. In *A Ford, Not a Lincoln*, a title taken from the president's characterization of himself, Richard Reeves wrote:

Amendments, motions to recommit and other parliamentary parlor tricks make it possible for Rep. Ford to assert that he voted for final passage of every civil rights bill during his tenure. Or he can let people know that up until the final votes, he fought to block every piece of civil rights legislation. He did both. . . . Whatever Ford's deepest feelings about civil rights—and friends said he had no deep feelings either way—he was able and willing to use that issue and others to trade for the valuable status of having no enemies in his own party.

Back in Ford's home country in Michigan, in a speech at Troy, Reeves heard him bring up busing sixteen times in seventeen minutes without being asked, "repeatedly implying that the Democratic Party and any fellow-travelers were dedicated to dragging blue-eyed children into the blackest wilds." As president, Ford erected a public monument to his opposition to busing—now the code word for desegregation—when Mayor Kevin White of Boston asked for U.S. marshals to help control violent antintegration demonstrations in the Irish neighborhoods of South Boston. "The court decision in that case in my judgment was not the best solution to quality education in Boston," Ford said. "I respectfully disagree with the judge's order." This tacit endorsement by the president was hailed by the mob, and guaranteed continuation of the turmoil that would beset the old abolitionist seat for years to come.

In his 1976 State of the Union address, President Ford made no mention of the problems and needs of minorities, nor did the subject engage the covey of congressional Democrats when they readied their primary campaigns for the nomination. The Southern Strategy was in effect for the Republicans, and was reinforced by the fact that George Wallace, pointing out that Franklin Roosevelt had also campaigned from a wheelchair, again entered the Democratic primaries. Wallace was generally recognized by the politicians and the media as a negative force in national politics, a spoiler who could not be elected but who could arouse a passionate minority against any Democratic candidate.

It was now clear that a substantial majority of the voters accepted, if they did not actively support, the civil rights claims of the black minority—at least until they infringed directly upon their own interests. The prudent politician, then, made obeisance to racial equality in principle and avoided discussing the means of achieving it. A similar approach to all sensitive social issues, Reeves believed, accounted for the increasing blandness of national campaigns in the television era. "Most politicians, particularly incumbents, have nothing against apathy, boredom or disdain among the electorate," he wrote. "They don't need enthusiasm; what can kill them is an excited minority." Wallace, the spoiler, provided a case in point:

Over the past few years I have talked with almost every other Presidential-class American politician about the Alabama governor, and their assessments of him are just about identical. He is, in their minds, an ignorant and dangerous demagogue playing on the fears and darkest impulses of a segment of the nation. But even though national polls indicated that as many as two-thirds of the American people were strongly anti-Wallace, these judgments stayed locked inside the minds of Humphrey, the Kennedys, McGovern, Rockefeller. They said nothing—even when Wallace's national support was only at 10 percent and their united voices might have destroyed him.

The inertial two-thirds was not their problem; they were afraid of an aroused 10 percent.

The man who finally removed Wallace from the national scene was another Deep Southerner, Jimmy Carter, and in so doing the Georgian proved the Southern Strategy invalid. Southern voters who had crossed over to the Republicans in 1972 came back in droves in 1976—demonstrating that they had no reluctance in joining forces with the black politicans who were now holding office throughout the region. The once lily-white Democracy of the South had taken on a salt-and-pepper complexion, and when Wallace again broke out the antibusing banner in the Florida primary, the magic was gone. After routing Wallace in head-to-head confrontation before a Southern constituency, Jimmy Carter began to be taken seriously by the media and was on his way to the White House. Racism had not disappeared in the South, or anywhere else, but it had lost its utility as a be-all, end-all appeal for votes.

JIMMY CARTER was an enigma to most Americans, including those who voted for him, and he remained one during the four years he occupied the White House. In his public style he seemed to work at conforming to one of the standard Southern stereotypes—emphasizing the corn-pone accent and big smile, posturing against the small-town backdrop of Plains, Georgia, that not only looked like a television set but seemed to be populated by soap opera characters. In action, however, he came through as the dedicated graduate of Annapolis, a physicist and systems engineer whose acknowledged hero was the Jewish martinet, Adm. Hyman Rickover, father of the nuclear submarine fleet in which young Commander Carter served. He wore his Southern Baptist piety proudly, but professed—and I think held to, as best he could—broad social concerns that involved tolerance for those he presumably judged, by the standards he set for himself, as sinful and weak.

These contradictions so fascinated William Lee Miller, a former visiting fellow at the Center, that he subjected the unlikely candidate to examination from his perspective as a professor of religious history with a special interest in ethics. Miller, a Northern Presbyterian who said he was born, at most, once, summarized his conclusions in the title of his book, *Yankee from Georgia*. His initial skepticism was dispelled by protracted observation of Carter on the campaign trail and in the White House, and he came away convinced of the deep sincerity of the man he described as "the autobiographical President"—one who seemed to deal with the problems of the world only in the first person singular.

Miller found that this Southern Baptist displayed all the characteristics associated with the New England ethos; Carter acted on the traditional Yankee assumption that "life should be predictable, managed, planned. . . . Straighten things out; be competent; save money, save time; time is money. Save time, use it wisely, because for a Puritan to do so is Godly and for a Yankee to do so is remunerative." In Plains, the older values of the nation's simpler past had been preserved in amber: "When the Civil Rights revolution ended the long moral isolation of the South and burst open the regional crust, Brother Jimmy, the Puritan-Yankee deacon and warehouse owner, was ready to step forth into the world bearing the marks of an older, almost forgotten America."

Jimmy Carter came along after my time in the South, and I never knew him, or any of those in the closed inner circle who could claim intimacy with this essentially lonely man. Most of my old friends among the politicians and journalists disliked him. The political writers were particularly put off, as their counterparts in Washington would be when he came to the White House as a self-proclaimed outsider. "The 'interfering spirit of righteousness' in American religious culture has set on edge the teeth of most of the country's better writers," Miller observed, "including many who write about politics for newspapers."

But there was more to it than reaction to an excess of piety. The Southern leaders who had taken their stand for desegregation looked with suspicion upon Carter, a latecomer to their cause whose personal ambition prompted him to disrupt their strategy. In 1966 when he made his first race for governor, the Georgia moderates were trying to resurrect Ellis Arnall and Carter's surprisingly strong showing against their candidate in the first primary was credited with clearing the way for the ultimate election of the pick-handle segregationist, Lester

Maddox. He won the office in 1970 by defeating another moderate, Carl Sanders, in a campaign in which he openly courted those who had defected to George Wallace's third party and was generally accused of "segging it up." He told Vernon Jordan, the black Georgian who would later head the National Urban League, "You *won't* like my campaign, but you *will* like my administraion." And he delivered on that promise, symbolically hanging a portrait of Martin Luther King in the statehouse lobby and taking an uncompromising stand in support of the rights of blacks.

At that point Carter's convictions on racial matters coincided with his ambition. To win the White House in 1976 he would have to do what Kevin Phillips believed could not be done —carry the black vote nationally while holding Southern whites in the Democratic ranks. When it was all over and he had narrowly squeezed past Gerald Ford, he was asked if he had incurred any personal political obligations along the way. He said he had only one major debt—to Andrew Young, the disciple of Martin Luther King who represented the Atlanta district in Congress. Young had reservations when he first announced support of his fellow Georgian in 1975, agreeing only to back him in the primaries in order to defeat George Wallace in Florida. But as he came to know Carter better through the grueling months on the campaign trail, he became a wholehearted convert—and his personal appearances before black and liberal audiences across the country, along with those of Coretta and Daddy King, helped turn out the vote that gave the Georgian his narrow victory.

Young was able to backstop the candidate when he blundered into sensitive territory with an offhand remark about preserving "ethnic purity" in urban neighborhoods. Daddy King helped out on another occasion, when Carter created a flap in fundamentalist circles, and aroused cries of hypocrisy elsewhere, by seeming to admit in a *Playboy* interview that he sometimes felt a pang of lust for strange female flesh, even though he never acted on it. Daddy cleared up the theological point: "They can't kill you for looking. Old as I am, they still look good. When I see a good-looking woman, I look, and I wipe my mouth . . . and I wish I could . . . but I'm a preacher!" However this absolution may have sounded in other circles,

Miller noted, it was highly effective at an interracial peanut roast in an Atlanta park in the year of Our Lord, 1976.

When he made his lonely pilgrimage around the country the year before the Democratic primaries, Carter, an unknown by national media standards, sought out small audiences of presumably influential people. He could not expect to make many converts, since those who practice politics rarely commit themselves so early to so long a shot. But, with those who were willing to listen, Carter managed to place himself in the futures book by undercutting in advance the principal charge his opponents would use against him when the primary campaign went public—that he was a naïve, parochial upward-striver seeking to exploit post-Watergate disillusionment with "Washington." He put in an hour and a half at the Center's conference table one morning when, unfortunately, I was away. A year later, as the election contest entered the home stretch, I listened to the tape recording of the wide-ranging exchange with the Center's skeptical intellectuals and set down my impressions in an article for *The Nation*:

He is not satisfactory to those on the left who believe that the materialistic American society is hopelessly corrupt and will respond only to radical restructuring. He is a moderate reformist who makes no promise of ideological innovation, holding that we can follow the welfare route to attain a tolerable degree of social justice within the limits of representative democracy and marketplace economics.

But he is a systems engineer by temperament and training, and there is no doubt that he would undertake a massive effort to shape up the flabby, inefficient federal bureaucracy—not necessarily to reduce its size but to improve the delivery of services. In that sense, then, he is no more satisfactory to those on both the left and right who believe the Republic's salvation requires the dismantling of the central structures of government and the transfer of autonomy to institutions closer to the people.

Jimmy Carter never managed to put together a national constituency of his own—except for the blacks, who again gave him more than 80 percent of their votes in 1980—and so his reformist designs bore little, if any, fruit. The diversion of events abroad, his failure to establish rapport with Congress and the other Washington power centers, the peccadilloes of his family and friends, the belittling condescension of his usual treatment by the media—all these things combined to render him largely ineffective in domestic affairs. The continued rise of inflation and unemployment coupled with the leveling out of national growth and income created an economic squeeze that was not of his making, but proved beyond his capacity to ameliorate. These conditions, as always, had their heaviest impact upon the black minority, and Jimmy Carter was unable to meet the high hopes he had aroused. Vernon Jordan, publicly criticizing the president for adopting conservative antiinflation policies that penalized poor blacks, sighed and recalled his friend's earlier observation that, while he might dislike his campaign, he'd like his administration: "I suppose Jimmy may have said last fall to business leaders what he said to me back in 1970."

One of the reasons for the national political writers' ambivalence, and frequent displays of irritation, in their treatment of Carter was the fact that he could not be properly slotted as either conservative or liberal. "Most of Mr. Carter's visceral commitments seem to be found not at the level of ideology but above it and below it: above it in the realm of moral affirmation; below it in the realm of managerial skill," Miller wrote. It was on the lower level that Carter failed. Nixon and Ford had wanted to eliminate much of the federal government's social programming, and thereby save money and reduce taxes. Carter, as he told audiences everywhere he went, wanted to "evolve an efficient, purposeful and manageable government for our nation"—which would include continuation and improvement of welfare services. His failure to make any progress in that direction would have particularly grievous consequences for his black constituency.

The Republicans blamed the inability of Nixon and Ford to reduce the percentage of federal welfare expenditures on the Democrats, who continued to control Congress after they lost the White House. But the controlling fact was that the general public had long since accepted the necessity of maintaining the federal role assumed under Franklin Roosevelt. The vastly changed, largely urban society could no longer depend upon the family unit to take care of its own aged, orphaned, or afflicted members, leaving it to private charity to look after the rest. Social security, veterans pensions, and subsidized medical care created a vested interest that cut across all classes. Unemployment benefits provided an essential cushion far up the wage and salary scale. All told, direct benefit payments to individuals accounted for 42 percent of the federal budget by 1980, much of it permanently funded through earmarked tax payments to guarantee immunity to annual appropriation. Thus there were effective, interest-based constituencies for all the major programs except those aimed exclusively at the poor—primarily the indigent aged, the physically handicapped, and mothers with dependent children. It followed that this was the area of federal spending that drew the most fire.

No one was prepared to argue that a person unable to earn a living because of infancy, old age, or physical disability should be left to starve. But there was a widespread feeling that welfare recipients included a substantial portion of the undeserving poor—louts who lived on public bounty because they were too lazy to work. Those who had always attributed this characteristic to blacks were confirmed in their prejudice by the fact that, being disproportionately impoverished, they were disproportionately represented on the welfare rolls, although they constituted well under half the total. There were certainly some welfare cheats, but they were mostly female, for the Aid to Families with Dependent Children program suspended payment when there was an able-bodied adult male in the house. In 1979 the record showed that 70.5 percent of those on the AFDC rolls were children, 58 percent of them under the age of six. Their mothers might be indolent, and some might even be producing additional babies in order to maintain welfare status, but it was nevertheless obvious that they couldn't leave small children untended while they went off to work.

There was, nevertheless, something about this situation that particularly agitated those overly imbued with the Puritan ethic, reinforcing their conviction that welfare dependency was, if not sinful, at least an indication of inferior moral character. The worst thing about this attitude was not that it was uncharitable, but that it tended to divert attention from the fact that welfare dependency was indeed a social evil, and had become one of the first magnitude as blighted welfare families passed into the third generation of existence at minimum subsistence level. By the end of the seventies there were children in the ghettoes who had never known their fathers or grandfathers to be regularly employed—if they had known them at all. Congress continued to pour billions into this debilitating system, whose bureaucratic superstructure consumed a large part of the total before it reached the recipients, while those who liked to consider themselves conservative continued to oppose efforts at basic reform.

Although it was immediately attacked as a do-gooders' raid on the Treasury, the War on Poverty represented a concerted attempt to break the poverty cycle, conceived not by a social planner but by an economist. Walter Heller, chairman of John F. Kennedy's Council of Economic Advisers, had raised the possibility of a frontal attack on hard-core unemployment with the late president before the assassination, and he got an immediate green light from Lyndon Johnson to go ahead with planning. Heller's premise was that the nation could no longer afford to treat poverty under existing practice, foreseeing that both the economic and social costs would continue to mount if the welfare system simply provided subsistence for the socially unfit and encouraged them to multiply. Instead, the primary federal effort should be aimed at salvaging the salvageable —primarily the young—by training and equipping them to become productive members of society. The ultimate effect would be to reduce the cost of unemployment benefits and welfare payments and increase productivity and the yield from the tax base. Johnson saw it the same way. In declaring "unconditional war on poverty" in his 1964 State of the Union message, he emphasized that "one thousand dollars invested in salvaging an unemployable youth can return forty thousand dollars or more in his lifetime."

The organizer of OEO, Sargent Shriver, gave priority to preparing people for jobs and jobs for people, as against simply improving social services. He recognized that providing ghetto youth with the kind of communication skills and motivation the children of the middle class acquired as a matter of course in their superior home and school environment would entail considerable time and per capita cost. But he was convinced the nation could afford it—rolling along as it was in those days in a kind of Keynesian euphoria induced by steady economic growth, controlled inflation, and increasing tax yield. Shriver saw the volunteer service aspects of OEO as an outlet for the energy of the idealistic middle-class young who had been attracted to, and disillusioned by, the Movement, arousing in them the spirit that had motivated the Peace Corps. "To eliminate poverty at home, and to achieve peace in the world, we need the total commitment, the large-scale mobilization, the institutional invention, the unprecedented release of human energy, and the focussing of intellect which have happened in our society only in war," he said. "We need what William James called 'the moral equivalent of war.'"

Before OEO had a fair test it came under the administration of a president committed to its demise. Gerald Ford carried out Nixon's prescription by abolishing the coordinating agency and scrapping the title. The surviving functions were distributed among existing departments and the steam went out of the drive to break the cycle of self-perpetuating poverty that continued to trap the majority of ghetto youth. The Nixon-Ford years, Vernon Jordan said, produced a "growing mood of passive indifference or outright opposition to issues of basic importance to black advancement such as affirmative action, youth job programs, scatter-site housing, and school desegregation. . . . The enthusiasm that illuminated the sixties has given way to the despair of the seventies." The resurgence of black optimism that marked the advent of Jimmy Carter did not last out his single term. The 1980 annual report of the National Urban League, released on the eve of the inauguration of Carter's successor, asserted that blacks faced an even bleaker future in terms of housing, education, and jobs, and now had added to it the prospect of increasing racial strife. In his introduction Jordan, only recently recovered from the near-fatal effects of an assassin's bullet, said that 1980 had been "a year of storm warnings, a year when long-simmering problems started boiling to the surface. . . . Deepening racial hostility, fueled by inequality and economic stagnation, threaten to tear our society apart."

Jimmy Carter was a great admirer of Reinhold Niebuhr, the theologian whose cautionary pragmatism was the antithesis of the resurgent religious fundamentalism that helped sweep the Georgia Baptist from office. He frequently quoted Niebuhr's melancholy dictum, "The sad duty of politics is to establish justice in a sinful world." Ronald Reagan, the hero of the self-proclaimed Moral Majority, came to the White House without providing any indication that he had given thought to what this might entail in the polarized society that had replaced the simpler red-white-and-blue America of his youth.

29

Flights from Reality

A quarter century after the chief state school officers of the South assembled to consider the Ashmore Project's appraisal of the region's segregated educational system I stood before their successors in a conference room at the Atlanta Biltmore hotel. We had convened the first meeting in deepest secrecy, under oath to deny that it ever took place if word leaked that the possibility of desegregation had been mentioned in the presence of these elected officials. The successor gathering was aggressively public—a session financed by the National Institute of Education to consider means of carrying word of the future needs of education to the grass roots. And now my audience had a pepper-and-salt complexion, for each school chief was accompanied by a black deputy who was no longer a token; as far back as 1970 the Southern school systems had showed up in the statistics as the least segregated in the nation, and now they were generally moving toward compliance with the spirit as well as the letter of *Brown*. In a keynote address I said:

No one could seriously argue that the race problem is solved, but I do think it is taking on very different dimensions. . . . It is fair to say that we have reached the point where we can assume that racism—which until recently was the absolute determinant in your educational arrangements—is now a secondary problem, and a soluble one. If we look at the whole of the educational structure, it would appear that the future of public education in the South is not significantly different from that facing schools and colleges everywhere in the nation.

The first question in the discussion period came from a black. "There surely have been a lot of changes on the surface," he conceded, "but do you think that, deep down, things are really different?" Yes, I replied, there is a profound change: "Twenty-five years ago the great majority of Southerners, white and black, believed the two races were fundamentally different. Now we know this is not so. And that's the root of the problem—blacks have turned out to be just like us, and we're no damned good." This backhanded assertion of common humanity drew no more than thin smiles from most of the superintendents but the laughter of their deputies shook the room.

"The people of Arkansas endure against a background not without certain pathological aspects," J. William Fulbright wrote in a characteristically erudite amicus brief urging reversal of the federal court order desegregating Little Rock's Central High School. "They are marked in some ways by a strange disproportion inherited from the age of Negro slavery. The whites and Negroes are equally prisoners of their environment." That was true enough, but the assumption Fulbright shared with most intellectuals left out the fact that the Southern environment also contained a remarkable reservoir of interracial goodwill. Had this not been so, the Southern cities could not have opened their public and private facilities to blacks so rapidly and with so little disorder. When the federal courts unleashed the spreading black protest movement and made it clear that there was no practical alternative to desegregation, ordinary white citizens proved to be ahead of their leaders; the new breed of moderate politicians who emerged in the 1960s did not produce the change, but were produced by it.

Overnight, as historical time is reckoned, the structure of institutional segregation was dismantled, and the submerged black population came into view—not only in the schools and colleges and public buildings, but in restaurants, theaters, bars and hotel lobbies, and behind the counters of retail establishments and the desks of banks and business offices. In the days of the Ashmore Project the closest we could get to the Biltmore at mealtime was the office of the Southern Education Foundation a block away, where we shared catered barbecue sandwiches with our black colleagues. Now Atlanta had become perhaps the most thoroughly desegregated city in the nation. When I came before the schoolmen for the second time, the city had a black mayor, a black police chief, and soon would have a black Chamber of Commerce president—and a Georgia governor had united white and black Democrats in a campaign that sent to Washington the first Southern planter to occupy the White House since Zachary Taylor.

Still, the question invoked by my citation of these dramatic changes was pertinent. My ironic reply recognized the widespread disillusionment among those of both races who had been sustained by soaring hopes in the glory days of the civil rights movement. The idealists had believed—perhaps had had to believe—that the inspired gallantry of blacks and their white supporters would usher in the beloved community of Martin Luther King's dream. It had, instead, only opened the way for the advancement of middle-class blacks who shared the material values of their white counterparts; these naturally adopted the prevailing approach to the power centers as they assumed leadership of a newly effective special interest pressure group, taking their place among the others contesting for political influence, and trading out to obtain it. How far this could go was demonstrated in the 1980 Democratic primaries when a majority of black Georgians voted for Herman Talmadge, who professed to be a reformed racist as well as a dried-out alcoholic. Black voters were willing to follow their leaders in a deal that ignored not only the candidate's messy divorce and censure by his senate colleagues but a long family history of blatant demagogy.

A certified idealist, Leslie Dunbar, a leading figure in the civil rights movement as director of the Southern Regional Council and head of the Field Foundation, found it necessary to heavily qualify his expectations of future progress as he surveyed *The South and the Near Future* for a Clark College publication:

We did not pass from a segregated to an integrated society; only in a relative sense have we come from an unjust to a more just society; most certainly we have not passed from a wandering in the desert by blacks and from moral squalor of whites into a "beloved community." We attained none of these. What was accomplished, however, is a vast enlargement of choice.

. . . The question for Southerners is whether they will try to wend their way as managers and technicians and dutiful consumers through such a rotting system, grabbing for its prizes or at least its crumbs; or will commit themselves to full rights and justice for all minorities, full respect for nature, full devotion to peace, full openness to visions of a new economy.

Still, the enlargement of choice was hardly insignificant in social terms since it had provided a status for blacks in the South comparable to the best they had enjoyed anywhere in the nation—and, in terms of their everyday dealings with whites, even a superior one, for at most points of contact there was less abrasiveness than was common in the great cities outside the region. Beginning in the seventies the tide of migration reversed, and by the end of the decade more blacks were returning to the South than were leaving. I knew a black college professor in California who said he spent his summers back home in South Carolina because he felt more comfortable there.

ALL of this was evidence of a significant tempering of racist attitudes, at least as they affected individual blacks. I had long ago concluded that it was virtually impossible for most whites to separate the myths of racial difference from the actuality until they had experienced sustained association with blacks on a more nearly equal basis than usually had been possible in the past. This, in my view, provided as compelling an argument for school desegregation as the requirements of equalized educational opportunity for minority children. In a 1979 poll, Lou Harris reported that "when whites who have contacts with blacks are asked about this experience, over 90 percent say it has been 'easy and pleasant.'" Yet the opportunity for such contacts remained limited outside the South, where the rising tide of antibusing sentiment had prevented effective opening of school systems to offset the restrictive effect of residential segregation. At the beginning of the seventies the percentage of black children in segregated schools in the major non-Southern population centers averaged 72.4; at the end of the decade it had been reduced only to 70.9.

The continued isolation of most whites from the mass of blacks was reflected in contrasting views as to the extent of black progress. In 1980 Gallup found that 68 percent of whites thought blacks fared as well as they did and 75 percent thought that there had been steady improvement in the quality of life for the minority. But only 44 percent of blacks thought their lot had improved, and 25 percent saw deterioration. In terms of the critical scale of family income—down from 60 percent of the white average in 1970 to 57 percent in 1979—the black view was obviously much closer to reality.

As the civil rights crusade began to wane, it became fashionable to use the analogy of the half-filled bottle to compare conflicting appraisals of the results achieved; those who measured progress from the point where the movement began saw the bottle as half full; those who measured against the goal of racial justice found it half empty. Like most clichés, this one obscured essential truths. Averages which treated the entire black population as an entity concealed what had become a highly significant internal differentiation; by 1980, in terms of income level, educational attainment, and type of employment, a third of the nation's blacks could be counted as middle-class and were more or less being treated accordingly. It was these who had been the primary beneficiaries of affirmative action; the rewards of their improved status were being passed on to their children in terms of motivation and expanded opportunity. For the most part it was the middle class that provided the third of all black youth who finished high school and went on to college, the same proportion as that for white youth.

These were the blacks who had become visible to white Americans, who generally applauded their progress. They were seen to be following in the path of previous "outsiders" who had earned their place in the larger society. In this view, the discrimination they still encountered was no different from that accorded Jews and Catholic ethnics a generation ago—largely a matter of gentlemen's agreements to protect the already diluted purity of what had once been uppercrust WASP neighborhoods, executive suites, clubs, and resorts. And here, it was pointed out, they had antidiscrimination laws on their side, if they chose to invoke them. This, according to increasingly influential neoconservative intellectuals, was the course of "natural" integration. In *The Real America* Ben J. Wattenberg contended that affluent blacks had no real problem with housing or schools:

Blacks with decent jobs, middle-class blacks, don't need . . . the artificial integration of scatter-sitism—they can buy their way into decent neighborhoods, black or white. Middle-class blacks, living in

good neighborhoods, black or white, neither need nor want busing—
they want good schools and they have the wherewithal to get them.

The experience of middle-class blacks hardly bore out this
hopeful finding. Even those who obviously could not be denied
purchase or rental of a residence found themselves steered
away from some of the most desirable locations by owners and
agents, and recognized that if they invoked their legal rights
they might guarantee the hostility of their new neighbors.
Difficulty in obtaining credit was a major problem, and prices
were often rigged. Statistics demonstrated the pattern. The
suburban ring around Detroit contained 73 percent of the
area's white families, and only 12 percent of the black; if
comparable income at various levels had been the determinant,
67 percent of the black families could have been suburban
residents. In Chicago only one-sixth of blacks with the necessary income lived in the suburbs; in Philadelphia, one-third; in
Boston, about one-fifth; in Baltimore, about one-tenth. By the
end of the seventies inflation of real estate prices and interest
rates had largely frozen these residential patterns; most
middle-class families, white or black, were effectively barred
from making initial entry into the suburban housing market.
It was true that many, perhaps most, middle-class blacks
still found it more comfortable to live among neighbors of their
own race, but even where there were clusters of fairly decent
housing in the inner city the residents were embedded in
poverty-stricken neighborhoods and denied ready access to
services and amenities whites of comparable status enjoyed as a
matter of course. The good, black neighborhoods Wattenberg
spoke of were few and far between—and were being emptied
of their most affluent residents as these chose to face the
uncertainties of flight to the suburbs rather than expose their
families to still further deterioration of the crime-ridden ghetto
environment. "It is impossible for the growing black middle-
class to achieve any approximation of the homogenous neighborhoods with high social and economic status so eagerly
sought by the white middle-class," Orfield concluded.

ALTHOUGH the psychological barriers were not yet entirely
down—and perhaps never would be, in this or any other
society—the American middle class was moving toward effec-

tive racial integration. If the spirit of brotherhood was less than universal, the basis for further progress was provided by the effectively neutral racial attitudes that had become the norm. Whitney Young of the National Urban League, commenting on the collapse of "massive resistance" in the South, dismissed prejudice as a primary factor in the overall plight of blacks. "Actually, what we've had in our society is about 10 percent of white Americans who have been actively resistant. But about 80 percent have been largely indifferent. So it hasn't been ill will or good will. It's been *no* will that's largely responsible."

That seemed a fair description of the situation as the nation passed into the eighties. If white Americans now accepted as near co-equals the third of black Americans who had achieved middle-class status, they continued to ignore the other two-thirds. Young cited the affluent New Yorkers who earned their living downtown in the predominantly black borough of Manhattan: "They keep their heads buried in the *Wall Street Journal* as the commuter train stops at 125th Street." This tunnel vision typified the men who assumed the places of power when Ronald Reagan moved into the White House. "The number of people remaining in poverty is very small and it grows smaller every year," wrote Martin Anderson, chief domestic policy advisor to the new president. "The war on poverty has been won except for a few mopping-up operations." Poverty for Anderson apparently equated only with outright starvation.

On the eve of the Reagan inaugural the Children's Defense Fund called the statistical roll. The benchmark for comparison was that used by President Kennedy in 1963 as the rationale for including improved economic opportunity among the civil rights of black Americans:

The Negro baby born in America today . . . has about one-half as much chance of completing high school as a white baby born in the same place on the same day, one-third as much chance of completing college, one-third as much chance of becoming a professional man, twice as much chance of becoming unemployed, about one-seventh as much chance of earning $10,000 a year, a life expectancy which is several years shorter, and the prospect of earning only half as much.

Examining the current statistical base, the Children's Fund found that the school dropout rate was still twice as high as for white teen-agers; the black child had half as much chance of finishing college and entering a profession, twice as much chance of becoming unemployed, and a life expectancy still five years shorter. If the family structure in general had been under assault in the new era of permissiveness, the black family unit had suffered the heaviest blows; four of five white children lived in two-parent families, while less than half of black children did; only one white child in thirty-eight lived away from both parents, while one in eight black children did.

The general decline of home discipline had been marked by an increase in school suspension rates for all children, but blacks were kicked out twice as often; black elementary and high school pupils were put into programs for the mentally retarded at more than three times the rate for white children. The cumulation of all these discrepancies showed up in the most appalling statistic of all: the unemployment rate for black youth, which had been twice as high as that for white teen-agers in the sixties, was now more than three times as high. In 1980, Department of Labor figures indicated that 36.3 percent of blacks aged sixteen to nineteen were jobless; in August 1981, as the pared-down Reagan budget began to cast a shadow across the economy, black teen-age unemployment had risen to 50.7 percent, the highest figure recorded since the department began breaking down statistics by age.

Marian Wright Edelman, President of the Children's Fund, cited these figures to explain "why millions of black children lack self-confidence, feel discouragement, despair, numbness, or rage as they try to grow up on islands of poverty, ill health, inadequate education, squalid streets with dilapidated housing, crime, and rampant unemployment in a nation of boastful affluence." No one came forword, publicly at least, to challenge the statistics, or Mrs. Edelman's interpretation of their meaning. Like the readers of the *Wall Street Journal* who manage to ignore Harlem, the Republicans busily engaged in putting together a new administration found no place on their list of priorities for the basic issues raised by the existence of a growing black underclass—although these had urgent practical consequences that went far beyond the question of racial justice.

Most of the men around President Reagan could, and did,

plead not guilty to charges of racism brought against them by some of the more frenetic black leaders. Reagan's infrequent references to racial matters were humane and conciliatory. "I want everyone to understand that I am heart and soul in favor of the things that have been done in the name of civil rights and desegregation," he said. His handpicked new head of the GOP, Richard N. Richards, rejected the Nixon-Ford Southern Strategy, declaring, "My goal as chairman of the Republican National Committee is to have this a party of opportunity and participation for everyone—for Hispanics, blacks, and whites; rich and poor; young and old; those from the big cities and small towns."

In endorsing the objective of a desegregated society the Republican leaders were conforming to majority public opinion, at least as it was measured by pollsters and recorded in recent election returns. In 1979 Lou Harris found that "the readiness of the American people to make new strides forward in reducing and eliminating prejudice is far greater than is commonly assumed by the establishment." He was right, I think, so far as basic attitudes were concerned. The doctrine of white supremacy had lost respectability; Harris reported that only 15 percent of whites were willing to admit that they considered blacks inferior. The term "racist" had become an epithet, and it was resented individually and collectively when it was applied it to those who did not actively support the black cause; Civil Rights leaders began to avoid the pejorative moral connotation by substituting the euphemism "insensitive."

POLITICS, of course, is not and never could be, a purely rational exercise. Racism was the cause of the inferior position most blacks still occupied in American society; if it had ceased to be a determinant this alone could not dispel the mythology that had grown up around the relationship between the races. In *American Myth, American Reality* James Oliver Robinson noted that the mythology took a peculiar turn in America because of the existence of the South, where the color line was established under slavery, and after abolition survived everywhere in the nation "to maintain a vision of black Americans as outsiders in American society, as people beyond the frontier (and thus savage, uncivilized natives)." But segregation did not prevent blacks from responding to the same values that were shaping the whole of the American culture:

Blacks seized upon the ideals of self-help, voluntary association, and education as part of their inheritance as Americans, and used them to demonstrate—to themselves as to others—their assimilation into American society. . . . The same forces and motives which press other Americans . . . raised money, built schools and hired teachers in black communities. *All* Americans agree that education is an important part of building a homogenous and egalitarian culture and of transmitting essential values and morality.

Blacks accepted segregation because they had no choice, but their mythology did not embrace the imputation of inferiority. Like their white neighbors, they were imbued with the spirit of traditional Protestant Christianity, which preaches that oppressors are morally inferior to the oppressed. The black spirituals drew upon the parables of the children of Israel. "The blacks were the Chosen People of America, sent to this land and suffering in it, in order to bring it redemption by making it truly free and by bringing its great promise of equality to fruition," Robinson wrote.

The theme of blacks as redeemers was inherent in the preachment of Martin Luther King, and its resonance with the religious inheritance of white America made possible the movement he launched. It turned up even in the introspective polemics of James Baldwin, who wrote off the civil rights movement as another failed slave revolt. "The intentions of this melancholic country as concerns black people have always been genocidal," he told a sympathetic audience of leftover white radicals in Berkeley,where he was honored as Regent's Lecturer at the University of California. But Baldwin first displayed his skill with words as a teen-age preacher at Harlem's Fireside Pentacostal Assembly, and he relapsed into a scatological version of the gospel of love when he appeared before an audience of black teen-agers at an Oakland high school: "No one under the sun understands the white American better than I do —better than his black brother does. And no one else in this world gives a shit about him. We are the only hope for him."

Presenting their demands in moral terms posed problems for the black leadership. King recognized this, and stressed the nonviolent, conciliatory aspect of his movement to defuse the resentment most whites felt when they were called upon to acknowledge their guilt and atone for it. His young associates did not always display his breadth of spirit. In the course of an extended interview for *Who Speaks for the Negro*, Robert Penn Warren was asked by Wyatt Tee Walker why he had taken it upon himself to probe the attitudes of the rising black leadership. Warren replied that among other things he wanted to examine his own reactions as a Southern white man. "It is very courageous of you," Walker said. Such a notion had never crossed his mind, the poet replied, but he added this entry in his notebook:

That was true, and yet at the same time, at hearing his words, there had been, deep down in me, a cold flash of rage. At the condescension —moral condescension. The Negro movement is fueled by a sense of moral superiority. No wonder that some sloshes over on the white bystander as condescension. The only effective payment for all the other kinds of condescension visited on black men over the years. Antidote indicated: humor. And not only self-humor.

Most of the black leaders have been blessed with an abundant supply of the antidote, and great skill in using it to ease the tensions that arise when established social conventions are deliberately violated. But when the young radicals took up the black cause in the sixties the saving grace virutally disappeared. Such humor as crept into the polemical onslaught of the establishment was usually corrosive and intended to shock, and those who took a more decorous approach to elders they considered corrupt, or at best obtuse, generally proceeded with grim singleness of purpose. Few members of my generation displayed a greater commitment to the black cause than Harris Wofford, but he wrote of his service as the principal civil rights advocate in the Kennedy inner circle: "I was too often amused at the ironies around me, and too prone to take the long view, to be fully effective with all the earnest people for whom each day and hour was a moment of truth. . . . I found myself increasingly irritated by the patronizing attitude of many white liberals who seemed to be moved primarily by a guilty conscience."

THE unreality of conservatives was manifested in their insistence that there really was no occasion for government action to meet problems that would take care of themselves in the natural, Darwinian order. It was matched in reverse by that of liberals who believed that they had learned what should be done from social studies and could produce instant progress if only the federal purse were unsnapped. The romantic populism of the period produced a drive for "maximum, feasible participation" of the ghetto poor in planning programs for their own relief. The assumption was that deprivation had somehow endowed the poor with collective wisdom and compassion instead of, as usually turned out to be the case, brutalizing them and reducing their capacity to manage their own affairs.

The poverty programs were launched on a wave of moral fervor brought on by revelation of appalling inner city conditions in such works as Michael Harrington's *The Other America*, which was treated to an extended essay review by Dwight McDonald in *The New Yorker* and managed to impinge upon the consciousness of the Wall Street commuters. The design and organization of the effort was largely left to social scientists imported from the universities. One of these, David Gottlieb, was instrumental in setting up the pilot project for the Job Corps, a residential training facility at a national park in the Maryland mountains. He had been summoned from the faculty of Michigan State University on the basis of a book on adolescence he had just published. Fifteen years later, safely back in academe, he recalled that he and his colleagues were still debating whether to greet the trainees with hot chocolate or cigarettes when the first bus arrived with a mixed load hastily recruited in pockets of white poverty in Appalachia and the black ghettoes of Baltimore:

And then the bus pulled up and these kids started getting off, and it became very, very clear that lower-income kids were a side of the moon we had never seen before. . . . We had no idea what these kids had suffered and what they had endured. . . . Then, suddenly, there were the kids, and there were the media, and the politicians and the bureaucracy, and there we were. . . .

The inevitable failures, dislocations, and occasional scandals produced a steady loss of support in Congress, where the money came from. The fact that the key poverty programs did manage to survive during the Republican years under unsympathetic or hobbled administration was largely due to the fact that the seniority system that preserved the racist status quo when congressional committees were dominated by diehard Southerners now provided the pro-civil rights minority obstructionist means to protect programs already in place. The Senate provided the remarkable spectacle of liberals filibustering to head off legislation that, as in the days of massive resistance, usually ignored the Constitution and sought to nullify the orders of the Supreme Court.

The Burger Court continued to hold firm on the principle of school desegregation, and in another area vital to blacks the justices upheld affirmative action programs setting aside job openings for minorities in public and private employment, and in the case of flagrant and persistent discrimination by public bodies they authorized Court-imposed quotas. In the landmark *Bakke* decision, they managed to find a means of effectively insuring that places were held for minority applicants in the limited enrollment of professional and graduate schools. This, it seemed to me, was further evidence that the issue of racial equality was not truly an ideological one, for the Court majority by the usual tests certainly had shifted from liberal to conservative. But the district judges, and on review the courts above, had to deal with the reality confronting a society ostensibly committed to ending all forms of racial discrimination—and they came to recognize the dire social consequences of continued failure to do so.

THE progression from civil liberties to civil rights not only increased the case load of the federal courts, but created areas of litigation outside the neat boundaries of classic jurisprudence. This was particularly true of affirmative action, with its requirement that appropriate federal authority be used to open the educational system and the workplace to a proportionate share of blacks—and, in time, of women and Hispanics. The only feasible way to determine compliance with the requirements imposed by contract upon those receiving federal funds or otherwise doing business with the government was to create a bureaucracy of administrative officers empowered to hear complaints, conduct investigations, and, where possible, negotiate settlements. But appeal to federal district court was provided, and often used by those seeking to resist or limit compliance. And congressmen opposed to affirmative action began insisting that the courts should have original jurisdiction in all cases—a means of putting the burden of obtaining relief upon the aggrieved individual under a procedure so cumbersome and expensive as to render it largely ineffective.

There could be no denying that affirmative action did serve to limit the traditional prerogatives of educators and employers. And there could be no doubt that such a system was subject to captious and exaggerated claims, since many of those who needed support to break through arbitrary admission, hiring, and promotion practices were likely to be in a state of high agitation, and backed by crusading organizations that had come into being to right what they considered a moral wrong. Almost any gathering of personnel managers brought forth complaints of "reverse discrimination" and bureaucratic harassment that allegedly forced lowering of performance standards. Against that, however, was abundant evidence that the existence of readily available, universally applicable enforcement machinery was indispensable to executives with a genuine desire to end discrimination, serving to minimize resistance of those presently favored, who naturally opposed changing the status quo.

In any case, experience both before and after *Brown* demonstrated that there was no way to dismantle the segregated society without affirmative action—taken in its broadest sense to include all government interventions required to establish and enforce nondiscriminatory standards in activities colored by the public interest. With experience, and the demonstration of general public approbation, compliance could become effectively voluntary—as was now the case with hotels, restaurants, theaters, and other places of public accommodation. But that could happen only after the federal executive, armed with appropriate statutes enacted by Congress, had moved to carry out the policy established by the courts.

As conservative politicians co-opted the libertarian demand that the government be taken off the backs of the people, and carried a national election under that slogan, there was growing danger that the burden would be shoved back on the courts. The political independence of the judiciary had made the civil rights movement possible, but some of the most thoughtful members of the bench thought they had reached, and perhaps even exceeded, the proper limits of relief through litigation. In Great Britain, where the same basic issue had arisen, Lord Hailsham, the Lord High Chancellor, warned, "Judges can be trusted—if they are asked to do what a judge is trained to do, to try a justiciable issue. If he is not given a justiciable issue, a judge will wander about the woods until the robins lay leaves upon his recumbent form."

A GOOD many judges, forced to supersede the authority of recalcitrant school boards in advancing desegregation, found themselves wandering in deep political woods at the close of the seventies. With antibusing as the rallying cause, the political process became polarized in the nation as it had in the South in the days before the Great Society breakthrough, and with the same result. A rational approach to the practical problems involved in dismantling the segregated society became virtually impossible, and this, as always, improved the fortunes of demagogues. The situation was particularly difficult for the new generation of black leaders just beginning to take their place in the mainstream. They knew, perhaps better than anyone else, the absurdities and inefficiencies that marred many of the federal programs, but they also knew that their concession would be less likely to lead to correction than to abandonment of the entire undertaking—and even the most maladministered provided benefits that were desperately need-ed. Moreover, their own constituencies were riven by the practicalities encountered in the effort to overcome the con-straints of residential segregation. This was particularly marked in the case of busing.

In the major cities it became evident that further integra-tion of the schools would require redistricting on a metropoli-tan basis, which would make busing feasible by bringing into the system white schools in the suburban ring. By the end of the seventies such metropolitan districting, although not yet ac-cepted by the Supreme Court, was seen by most experts as the only possibility for desegregating the schools of the five largest districts—New York, Los Angeles, Chicago, Philadelphia, and Detroit—which now contained more than a third of all the black children outside the South, and a rising proportion of newly arrived Hispanics and Orientals.

Against this background there was no longer any consistent black pressure for court-mandated busing, although its symbolic importance was such that no national black leader could afford to reject it, or even to use the retreat fashioned by white liberals who now said they were for busing in principle so long as it wasn't *forced*, and piously added that they were sure a better way could be found to integrate the schools. In the 1976 election no Democratic candidate in the presidential primaries, including Jimmy Carter, offered an unqualified endorsement. Ronald Reagan stated his position by declaring that "busing has been a failure and is not accomplishing the purpose, the worthwhile purpose that gave it birth." His election reinforced this effort in the House to effectively eliminate the authority of the federal government to enforce court-ordered busing, and in the Senate a last-ditch filibuster by a maverick Republican, Lowell Weicker, Jr., of Connecticut failed to slow the steamroller. Only thirty senators were willing to be counted in opposition to Jesse Helms of North Carolina, an uncompromising throwback to pre-Great Society days. In California Willie Brown, black speaker of the state house of representatives, read the handwriting and offered this advice to his fellow politicians: "What the officeholder now has got to do is say, up front, that busing is no longer an issue."

RONALD REAGAN came to the White House as an undeviating advocate of 100-proof free enterprise who also believed that Western capitalism and Eastern communism might be headed for Armageddon. His professional skills as a communicator enabled him to present his case with good-humored charm, and moderates tended to discount his apocalyptic rhetoric by noting that as governor of California he actually hadn't tried to change things much—in part because liberal Democrats controlled the legislature, but also because there were then no compelling issues at the state level that required drastic action. The situation was entirely different when a dispirited electorate turned out only 53.9 percent of its qualified voters in the election that made Reagan president.

The political realities of 1981 were uncontrolled inflation, high unemployment, a stagnant economy, and a deteriorating position in world affairs. President Reagan's approach was foreordained: deep tax cuts to stimulate the private sector, massive increases in military appropriations to improve the American position vis-à-vis the Soviet Union, and drastic cuts in domestic spending to balance the budget as, in his view, the only brake against inflation. This program not only would require severe curtailment of social programs, but would reverse the Keynesian fiscal policies that for a generation had been depended upon to flatten the curve of recession, control inflation, and stimulate growth to provide tax income to pay for goods not readily available in the private sector—low- and moderate-cost housing, health care, urban transporation, and the like.

Ever since New Deal days a majority of Democrats and Republicans, with some differences on priority and method, had been in general agreement that the Keynesian formula was essential to the functioning of a modern industrial society. They had agreed, too, that the central government must provide measures—unemployment insurance, welfare payments, old-age pensions, medical insurance, environmental protection, job and product safety regulation—that would protect individuals against circumstances beyond their control.

Government activity had contracted and expanded in some of these areas as political balance shifted between the parties, and in recent years there had been bipartisan agreement that the federal bureaucracy was getting out of hand. Jimmy Carter also brought to the White House a neopopulist bias against the central government; no Republican orator ever surpassed the Georgian's campaign denunciation of "the horrible, bloated, confused, overlapping, wasteful, insensitive, unmanageable bureaucratic mess in Washington." But there had been no effective effort to dismantle the essential elements of the structure; even Richard Nixon conceded that all Americans, including Republicans, had become Keynesians. Ronald Reagan, however, was committed to as near a return as possible to the classic tradition which holds that economic decisions should be left to the freely competitive market.

The threat this regressive philosophy posed for blacks, two-thirds of whom were directly or indirectly dependent on threatened federal programs, was unmistakable. Black leaders with popular constituencies were unanimous in their opposition to the Reagan candidacy, although a good many less political middle-class individuals felt secure enough to declare a pox on both candidates, and a few black neo-conservatives turned up in the Reagan advisory group. The most prominent of these, the economist Thomas Sowell, was associated with the Hoover Institution at Stanford, which was slated to provide the kind of academic backstopping for the new administration the Brookings Institution had furnished recent Democratic regimes.

"A creative role for the federal government is almost a contradiction in terms," Sowell asserted in support of his thesis that genuine economic advancement for blacks could only be made through the private sector. He denounced affirmative action to open educational and employment opportunities as embodying a demeaning message that minorities are losers who will never have anything unless someone gives it to them, a message he found "destructive of society in general and minority youth in particular." At a San Francisco meeting called by the Institute for Contemporary Studies, which provided position papers for the Reagan transition teams, the president's senior White House policy advisor, Edwin Meese, III, listened approvingly as a procession of black speakers proclaimed an era of transition from civil rights to economic determinism—and in the process denounced busing, rent controls, affirmative action, the minimum wage, and any and all "dependency-encouraging" welfare programs.

There was no one present to speak on behalf of those below the bottom line practical men are wont to cite—in this case the poverty line that sets off some 25 million Americans from the benefits of the marketplace. There was nothing in the self-help formula that could improve the lot of most of those on welfare. In California, epitome of the prosperous Sun Belt, these included 700,000 of the blind, aged and disabled, and 1.4 million members of families with dependent children. If jobs could be found to pry all the able-bodied cheats off the rolls under what Reagan in his Sacramento days called "workfare," a substantial number still would be left. Could the amount of the dole be reduced? Under state policy that adjusted benefits for inflation, and made California's payments among the highest in the nation, a mother with two dependent children received $463 a month at the beginning of 1981. At the opposite end of the scale, in Arkansas, the monthly payment was $142, and had not been increased in four years.

Anyone who had recently passed through a supermarket checkout counter would have difficulty seeing how an adult and two children could survive on less, but the new administration's budget reduced federal welfare funds by an amount that, in the case of Arkansas, represented a third of the total previously allocated by the state to the dependent children's program. The response of Gov. Frank White, a supply-side Republican, was to cut the monthly payment by 17 percent. These figures were an inescapable element in the calculus that came to be dubbed "Reaganomics."

30

Below the Bottom Line

*I*n 1980 the census takers again went forth to count heads in the Other America, that terra incognita below a poverty line established by federal reckoning at $4,190 in annual income for a single person, or $8,410 for a family of four. The final count was delayed when city administrations in the larger metropolitan centers challenged initial figures on the ground that a substantial portion of the minority population was beyond the ken of the enumerators, having no permanent abode or forwarding address and no disposition to answer a stranger's questions. The Census Bureau conceded that it had missed 5 percent of the blacks and 4.4 percent of the Hispanics, but insisted it could do no better. If these invisible poor had lost their human identity they remained a budgetary concern, since the federal allotments that kept most big cities nominally solvent were based on the census count.

The adjusted 1980 figures would show significant changes in the racial and ethnic composition of the population. Blacks, at 26,488,218, were up from 11.1 percent to 11.7 percent. Hispanics, at 14,605,883, were up from 4.5 percent to 6.4 percent—but that figure was deceptively low since 5,804,648 of those who chose to list themselves as "other" rather than as black or white were of Hispanic origin. In the backwash of the Southeast Asian war, Orientals had increased from 1,518,721 to 3,500,636. The American Indian, Eskimo, and Aleut population had nearly doubled, from 827,268 to 1,418,196.

Imbedded in these gross figures were the contours of the black underclass, and the other clusters of American poor with whom its members must compete for subsistence, and for opportunities to rise above the poverty line. In 1979, 25,214,000 Americans—11.6 percent of the population—were officially certified as poverty stricken; by 1980 the total had risen by 3.2 million to 13 percent. These included 8.9 percent of the white population, 30.9 percent of the black, and 21.6 percent of the Hispanic. Among adult blacks 27.2 percent of males were classified as poor, and 34.1 percent of females; among those under sixteen the percentage soared past 40 percent.

The vast bank of data assembled in the new census now became grist for the mills of the social scientists, a process aptly described by Ralph Ellison: "Prefabricated Negroes are sketched on sheets of paper and superimposed on the Negro community. Then when somebody thrusts his head through the page and yells, 'Watch out there, Jack, there's people living under here,' they are shocked and indignant." For the people living under there the statistics took on new and urgent importance in 1981. The chief domestic policy advisor to the Reagan administration reached his conclusion that the war on poverty had been won by adding to the income of the poor the cost of food stamps, public housing, day care, and other federal assistance, thus lowering the poverty line so as to set off only 3.4 to 6.4 percent of the population.

This kind of numbers game was not new to Washington, nor was the tendency of the media to treat it as a contest between resurgent conservatives with hearts of stone and failed liberals whose hearts were so soft they frequently bled. "As in 1964 the federal policy-makers are redefining poverty," the *Washington Post* observed. "While in the 1960s the 'experts' were heavy on humanism the new wave talks statistics." Still, no one questioned the fact that the dire condition of the economy required drastic budgetary action; and, after four years of Jimmy Carter's toothy homilies, what was called "compassion fatigue" was so prevalent among the surviving Democrats there were few to argue against reconsideration of the government's social programs. John Kenneth Galbraith, whose support of a managed economy put him at the opposite end of the spectrum from the Reagan policy-makers, conceded "that the expenditure on public welfare services has involved no careful judgment on need or cost; more has been believed to be better. And the quality of public administration has been seriously deficient."

Anyone who traced the curve of progress made by the black minority in the last generation could agree with President

Reagan's basic premise—that consolidation of the gains of the civil rights era depended upon control of inflation and resumption of steady economic growth. If this could be achieved it should follow that the newly won status of middle-class blacks could be maintained and improved, and upward mobility could be insured for those who occupied a place somewhere above the poverty line but still below that of the more or less integrated upper third. This middle group of "working poor" included many who had only recently achieved economic self-sufficiency—those whose stable family background had protected them against the ravages of the ghetto and enabled them to take advantage of the lowering of the color bar. For these, the economic turnaround the Reagan administration so confidently predicted could not be long delayed. They were among the last-hired and the law of the marketplace had already put many on the unemployment compensation rolls, the last handhold of the private economy they could cling to before being pushed back into the welfare pool.

Yet it was precisely these working poor, and the underclass blacks who sought to join them in the job market, who were most adversely affected when the Reagan budget went into effect at the end of September and produced what the president conceded was a deepening recession. The pattern of appropriations made it clear that the administration's intent was not to attack the undoubted waste and inefficiency of some of the affirmative action programs, but to scuttle them entirely. With the advent of the new fiscal year the last remnant of OEO, the broad-based National Advisory Council on Economic Opportunity, was disbanded. Its final report concluded: "At present there exists an air of suspended disbelief over the radical changes that have occurred in the past months. That is because the layoffs, the shutdowns, the cutbacks, and the reduced paychecks have not yet reached ground level. . . . October 1, 1981, will be remembered as a day of infamy, for it will mark the worst massacre of social and human services in American history."

The immediate impact of the budget cuts, however, was only the surface manifestation of the massive change in direction. "The economic program of the Reagan administration," wrote James Tobin of MIT, the current Nobel laureate in economics, "manifests a conservative counterrevolution in the theory, ideology and practice of economic policy." Professor Tobin spelled out the implications:

The ideal of capitalism in a democracy is a fair race from an even start. Big prizes go to the swift, but all participants are rewarded—the more rewarded the faster everybody runs. True, economic and social outcomes are highly unequal. The excuses are that the racers all have the same opportunities and that the differential prizes generate even larger rewards for all participants.

Opportunities are actually far from equal. We Americans escaped the feudal castes of the Old World, but erected our own racial, religious and ethnic barriers. Even as these are overcome, the hard fact remains that the children of high economic and social status gain a head start—better education at home and at school, better nutrition and medical care, as well as more gifts and bequests of worldly goods . . .

Wealth breeds wealth and poverty breeds poverty. . . . Here, as in other democracies, governments have sought to arrest the momentum of inequality by free public education, social insurance, "war on poverty" measures and progressive taxation. The U.S. budget and tax legislation of 1981 is a historic reversal of direction and purpose. Existing institutions, commitments and "safety nets" can't be rapidly dismantled, but the message is clear enough: Inequality of opportunity is no longer a concern of the federal government.

The "supply-side" economic theory offered as the basis for the new tax program called for three straight 10 percent across-the-board annual reductions in the income tax. This was offered as a means of benefitting all taxpayers, and of releasing funds for private investment that would stimulate economic growth and ultimately improve the lot of those whose income was too low to make a tax cut significant. But the chief architect of the Reagan economic program, Budget Director David Stockman, in remarkably unguarded, and undeniable, taped interviews with William Greider of the *Washington Post*, confessed that the real objective was to lower the top income-tax rate from 70 to 50 percent, and to grant other benefits to those in the upper brackets through lowered capital gains rates and inheritance taxes. The across-the-board formula, he conceded, "was always a Trojan horse to bring down the top rate. It's kind of hard to sell 'trickle-down,' so the supply-side formula was the only way to get a tax policy that was really trickle-down. Supply-side is trickle-down theory."

The effort to turn back the clock was not limited to the budget, where the generally accepted need for some curtailment of government spending helped generate support in Congress. There was no real issue of cost involved in extension of the Voting Rights Act, which in its ten years of existence had been instrumental in bringing blacks fully into the political process by employing federal authority to eliminate restrictions on the ballot. The measure passed the House by a vote of 389 to 24, and its supporters included most of the Southern congressmen who represented what once had been lily-white districts. In the face of this overwhelming approval by politicians immediately concerned with the result, the president first indicated that he would endorse the House measure, but a last-minute ideological intervention by Attorney General William French Smith caused him to reverse himself and add qualifications the civil rights leadership declared would render the act meaningless. The attorney general, it seemed, had an even more stringent commitment to the "new" federalism than did the president—and he was in charge of the Justice Department, which could, by simple inaction, effectively invalidate most of the antidiscrimination measures still on the books.

To AN extent the ideological changing of the guard in Washington, and the apparent abandonment of the old bipartisan Keynesian consensus, served the useful purpose of raising what the economics writer Robert J. Samuelson called blockbuster questions—"ones that people won't ask, not only because they're afraid of the answer but also because they don't even want to be associated with the question." Unfortunately, the blockbusting disposition did not extend to considerations of the future of the black underclass, and its impact upon society at large. It could no longer be assumed that there was in that inchoate mass a significant proportion of able-bodied adults who had the capacity to make their own way in a free enterprise economy, but were locked out by the repressions of a racist society. The kind of men and women who could be expected to benefit from the "urban enterprise zones" President Reagan proposed as a stimulus for private sector employment still could be found in the ghettoes, or at least on their fringes—but they had long since separated themselves as best they could from the socially maimed who surrounded them, and they would depart entirely once their incomes permitted.

The blockbuster questions had to do with those who were in fact unemployable, not because of their current circumstances but because of their lack of inner resources. It was possible to see these coming, and their numbers were certain to increase if programs like Head Start, CETA, and the Job Corps went by the boards. The odds were long that an adult who had passed through teen age without acquiring the skills and motivation required for a regular job would wind up a ward of government, as a convicted criminal or a disability case. If such as these were to be salvaged, the process would have to begin when they were very young, and the public school would have to be the primary instrument. But the educational system was under attack from both right and left, and its popular support was declining at a rate that was prompting politicians to reconsider the traditional American commitment to public education as the ultimate social panacea.

I had an opportunity to observe the effects of the change in political climate at close range when I served as a consultant to Shirley Hufstedler during her brief tenure as the nation's first secretary of education. Mrs. Hufstedler, as a member of the Ninth Circuit Court of Appeals, the highest-ranking woman judge in the nation, was an ideal choice; sensible, energetic, free of the prejudices of the professional educator, she thought it might be possible to lift educational policy making above the stultifying bureaucratic morass into which it had sunk. It turned out not to be, at least in the brief time allotted to her. Taking office in an election year, the new secretary was immediately subject to the pressures of a presidential campaign in which the winner greeted her appointment by pledging to abolish her department.

Still, Secretary Hufstedler encouraged me to ask the blockbuster question that had prompted me to sign on in the first place: What does the government propose to do to carry forward its mandate to equalize educational opportunity in the critical urban areas where demography and political pressure have combined to prevent busing? There was general agreement among the senior professional staff that the question was in order; there was also general agreement that it was too hot to handle. The educational bureaucrats added to the protective, non-decision-making instinct of the civil servant inhibitions brought over from the academy, where pedagogues, behavioral and social scientists, and philosophers had been immersed in disputation over the nature of the learning process ever since John Dewey enshrined progressive education at Columbia Teachers College in the 1920s.

It was, certainly, a legitimate controversy—one rooted in questions of nature versus nurture that had occupied scholars all the way back to Aristotle. The extent to which learning capacity is influenced by genetic inheritance and by environmental conditioning is a proper concern for anyone trying to fashion a curriculum or instruct a classroom full of students. But there never had been, and perhaps never could be, definitive answers, and the usually garbled by-product of the academic controversy fueled exchanges among those who treated the problems of public education in ideological terms— elitists versus levelers and, by extension, segregationists versus integrationists, and, most numerous of all, sentimentalists who wanted to "get back to basics." The polemics they produced colored the treatment of the issue by the media and in turn fed back to the academy. These arguments were intensified by the claim of some experts that a genetic differential produced black averages below those for whites in the IQ and aptitude tests used to slot students into the system all the way from kindergarten to graduate school. Experts with equivalent credentials contended that any racial differential was accounted for by the inferior social environment that inhibited the development of communication skills in underclass children—and was compounded by the use of such tests to separate them from more fortunate peers whose example would improve their performance.

Most of the ranking experts of both persuasions appeared at the Center, and it seemed to me that in this instance, as in most of those that had a bearing on racial matters, the great failing of the academicians was the virtually automatic rejection of what they scorned as the popular, or commonsense approach. Obviously laymen were unqualified to deal with a complex scientific question requiring mastery of an esoteric body of theory. But they were capable of observing the results achieved by the educational system, which during the melting-pot era had demonstrated that ethnic differentials had no place in the determination of public school admission policy beyond indicating need for remedial training. Children from a variety of cultural backgrounds, many of them from families who spoke no English and were afflicted by extreme poverty, passed through the grades along with WASP peers, under the instruction of WASP teachers, and emerged able to cope with what had been an alien environment—and a good many demonstrated that they could compete on equal terms with the best and brightest the dominant culture produced. Such also had been the experience when middle-class blacks began to attend school with middle-class whites.

It did not follow, however, that this pattern of progression was automatically available to black underclass children. What was missing in their case was the stable family background that offset the effects of poverty with loving care, provided motivation, and fostered development of communication skills. An effective substitute, for the latter at least, could be provided by the schools if they had access to the children early enough, and the means to give them the individual attention such tutelage required. What was needed to salvage these youngsters—and to adequately serve an increasing number of middle-class children of both races—was a new approach to preschool and primary education.

As it developed toward the end of the nineteenth century the public system was designed to serve the nuclear family: a wage-earning father, a housekeeping mother, and one or more children living in a stable, homogenous community. The neighborhood school this concept produced no longer accorded with the reality of the typical family situation. In a permissive, highly mobile era the traditional nuclear family was disappearing; by 1980 more than half the women of childbearing age were working full time, and an increasing number were single. "We have moved from a society dominated by one type of arrangement, the husband-provider nuclear family, to a more variegated society with many types of households, no one of which predominates," Daniel Yankelovich wrote in *New Rules*. The burden of nurturing the small children of these parents was no longer being borne by the family in the conventional way—and certainly it wasn't adequately being taken care of by the makeshift day-care centers that kept small-fry off the streets.

Overcrowded schools in the inner city and empty classrooms in the suburbs were the product of changing demography and an altered birthrate that attested to the need for functional reconstruction of the public school system. To exalt preservation of the neighborhood school as justification for opposition to busing, or to the metropolitan districting which in most cases would make it practicable, was simply to ignore the central problems of urban society as a whole. Jimmy Breslin described the result in the *New York Daily News*:

In 1957, New York's public schools were 68 percent white. During 1980, only 27.8 percent of a total attendance of 963,000 were white. . . . At this rate, in five years the schools, and perhaps the city, will belong to everyone who is not white and the word "minority" will have the same meaning in New York that it has in Zimbabwe.

Any other discussion about the city at this time is merely a diversion. The calamity for all is that a school system of blacks and Latinos is one that at best will be ignored and at worst will be probably wrecked by government, which remains white.

FAILURE to devise a system that could salvage underclass youngsters was inescapably linked to the problem ranked first by most city-dwellers—crime. This could no longer be written off as a discrepancy between perception and reality; the statistics showed a marked, continuing increase in crime in general and violent crime in particular, twofold in a few years in most cities. Attorney General Smith began his tenure by declaring that violent crime was "out of control," and announced appointment of still another high-powered commission to consider what might be done to strengthen the criminal justice system. Chief Justice Warren Burger weighed in with a speech before the American Bar Association asserting that "today, the proud American boast that we are the most civilized, most prosperous, most peace-loving people leaves a bitter taste. . . . Today we are approaching the status of an impotent society, whose capability of maintaining elementary security of the streets, in schools, and for the homes of our peoples is in doubt. . . ."

For the first time since the postwar period, many homicides

were gang-related, often involving shoot-outs between black and Hispanic teen-agers. Other homicides were characterized as random, which was particularly alarming since, having no evident cause, they were not affected by the usual precautions. Most of the killings, muggings, rapes, burglaries, and hold-ups were committed by men and women in their teens or early twenties. There was no clear racial pattern, but the number of blacks among both criminals and victims was disproportionately high and—the most alarming aspect to whites—violent encounters had become commonplace outside the ghettoes.

This pattern seemed to me an indication that another casualty of the changing times was the traditional black matriarch, the mother or grandmother or aunt whose strength and dignity sheltered her own young and others of her extended family. She was a fixture in the Greenville slum that gave me my first insight into the condition of poor blacks fifty years ago, the source of the only stability to be found in that island of misery. Her kind still survived in the South, imposing discipline and instilling ambition in children within their reach, but the very upward mobility they inspired had removed from the urban ghettoes most of the younger women who saw them as role models.

When an athletic superstar emerged on a Southern campus to become an instant millionaire he usually acknowledged his debt by buying a home for the aging black woman who had seen to it that he protected his health and stayed with his studies. One of these, Mike Williams, a quarterback at Louisiana's Grambling College, was profoundly shocked when he came to New York to be looked over by the pros. "The first time I saw Harlem I cried," he said. "It's unbelievable, all the little kids running around in the middle of the night. And the old people just sit, like they'd given up. It's like they've told themselves this is the way it's supposed to be and they just accept it. Harlem is like a human junk pile."

An increasing number of those with nominal responsibility for nurturing ghetto children were still children themselves— victims of what the activist preacher Jesse Jackson called "an epidemic of teen-age pregnancy." The government's figures showed that more than 50 percent of the black children born in 1980 were illegitimate. Breaking down the count for the

District of Columbia, where the total stood at 60 percent, the *Washington Post* found that 95 percent were borne by teen-age mothers, whose progeny accounted for 90 percent of low-birth-weight babies—those who run a high risk of health problems that harm mental and physical development. The end product of this kind of casual parentage could be seen in the fact that 75 percent of the black teen-agers in the District's juvenile detention facilities were themselves illegitimate.

Those who survived into their teens in such an environment were effectively without self-imposed restraints on their behavior, and could see no alternative to crime as a source of income and an outlet for their energy. Virtually their only contact with whites was with those whose job was to impose restraints upon them: police, court officials, and prison attendants. The more intelligent, in whom a spark of conscience survived, were likely to be the most dangerous; an edge of rage added to sullen resentment could provide rationalization for the most extreme brutality. From his cell in Soledad Prison, George Jackson, who had been nurtured by the criminal justice system since his early teens, expressed his view of the white world in a letter to Angela Davis: "They hate us, don't they? I like it that way, that is the way it is supposed to be. If they didn't hate me I would be doing something very wrong, and then I would have to hate myself. I prefer it this way."

The young criminals produced by the ghetto reduced to irrelevance much of the public debate inspired by the mounting crime statistics. They could not be absolved, as radical cant would have it, on the ground that past failures of a racist society had shaped their destiny. They might be entitled to compassion, but they constituted a clear and present danger, and there was no reason to believe that, once hardened, they would respond to reform of the criminal justice system—whether it be by providing tougher laws, judges, and prisons, or by making the system more humane. For twenty years I asked every criminologist who came to the Center for his best judgment of the effectiveness of capital punishment and stringent prison sentences as deterrents to violent crime. The answer was that there was no way to determine what effect they have—for the good reason that the statistics cover only those who had already committed a crime and could not include those who had restrained the impulse out of fear of punishment.

By the seventies the recidivism rate had undercut the once-prevalent belief that a significant number of criminals could be rehabilitated in prison, and in fact the effort had been largely abandoned. Prisons had become warehouses where predators were isolated from their potential victims. The cost of bed, board, and security—on the average $50,000 per cell for construction, $17,000 per annum for maintenance—provided the primary pressure for reducing the population of the already overcrowded penitentiaries through plea bargaining, suspended sentences, and parole. In the typical case of New Jersey, arrests averaged over 400,000 annually, while the state prison system could accommodate only 7,000 inmates. The fact was that offenders were most often returned to the streets not because the courts were excessively lenient but because there was no place to put them—and the United States already imprisoned a higher percentage of its population than any other industrialized nation except South Africa and the Soviet Union.

I found it difficult to imagine a beefed-up criminal justice system serving as a deterrent in cases typified by the perpetrator of the last murder recorded in Los Angeles in 1980—the fatal shooting of an elderly man who protested the noise emanating from a New Year's Eve party. The police blotter provided a shorthand biography of the thirteen-year-old boy who fired seven bullets into the victim: He was being nurtured by a gang that included his older brother and sister; he had an arrest record for burglary, vandalism, and assault; his father, a convicted drug dealer, died in prison; he didn't know where his mother was; and he was under the influence of alcohol at the time of the murder.

It was the opinion of one who viewed the scene from the perspective of the judicial bench that such as these were simply in transit from one warehouse to another. Judge Paul Egly, who in 1976 was assigned to preside over the litigation that marked Los Angeles's convulsive experience with court-ordered school desegregation, said that in the days when he was hearing criminal cases he used to wonder why so many of the defendants were blacks and Latinos. "I think I have learned the answer in the four years I've been listening to the Los Angeles [school] case," he said. "In my opinion there is a direct correlation between the ability of the child to compete in our society and the crime rate. . . . We've said these people should be warehoused until they're sixteen or so and then forget it. That's exactly what the Los Angeles Unified School District has been doing. . . . When we end up, we have produced a large number of children who cannot function in our society."

BLACK leaders expressed apprehension that the correlation between the rise of crime and the continued deterioration of the inner cities would bring a new wave of racial strife. There were stirrings out on the fringes, where the sensation-prone media helped promote a resurgence of the Ku Klux Klan. In so staid a community as Portland, Oregon, handbills distributed by the Christian National Socialist White People's Liberation Front incited action against a comprehensive list of traditional scapegoats: "Death to Jew-Communist pigs! Deport Niggers, Mexicans, Cubans, and Queers!" But it was not just bigots and frightened little old ladies with bars on their windows who thought they saw a rising black menace. Judith Coburn, a veteran of The Movement, was awash in her own guilt when she recognized that she automatically assumed that the burglar who broke into her Venice apartment was black. She had moved to Los Angeles's oceanfront bohemia seeking spiritual liberation in a "community that sneers at white flight; integrates its schools; hires organizers to resist developers against the poor; and tolerates its bag ladies, junkies, vandals, and psycho vets." She found only terror:

I walk the streets on ambush. Fear turns me racist. Me, the gal who learned what a hero was from a 15-year-old black girl in Selma and who picked up a little *joie de vivre* from the jiveass Little Richard fans who hung out in the Pittsburgh ghetto where I worked. Me, the lady who thought she'd figured out something about minorities in a semester as the only white student in an all-black college in Hampton, Va. . . . But now I just keep moving on the streets, avoiding eye contact with my neighbors—the black and brown ones, that is, the men.

Crime had become a dominant issue in local politics in most major cities. A *Los Angeles Times* poll found that 82 percent of the residents felt unsafe on public transportation at night, and 72 percent were afraid to walk their neighborhood streets alone after dark. If the dangers were exaggerated, the fears were real. Understandably, the first reaction was a demand for more police, but the polls seemed to show that the public did not regard organized repression of blacks as a solution; on the contrary, only 3 percent nationwide saw the crime wave as racial in character. Asked to identify the primary cause, 39 percent cited the weakened economy, 36 percent the general decline in moral standards, and 24 percent drugs.

Although many felt that its simplistic preachments encouraged a rising intolerance against any who did not share the values of fundamentalist Christianity, the new force in right-wing politics that called itself the Moral Majority firmly rejected racism. There were usually black faces in the choirs that backed up the electronic evangelists, and the most prominent of these, the Reverend Jerry Falwell, specifically repudiated his earlier support for segregation and asserted that his activist role in politics was undertaken in the spirit of Martin Luther King. "It was only as I became a real student of scripture that I saw that [segregation] is not in the Bible," he said. "As a matter of fact, the opposite is there."

Public opinion seemed to reflect a general awareness that the social pathology of the ghettoes could not be effectively treated in isolation, and must be cured if the cities were to regain their health. Most of those who opposed busing—and by 1981 Gallup found that this included 80 percent of whites—insisted that this stemmed from understandable unwillingness to support a system that might require their children to attend schools in the inner city; less than 5 percent of those polled objected to attendance at a school containing a few blacks, and the level rose only to 23 percent in the case of 50-50 division between the races. These figures were supported by experience in the South, and in smaller cities elsewhere, where busing had not transferred whites to schools located in high-risk neighborhoods.

Wherever local authorities committed themselves to finding a workable solution, conforming not only to the letter but to the spirit of *Brown*, they had generally succeeded. *Newsweek*, in the course of a gloomy 1981 survey of the nation's public schools, cited as a shining exception Little Rock's Central High, once the prime symbol of massive resistance to court-ordered desegregation. "Today Central is once again a national symbol —as one of the best public high schools in America," *Newsweek* concluded. "Sixty-five percent of the seniors go on to college, and fifty-seven percent of the student body is black. Central, indeed, provides solid proof that racial harmony and academic excellence are not mutually exclusive." The question the Reagan administration had not yet faced, or even acknowledged, was whether racial harmony was possible without a public school system that made available a common educational experience to blacks and whites.

THE continued existence of the black and Hispanic underclass was often cited as evidence of the failure of the extensive federal interventions of the past. Vast sums had been spent on urban renewal programs intended to break up the ghettoes and redistribute the poor in subsidized scatter-site housing, but most poor blacks and Latinos were still huddled in overcrowded, substandard tenements or inferior public housing. To use this as an excuse for curtailing the federal effort was equivalent to denial of the vote to blacks in post-Reconstruction days on the ground that there was no way to keep white men from stealing it. The fact was that connivance of private developers and public officials had diverted most of the benefits of subsidized urban renewal to the middle class. When "gentrification" brought an influx of prosperous young couples to reclaim a decaying inner-city neighborhood, the resident poor were simply pushed aside into even more crowded and squalid quarters. When I asked what happened to all the blacks who occupied Capitol Hill in Washington after it began to be remodeled along the lines of fashionable Georgetown, I was told that they seemed to have disappeared into the dismal confines of Anacostia Flats, where the bonus army once pitched its tents.

There was nothing in this experience to encourage the assumption of the Reagan administration that it could open opportunities for underclass blacks by using tax incentives to stimulate private sector "enterprise zones" that would provide jobs and services for ghetto residents. In the aftermath of the long hot summers there had been a concerted effort by public-spirited businessmen to locate branches and foster black-owned enterprises in places like Watts and Bedford-Stuyvesant—usually through partnerships that provided not only capital but managerial support and training. None met with marked success, and most were counterproductive failures. Experience underscored the obvious fact that most of the highly motivated blacks had responded to the opening of employment opportunities outside the ghettoes, leaving behind a crime-ridden environment that made it imprudent for a private investor to risk his capital.

A task force of Los Angeles civic leaders, undertaking what was billed as a "fresh and optimistically realistic look" at Watts on the sixteenth anniversary of the holocaust, glumly concluded: "There has been very little change. . . ." There were some signs of rebirth in perhaps the most thoroughly devastated slum area in the nation, the South Bronx, where blocks of abandoned apartments were put to the arsonist's torch or vandalized until they had to be pulled down and bulldozed away. Neighborhood associations organized by clergymen and social workers undertook cooperative efforts to make decaying buildings habitable and provide community services. But, while this involved active participation by the private sector, it also required heavy government subsidy. And this kind of rehabilitation did not include, but necessarily excluded, trouble-making underclass families, leaving middle-class residents isolated in enclaves of their own kind.

If the use of government funding to make available housing at prices well below the market induced some Bronx residents to resist the wholesale flight that greeted the incursion of black and Hispanic poor, these were so few the bait had to be extended to potential home buyers and renters in less afflicted sections of the city. Mayor Edward Koch, who had written off the black vote and created a solid political base among New York's ethnics, did not blink at the charge of gentrification: "I happen to believe it's helpful to an area that is perceived as low income, near the bottom of the poverty ladder, to have an infusion of middle-class people—black, white, and Hispanic—to upgrade the area." Such settlements on the criminal frontier no doubt served a useful purpose, but they met neither the challenge posed by the underclass nor the criteria President Reagan established for self-sustaining enterprise zones.

Reagan's doctrinaire commitment to localism and private enterprise extended even to education. He strongly favored provision of tax credits for payment of tuition to private schools, which had expanded greatly to provide a refuge for parents withdrawing children from the debilitated public system. The freedom of choice this was supposed to enhance would hardly extend to the children of the poor, who would be consigned to schools formally recognized as inferior and left devoid of the middle-class support upon which the system had always depended. The process was already far advanced in the cities where white flight had left behind a dominantly minority public school system.

"What we're dealing with," Judge Egly said, "is a large minority school district in which the children are truly isolated from the mainstream of American society, if you assume that the mainstream is the white society. We're talking about children who, by the time they are in the fourth or fifth grade, are considered to be failures." The objective of busing was to break through such cultural isolation by exposing deprived black children to the company of middle-class white peers in schools that met the prevailing norms of faculty and facilities. The more expensive alternative was to create ghetto schools specially designed and staffed to offset deficiencies of home environment.

When the California Supreme Court reversed itself and undercut Judge Egly's four-year effort to apply its previous "reasonable and feasible" equalization standards, there was left only the wan hope that the upheaval had opened the public's eyes to the nature and gravity of the problem. "In a sense, busing was a club with which to get society's attention to a desperate need for change," said Monroe E. Price, a UCLA law professor who served as a court-appointed referee. "Now that the club is gone, Los Angeles's minority children deserve to retain the attention that judicial coercion won for them." But effective change within existing segregated schools would require expenditures far greater than those involved in busing— and the Reagan program called not only for a reduction in the total of federal aid but a block grant formula that would remove the categorical requirement that such funds be spent on programs of direct benefit to underprivileged children. Watching the dismantling of the Department of Education,

Shirley Hufstedler warned that the new policies meant "the destruction of what took years and years to build up. It's a scorched earth policy, but people don't smell the smoke yet."

EVERY lesson to be drawn from history imbued blacks with distrust of the pre–New Deal concept of federalism espoused by Ronald Reagan, and so minority leaders with popular constituencies had unanimously opposed him, with some 80 percent of the black vote going to the doomed Jimmy Carter. Their minds had not been changed when the president, still celebrating his sweeping triumph over the Democrats in the battle of the budget, appeared before the NAACP's national convention in Denver, where he told his grimly silent audience he would not "concede the moral high ground to those who show more concern for federal programs than they do for what really determines the income and financial health of blacks—the nation's economy." And, in a notable display of *chutzpah*, he declared that those who said his domestic policy discriminated against the poor—among whom were all those on the platform except Nancy Reagan—had been confused "by some who are either ignorant of the facts or . . . are practicing, for political reasons, pure demogoguery."

In any confrontation involving race there was likely to be more than a trace of demagoguery on both sides. But what was striking about this encounter was its pointed revelation of the president's perception of the condition of black Americans. The affluence and personal style of the NAACP members assembled in Denver attested to their middle-class status; the fact that their organization could command the presence of a president whose election they had opposed demonstrated that they were not without political clout. To Ronald Reagan this was evidence of the validity of his domestic policy advisor's claim that the war on poverty had been reduced to a rearguard action. But even the most successful blacks were constantly reminded that a majority of their people had not yet attained the status of those who could afford a trip to Denver. And most of those whose family income had risen above the 1980 median—$21,900 for whites, $12,670 for blacks—had been beneficiaries of the programs the president condemned as failed experiments perpetrated by self-serving liberals.

The connection between his professed aversion to racial discrimination, and his obligation, as president, to do something about it, continued to elude Reagan. In 1982 the Internal Revenue Service, with prior clearence from the White House, reversed its standing policy—and the current position of the Justice Department in litigation before the Supreme Court— to grant tax exempt status to two private educational institutions which openly denied equal treatment to blacks on grounds of religious conviction. In the face of protests from all quarters, including the Republican leadership, the president declared that all he had in mind was obtaining Congressional approval for such action rather than relying on administrative fiat. His letter to Congressional leaders contained an unexceptionable statement of principle:

I share with you and your colleagues an unalterable opposition to racial discrimination in any form. Such practices are repugnant to all that our nation and its citizens hold dear and I believe this repugnance should be plainly reflected in our laws.

But, even after that, the action of IRS was allowed to stand pending Congressional action. And the president seemed to be genuinely puzzled as to what all the shouting was about.

This kind of myopia, still prevalent in the white community, left the black leadership subject to the critical double standard employed by intellectuals who accused them of reverse racism—of relying on what Thomas Sowell labeled a "blacker than thou" appeal to rally their following. When the presidential candidates came to pay their respects to the Urban League at its 1980 convention, the Washington columnist Joseph Kraft appraised the response as evidence of the pathos of black leadership:

. . . they did not want to acknowledge the black ascent to middle-class status or the responsibility that it implies. . . . Far more appealing to the convention was putting the monkey on the back of race prejudice and government failure. . . . Through the workings of a vicious circle, it happens that the unwillingness of middle-class blacks to shoulder responsibilities commensurate with their gains causes leaders to lose followers and race tensions to rise in a way that has to haunt all America.

The fact was that the black leaders themselves were increasingly concerned over the tendency Kraft cited. Affluent blacks were enrolling their own children in private schools and withdrawing from civic activity to an extent that drew a blast from a member of Washington's virtually all-black city government, Councilman John Ray: "They don't do a damn thing except work, drive 280Zs, listen to music, and watch football. . . . Martin Luther King and Malcolm X opened doors for them but they don't act like they know it. Successful young blacks today are among the greatest opponents of social programs. . . ." On the list of the twenty-five black Americans chosen as most admired in a 1980 poll of *Ebony*'s 6 million middle-class readers only one—the Reverend Jesse Jackson—could be said to be actively engaged in carrying on Martin Luther King's mission on behalf of the underclass.

By American standards this was a natural progression. When blacks adopted the Protestant ethic as it had evolved under popular government, they became subject to the temptations cited by John Adams when he posed these questions to another founding father, Thomas Jefferson: "Will you tell me how to prevent riches from becoming the effects of temperance and industry? Will you tell me how to prevent riches from producing luxury? Will you tell me how to prevent luxury from producing effeminacy, extravagance, vice and folly?" The only effective restraints on the corruptions of liberal democracy developed in what has been called, to the discomfiture of theologians, the "civil religion"—the secular faith, generally accepted although not always acted upon, that provided a common moral standard and an essentially self-enforcing ethical code. Alexis de Tocqueville noted that the new American republic, while exalting individual freedom in its Constitution, nevertheless assumed limits on permissiveness: ". . . while the law permits the Americans to do what they please, religion prevents them conceiving, and forbids them to commit, what is rash and unjust."

The great force of the civil rights crusade derived from the unmistakable injustice of a caste system that penalized and degraded all blacks; this blended the self-interest of the minority with the moral response of the majority. Martin Luther King was aware that the equation was changing as the formal barriers of segregation were removed. The besetting problem, as he came to see it, was no longer racial discrimination but the inability of the American system to deal with poverty—to make provision for those who had become economic displaced persons as a result of the rapid changes brought on by revolutionary advances in technology. At the time he was assassinated at Memphis he was completing plans for the Poor People's March on Washington—a pilgrimage intended to bring together impoverished blacks, whites, Puerto Ricans, Chicanos, and Indians to settle, like Coxey's Army of the Populist era, in an encampment to be called "Resurrection City." The mules that drew his funeral cortege through the streets of Atlanta had been chosen to lead the procession of the poor to the capitol.

The march was a fiasco, and probably would have been even if King had lived to lead it. Television was now the primary instrument shaping the nation's consciousness, and it depended upon brief flashes of high drama, not protracted exposure of squalor as a reminder of society's failure to take care of the least of its citizens. And the concept of a poor people's movement was based on the dubious assumption that common misery resulted in common purpose. In the case of blacks the reverse had been true. Those of a different color or culture who were also subject to deprivation had always resisted joint effort—poor whites because of unwillingness to acknowledge any degree of equality with blacks; Hispanics, Indians, and Orientals because linguistic differences and pride of identity caused them to resist acculturation.

As a final irony, blacks had come into competition for government support by other groups that insisted that they were also entitled to the benefits of affirmative action programs originally designed to offset the unique disabilities imposed by slavery and segregation. Thus they found themselves facing new competition for jobs, promotions, and educational advancement, from women, the aged and the physically handicapped. These so-called liberation movements provided some effective allies for blacks in upholding the principle of affirmative action, but in practice they often produced sharp conflicts of interest. With all this came a new flood of immigrants, legal and illegal, who swamped the shrinking market for unskilled labor. When Fidel Castro emptied his prisons to dispatch a new wave of Cubans to Miami in 1980, I was reminded of Bill Baggs's wry observation after those who fled the revolution first were welcomed as certified anti-Communists: "We've got a new definition of a nigger down here in Dade County. It's a black man who can't speak Spanish." Festering resentment of Miami blacks against what they deemed to be preferential treatment accorded Hispanics helped fuel 1980's only major race riot.

EVER since I first began considering the role of blacks in shaping our national history I have been impressed by the profound influence they have exerted simply by being present, and this initially against their will. They have constituted a challenge not only to our moral standards but to our basic concepts of governance. If the Americans who exercised power usually managed to immunize their consciences against the palpable injustices of the system, they still kept running up against the high cost of maintaining a substantial portion of the population in a state of subjugation. Until the middle of this century this presumably was offset by the fact that holding blacks in thrall permitted their exploitation as a source of cheap labor. But that was no longer the case. For a generation the unskilled had been surplus population, a growing financial burden rather than a benefit.

The experience of the sixties demonstrated that there was no substance to the romantic Marxian delusion that disadvantaged blacks might constitute a *lumpenproletariat* that could touch off a class war and force the redistribution of wealth. But the social pathology that made the underclass unorganizable also was producing able-bodied criminals at a rate that destroyed the domestic tranquility essential to a civilized community. These restive blacks were forcing the nation to consider whether it was willing to adopt police state methods to restore and maintain order—at the cost, necessarily, of undermining the civil liberties of all Americans.

"In the end there is no escaping the questions of race and crime," Charles Silberman wrote in *Criminal Violence, Criminal Justice*. "To say this is to risk, almost to guarantee giving offense; it is impossible to talk honestly about the role of race in American life without offending and angering both whites and blacks. . . . The truth is too terrible on all sides; and we are all too accustomed to the soothing euphemisms and inflammatory rhetoric with which the subject is cloaked."

So it was that the initial response of those who came to power with President Reagan was insistence that such an issue did not exist; they contended, as my Southern forebears had, that there was no race problem, at least not one that required the ministrations of the central government. This was inherent in the grand design of the new administration. One of its basic premises was that the urban crisis could be alleviated through a process of social Darwinism sustained by benefits trickling down from a stimulated private sector. Another was that such dislocations as might remain could best be dealt with by restoring responsibility and authority to state and local government. Past performance cast grave doubt on this proposition, and there was a compelling new factor: even before the Reaganauts began shutting off the spigots of the federal treasury, popular tax revolts had occasioned a reordering of priorities in every state capital and city hall—with the special interests of nontaxpayers relegated to the very bottom of the agenda.

Such a radical reordering of the governmental process was defended on the ground that it represented a necessary response to popular reaction against the shift in values and mores that followed the leftward ideological surge of the sixties. Those who fancied the cyclical theory of political change took comfort in the belief that when the pendulum completed its swing between the extremes it would, as before, respond to the pull of the center. That possibility now depended, to a large extent, upon those whose presence represented a new element in the American polity—the black politicians, lawyers, judges, teachers, business executives, journalists, artists, athletes, military officers, engineers, and astronauts, who did not yet proportionately represent the minority population but might be numerous enough, and determined enough, to help insure that there would be no closing of the access routes that had opened to them.

Near the close of the era of second-class citizenship for blacks Kenneth Clark rode the train south from New York with Thurgood Marshall, bound for Charleston to try *Briggs* before Judge Waties Waring. Late at night, pounding down across

Virginia, the weary Marshall sighed and said, "You know, Kenneth, sometimes I get awfully tired of trying to save the white man's soul." The ultimate victory in *Briggs*, brigaded with *Brown*, had changed the contours of race relations, but the burden of redemption remained.

It was in this light that blacks, as blacks, still had something to say to whites. Pauli Murray, noting that she was old enough to identify herself as the granddaughter of a slave and the great-granddaughter of a slaveowner, cited her historical roots, not as a reproach, but as "a reminder to white Americans that we are in fact related and cannot be excluded from the family table." In the course of her seventy years this indomitable woman had been, among other things, a civil rights lawyer, an Episcopal priest, and a professor at an African university. She had derived from that experience her abiding "conviction that the late Dr. Martin Luther King was on the right track." That track still pointed in the direction of the beloved community.

A generation ago, about the time Thurgood Marshall was heading south for Charleston, I noted in *An Epitaph For Dixie* that, while I entertained doubt as to the perfectibility of man, I had come to believe that most of us were better than we usually had a chance to be. My meliorist faith has been confirmed by the changes brought about under the renewed constitutional commitment to civil liberties, and the uneven progress toward endowing all Americans with accompanying civil rights. If it is not now halted, this progression may be reckoned the most profound social change mankind has accomplished without resort to violence. The record of my time demonstrates that it *is* possible to change hearts and minds—not by exhortation, or coercion, but through governance that recognizes the possibilities, as well as the limitations, of our pluralistic heritage.

Acknowledgments

I hope my debt to the authors whose works I have drawn upon for background is adequately acknowledged in the citations in the text. The narrative also identifies some of those who made personal contributions to my understanding of the events described here.

Among those who provided direct assistance in the course of the writing I owe a special obligation to Harold C. Fleming of the Potomac Institute, who, as he did in the case of my first work in the field, contributed invaluable information, insight, advice and encouragement. Carl F. Stover of the National Academy of Public Administration screened the manuscript in its penultimate form. Bryant Rollins of Mountaintop Press provided the perspective of his own experience as a black American. Gladys Justin Carr, editor-in-chief of McGraw-Hill, and her assistant editor, Leslie Meredith, saw the final version through publication.

My brother William, and Betsy and Robert S. Campbell, choice companions of my youth who remained in the home country, checked my memory of events cited in the early chapters. For later developments I have relied particularly on Tom Fesperman, John A. Griffin, John Popham, Judge Henry Woods, Knox Banner, Edwin E. Dunaway, and Fred Darragh. Hugh Patterson, Robert Douglas, Charles Allbright, and other former colleagues on the *Arkansas Gazette* responded generously to the calls I made upon them. My daughter Anne checked out sources in the Library of Congress. Nancy Andon provided indispensable aid in readying the manuscript for publication.

Finally, a grant from the Ford Foundation made it possible for me to devote the time and undertake the travel and research *Hearts and Minds* required. I am particularly grateful to Chairman Alexander Heard.

Index

Harry S. Ashmore was born in Greenville, South Carolina, in 1916. He attended the public schools there and Clemson College. A Nieman Fellow at Harvard, Mr. Ashmore was awarded LL.D. degrees by Oberlin, Grinnell, and the University of Arkansas. He has been a political correspondent for the *Greenville News*, editor of the *Charlotte News*, executive editor of the *Arkansas Gazette*, correspondent for the *New York Herald Tribune*, columnist for the *Los Angeles Times* syndicate, and editor-in-chief of *Encyclopaedia Britannica*.

He is the author of *An Epitaph for Dixie, The Negro and the Schools, The Other Side of Jordan, Mission to Hanoi: A Chronicle of Double Dealing in High Places, The Man in the Middle, Fear in the Air,* and *Arkansas: A History*.